AF380634

DESPERATELY YOUNG

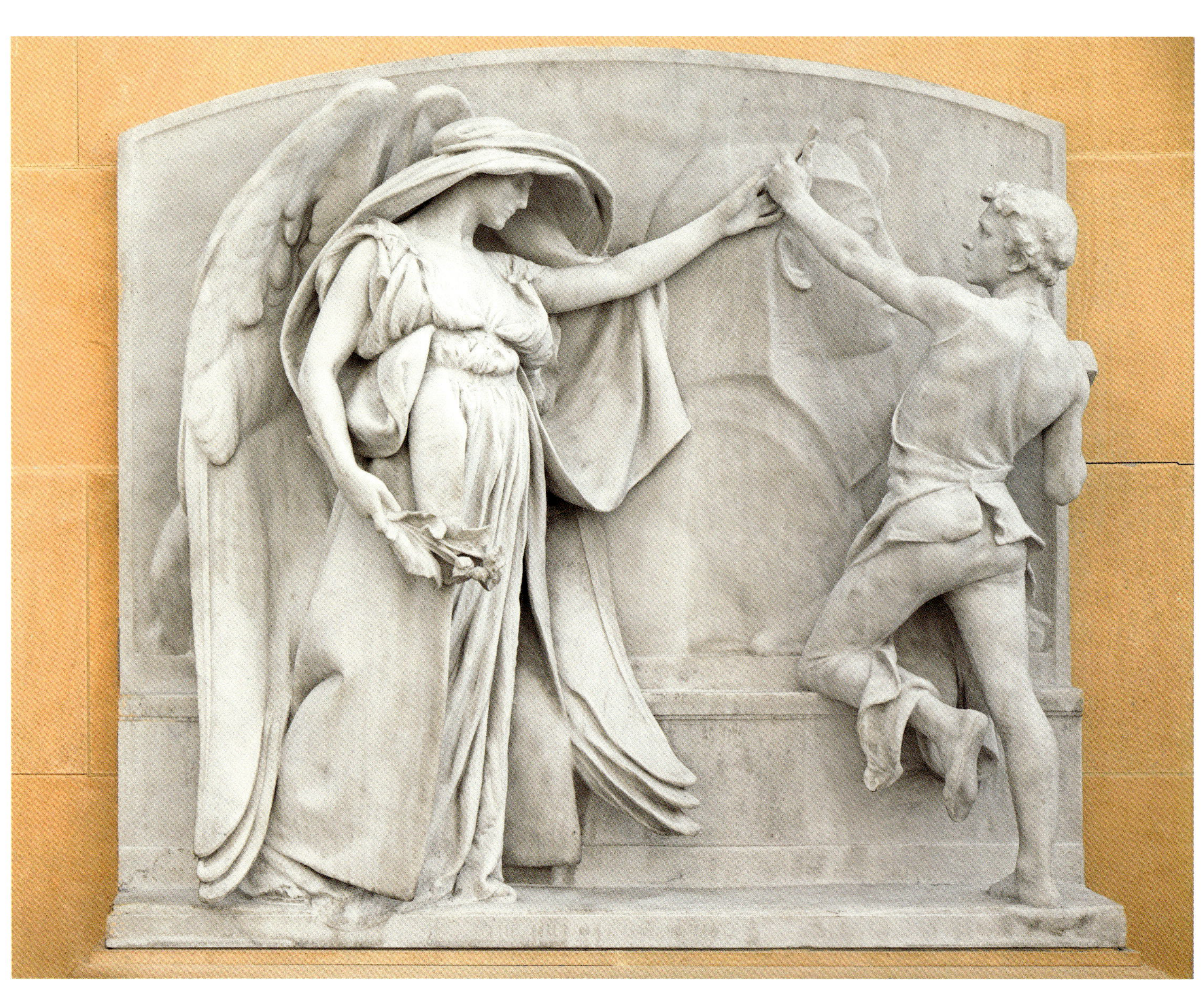

DESPERATELY YOUNG
ARTISTS WHO DIED IN THEIR TWENTIES

Angela Swanson Jones and Vern G. Swanson

ACC ART BOOKS

This book is dedicated to my husband Jason Blair Jones

ISBN: 9781788840842

British Library Cataloguing-in-Publication Data
A catalogue record for this book is available from the British Library

Cover Illustration:
Egon Schiele
Self-Portrait with Chinese Lantern Plant, 1912, oil on canvas, 32.2 x 39.8 cm (12⅝ × 15⅝ in)
Courtesy of Leopold Museum, Vienna

Frontispiece:
Daniel Chester French
The Angel of Death and the Sculptor from the Milmore Memorial, 1889–93/marble 1926,
marble sculpture, 233.5 × 255.3 cm (91⅞ × 100½ in)
Metropolitan Museum of Art, New York City, Gift of a group of Museum trustees, 1926/Alamy

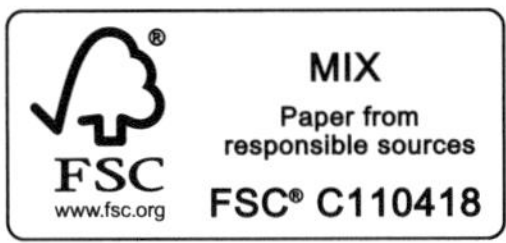

Printed in Slovenia
for ACC Art Books Ltd, Woodbridge, Suffolk, England

www.accartbooks.com

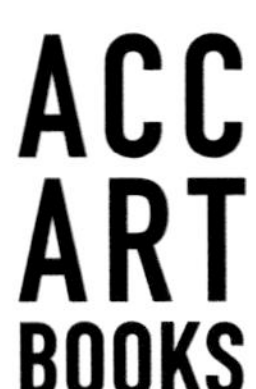

CONTENTS

INTRODUCTION

In the roll-call of the dead, to be remembered is to give meaning to their lives and deeds.

Anon.

At the entrance to the Repin Institute of Fine Arts in St Petersburg, there is a marble wall on which the names of student artists killed in action are written in gold lettering. The entire class of 1942 was sent to the front line, barely armed and with little military training. Less than half of them came home alive. Likewise, in the old Leningrad Union of Soviet Artists building there once were hundreds of photographs, along the grand stairwell, of young artists who died giving service to the motherland during the Great Patriotic War (World War II). Socialist realism expert, Dr Vern G. Swanson remembers:

> Each time I visited this wall I would choke up at the immensity of our loss. Some of these were great artists, and it chills and saddens one to think of these young people never living out the full extent of their artistic potential. I wanted to see every artist's face again and hear my friend Igor Nazareychuk pronounce their names one more time. As painful as it was, I just didn't want them forgotten.

What would the heights of Soviet art have been if this generation of creative souls had lived? One can only imagine that socialist realism would have been twice as impressive. This book seeks to recognise and honour artists who, like these, didn't live long enough to satisfy the hunger we have for more of their work. In short essays, the lives, influence and unfulfilled promise of 109 artists are explored. These artists have been gleaned from a broad range of artistic styles, eras, mediums and geographic locations with the only steadfast criteria being that they died before their 30th year and they had something to say. For this reason, certain groups of artists may appear underrepresented; for this we can be grateful that their lives were not as abruptly truncated as those featured in these pages.

While each artist's story is unique, readers will soon recognise emerging trends and patterns. For example, a number of artists came from artistic families where relatives offered them their first tutelage. This gave many the much-needed head start to achieve excellence in the short time allotted to them. Several artists died soon after marriage or the birth of a child. Perhaps the added stress of these new family relationships hastened the deaths of such artists as Baldry, Bunker, Nuijen and Bromley.

A surprising number fell victim to the scourge of tuberculosis, which spread rapidly in the confined space of artists' studios, particularly where alcohol consumption was high. Then there is the phenomenon of Rome and its environs which saw the death of no fewer than 20 artists in this book, seven of whom were Prix de Rome winners. Hazardous travel and unsanitary conditions made their stay in the Eternal City ironically short. The enticement of war led some hot-headed artists, such as Bazille, Hatton and Regnault, to volunteer, while others reluctantly joined the soldiers' ranks – both meeting the same unfortunate fate.

Through poignant stories, readers will marvel at what these young artists accomplished in so short a sojourn, despite the seemingly insurmountable obstacles in their path. It has not been possible to fully include here all the desperately young artists researched by the authors; the names and dates of those omitted are listed in remembrance at the back of this book (see page 249). It is not with morbid fascination that this book is written, but with abiding honour, recognition and consolation.

Jean-André Rixens
The Glory (Muse of art placing golden wreath on departed artist), 1883, oil on canvas, 56 × 38.5 cm (22 × 15⅛ in)
Musée de Augustin d'Hazebrouck

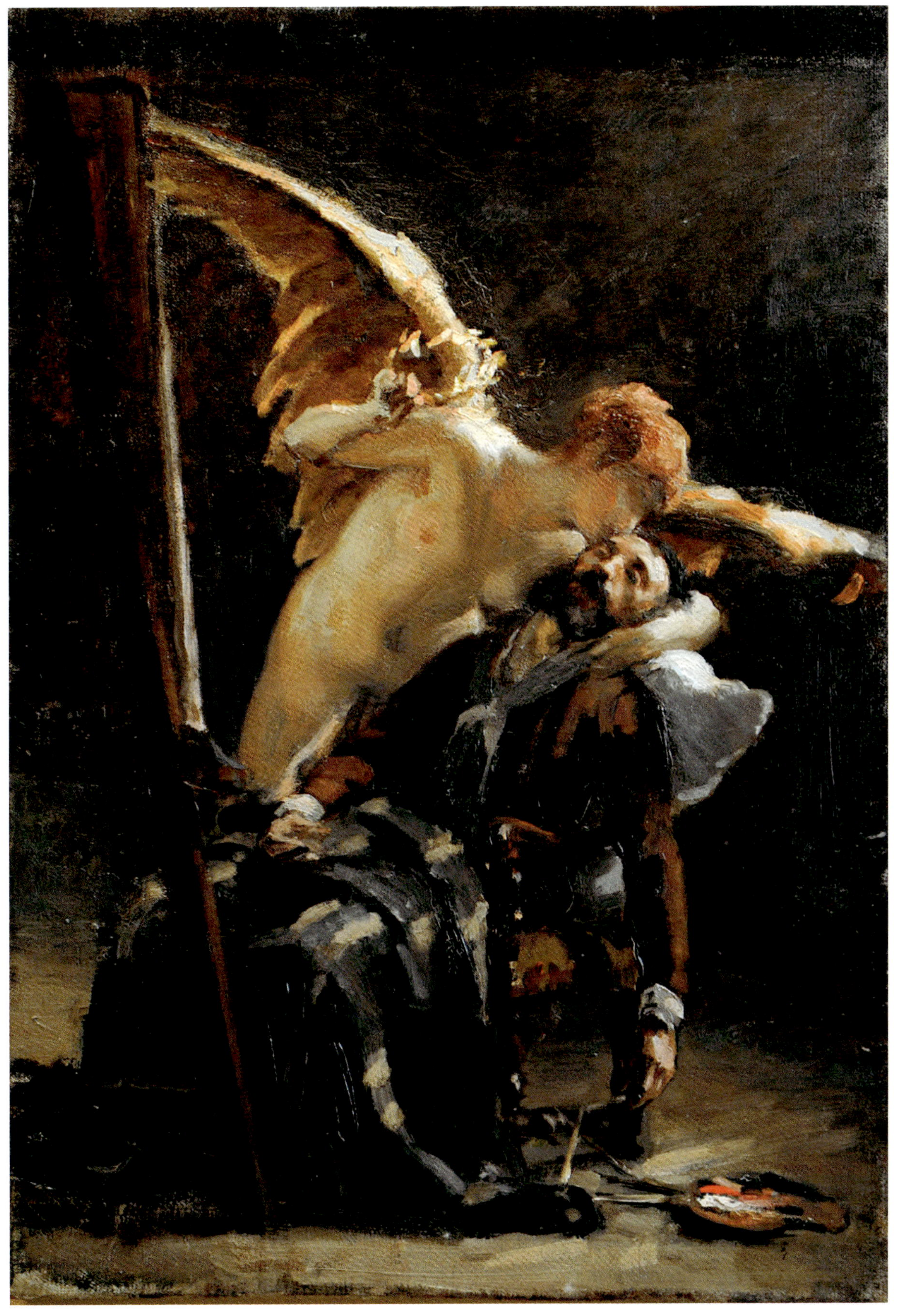

HYPOTHETICALS OF SHORT-LIVED ARTISTS

How many artists' lives were cut short before they reached their true potential or filled the measure of what their full oeuvre ought to have been? While there have been millions of visual fine artists through the millennia, there has never been an overabundance of truly significant grand masters. How has the larder of art museums and private collections been diminished by these artists' early passing? Did each make their maximum contribution despite the brevity of their days? Sandy Askey-Adams speaks to these sentiments:

> All their artistic achievements happened fast within their brief existence. Certainly, they did not know how long a life span was ahead of them. They buried their heads in excelling in their work. That was all that mattered to them.[1]

Tragically, some despairing artists decided for themselves 'how long a life span was ahead of them' – they committed suicide. It would be impossible to compile a definitive list of those artists who cut short their own lives, because so often it was purposely disguised. Such was the case for Christopher Wood (1901–1930), who died by throwing himself under a train, but the incident was reported as an accident according to his mother's wishes. However, had Wood's mental health not deteriorated to such a degree, would his famed naive style have evolved into something more remarkable than it already was?

Alcoholism has always played a devastating role in the health of artists, and even contributed to the death of some – the Japanese artist Kaita Murayama (1896–1919), for example, and the Dutch painter Andries Dirksz Both (c.1612/13–1642).[2] More recently, illegal harmful drugs have claimed many lives. In popular culture the '27 Club' has been the term used to identify actors, musicians and visual artists who died at the age of 27, commonly from drug and alcohol abuse.

Such was the case for the painter Jean-Michel Basquiat (1960–1988), who died of a heroin overdose, and photographer/installation artist Dash Snow (1981–2009), who killed himself with beer, rum and heroin. However, the 27 Club is anecdotal even if their deaths were not. In fact, many more fine artists died at the age of 28 and 29, as is evident in this book. In these cases, it is difficult to say, 'They were meant to die young', for none were. However, would they have been the artists they were without the influence of these substances to stimulate their artistic drive? It was perhaps an occupational hazard not worth taking.

In earlier times, when adequate medical care was unavailable, illnesses like cholera, dysentery, influenza, pneumonia, typhoid fever and, uppermost, tuberculosis claimed the vast majority of the artists who died young. But even then (as far back as seven centuries ago) most artists lived well into their fifties or even eighties. How long would the masterful Achille-Etna Michallon (1796–1822) have lived if he had had access to penicillin during his brief bout of pneumonia?

If he had lived longer, his story may have played out more like that of the great

American painter Minerva Teichert (1888–1976). As a young woman she lay at death's door with the Spanish influenza, the severity of which turned her hair completely white. However, she pulled through and gave the world a rich and vivid oeuvre of paintings and murals documenting the American West like no artist before her. If only Michallon had been so fortunate.

Each of these artists, whether traditional or avant-garde, had demonstrated their considerable abilities to some degree before their death. We know not of those other countless unlisted souls who, either by death or differing vocations, never got to grow to the stature of Michelangelo, Ingres or Bouguereau. Although some artists, such as Tommaso Masaccio, Geertgen tot Sint Jans and Richard Parkes Bonington, certainly came close. But, each of the artists here below had their story and all are missing the final chapters of the book on their life and art. The phrase *'Ars longa, vita brevis'* certainly applies here.

One almost wishes that those 'born under Saturn' could take some of the extra years granted to older artists (in which their elderly efforts in art suffered from various banalities). For example, a wonderful Utah landscape artist LeConte Stewart (1891–1990), who died at the age of 99, artistically had a rather bad late period. What if we could give to the unparalleled master Masaccio (1401–1428) 10 of LeConte's latter years, and to Jean Frédéric Bazille (1841–1870) another 10? Certainly, art history would have been blessed with further treasures.

For some death came swiftly, abruptly halting their artistic progress. This is poignantly portrayed in *The Angel of Death and the Sculptor from the Milmore Memorial* (1889–93/marble 1926; see frontispiece) by Daniel Chester French, where a strong young artist raises his chisel to carve at a bas-relief of a sphinx. To the sculptor's left, the winged Angel of Death approaches, clutching a bouquet of poppies (a symbol of death) and, laying her hand on the artist, stills his action. She will spirit him away, and his fame will now rest on the works he leaves behind, for one can only speak in hypotheticals regarding what his full potential would have been. Historian B.H. Roberts aptly remarks upon the bitter-sweet nature of these desperately young artists' passing: 'It is sad for friends to part, but there is something grand in being taken while there is yet some power in life.'[3]

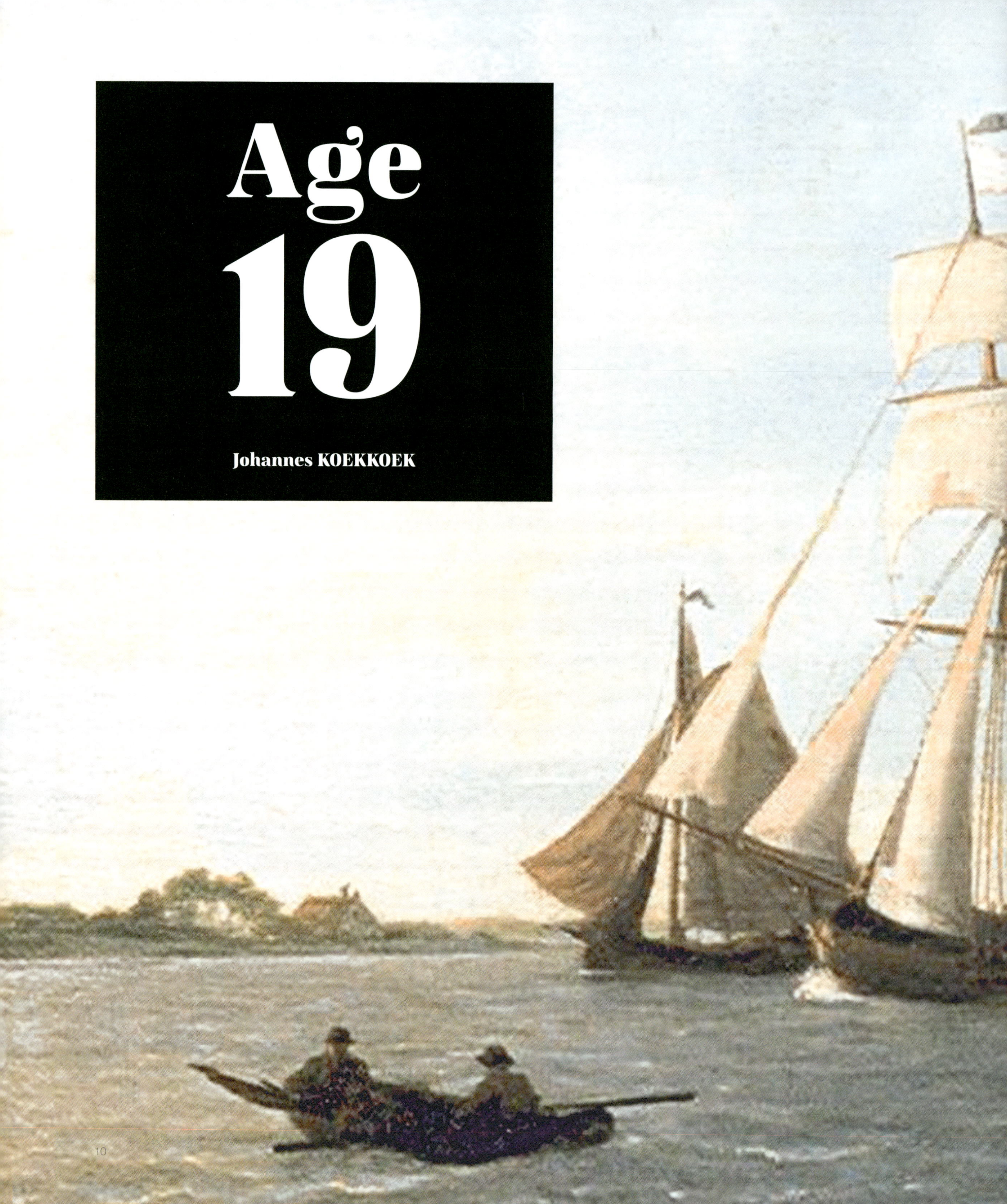

Age
19

Johannes KOEKKOEK

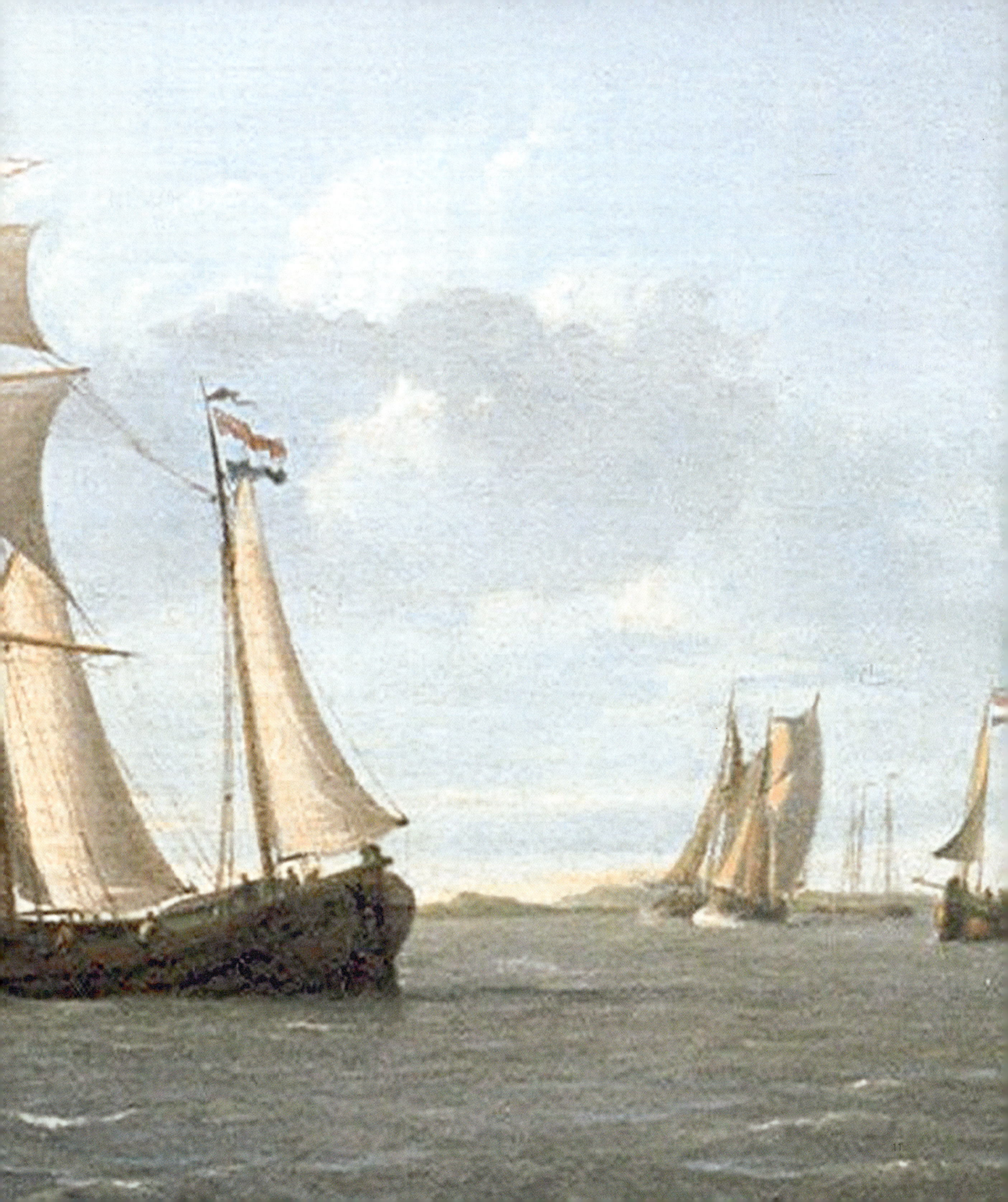

Johannes KOEKKOEK

Middleburg, 8 Dec 1811 – 28 Apr 1831, Breda
Dutch, 19 years, 4 months, 21 days

Johannes Koekkoek (meaning 'cuckoo' in Dutch) was the third artist son of Anna van Koolwijk and Johannes Hermanus Koekkoek (1778–1851). His father was a Dutch romantic landscape painter, lithographer and founding member of the larger Koekkoek dynasty of 16 significant artists. His older brothers Barend Cornelius Koekkoek (1803–1862) and Marinus Adrianus Koekkoek (1807–1868) went on to become two of the leading cityscape and landscape artists of Dutch romanticism. Johannes began to be active professionally around 1826, at the age of 15, in his father's studio. While his technique and personal style are still too youthful to say much, his rich talent assured a successful future like his many famous artistic relatives.

Sailboats on Calm Inland Water (1829) shows that the 18-year-old artist painted very much in the marine genre of his father. In fact, Johannes was his father's promising successor. He was the bearer of his first name and shared the same intense interest for depicting ocean, canal and river views. This refined panel painting demonstrates his maturity for one so young. His marine paintings such as this were poetically calm while others had a tempestuous stormy appearance. If more could have been produced by his hand, would he perhaps

have surpassed his father's legacy? Sadly his oeuvre is very small, barely 20 known works. Fortunately, the mantle of Koekkoek marine painting was picked up by his very able younger brother Hermanus Koekkoek (1815–1882) and by Johannes's nephew and namesake – Johannes Hermanus Barend Koekkoek (1840–1912).

The cause of his early death is not certain, but one theory has it that pneumonia or consumption forced him to abandon sickly conditions in low-lying Amsterdam. He possibly made it as far as the inland crossroads city of Breda to the south, before he grew worse. So weakened, he was obliged to remain there until the end, just as the hope of spring was coming on. With his sad demise it will never be known how his career and later work might have developed, although it can be said with certainty that his art was comparable to that of his siblings, which is saying much. There is no account of any contemporary critical appraisal of his art, however art historians today describe the early departure of this gifted artist thus: 'He was a flower of a painter that did not fully blossom because he was nipped in the bud' and 'To the loss of the art world; he was the harbinger of the best expectations because of the promise that he had displayed.'[4]

Johannes Koekkoek
Sailboats on Calm Inland Water, 1829, oil on panel, 32.2 × 44.8 cm (12⅝ × 17⅝ in)
Simonis & Buunk Kunsthandel, Ede

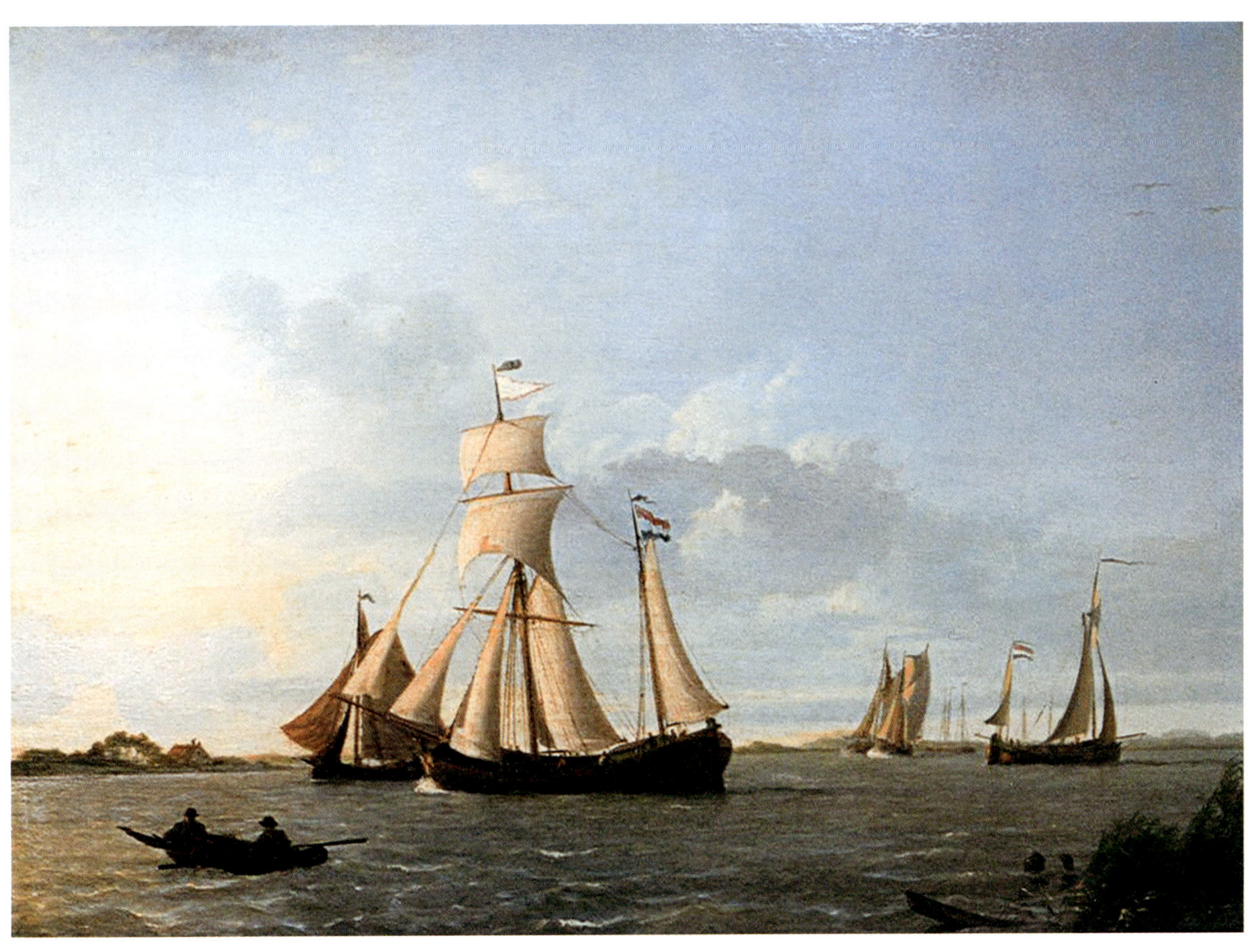

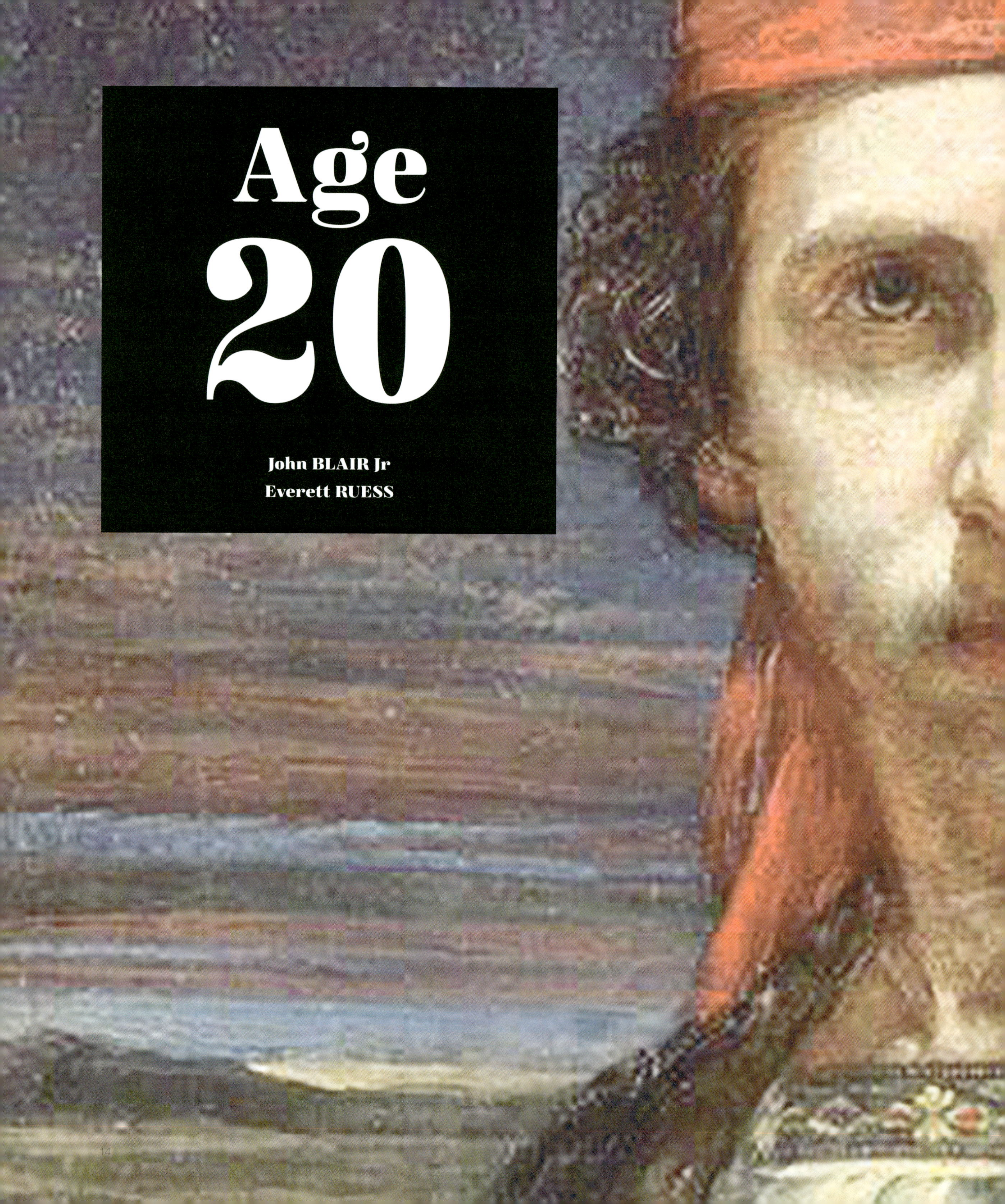
Age
20
John BLAIR Jr
Everett RUESS

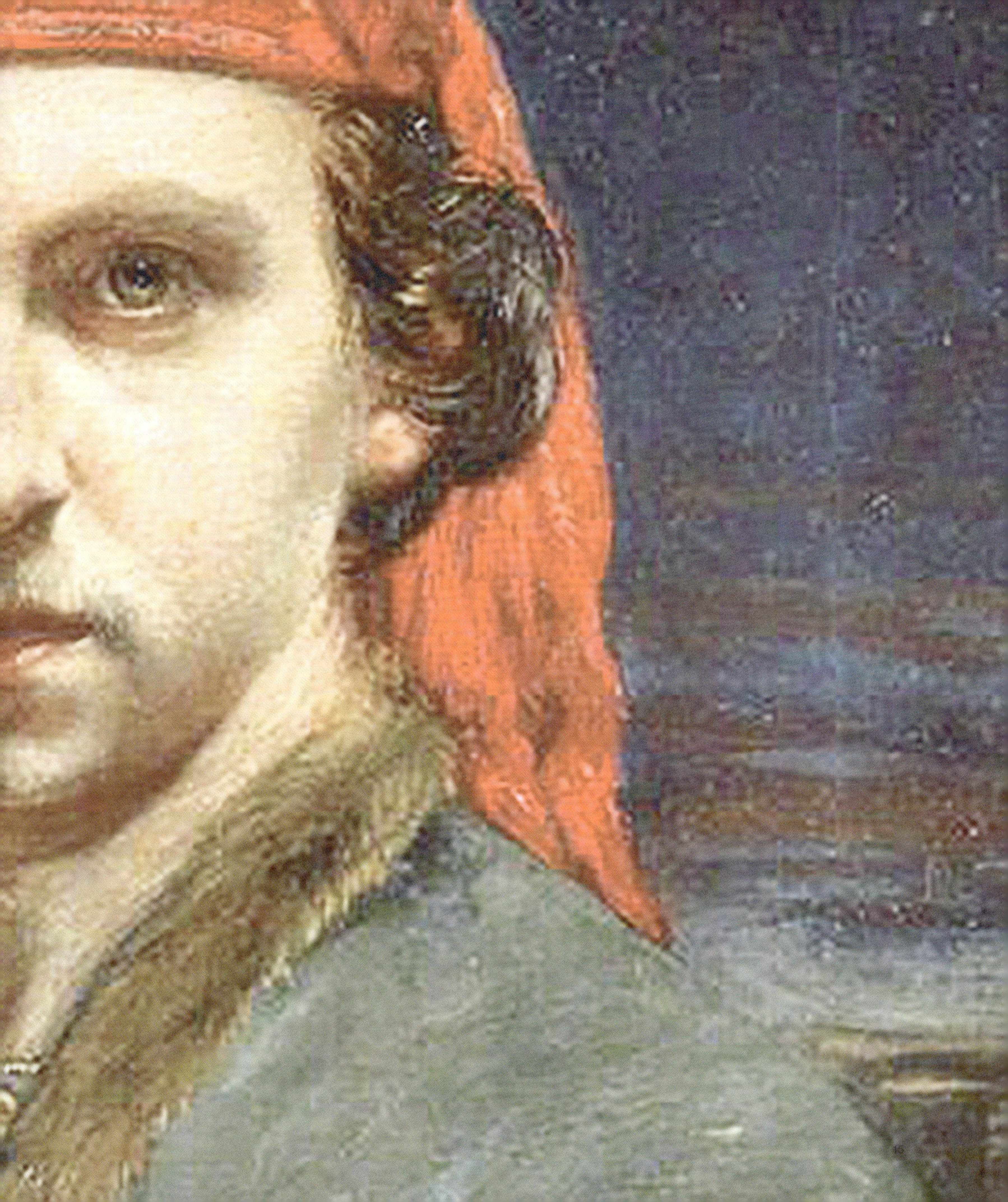

John BLAIR Jr

Paisley, 8 Mar 1839 – 11 Oct 1859, Newmilns
Scottish, 20 years, 7 months, 4 days

The young portrait painter John Blair was born in Paisley near Glasgow, the fifth of seven sons and five daughters. His father laboured in the cotton, cloth and carpet mills to support a family of 14. Somehow, with dire need all about him, Blair was able to see his future in art, encouraged no doubt by Paisley's thriving arts community. His poor health may also have prevented him from mill work and propelled him into fine art. Blair became a star student of the Paisley Government School of Art and Design (founded in 1846), and died just as he was preparing to begin his studies at the Royal Academy of Arts in London.

His excellent oil titled *The Exile – Self Portrait* (c.1859) in the Paisley Museum and Art Galleries hints at the genius this young artist possessed. The work, a self-portrait of the artist, presents a turbaned young man with a soulful face and a wild desert landscape behind. Its enigmatic title reveals his perception of himself as something of a lost sheep – not long for this world. Jan Patience writing for *The Herald* rivets our attention to this piece:

> I found myself drawn to a cracking self-portrait by one John Blair called *The Exile*. A young man gazes at us unflinchingly. He is wearing a scarlet eastern-style turban, and a green fur-lined coat. An almost abstract sunset glows in the background. [5]

Blair's demeanour and styling hint that he might have been a bit of an eccentric.

Blair died on the threshold of what should have been a very successful career. In an attempt to earn money for his studies in London, he took as many portrait commissions as possible, which caused great stress to his frail body. He had suffered from consumption (tuberculosis) for some time and now, under this added strain, his health completely collapsed. At the time of his death he was painting portraits in Newmilns, Ayrshire about 25 miles south of Paisley. His obituary, printed in the *Paisley Herald and Renfrewshire Advertiser* on Saturday 15 October, exalts:

> We regret to notice in to-day's obituary, the death of Mr. John Blair, a young townsman who had life been spared, had every prospect of reaching an eminent position as an artist. Though but 20 years of age, he had already manifested powers and achieved a position, which were sufficient to justify the high hopes entertained regarding him by all who had watched his career. Not only had the highest honours awarded in the Paisley School of Art been conferred upon him, but twice had he secured the large National Medallion, and that for works demanding the possession of the higher attributes of the artist… Though constitutionally of delicate health all who knew of his rare gifts, and had watched their gradual development, hoped that with mature years, more stable health would come; but these anticipations have now been blighted, and during the past week one more had been added to that mournful roll of young men of high promise, removed from the arena when their powers had been tested, and a life apparently of honour and success lay before them.

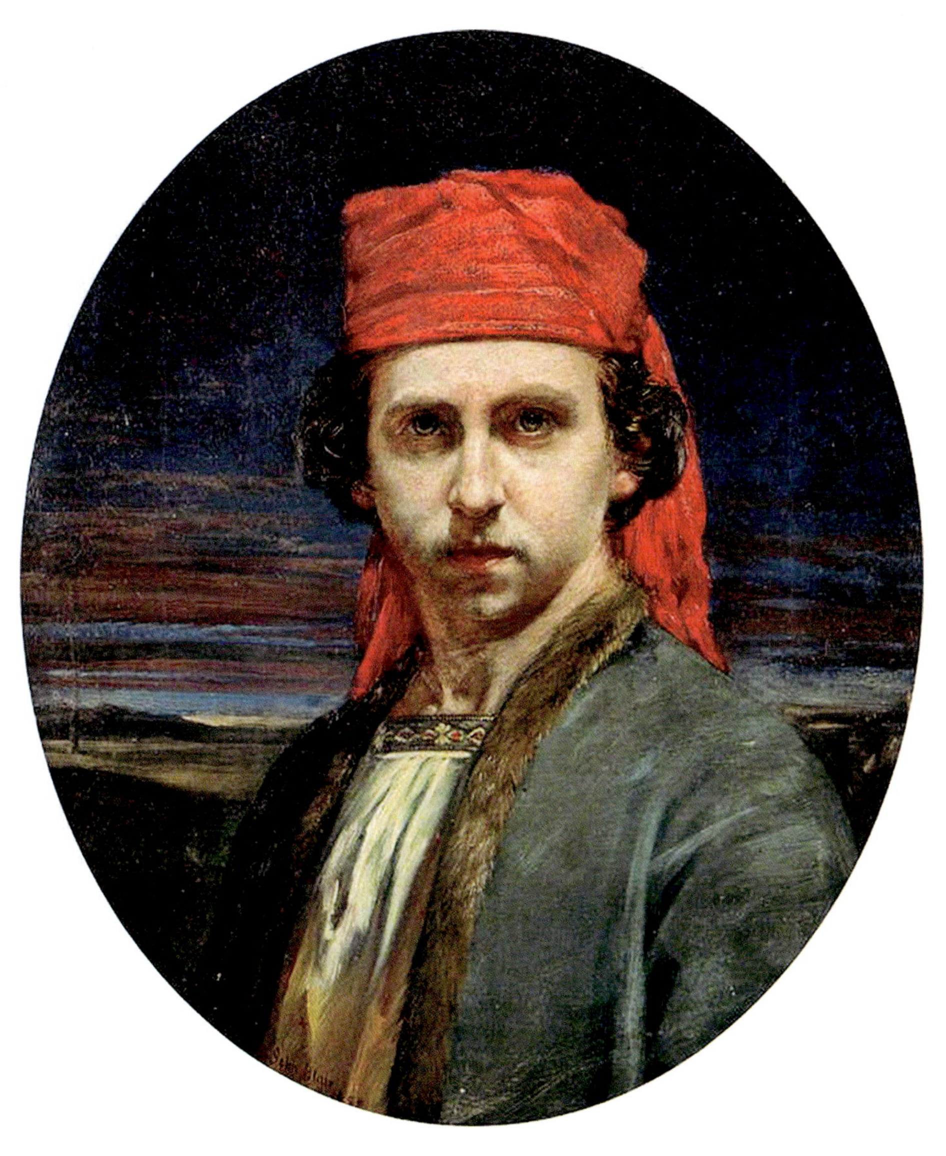

John Blair Jr
The Exile – Self Portrait, c.1859, oil on paper, 32 × 27 cm (12⅝ × 10⅝ in)
Paisley Museum and Art Galleries

Everett RUESS

Oakland, California, 28 Mar 1914 – c.Nov 1934, near Escalante, Utah
American, approx. 20 years, 8 months

The enigmatic vagabond Everett Ruess was a poet, writer, printmaker, watercolourist and draughtsman who explored the High Sierra, the California coast and the remote wilderness areas of Utah, Arizona, New Mexico and Colorado – invariably alone. From 1930, at about 16 years of age, he travelled the dangerous badlands of the West by horse and donkey, trading his art for supplies as he went. He learned to speak Navajo, and participated in a Hopi religious ceremony, fully engaging in everything as he pushed further into isolated regions.

Ruess was an ardent diarist and prolific letter-writer, and was intellectually mature for his age. In his final letter to his brother Waldo, he said, 'As to when I will revisit civilization, it will not be soon. I have not tired of the wilderness; rather I enjoy its beauty and the vagrant life I lead … It is enough that I am surrounded with beauty … This has been a full, rich year. I have left no strange or delightful thing undone that I wanted to do.'[6] Shortly thereafter he disappeared into thin air.

His mysterious fate has turned him into a folk hero. He wrote, 'And when the time comes to die, I'll find the wildest, loneliest, most desolate spot there is.' Ruess was not suicidal, but rather just attached to his eccentric lifestyle. Ruess was last seen along the Hole-in-the-Rock Trail in the Grand Staircase-Escalante National Monument on 21 November 1934. His two burros were later found at Davis Gulch along the Escalante River, but Ruess had vanished. Remains were found in 2009 that seemed to be Ruess's but were later determined to be those of a Native American. Some say he fell from a cliff, or drowned in a flash flood, or was even killed by Ute Indians for his burros. Locals from Utah's southern desert say that Ruess was probably shot for killing and eating a rancher's cattle near the small outpost of Escalante, Utah.

His powerful linoleum prints such as *Granite Towers* (c.1933) and *Monument Valley* (c.1932), and watercolours of the naked Western landscape such as *Desert Light* (c.1933) demonstrate that he had abundant talent. He once wrote, 'The world does not want art, only artists do.' He lived an anti-urban lifestyle and for him 'his wanderlust and his art became inseparable.'[7] Looking much like a young Leonardo DiCaprio, this wanderer penned, 'I prefer the saddle to the streetcar and the star-sprinkled sky to a roof, the obscure and difficult trail, leading into the unknown to any paved highway, and the deep peace of the wild to the discontent bred by cities.'

Everett Ruess
Granite Towers, c.1933, linocut print 39/50, 19.7 × 15.2 cm (7¾ × 6 in)
State of Utah Alice Merrill Horne Collection, Courtesy of Utah Division of Arts and Museums, Salt Lake City, Utah

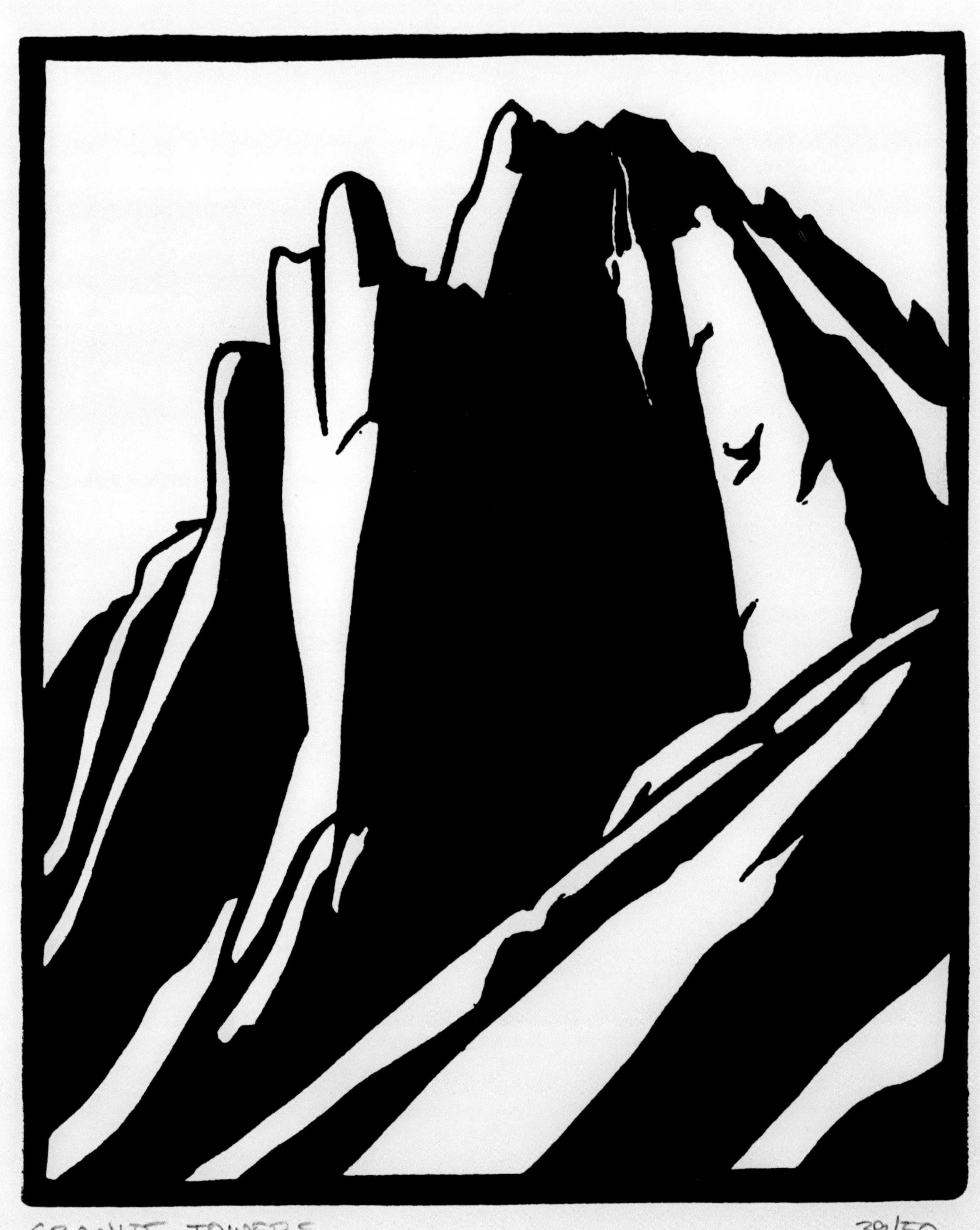

GRANITE TOWERS
39/50

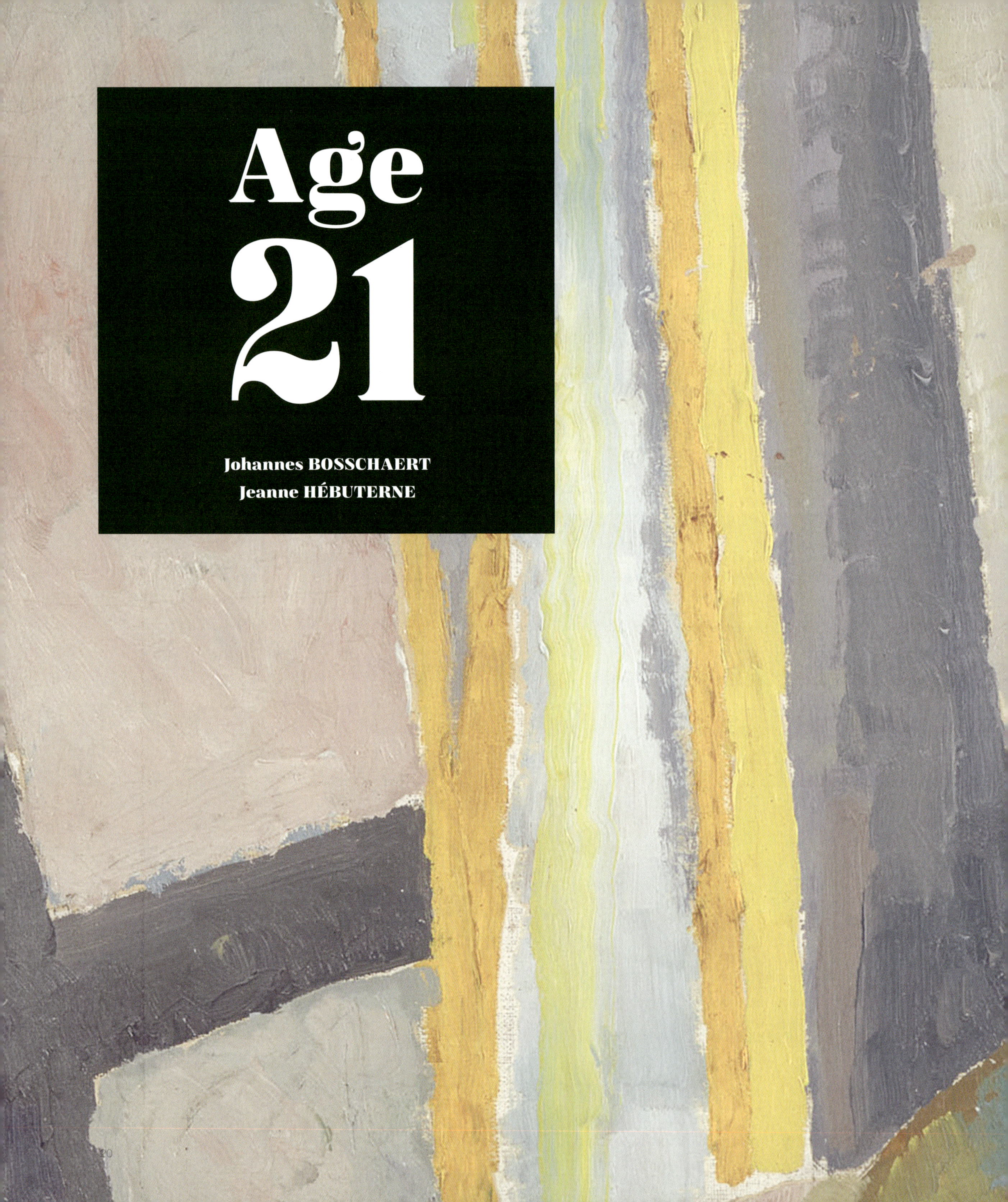
Age
21
Johannes BOSSCHAERT
Jeanne HÉBUTERNE

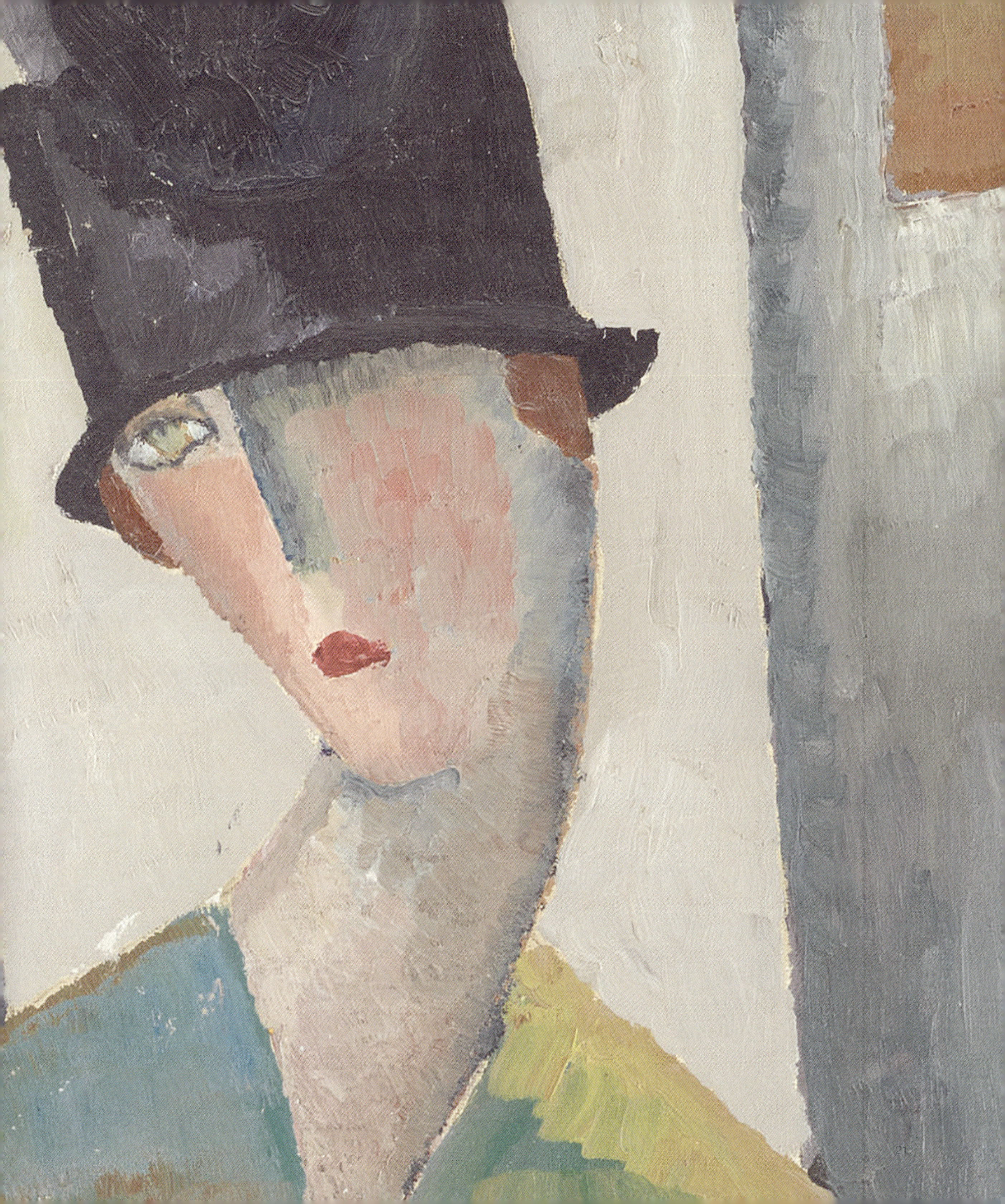

Johannes BOSSCHAERT

Middelburg, 1606/8 – 1628/9, Dordrecht
Dutch, approx. 21 years

Johannes Bosschaert was the eldest of three floral still-life painters, all sons of the noted mannerist floral still-life artist Ambrosius Bosschaert the Elder (1573–1621). The father was born in Antwerp where he studied art and had a workshop. However, since he was a Protestant in a Catholic country, he moved to the Netherlands because of the threat of religious persecution. He settled in Middelburg (1587–1613) in the southern Dutch province of Zeeland. There he joined the city's Guild of Saint Luke, and years later became its dean. Ambrosius Bosschaert established himself as one of the Netherlands's leading painters in the fashionable floral-painting genre.

It was in Middelburg that Ambrosius married Marie (the daughter of a prosperous wool merchant) and where his children were born. Marie's brother was the remarkably talented artist Balthasar van der Ast (1593/4–1657) of Middelburg, who studied painting with Bosschaert and lived with the family after his father died in 1609. When Ambrosius died in 1621, his children, in turn, studied with Van der Ast.

For reasons not altogether clear, the Bosschaert family moved frequently, perhaps for commissions and fresh markets. With Van der Ast, the Bosschaerts moved to

Amsterdam (1614), Bergen op Zoom (1615–16), Utrecht (1616–19) and Breda (1619). The family returned to Utrecht in 1619. After the father's death two years later, Uncle Van der Ast ran his workshop and the three brothers began working there. Younger than Johannes were Ambrosius Bosschaert II (1609–1645) and Abraham (1612–1643); all painted table-top floral still-lifes in the style and manner of their father and uncle.

Of the three sons, Johannes could have been the most talented. His oeuvre was small but had all the inklings of strong potential within the 'family' genre, demonstrating his father's delicacy of colour and his uncle's subtle tonalities. Johannes's *Still Life with Tulips and Frog* (c.1628) demonstrates the energy he infused into the traditionally staid genre. His still-lifes veritably teem with amphibian and insect life, adding dynamism to his compositions. Being immersed in the family dynasty, he began his professional career early and vigorously. Because his oeuvre is difficult to distinguish from that of the other Bosschaerts, it cannot be said that he broke new ground. At only 21 years he hardly had a chance to find his own voice. Sadly, Johannes's two brothers died young as well, whisked away by unknown causes (possibly tuberculosis).

Johannes Bosschaert
Still-Life with Tulips and Frog, c.1628, oil on panel, 46 × 64 cm (18⅛ × 25¼ in)
Nationalmuseum, Stockholm

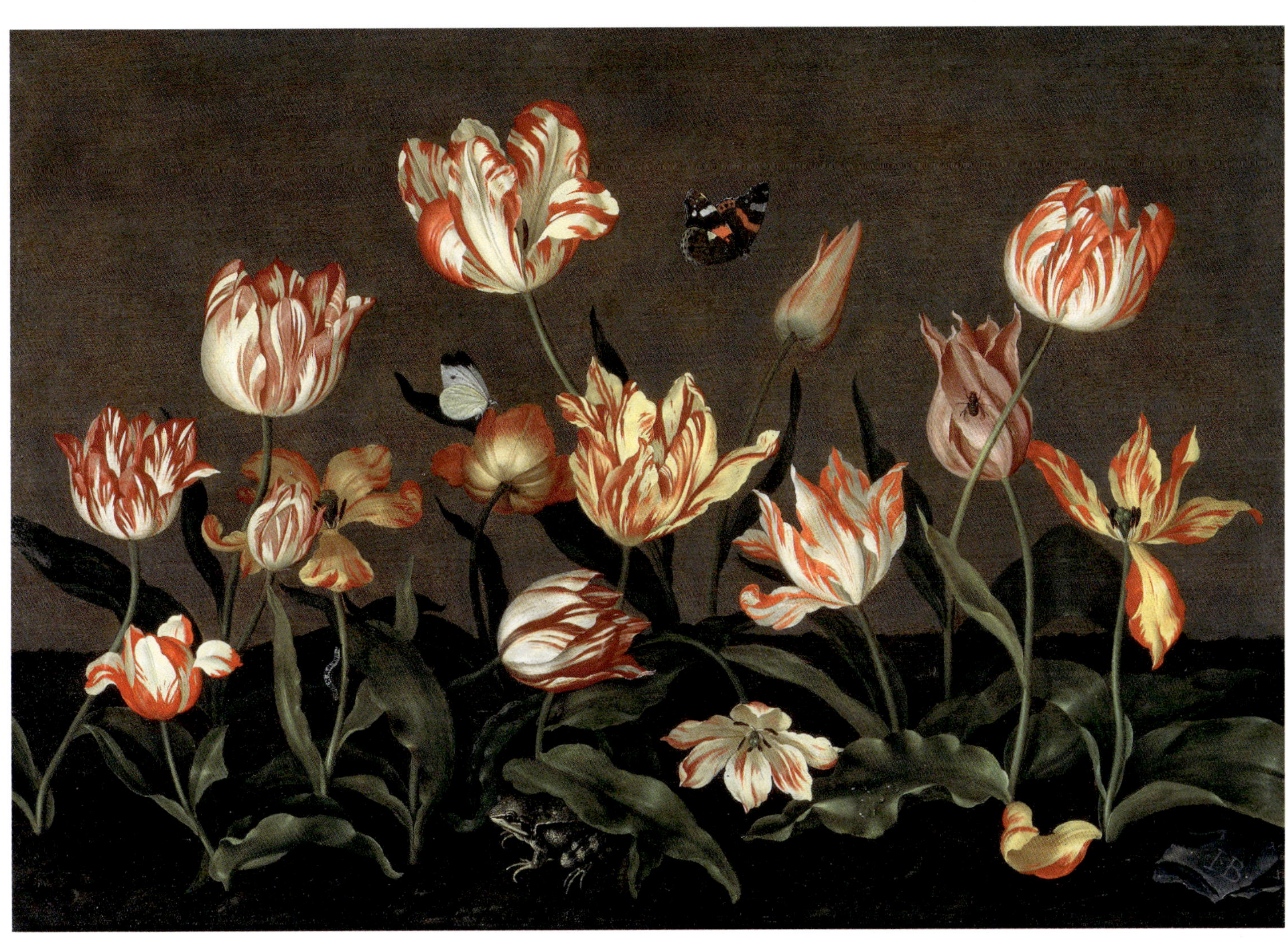

Jeanne HÉBUTERNE

Meaux, 6 Apr 1898 – 26 Jan 1920, Paris
French, 21 years, 9 months, 21 days

Hébuterne has long been considered a minor painter, but in the 21st century her reputation as an artist has staged a revival. She is most famous for being the common-law wife and model of Amedeo Modigliani and the mother of his surviving daughter. Modigliani produced more than 20 finished oil portraits of Hébuterne, however Hébuterne had ambitions of her own to be a painter. Encouraged in art by her parents and elder brother, Hébuterne studied drawing at the École des Arts Décoratifs and then the Académie Colarossi in Paris.

Hébuterne continued drawing and painting even after meeting Modigliani at the Académie in the spring of 1917, and later moving in with him. While her style was influenced by les Fauves, Nabis and Modigliani himself, Hébuterne demonstrated notable stylistic differences from her husband even when treating the same subjects and models. Her paintings, such as *Femme au chapeau cloche* (1919), were certainly experimental and au courant for her day, but they also displayed a certain quality and quiet confidence.

Sadly, her short career came to an abrupt end when, on 24 January 1920, Amedeo Modigliani died of tuberculosis. The distraught Jeanne Hébuterne was brought by her family to their home on rue des Amiaux, Paris. It was there that Jeanne threw herself out of the fifth-floor apartment window just 40 hours after Modigliani's death, killing herself and her unborn child. She was just 21. Her family, who blamed her demise on Modigliani, buried her in the Cimetière parisien de Bagneux. Nearly 10 years later, at the request of Modigliani's brother, Emanuele, the Hébuterne family agreed to have her remains transferred to Père Lachaise cemetery to rest beside Modigliani. Her epitaph aptly reads, 'Devoted companion to the extreme sacrifice'.

Hébuterne never exhibited during her lifetime and after her death her art was hidden and forgotten. Her oeuvre is also very small, with Christie's estimating only around 25 extant paintings in the world. However, since the year 2000, numerous exhibitions have been mounted, displaying her paintings alongside those of Modigliani. In 2008 a monograph and catalogue raisonné, dedicated solely to her life and work, was published, finally recognising her youthful talent. 'To die at such a young age, just when her skills as an artist were beginning to reveal themselves, was a tragedy,' Valerie Didier Hess of Christie's states. 'Who knows what she could have done had she lived, with or without Modigliani.'[8]

Jeanne Hébuterne
Femme au chapeau cloche, 1919, oil on canvas, 92.2 × 65.3 cm (36¼ × 25¾ in)
Christie's Paris

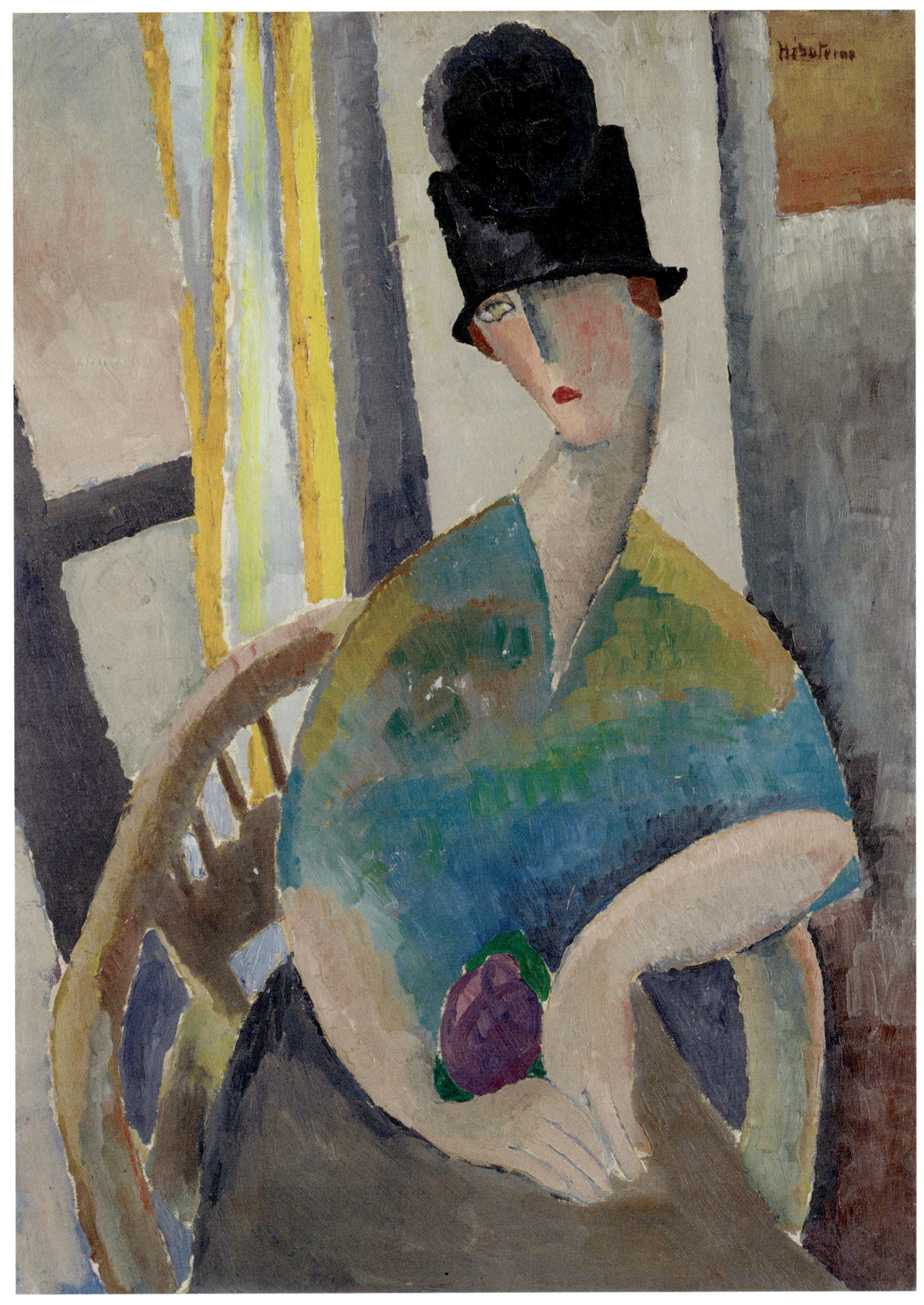

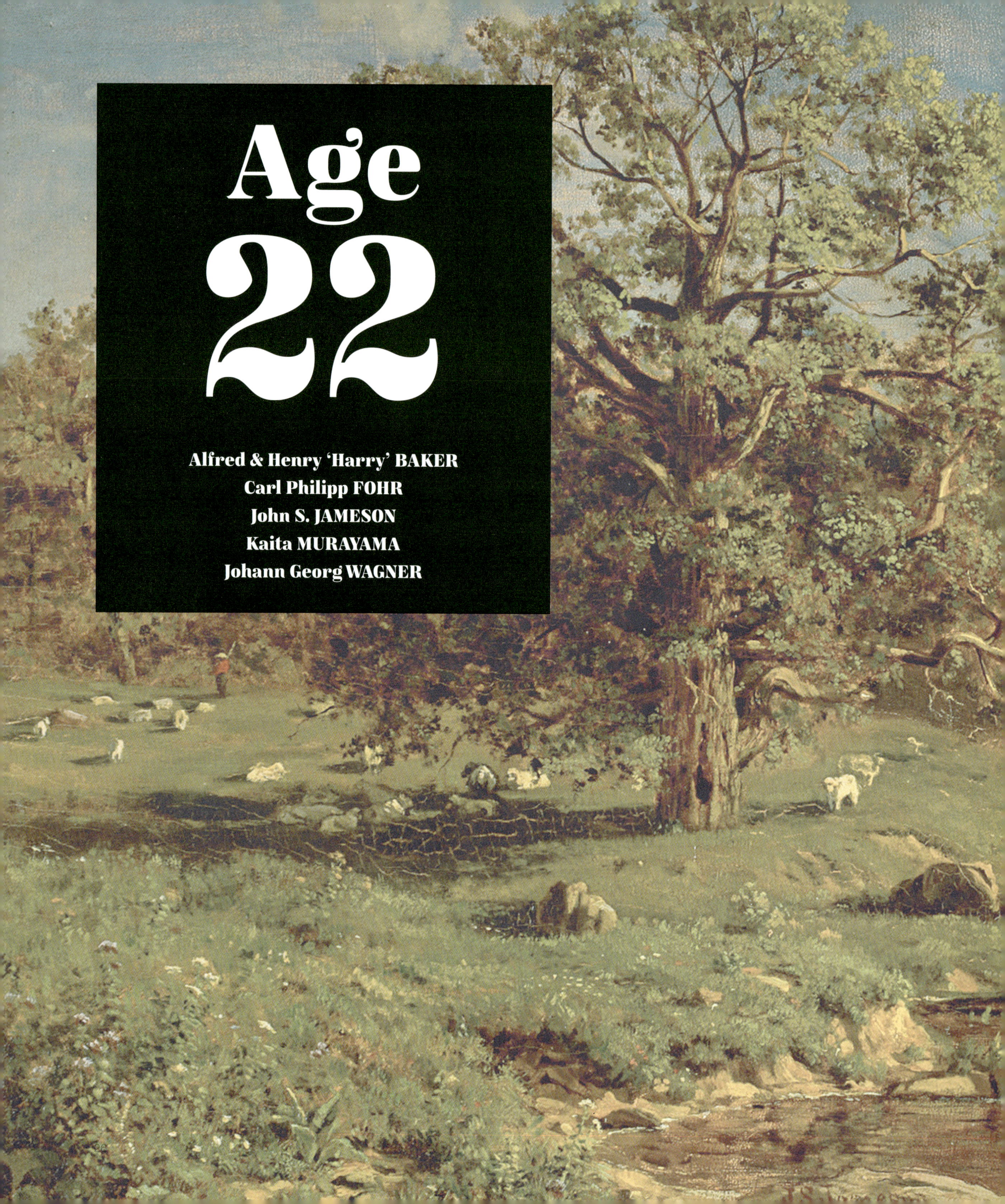

Age
22

Alfred & Henry 'Harry' BAKER
Carl Philipp FOHR
John S. JAMESON
Kaita MURAYAMA
Johann Georg WAGNER

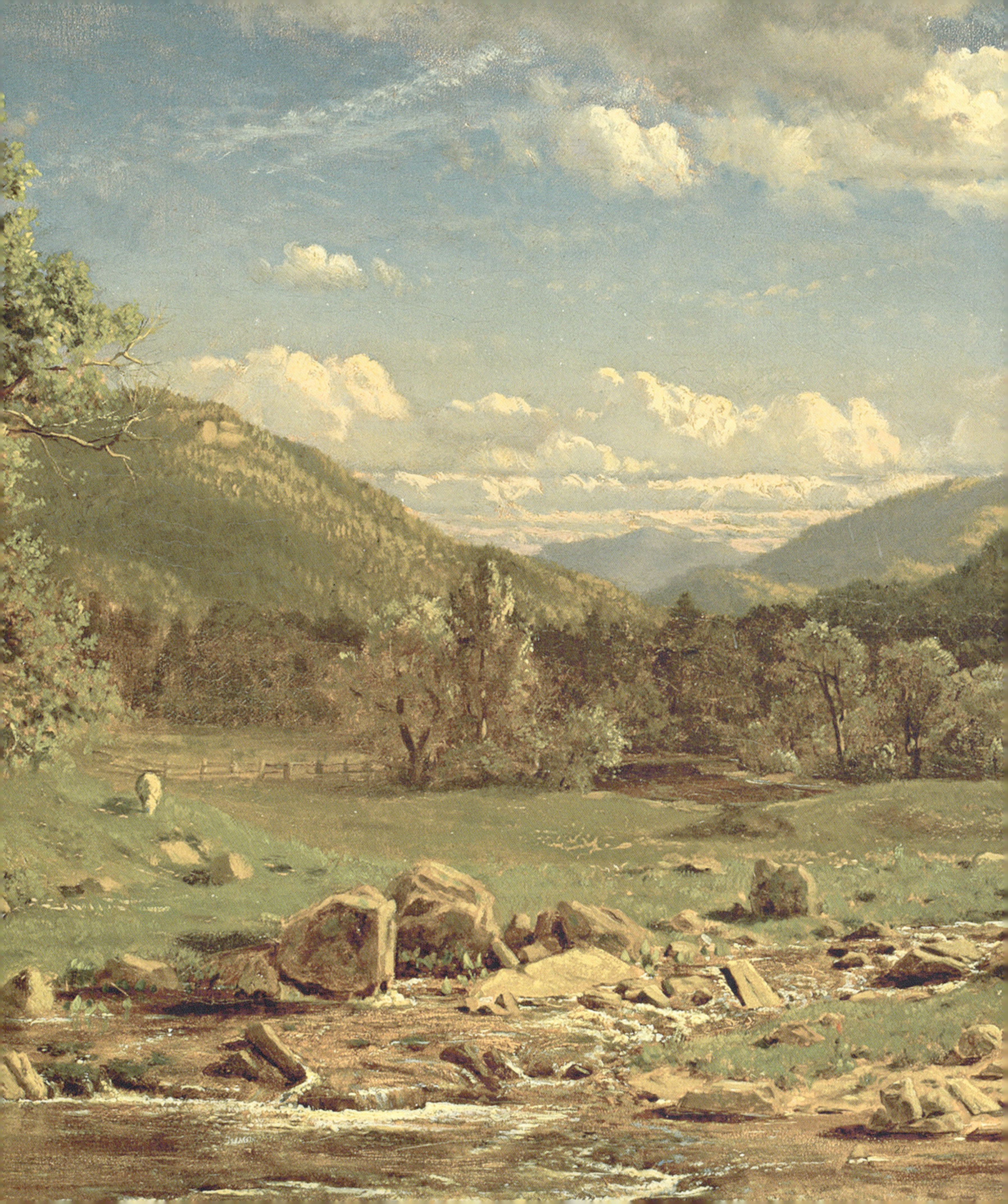

Alfred & Henry 'Harry' BAKER

Birmingham, 1850 – 1872, Birmingham[9]
British, approx. 22 years

Birmingham, 1849 – Jan 1875, possibly Christchurch
British, approx. 25 years

Of the four artist sons of landscape painter Samuel Henry Baker (1824–1909), only two reached their artistic maturity. The eldest, Henry and Alfred, were just in their early twenties when they died. In contrast, their younger brothers Oliver (1856–1939) and Harold (1860–1942) lived long, notable lives. Oliver became a painter, designer and silversmith, gaining fame for his role in developing the 'Cymric' silverware line for Liberty & Co. Likewise, Harold was a distinguished photographer, becoming the official photographer for *Birmingham Magazine of Arts and Industries*, as well as other publications.

The Bakers were clearly a family of great talent, all educated in their father's studio. Studying art with one's father clearly was an advantage; and for artists who left the scene at 22 and 25, it was indispensable. After leaving the Handsworth Bridge Trust Grammar School at the age of 15, Alfred entered the Birmingham School of Art where his father was a professor. Henry most likely obtained a similar education. Both brothers painted the bucolic countryside of North Wales, the Midlands and southern England. Their subjects were largely plein-air rural farms, fields, cottages and farm animals. As seen from extant works, they followed in the stylistic and subject footsteps of their noted father.

Henry and Alfred exhibited mainly at the Birmingham Society, and the Royal Society of British Artists on Suffolk Street, London. Their paintings did not escape the notice of critics. A review in the *Art Journal* shortly before Alfred's death mentions him in prescient terms: 'His [Samuel H. Baker's] son gives promise of fame hereafter, and not far off. *Harvest in the Vale of Llangollen* and *Moel Seabod* are admirable landscapes by Alfred Baker.'[10] The Birmingham Museum Trust collection possesses one oil by Alfred, *Cow Lying on the Ground* (c.1870), and one by Harry, titled *Selly Manor* (c.1870).

It is not known how the two young men died. Alfred, the younger and more talented of the two, died first in 1872. The Birmingham Museum's catalogue notes that, 'A very promising career was cut short by his early death in 1872, when he was not quite twenty-two years of age.'[11] Henry painted and exhibited for a couple more years. At the time of his death he lived in the Bournemouth area, and most likely died at Christchurch, England in January 1875. Had they lived, would Alfred and Henry have reached the technical excellence of their father in landscape painting, or would they, like their younger brothers, have explored new mediums and styles? These are questions their early deaths leave unanswered.

Henry 'Harry' Baker
Selly Manor, c.1870, oil on canvas, 30 × 46 cm (11¾ × 18⅛ in)
Courtesy Birmingham Museum Trust

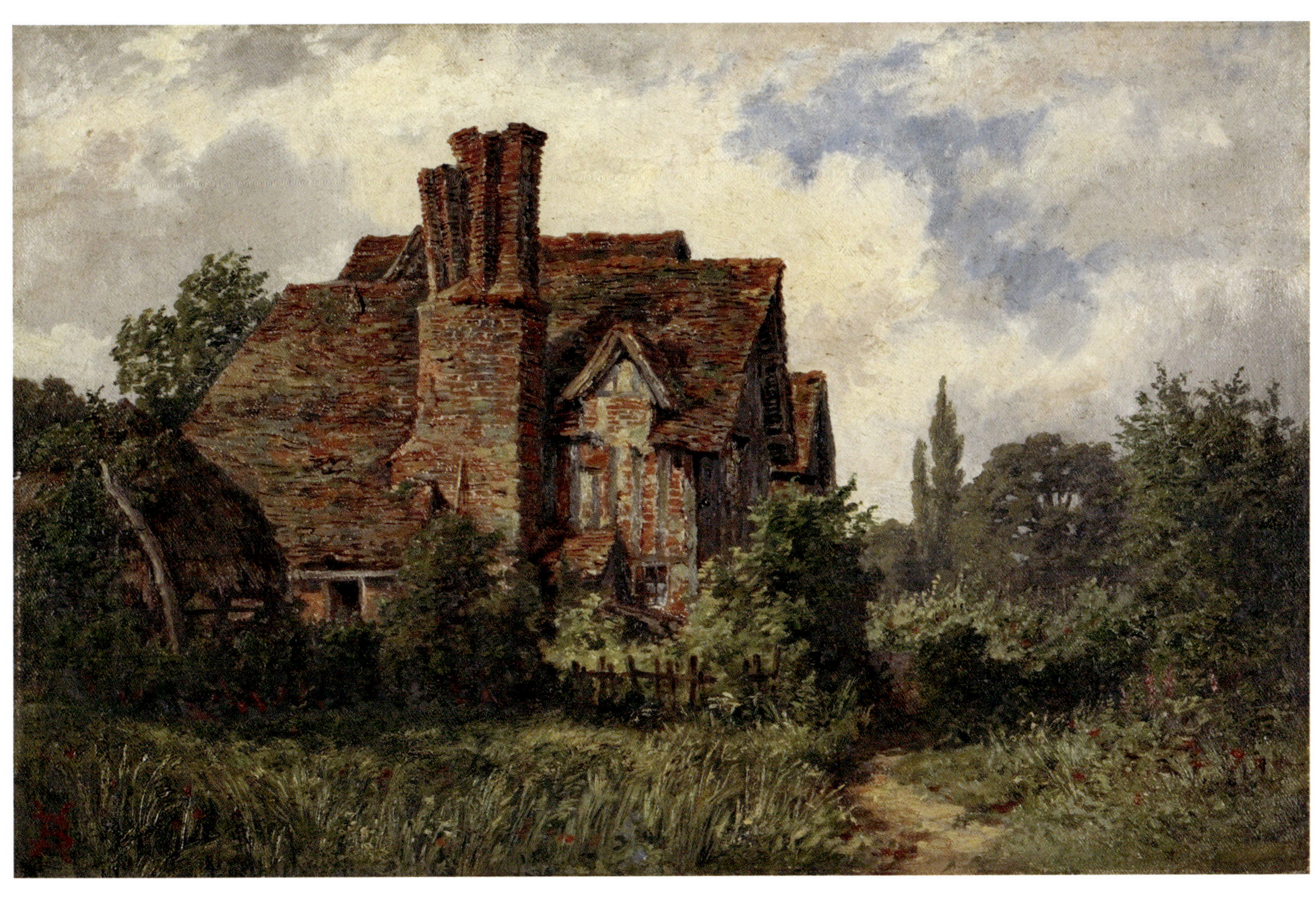

Carl Philipp FOHR

Heidelberg, 26 Nov 1795 – 29 Jun 1818, Rome
German, 22 years, 7 months, 4 days

The death of the young Carl Philipp Fohr came as a great shock to the artist community of Rome. Fohr had been swimming with fellow artist friends Carl Barth, Johann Anton Ramboux and Samuel Amsler in the river Tiber when he began to struggle. Although Barth risked his own life to rescue his dear friend, he was unsuccessful and Fohr drowned. As one friend Philip Dieffenbach lamented, 'Just as he began to get a name for himself as an artist, the waves of the Tiber's current tore him away.'[12]

In order to raise funds to build a monument in Fohr's memory, Amsler made a print after a portrait by Barth of the young artist. Barth was himself so overcome with grief at Fohr's loss that he could not produce the print himself. In the end a modest stone plaque was erected for Fohr in the famous Non-Catholic Cemetery in southern Rome, which also hosts the remains of many notable artists and poets. Although small, his memorial is in a prominent place in the cemetery beside the great Pyramid of Cestius.

In his brief but eventful lifetime, Fohr embodied the romanticism of his age. He was largely self-taught as a youth. After being 'discovered' by the artist Georg Wilhelm Issel, he won the patronage of Princess Wilhelmine Louise of Baden who provided him with an annual stipend. Although Fohr studied briefly at the Munich Academy in 1815 and again in 1816, his independent spirit made him at odds with the regimented instruction, and he left. Returning to his hometown of Heidelberg, he joined the Burschenschaft – a young political group dedicated to freedom and German unification. Fohr also began wearing his hair long and dressing in 'old German' costume, which can be seen in his memorial portrait. In autumn 1816, Fohr walked on foot from Heidelberg to Rome, a trek that took over a month.

He fell in well with the artist community of Rome, except for the unfortunate incident of a pistol duel he fought with artist Ludwig Ruhl in March 1817. Both artists were unharmed, but never again were they friends. Fohr shared a studio with the landscape artist Joseph Anton Koch and had frequent contact with the Nazarenes. Fohr became noted for his stern portraits, mediaeval German mythological scenes, and sublime landscapes such as *Waterfalls at Tivoli* (1817). What remains of his life's work consists of sketch-books, drawings and only seven oil paintings, just fragments that testify to his ability. However, his precocious talent was readily recognised by his fellow artists as 'a cult of great promise unfulfilled'. Or as his friend and biographer Dieffenbach wrote, if he had lived but 'ten years longer, the Fatherland would have boldly placed him among its first artists.'[13]

Carl Philipp Fohr
Waterfalls at Tivoli, 1817, oil on canvas, 74 × 105 cm (29⅛ × 41⅜ in)
Städel Museum, Frankfurt

"

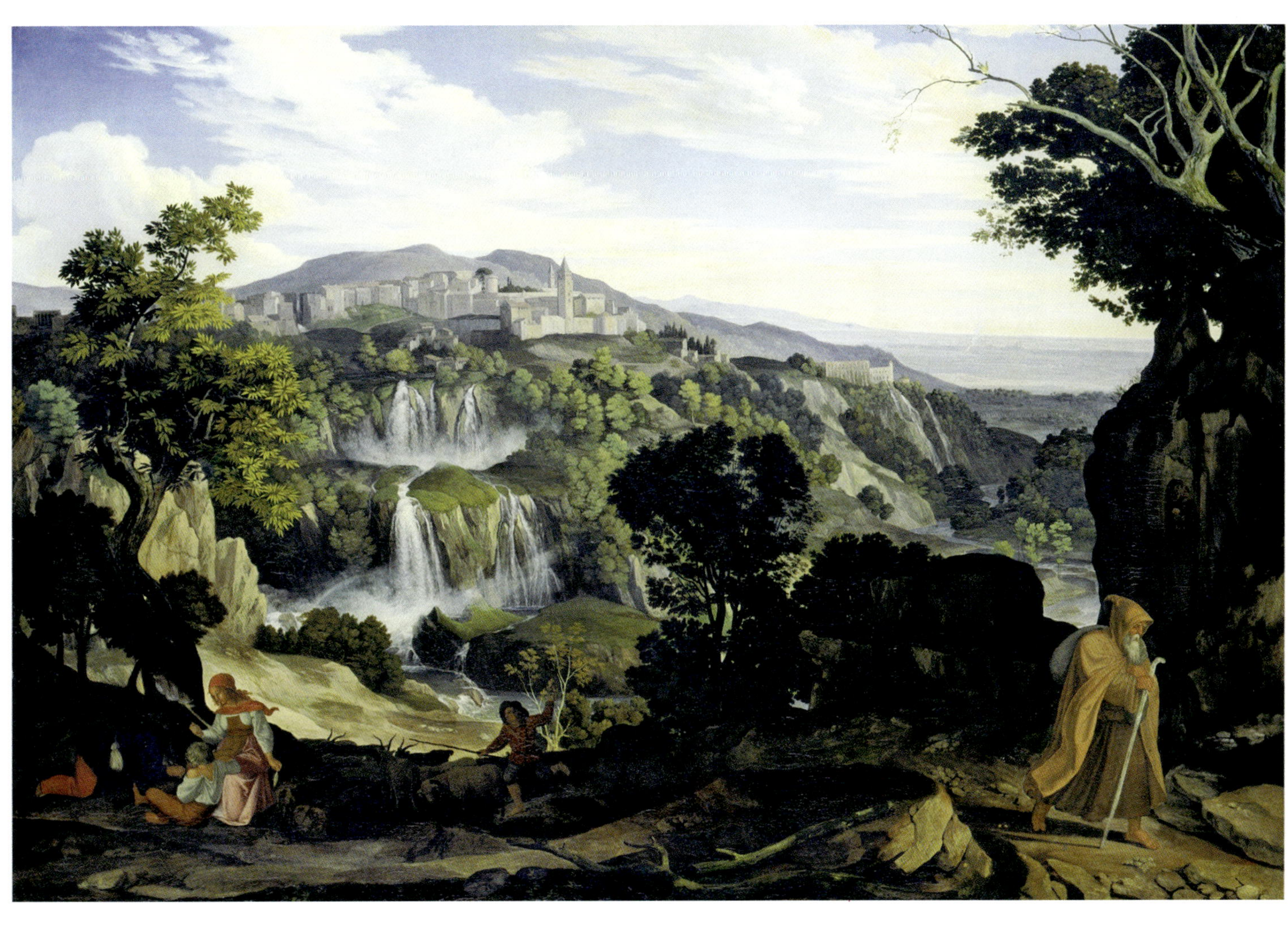

John S. JAMESON

Hartford, Connecticut, 25 Mar 1842 – 31 Aug 1864, Andersonville, Georgia
American, 22 years, 5 months, 7 days

A man of many talents, John S. Jameson was very gifted in both music and painting, and often wondered which had the greater claim upon him. In 1853, his family moved to New York City and he later enrolled in drawing classes at the National Academy of Design. He also painted at the Tenth Street Studio where he befriended Frederic Edwin Church (1826–1900) when he was completing his famed canvas *The Heart of the Andes*. Other illustrious acquaintances included John W. Casilear and Sanford R. Gifford, thus giving Jameson a path to becoming a Hudson River artist. Tragically, Jameson's oeuvre amounts to only about 25 to 30 finished paintings.

After a couple of years of wanting to enlist in the Civil War but deterred by friends, Jameson wrote, 'I should be ashamed to be staying at home at my ease, while others were fighting at the front.'[14] In January 1864, Jameson joined the 1st Connecticut Cavalry of the Union Army where he was eventually made a sergeant. He made 13 sorties with the Cavalry before being captured while refilling his canteen at a river near Reams Station, Virginia. He was sent to the infamous Confederate POW camp of Andersonville.

This death camp was an overcrowded, unsanitary and disease-ridden sprawling stockade in Southwest Georgia. During the 14 months Andersonville served as a prison, nearly 13,000 Union prisoners died, approximately 28 per cent of its inmates. The prison's commander, Captain Henry Wirz, was later tried and executed for cruelty and murder of prisoners, one of only two people convicted for war crimes during the Civil War. Already delicate of health and suffering from diarrhoea, Jameson succumbed to these intolerable conditions at the youthful age of 22 years.

After his death, Jameson's mother wrote to Frederic Church, expressing her appreciation for his friendship with her son. Church replied, 'Of all the younger Artists whose personal acquaintance I have made, and whose works and characteristics of mind and heart came to my observation, no one has interested me so much as your son, or held out better grounded hopes of future high excellence.'[15] Such paintings as *Saranac Waters* (1863) and *Grazing Sheep at Headwaters of a Stream* (1862) ratify these expectations. The latter painting, which sold at Heritage Auctions, Dallas in 2018 for US$250,000 (£192,000), is a testament to the skill and appeal of his art.

At the 1866 Artists' Fund Society's meeting, 'the young, brave, and enthusiastic John S. Jameson' was eulogised by president John F. Kensett, a prominent Hudson River landscape artist. He lamented that, 'Had his life been spared, the rare qualities of Jameson's mind – his exquisite taste and accomplishments, and fine promise of future excellence in his art would have reflected honour upon this Society and upon the country of his birth.' He continued, that through his 'patriotic sense of duty to his country' he has been interred in 'the loathsome fields of Andersonville.'[16]

These eulogies express well the art community's grief from the loss of this brave artist; however, none is quite as lyrical as that by the author Harry Willard French. Writing in 1879, he penned these few words of solace: 'Many a bright star of promise fell, shaken from its path toward a glorious zenith by the convulsions of that bitter conflict – probably none brighter than the promise in John S. Jameson.'[17]

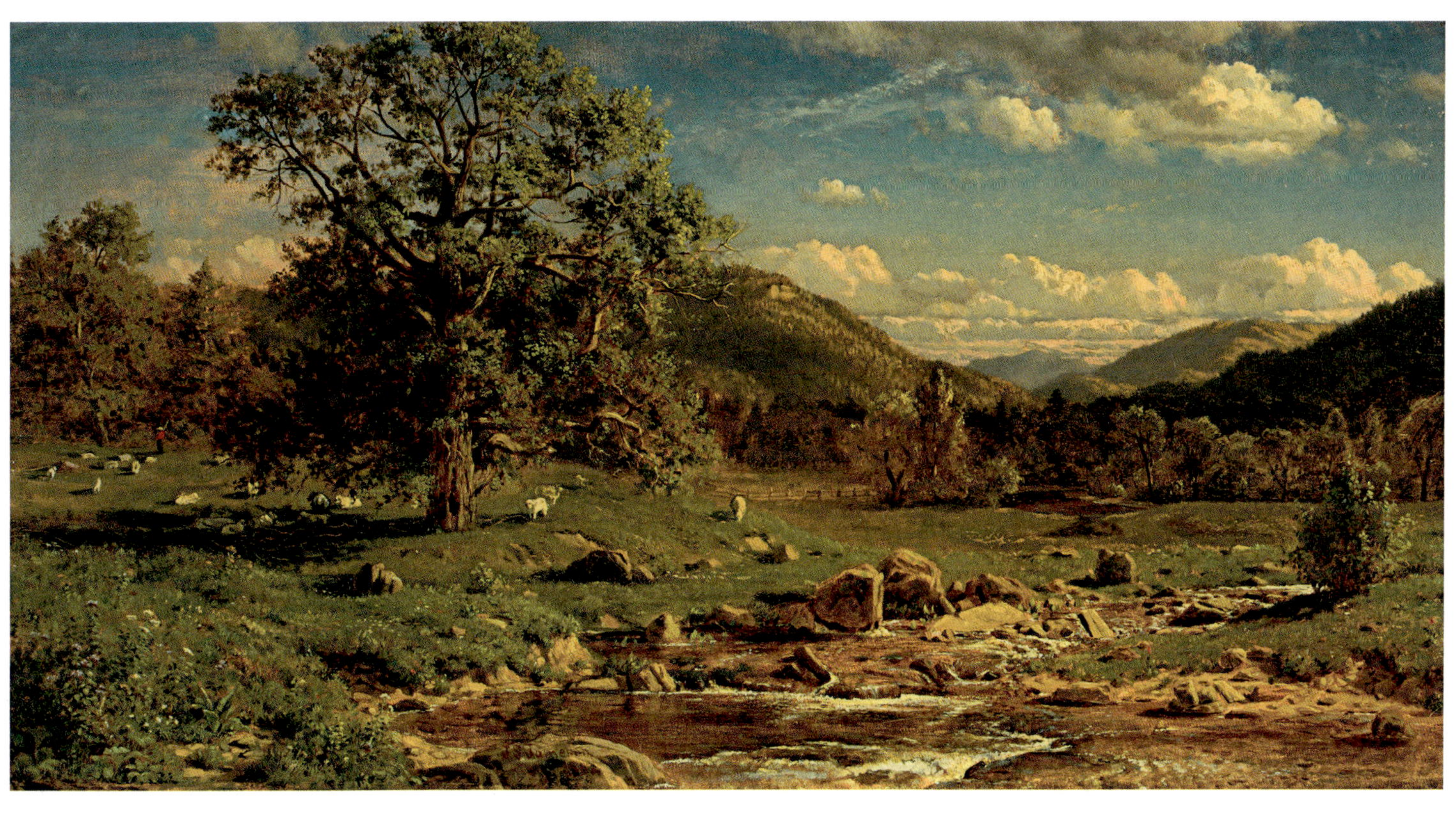

John S. Jameson
Grazing Sheep at Headwaters of a Stream, 1862, oil on canvas, 45.7 × 83.8 cm (18 × 33 in)
Heritage Auctions, Dallas

Kaita MURAYAMA

Okazaki or Yokohama, 15 Sep 1896 – 20 Feb 1919, Tokyo
Japanese, 22 years, 5 months, 6 days

Just as he was beginning to make a name for himself in art, Kaita Murayama died of tuberculosis aged only 22. As a youth, Murayama's expressionistic talents were recognised by his cousin, the famous artist Kanae Yamamoto (1882–1946). Yamamoto gave him a full set of oil paints and encouraged him to pursue a career in painting. The family's move to the artistically rich city of Kyoto also served as an inspiration to the young painter's fertile mind.

Finally, in 1914, the 18-year-old moved to Tokyo and studied at the Fine Arts Academy under Kosugi Misei (1881–1964), a founder of the Western-style Pacific Painting Society. Murayama's own art developed into a bold, Western-inspired modernist style, described as 'muscular, robust and emotional' and even 'wild'.[18] When he exhibited in 1914, one of his paintings was purchased by Taikan Yokoyama (the grand master of Nihonga painting), hinting at the successful career that lay before him.

Unfortunately, Murayama was an alcoholic, involved in several ill-fated love affairs, and along the way had contracted tuberculosis. In late 1918 during a trip from Bōsō, he was taken to the hospital with hemoptysis. It is said that one night he wandered into the cold air and was discovered early the next morning collapsed in a field. Overcome by his coughing of blood, he died shortly thereafter. Murayama's art was once considered very rare, only 27 known oils, with some of his paintings gaining widespread recognition. His canvas *Kosui no Onna* ('Lake and Woman', 1917, Pola Museum of Art) has been affectionately called the 'Mona Lisa of Japan'.[19]

In 2019, an Okazaki exhibition revealed more than 100 previously unknown works, displaying the breadth of his production and the diversity of his style. Murayama was also known for his writing. Two volumes of his prose published posthumously (1920–21) 'set the Japanese literary world abuzz.' Felled by the disease that claimed so many artists, Murayama is thought to have been one of the most 'vibrant and original painters of the Taishō period.'[20] Murayama wrote in the waning days of his life this haunting poem predicting his own demise: 'The tree trembles in the wind. The dark leaves flutter like the eyes of the grim reaper. The sky is staring at the tree. The tree continually trembling. Then me. The wind blows away in the sky. Life is going to disappear.'

Kaita Murayama
Self-Portrait Wearing a Paper Balloon, 1914, pencil and wash on paper, size unknown
Private collection

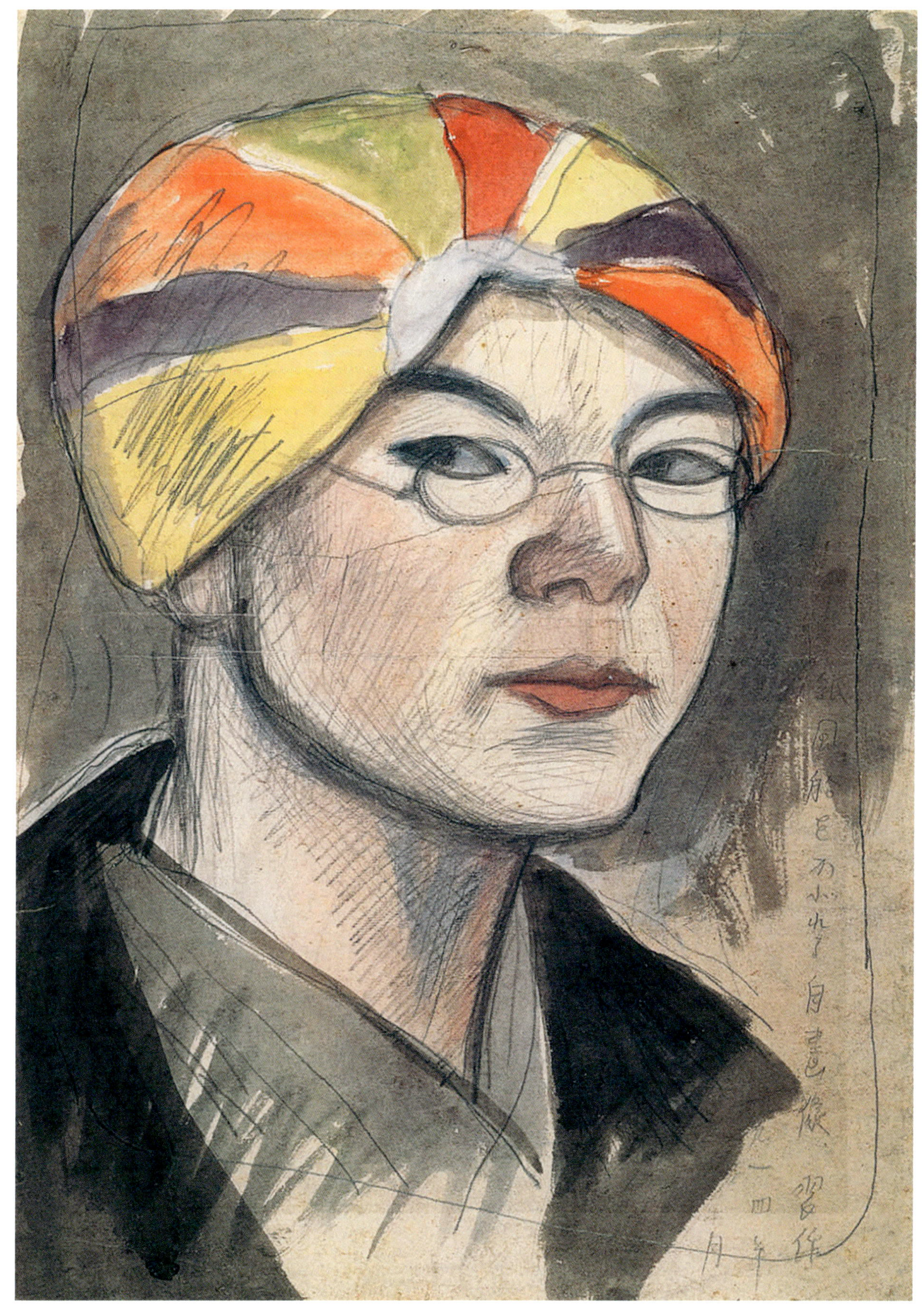

Johann Georg **WAGNER**

Meissen, 26 Oct 1744 – 14 Jun 1767, Meissen
German, 22 years, 7 months, 20 days

Johann Georg Wagner benefitted greatly from being born into a Saxon artistic family. His mother was Maria Dorothea Dietrich Wagner (1719–1792), a gifted painter of landscapes and historical subjects in oil and gouache. Two of her paintings can be found in the Städel Museum, Frankfurt. The young artist was first taught by her and his father Johann Jakob Wagner, then by Maria's father, the elderly painter and etcher Johann Georg Dietrich (1684–1752), Weimar court painter. Furthermore, Johann's uncle was the noted court painter Christian Wilhelm Ernst Dietrich (1712–1774) of Dresden. Uncle Dietrich taught Johann from 1758 when he was only 14. Wagner worked very much in his uncle's style, and his early work is often confused with his uncle's.

Family legend has it that Joseph Roos (1726–1805) of Vienna was asked to teach the boy-prodigy but refused because Johann was so advanced in his skills. However, Roos agreed to give him assignments, and thus influenced Wagner in the style of Italianate landscape and animal painting. For a short time, Wagner was even the workshop foreman for Roos. This head-start meant that he was an extremely competent draughtsman, etcher and painter in gouache and oil by his late teens and early twenties. Some of his drawings are listed with dates of 1760, and his earliest known painting just two years later.

Probably because of his declining health, Wagner became a pensioner in 1765. Then, to supplement his income, he took a position as an assistant teacher at the Dresden Academy of Art. His fame was secured when the Parisian engraver and art dealer Johann Georg Wille began selling Wagner's originals and engravings after his artwork in the French art market. François Boucher was influenced by his gouache technique and propagated it into French society. Thus, small cabinets filled with gouache paintings and drawings, known as 'coloriés d'après' and 'dans la manière de Wagner,' became the fashion. Amazingly the 'Wagner style' was then reintroduced to Germany where it had begun, and especially into Wagner's hometown where the Meissen porcelain works of Carl Gottlob Ehrlich and Johann Friedrich Nagel used it to great effect.

We can see in his paintings a certain youthful immaturity which is not apparent in his drawings, which have the deft touch of a master. He was mostly an artist of rustic hilly Saxon landscapes with figures, huts and farm animals. His unique use of gouache as seen in his *Hilly Landscape with Waterfall, Jetty, Ruins and Herd* (1765, Albertina, Vienna), though minor in-and-of itself, had a great effect on his contemporaries. His pen and ink with wash drawings, such as *Hilly Landscape with Farmhouse and Cattle* (Albertina, Vienna), possess an elegance of simplicity. His uncle Dietrich encouraged him to do 'malerradierer' (engravings and prints) and in the nine-autograph works, his subjects were mostly figurative. Wagner died of unknown causes, but since he was a pensioner at the age of 20, we imagine it was a wasting disease such as tuberculosis. His flower of artistic genius gave us but a glimpse of what was to bloom. Fortunately, his influence on the arts was greater than he was.

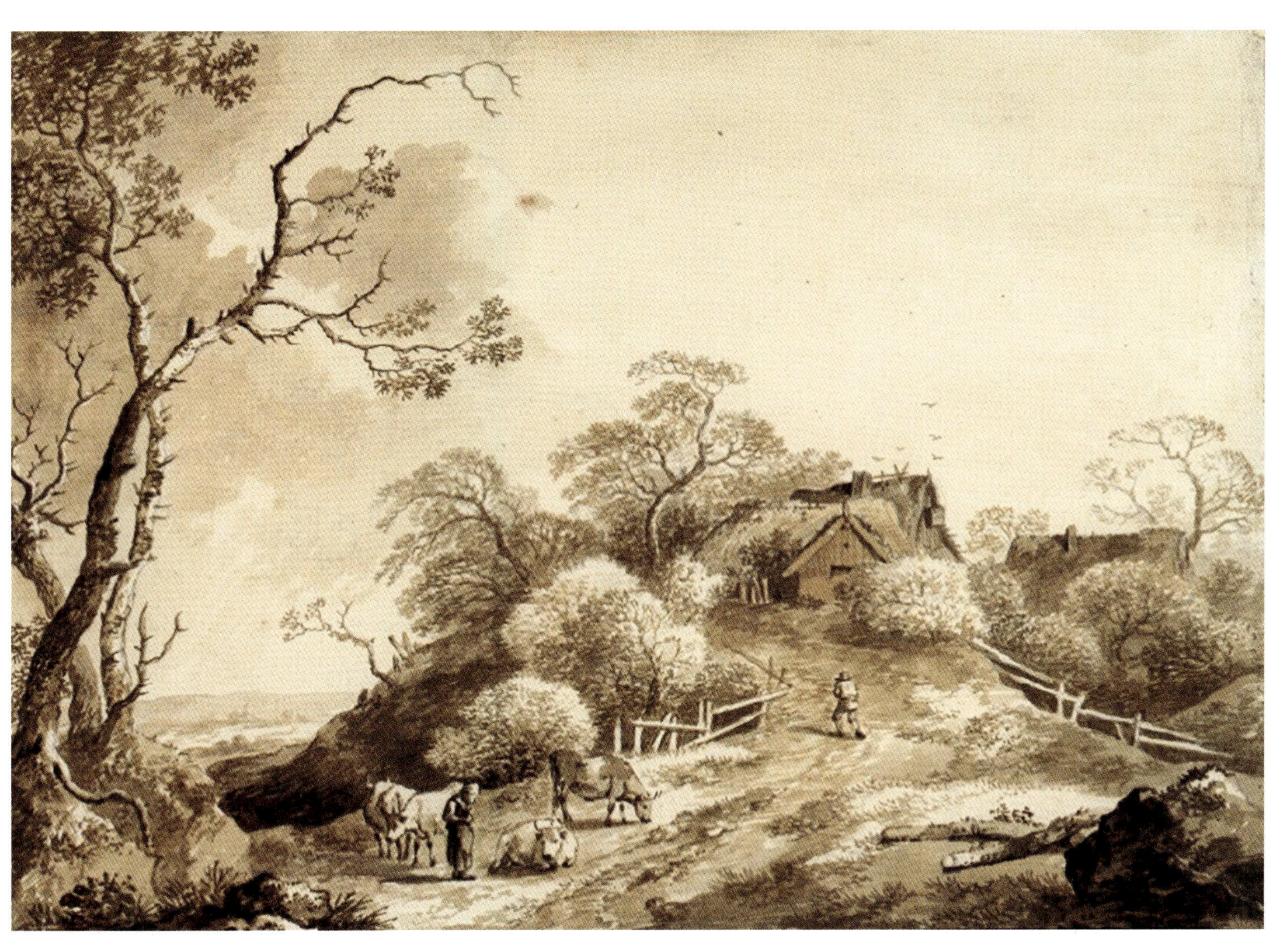

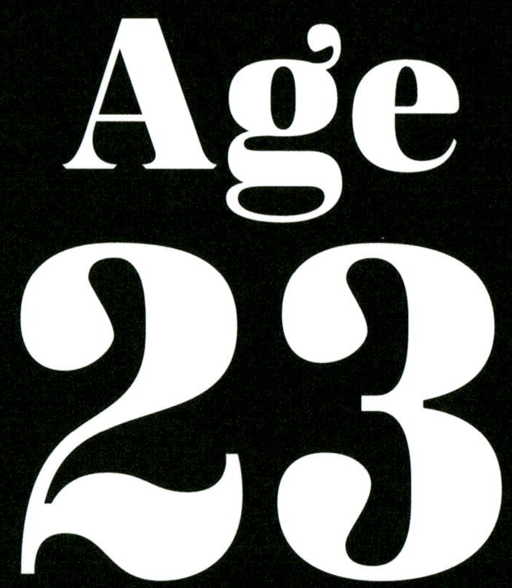

Age 23

Samuel FORDE

Henri GAUDIER-BRZESKA

Frederick Trevelyan 'Trev' & Howard GOODALL

Maurycy GOTTLIEB

Hermann STENNER

Fyodor Aleksandrovich VASILYEV

Pierino da VINCI

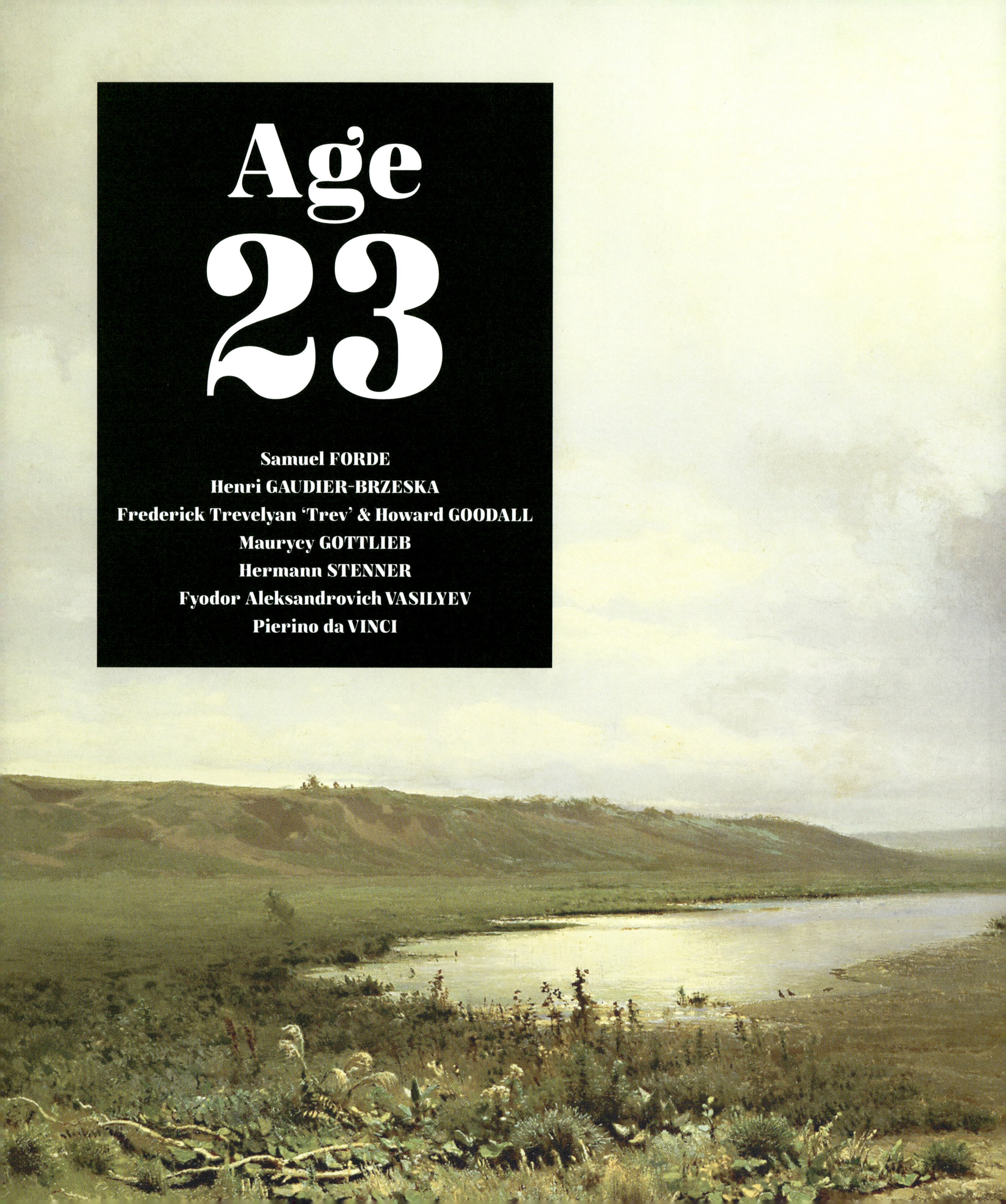

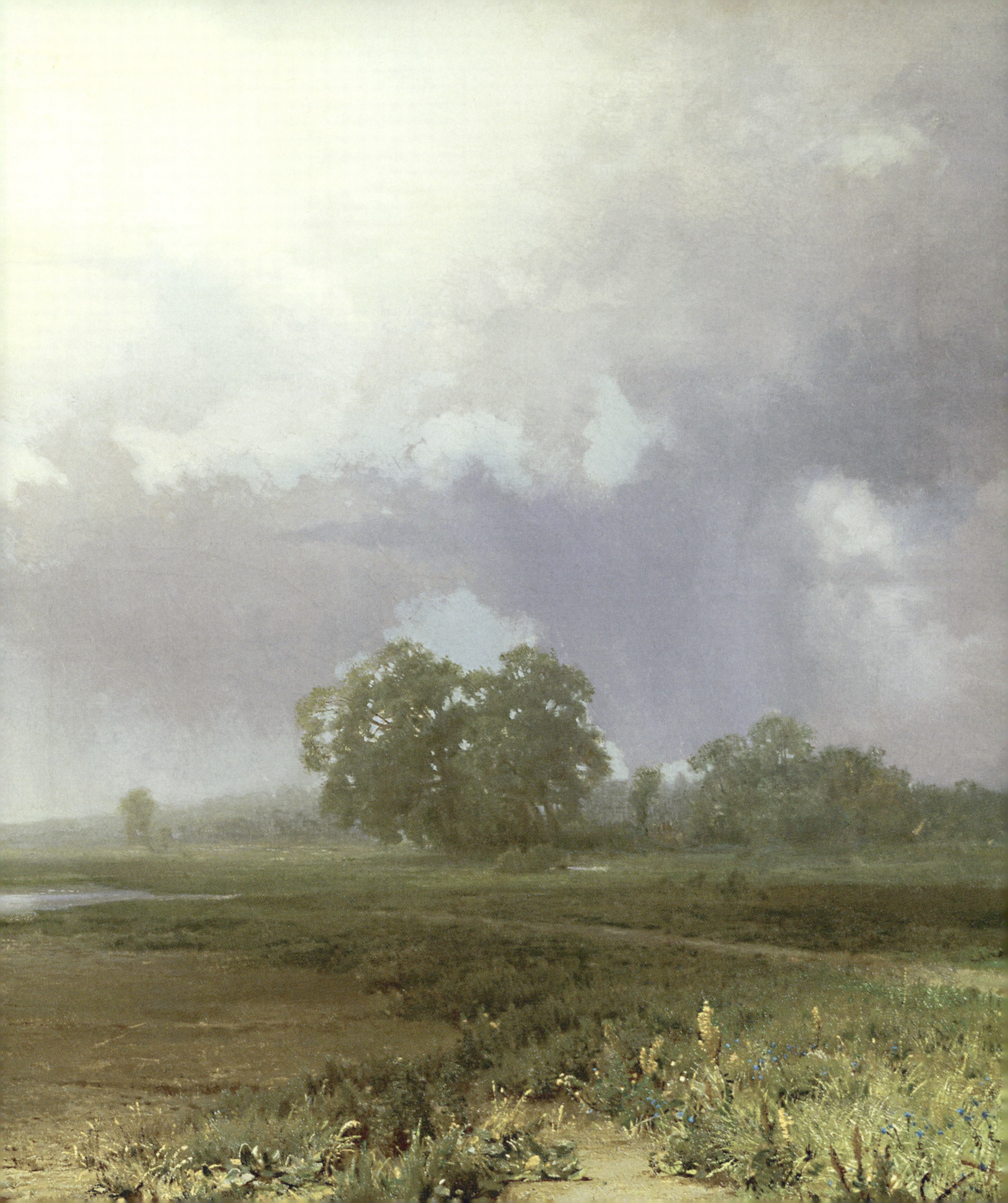

Samuel **FORDE**

Cork, 5 Apr 1805 – 29 Jul 1828, Cork
Irish, 23 years, 3 months, 25 days

Though born into impoverished circumstances, the young painter Samuel Forde may well have risen to the highest ranks of the artistic profession, had fate not made other plans. Forde's father was a failed tradesman who left the family for America when the artist was very young. His elder brother William, a talented musician, supported the family and was able to fund Forde's schooling, where he eagerly learned languages and literature. Very early on, Forde's artistic talent manifested itself, and at the age of 13 he enrolled at the Cork School of Art with fellow student and friend Daniel Maclise. There Forde learned distemper painting for theatre props and mezzotint engraving, and for a time he worked at the Cork theatre. He also became a teacher at the School of Art at just 16 years of age and later became Drawing Master of the Mechanic's Institute, Cork.

Influenced by the theatre and his love of literature, the artist liked ambitious pictures, in both size and subject. This can be seen in his oil, *A Vision of Tragedy* (1826), a grandiose, multi-figure composition inspired by John Milton's poem *Il Penseroso*. Unfortunately, by October of 1827, Forde's lungs had become infected with tuberculosis and he slowly began to wilt under his consumptive symptoms. Despite his illness, the young artist continued his rapid work pace. In November of 1827, he painted *Crucifixion* for the Chapel of Skibbereen. Working through the night, he completed the large painting in just 48 hours.

In early 1828, Forde commenced his final work – the nearly finished *Fall of the Rebel Angels* (Crawford Art Gallery, Cork). The painting is a massive, spectacular depiction of the war in Heaven (Rev 12), where Satan and his spirit angels are hurled to Earth. Hoping this painting would bring him fame, he died before its completion. Nevertheless, even in its unfinished state, one contemporary wrote that the painting 'is in itself an almost imperishable record of his genius – sufficient to have placed him in the first rank of his profession.'[21] Another writer called *Fall of the Rebel Angels* 'a relic of youthful talent and intellect, seldom or never surpassed.'[22]

Similarly, upon seeing his art, Sir David Wilkie declared they could have been by the old masters.[23] Forde had planned a series of paintings dedicated to great tragedies including Oedipus, *Macbeth* and *Romeo and Juliet*. Unfortunately, these would never be. He died at just 23 years and was buried in St Finn's churchyard in Cork. His work can be seen in the Crawford Art Gallery in Cork and shows that he could have been a major artistic force in Irish painting, at least during the period in which large literary pictures remained in vogue.

Samuel Forde
Fall of the Rebel Angels, 1828, oil on canvas, 295 × 235 cm (116⅛ × 92½ in)
Collection of the Crawford Art Gallery, Cork

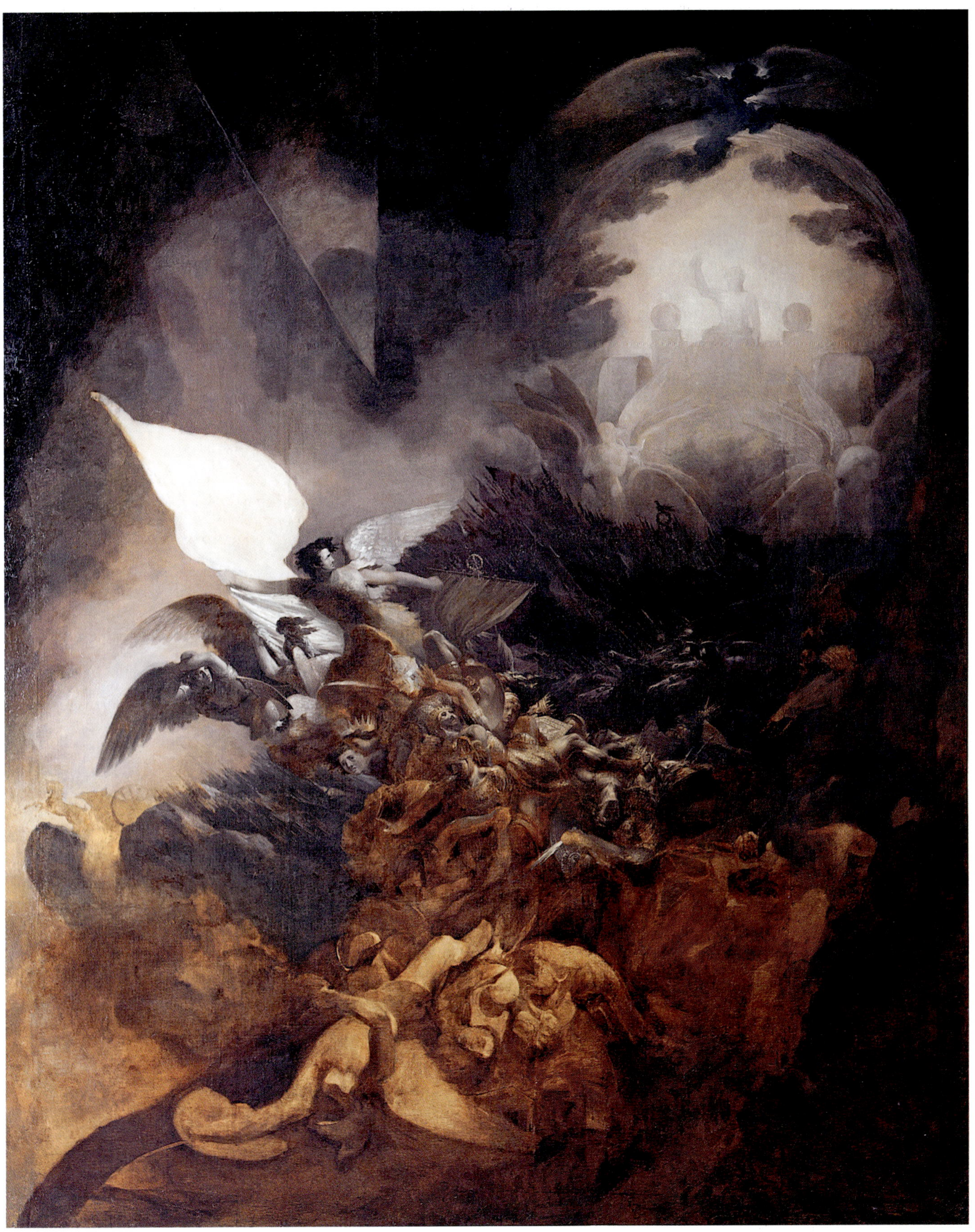

Henri GAUDIER-BRZESKA

Saint-Jean-de-Braye, 4 Oct 1891 – 5 Jun 1915, Neuville-Saint-Vaast
French, 23 years, 8 months, 2 days

Gaudier-Brzeska is generally regarded as one of the most significant sculptors of his generation. His primitive abstracted aesthetic and direct carving style have had a profound influence on later British sculptors including Henry Moore and Barbara Hepworth. This legacy is especially extraordinary in light of his extremely brief career. Although he kept a sketch-book and loved to draw from an early age, he didn't undertake sculpture until 1910. In fact, the majority of his art was produced between 1911, when he arrived in London to avoid the draft of World War I, and September 1914, when he finally enlisted in the French army, amounting to around three years of productivity. But what a prolific three years those were, producing approximately 2,000 drawings and more than 100 sculptures.

Born Henri Gaudier, the son of a carpenter in France's picturesque Loire Valley, Gaudier was trained to become a businessman. At just 16 years of age he pursued business studies in England, Wales and Germany for two years. Eventually, he returned to France and took residence in Paris where he met Zofia Brzeska, a Polish woman twice Henri's age, and whose influence was so strong and lasting that he hyphenated his own name to include hers.

When the pair moved to London in 1911, he began developing his sculptural skills in earnest, taking inspiration from Rodin, and African and Oceanic art he viewed at the British Museum. His *Red Stone Dancer* (c.1913) is considered one of the masterpieces of the Tate Collection in London, and *Birds Erect* (1914, MoMA) highlights his brilliant use of three-dimensional abstraction. He was also closely associated with the Vorticist movement, in which he was one of the 11 original signers of the Vorticist Manifesto. Gaudier-Brzeska lived in poverty during these London years and suffered from mental health issues.

Once he joined the French army in 1914, he fought with little regard for his personal safety. While this earned him two promotions for 'gallantry', he also took great risks. On one occasion he pinched an enemy rifle and carved the butt into a sculpture. Tragically he was killed in an infantry charge at Neuville-Saint-Vaast, in northern France on 5 June 1915. It was said of him, 'After his death he was remembered as a tragic example of an unfulfilled genius.'[24] The poet Ezra Pound, who later wrote a book and organised a memorial exhibition of the artist, wrote this touching tribute: 'a great spirit has been among us, and a great artist is gone'.[25]

Henri Gaudier-Brzeska
Birds Erect, 1914, limestone sculpture, 67.6 × 26 × 31.4 cm (26⅝ × 10¼ × 12⅜ in)
Museum of Modern Art, New York, Gift of Mrs W. Murray Crane

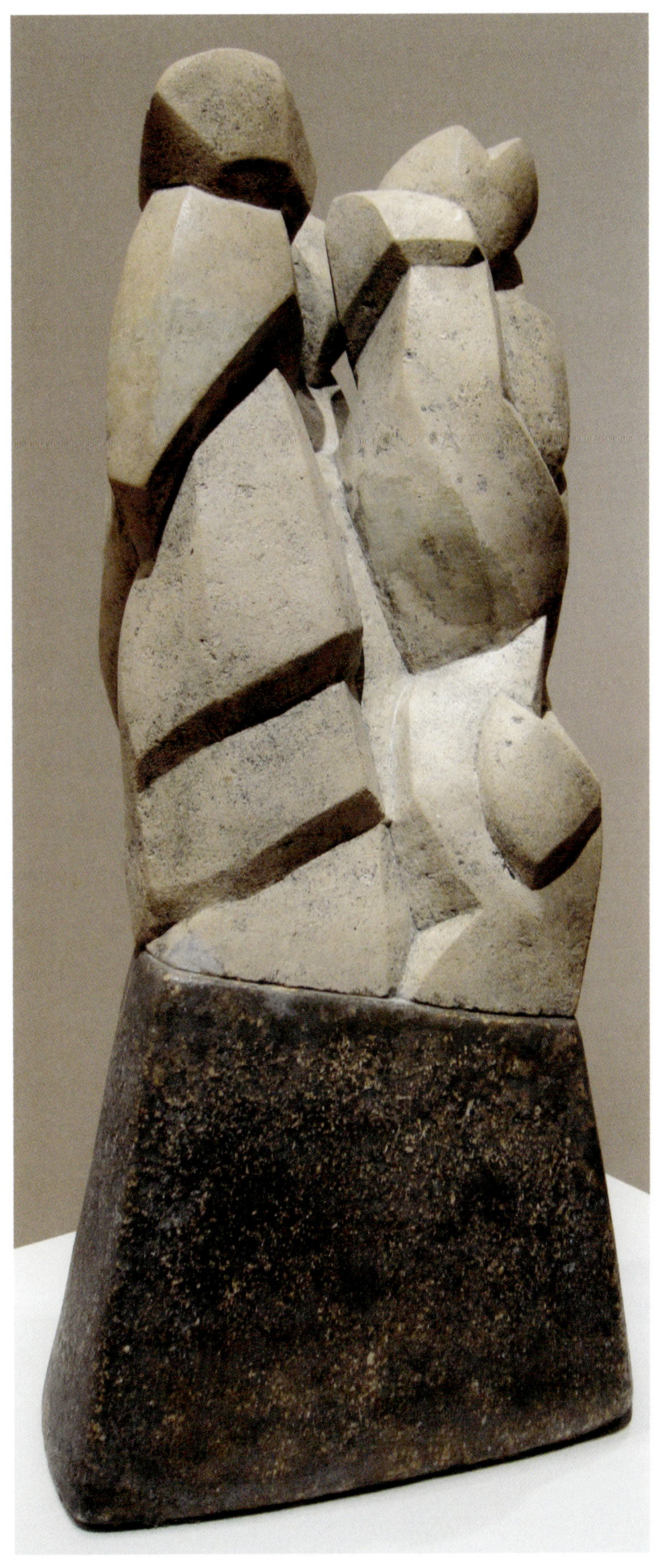

Frederick Trevelyan 'Trev' & Howard GOODALL

London, 24 Aug 1848 – 12 Apr 1871, Capri
British, 22 years, 7 months, 20 days

London, 19 Jul 1850 – 17 Jan 1874, Cairo
British, 23 years, 5 months, 30 days

The brothers 'Trev' and Howard Goodall were sons of the famous painter Frederick Goodall RA (1822–1904). Both attended the University College School and then the Royal Academy Schools. Trev, in particular, earned distinction at the Academy, winning multiple medals. In 1869, his most famous painting *The Return of Ulysses* (Art Gallery of New South Wales) earned him a gold medal, books and a scholarship of 25 shillings. Trev was described as a man at the start of 'a highly successful career as an artist and was considered one of the rising young men of the day.'[26] He received multiple portrait commissions and between 1868 and 1871 exhibited four to five works each year at the Royal Academy.

Unfortunately, what followed next would have profound repercussions on both brothers's lives. In the spring of 1871, Trev and Howard were studying the ruins in Pompeii for a few weeks. Awaiting the return of their father from Cairo, they visited the Isle of Capri with others of the English colony. Howard was showing off his pistol to the group when it accidentally fired. The bullet hit his brother, critically wounding him. Trev lingered in agony for days, and then inflammation set in. The young artist passed away on 12 April.

Before his death Trev had expressed the wish that his painting *The Return of Ulysses* be given to Edith Sparrow (1853–1911), the young red-headed beauty whose portrait he painted in 1869 and again in 1870. His painting of her, *Edith, Eldest Daughter of Arthur Sparrow, Esq.* (1869) was exhibited at the Royal Academy. Apparently, he harboured a tenderness for her, as he bequeathed her the greatest work he had ever produced. Edith Sparrow kept the painting her entire life and never married,

begging the question: had Trev been the love of her life as well? The *Art Journal* eulogised the young artist thus: 'He had already given ample proof of talents that promised, in a remarkable manner, to sustain the reputation which this family of artists has so long enjoyed … His premature death, at the early age of twenty-three, is not only a heavy affliction to his family, but a loss to Art.'[27]

Trev's untimely death must have left Howard guilt-ridden. Depriving his brother of art, love and life must have been a heavy burden to carry. Furthermore, contemporary reports indicate they had been very close, and he undoubtedly missed Trev's companionship. Howard, nonetheless, continued pursuing art. His most famous painting, *Capri Girls Winnowing Corn* (Collection of Museums Sheffield) was exhibited at the Royal Academy in 1873, and was praised by one reviewer as 'a picture which approaches nearer to the quality of pictorial beauty than any other in the room.'[28] Howard was considered to be an artist 'of more than ordinary good promise.'[29]

It is a strange coincidence that Howard died at nearly the exact same age as his brother. In January 1874 Howard travelled to Cairo to paint Orientalist scenes such as his father had before him. However, upon his arrival he was suffering from an unknown illness. He died shortly thereafter. While Trev died at the age of 22 years, 7 months, 20 days, Howard died at 23 years, 5 months and 30 days. Could Howard have inflicted some self-harm on himself through a desire not to 'outlive' his beloved brother whom he had deprived of life? Regardless of the cause, Howard's death left his father bereft of two gifted artist sons, both of whom had the potential to carry on the family's rich artistic legacy.

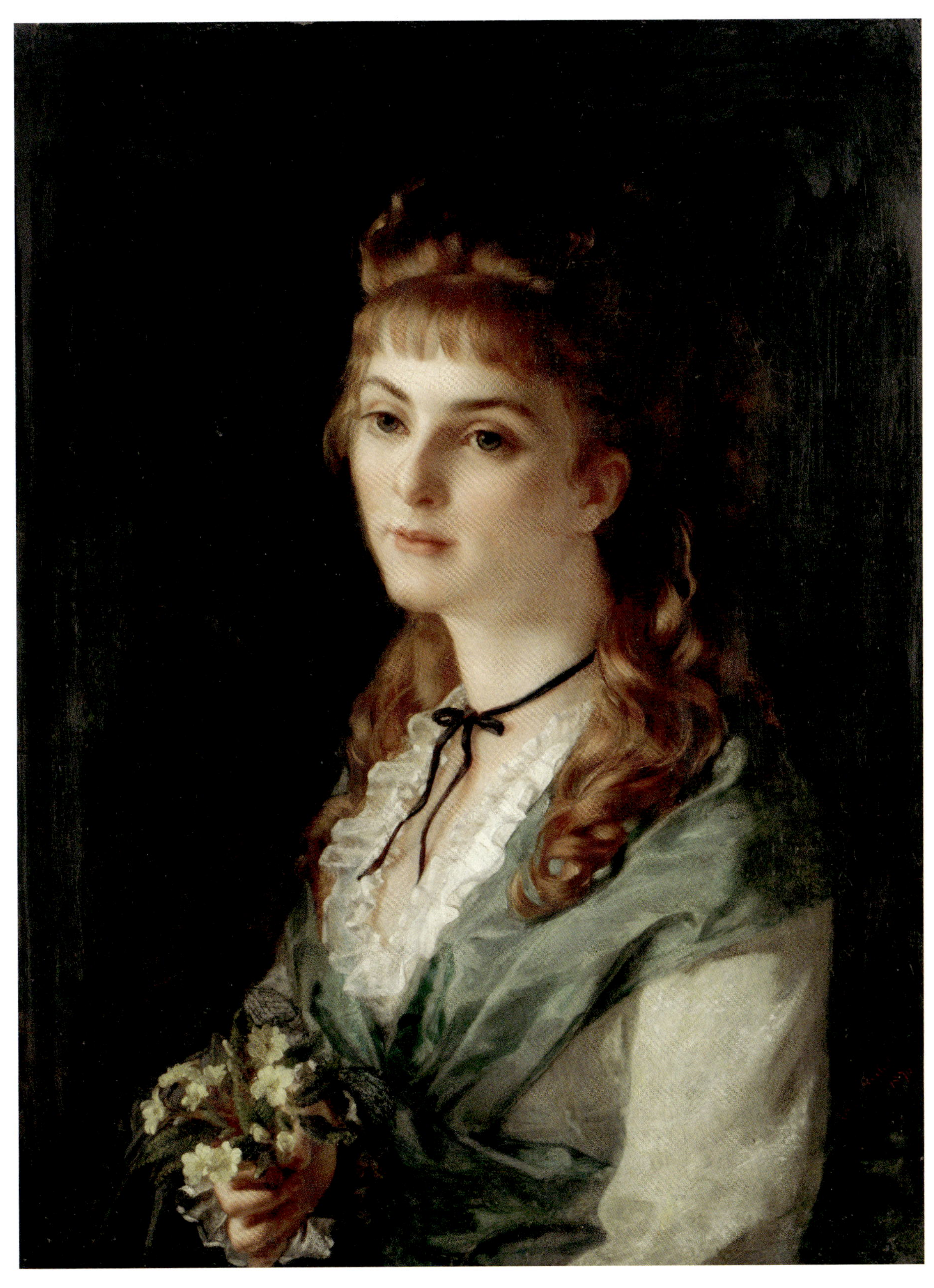

Frederick Trevelyan 'Trev' Goodall
Spring ('Portrait of Edith Sparrow'), 1870, oil on canvas, 68 × 50.8 cm (26¾ × 20 in)

Maurycy GOTTLIEB

Drohobycz, 21 Feb 1856 – 17 Jul 1879, Kraków
Polish, 23 years, 4 months, 27 days

The realist painter Maurycy Gottlieb was born to a Jewish-Polish family. Throughout his short life, both his Polish heritage and his Jewish roots profoundly shaped his artistic outlook. At the age of only 15, he gained admission to the Academy of Art in distant Vienna. Two years later, Gottlieb returned to his beloved Poland to study with noted history painter Jan Matejko (1838-1893) at the Kraków Academy of Art. Gottlieb soon became one of Matejko's best students, but unfortunately not everyone was so accepting. After just a short time at the Academy, Gottlieb angrily left because of the intense anti-Semitism shown to him by his fellow students.

In 1875, Gottlieb enrolled in the Munich Academy of Art. He thought that Munich might be fairer to the Jews because of German Unification and the concurrent Jewish Emancipation, which afforded Jews equal civil rights. There he studied with Karl Von Piloty and Alexander Von Wagner. In Munich the artist felt comfortable to explore Jewish themes in his art, and his Shakespearean painting *Shylock and Jessica* (1876) won a gold medal. The following year, Gottlieb returned to Vienna where he painted his masterpiece *Jews Praying in the Synagogue on Yom Kippur* (1878). In October 1878, the artist travelled to Italy where he met his old teacher Jan Matejko. Matejko convinced Gottlieb to come back to Kraków to work on a series of monumental paintings of the history of Polish Jews. Feeling both intrigued and validated, Gottlieb returned to Kraków in 1879 and feverishly began to work on the project he hoped would change public perception of Jews in Poland. Sadly, the project would never be completed.

At the height of his creative power, Gottlieb died in July of 1879. His painting *Christ Preaching at Capernaum* (1878-79) remained unfinished on his easel. Unrequited love would be Gottlieb's undoing. The woman who modelled for Jessica in his award-winning painting was Gottlieb's love-interest Laura Rosenfeld. He proposed and she accepted, but then later rejected his offer. Even though Gottlieb was soon to be engaged to another woman, the news of Laura's marriage to a banker in Berlin may have led to his premature death. Yemima Hovav explains: 'His sudden death was attributed variously to complications arising from an ear infection, angina, or a neck growth, but his depression also sparked rumors of suicide, which Rosenfeld herself believed.' [30] The hypothesised suicide may have been caused by exposure to the elements, from which he caught a cold and swiftly died.

It was once believed that because of Gottlieb's short life and the Nazis purge of Jewish art, there were only a few surviving pictures by the artist. However, with the fall of the Soviet Union more than 200 works were discovered. These have convinced a number of critics to believe that Gottlieb was the best of his generation. We might assume that with his studio discipline and spectacular talent, he would have been prolific and tremendously influential. It was all waiting to be seen, but the future never came.

Maurycy Gottlieb
Jews Praying in the Synagogue on Yom Kippur, 1878, oil on canvas, 245.1 × 191.8 cm (96½ × 75½ in)
Tel Aviv Museum of Art, Gift of Sidney Lamon, New York, 1955

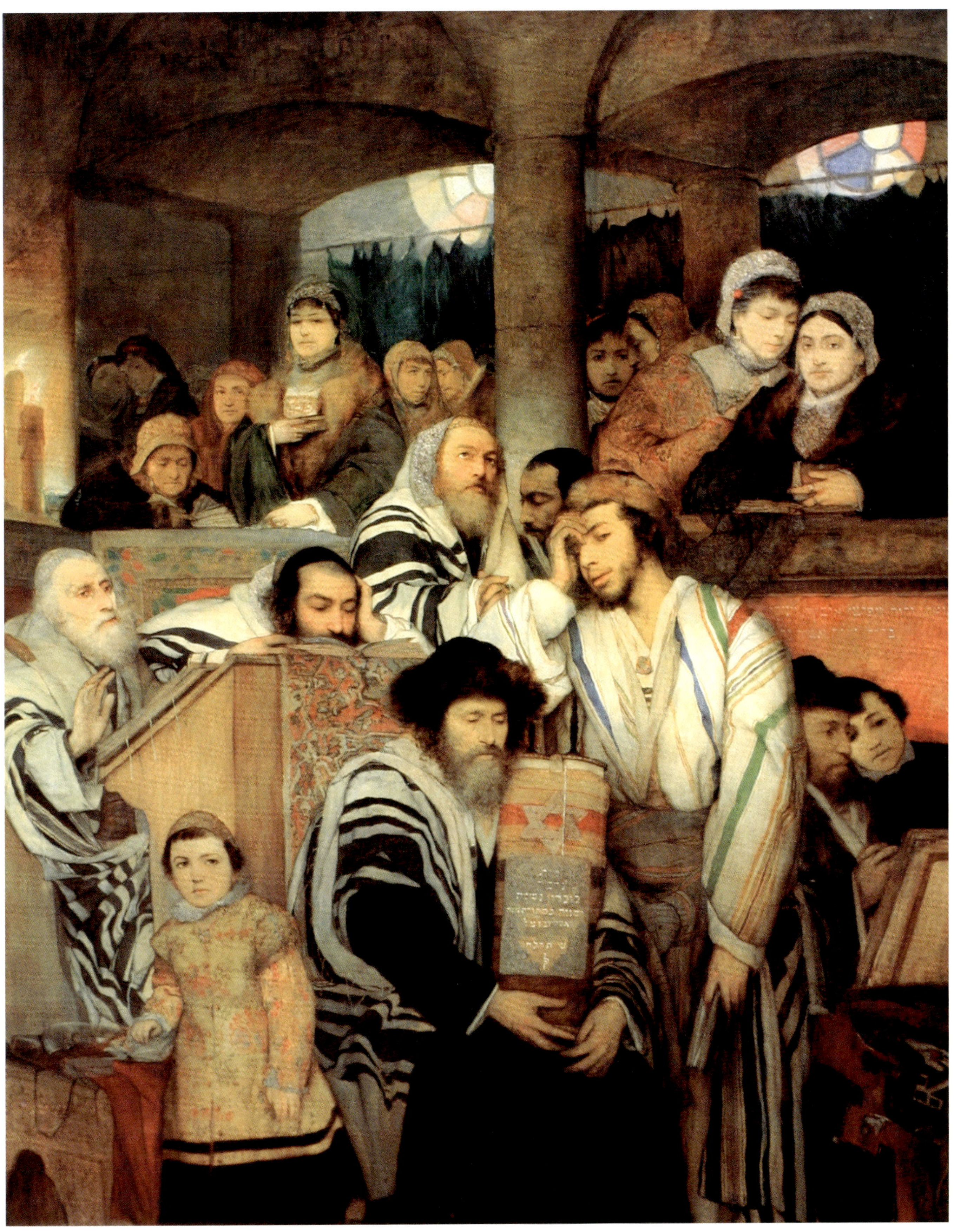

Hermann STENNER

Bielefeld, 12 Mar 1891 – 5 Dec 1914, Iłów
German, 23 years, 8 months, 24 days

Stenner was an important expressionist painter and graphic artist. He was a student at the Stuttgart Academy, first under Christian Landenberger and then the progressive Professor Adolf Hölzel (1853–1934). Under Hölzel's tutelage, Stenner quickly developed his own bold style. From his first solo show in 1911 onwards, Stenner participated frequently in many important exhibitions, including the 1914 expressionist exhibition *Die Neue Malerei* at Galerie Arnold in Dresden. In addition to his landscapes, nudes, still-lifes and portraits, Stenner painted many semi-reverential Christian paintings and drawings, including *The Black Cross* (1913), *Resurrection* (1913) and *Saint Sebastian* (1914).

Stenner's big break came in 1914 when he painted murals for the main hall of the Werkbund exhibition in Cologne with fellow students Oskar Schlemmer and Willi Baumeister. Their murals excited both praise and outrage, and brought much attention to the burgeoning young artists. However, Stenner's position at the forefront of avant-garde art did not last long. With the outbreak of World War I, Stenner and Schlemmer volunteered and were assigned to the 119th Grenadier Regiment 'Queen Olga'. After two months on the Western Front his regiment was transferred to the Eastern Front in Poland. There Stenner was tragically killed during an attack on Iłów. He was buried there in a mass grave. Even though he was only 23 years old at his death, he created around 300 oil paintings and more than 1,500 watercolours, drawings, linocuts and lithographs.

Upon Stenner's death, his esteemed artist friend Willi Baumeister lamented, 'He would have been one of Germany's best painters.'[31] In 1917, an art critic observed, 'Stenner, perhaps the most hopeful of them all [Hölzel's students], died a hero's death. What tremendous possibilities were revealed in the color rhythms he left behind.'[32] In 2019, at his hometown of Bielefeld, Germany a gallery has been named in his honour – Kunstforum Hermann Stenner. As a German expressionist, Stenner would have climbed to considerable fame, but dying at such a young age, he unfortunately lost his opportunity to become a household name.

Hermann Stenner
The Black Cross, 1913, oil on canvas, 49 × 50.5 cm (19¼ × 19⅞ in)
Private collection

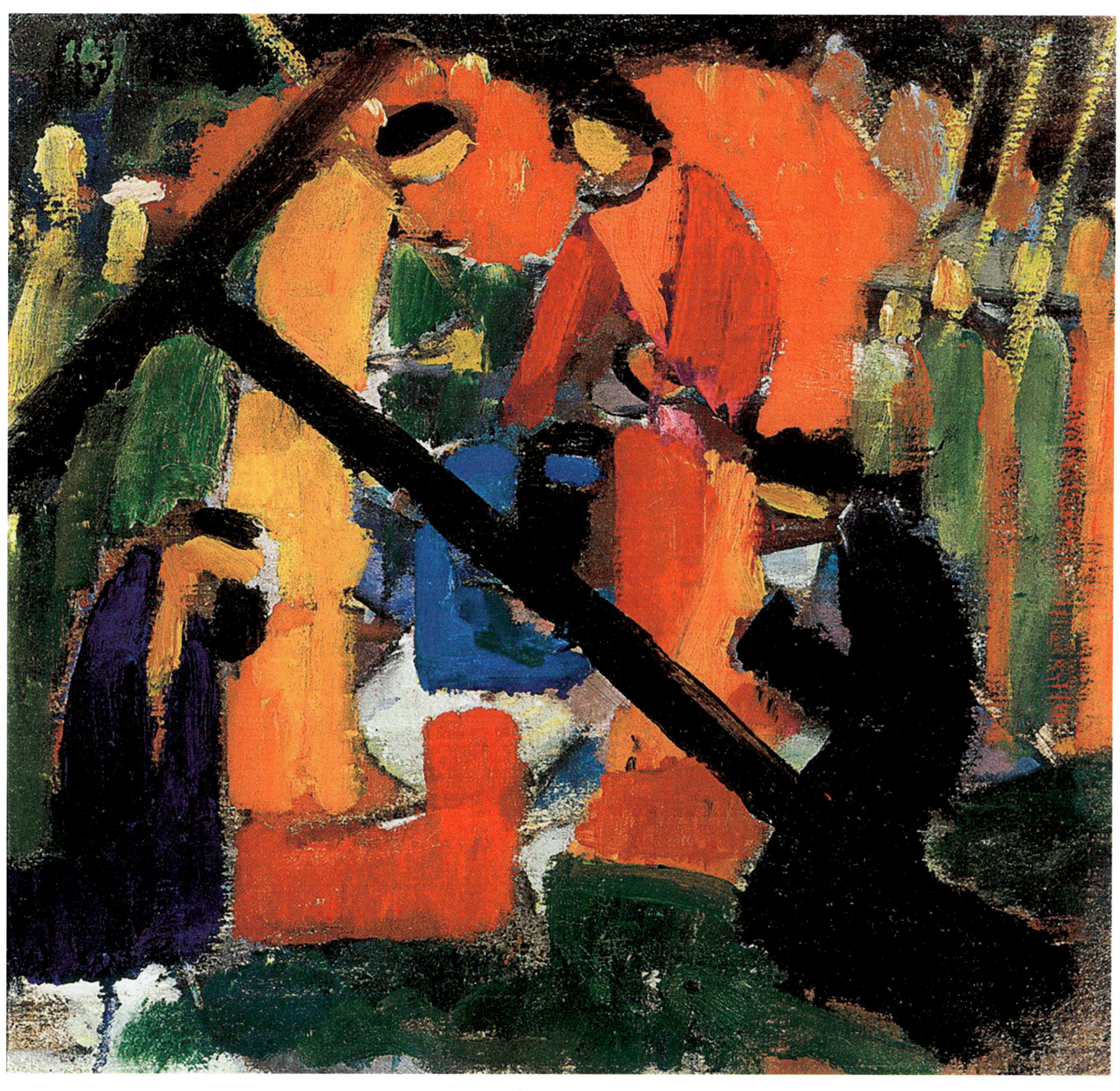

Fyodor Aleksandrovich VASILYEV

Gatchina, 22 Feb 1850 – 6 Oct 1873, Yalta[33]
Russian, 23 years, 7 months, 15 days

In the briefest of careers, Fyodor Vasilyev brought to Russian landscape painting a poetry and naturalism never before conceived. Unlike so many precocious talents, Vasilyev did not come from an artistic family. He was born illegitimately, four years before his parents' marriage. His father was a low-level government official, and after his death the young Vasilyev became the mainstay of the family. At the age of 12 he worked as a postman's scribe, and then as an assistant to a painting conservator. Being around pictures inspired him towards fine art and he enrolled in evening classes with Pyotr K. Sokolov at the Society for the Encouragement of Artists (1863–67).

Conveniently, the noted landscape painter Ivan Ivanovich Shishkin (1832–1898) fell in love with Vasilyev's sister Evgenia in 1866, and Vasilyev began taking lessons from him. Shishkin introduced Vasilyev to the great painters of the day, and Ilya Repin took him under his wing. In October 1868, Shishkin married Evgenia and became not just the young artist's teacher and mentor but also his brother-in-law. However, by the end of the decade, Vasilyev's expressive voice and technical proficiency had progressed to such a degree that he began to be Shishkin's competitor. In 1870, at the age of 20, Vasilyev cruised down the Volga with Repin and Yevgeni Makarov, painting as he went. Though young, his Volga landscape paintings were critically accepted, and he was invited to become a member of the influential Peredvizhniki (Society for Travelling Art Exhibitions). The following year, when Vasilyev exhibited his masterpiece *Thaw* (1871), he became instantly famous.

The young artist was moving from success to success with no end in sight, until he fell ill in the winter of 1870. Vasilyev had only caught a bad cold, but doctors diagnosed lung disease, which worsened by spring. The 'boy wizard', as he was called by Repin, was soon thereafter diagnosed with tuberculosis. For his health, he was ordered to leave St Petersburg for the warmer climate of Yalta on the Crimean peninsula.

Vasilyev arrived at Yalta in July of 1871, but for some reason he was unable to attune himself to the new surroundings, with its mountainous terrain and crystal clear atmosphere. He quickly turned to painting the plains just to the north, to great effect. The captivating landscape *Wet Meadow* (1872) was painted indoors (because of his affliction) entirely from sketches and memory. Vasilyev's homesickness and loneliness at this time were palpable. Eventually, however, he caught the vision of the south with his *In the Mountains of the Crimea* (1873), sadly his last oil. His health gradually withered, and he died in the autumn of 1873. His sister Evgenia Shishkin, afflicted with the same disease, died the following year.

A posthumous exhibition in St Petersburg was a great success and everything sold prior to the opening. Fortunately, the tragic brevity of his life did not tarnish his legacy, which glows brightly to this day. Vasilyev introduced lyrical landscape painting to Russia. Before him, it was crisp and linear, but afterwards it was more influenced by the atmospherics of lighter values and Barbizon landscapists. Painter Nikolai Ge aptly said of Vasilyev, 'He discovered for us the sky.' His enchanting vision and original beauty of romantic nature deeply affected the Russian national school, including Isaac Levitan. Had he lived, Vasilyev surely would have, through his talent, foresight and larger oeuvre, impacted the history of Western art dramatically.

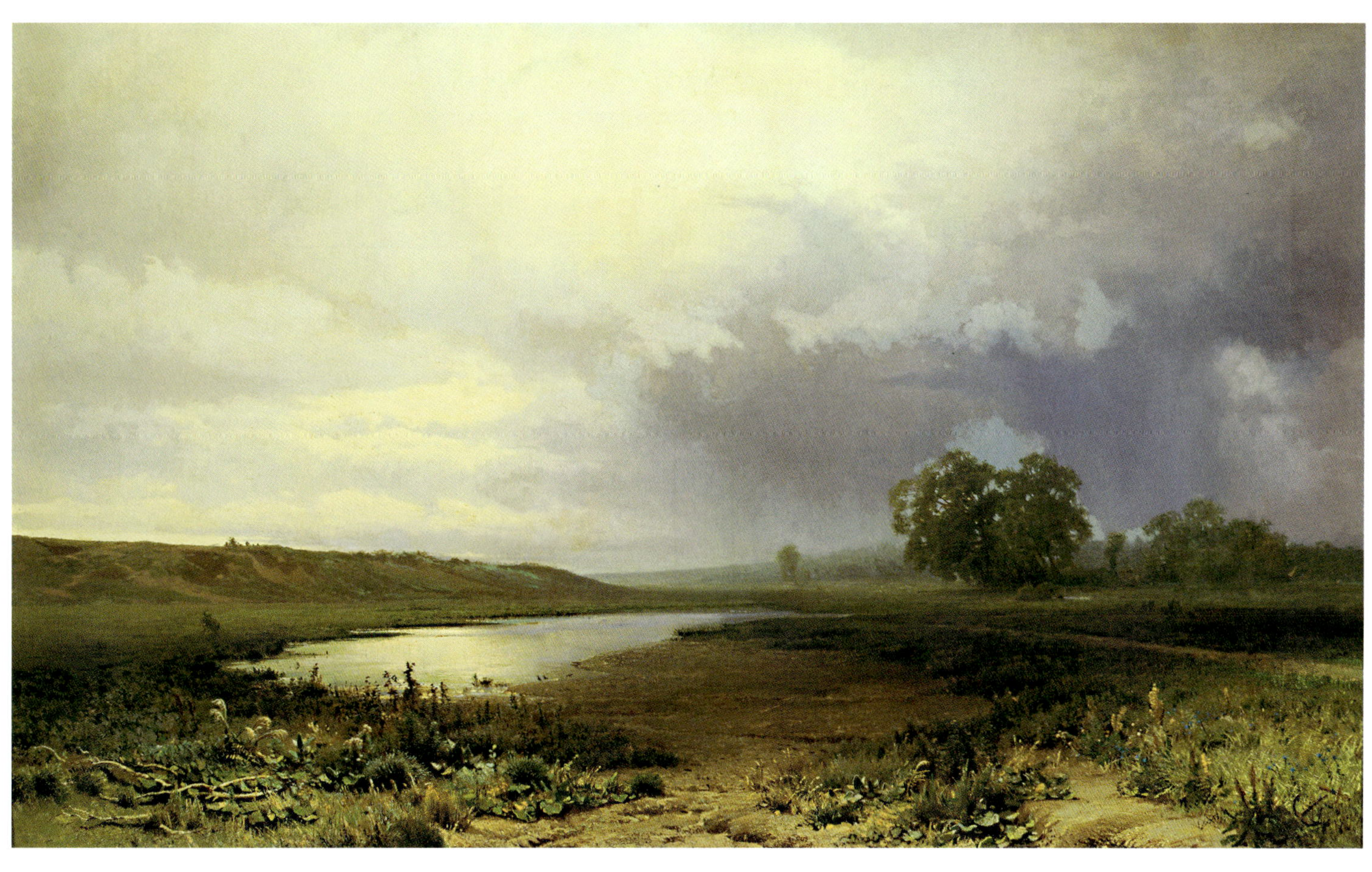

Fyodor Aleksandrovich Vasilyev
Wet Meadow, 1872, oil on canvas, 70 × 114 cm (27½ × 44⅞ in)
State Tretyakov Gallery, Moscow

Pierino da VINCI

Vinci, c.1530 – c.1553, Pisa
Italian, approx. 23 years

Pierino (born Pier Francesco di Bartolomeo di Ser Piero da Vinci) was the precocious sculptor son of Bartolomeo da Vinci, Leonardo's younger brother. Leonardo da Vinci passed away about 10 years before Pierino's birth, but when the gifted nephew began to exhibit a proclivity towards the arts, he was seen by his family as the heir to Leonardo's talent. Pierino's brief life was recorded in Giorgio Vasari's *Lives of the Most Excellent Painters, Sculptors, and Architects*. Although contemporary, Vasari's fanciful rendition of the young artist's story makes it difficult to decipher fact from fiction.

In one such passage, Vasari states that when Pierino was three years old, an astrologer and a priest of chiromancy (palmistry) visited the family's home. After viewing the child's forehead and hand, they proclaimed that Pierino possessed the 'greatness of his [Leonardo's] genius' and that he would be proficient in the 'mercurial arts' but sadly his life would be very short.[34] Although this tale could very well have been fabricated posthumously, it is nonetheless spine-tinglingly foreboding.

At 12 years of age Pierino studied under the sculptor, Baccio Bandinelli (1488–1560) and, shortly thereafter, Niccolò Tribolo (1500–1550). He assisted Tribolo in sculptures for the fountains at the Medici Villa di Castello, and all were astonished by his development and skill. Luca Martini became Pierino's patron when he was not yet 17, and soon after he went to study in Rome for a year. In Rome he was greatly influenced by the art of Michelangelo, as evidenced by his masterful marble *Young River God with Three Children* (c.1548, Musée du Louvre). For this reason, and because of Pierino's consummate skill, several sculptures by Pierino have at one time been misattributed to Michelangelo.

Fittingly, Pierino's last work was a marble funerary monument of Baldassarre Turini for Pescia Cathedral, which was left unfinished. On a trip to Genoa with Luca Martini, Pierino contracted malarial fever in the early months of 1553. Wishing to return to Pisa, the feverish artist travelled by boat and litter, arriving in Pisa very late at night. The next morning Pierino died, at the tender age of 23. Vasari described the artist thus: 'his genius was admired by all, being much more perfect than could have been expected in one so young, and it was likely to grow even more and to become greater, and equal to that of any other man in his art.'[35] Unfortunately, we will never know what heights this artist could have attained. Leaving behind a remarkable oeuvre of sculptures, one might better say he was more the heir of Michelangelo's talent than his uncle Leonardo's.

Pierino da Vinci
Young River God with Three Children, c.1548, marble statue, 130 cm (51¼ in) high
Musée du Louvre, Paris

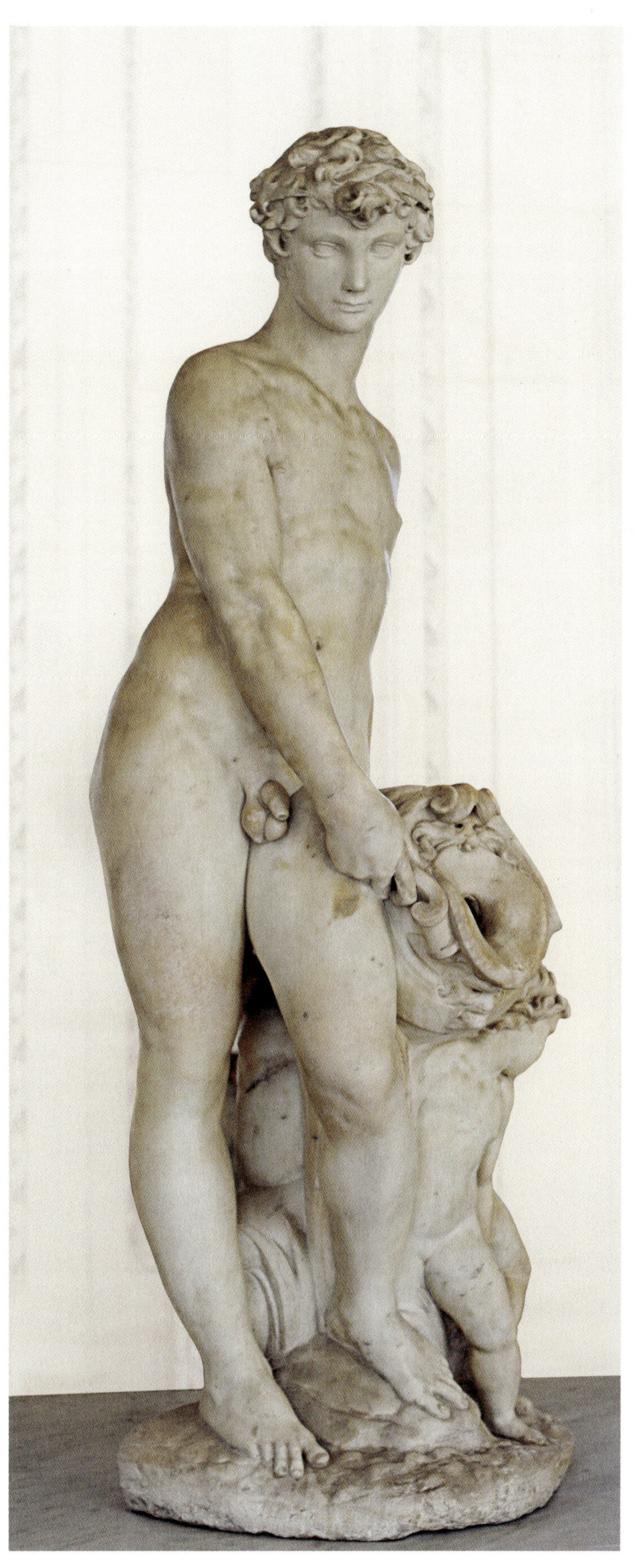

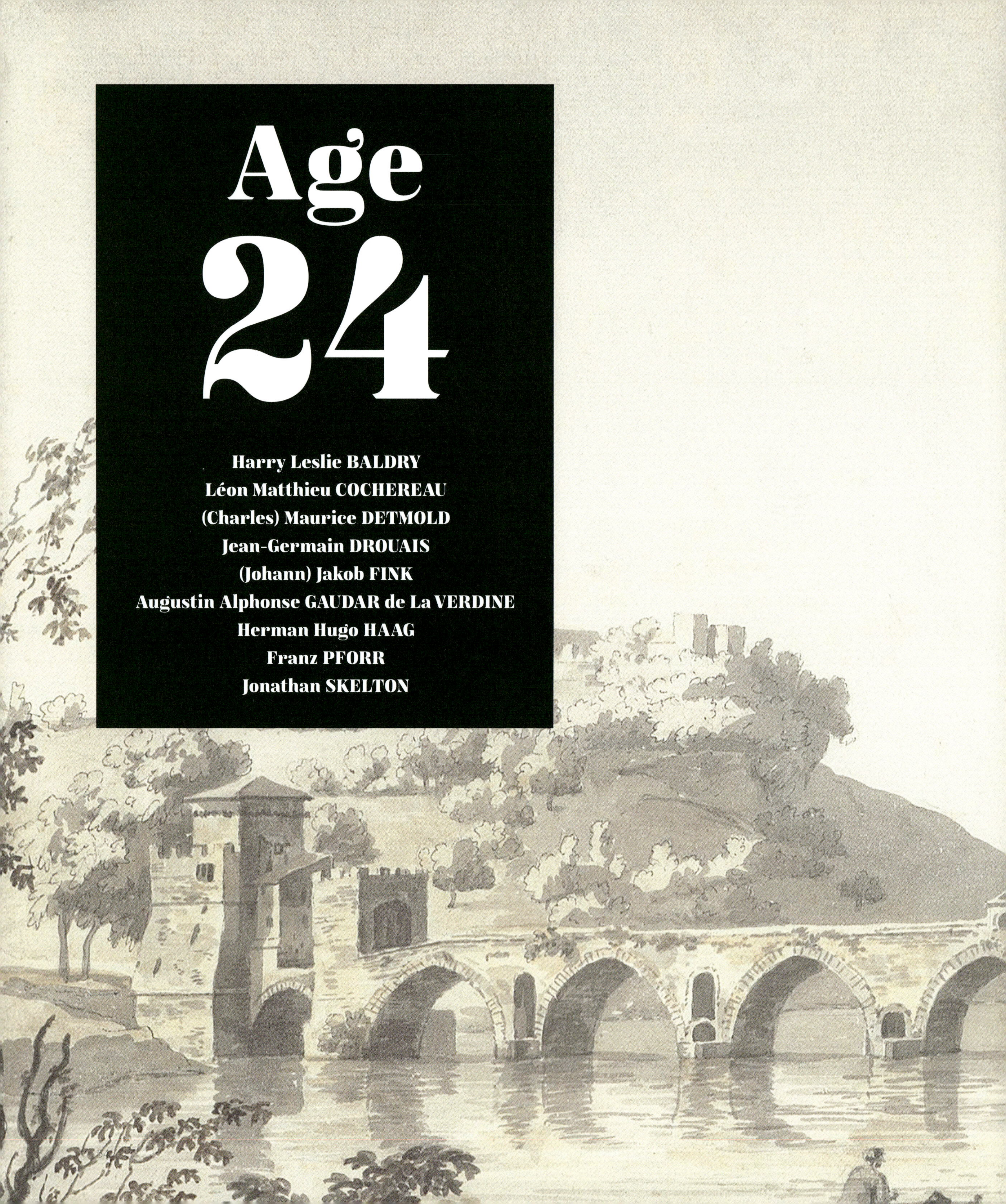

Age 24

Harry Leslie BALDRY
Léon Matthieu COCHEREAU
(Charles) Maurice DETMOLD
Jean-Germain DROUAIS
(Johann) Jakob FINK
Augustin Alphonse GAUDAR de La VERDINE
Herman Hugo HAAG
Franz PFORR
Jonathan SKELTON

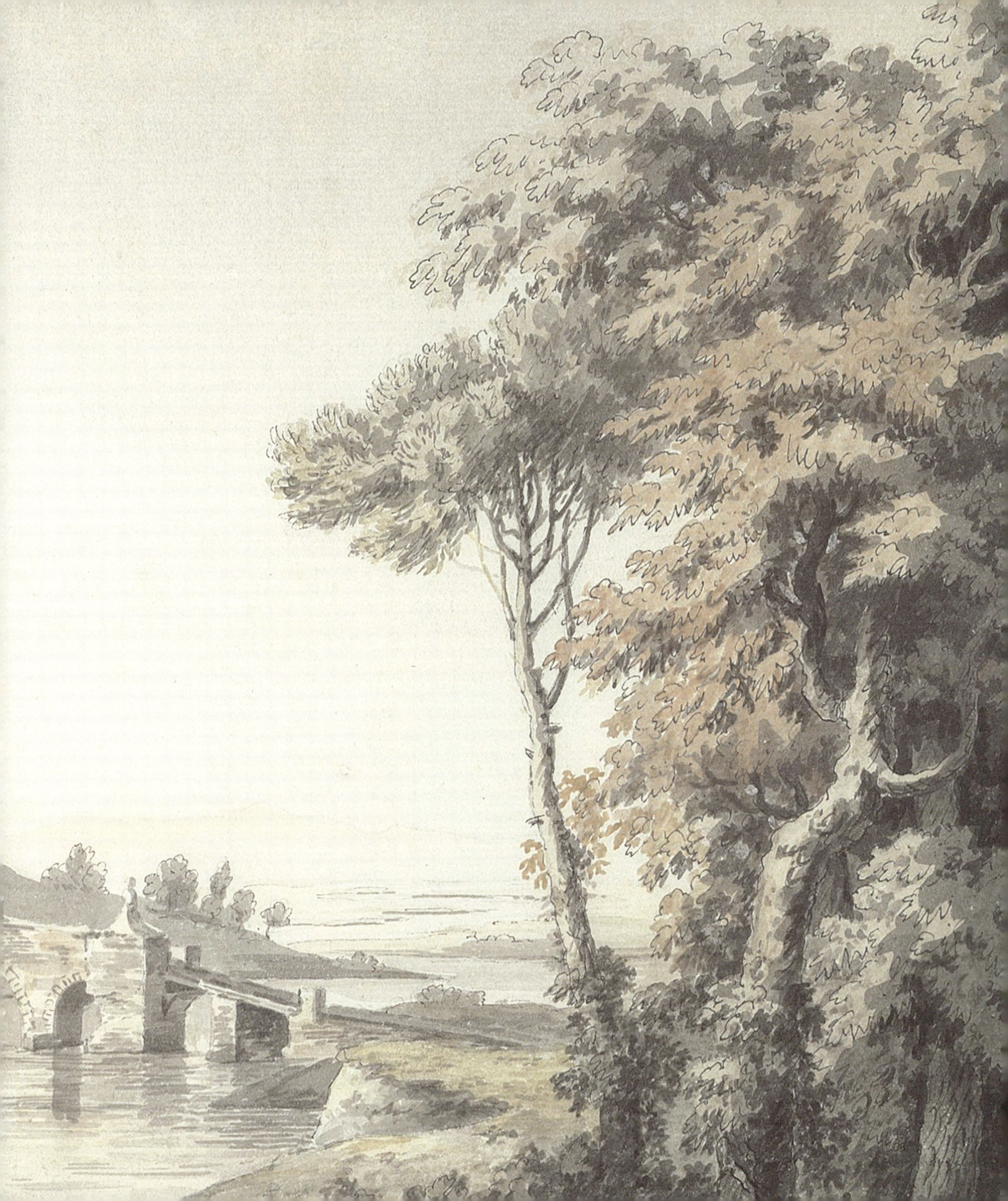

Harry Leslie BALDRY

Norfolk, baptised 21 Jan 1866 – 29 Aug 1890, London
British, 24 years, 7 months, 9 days

Harry Baldry was born into an artistic family of 13 children in an old manor house in Norfolk. Son of the portrait painter George W. Baldry (1835–1929), Harry and his twin sister Grace Baldry (1866–1931) were first tutored in art by their father. Harry painted genre scenes in the manner of Marcus Stone and was also a serviceable portrait painter. He was active between 1883 and 1890, and exhibited six pieces at the Royal Academy of Art, London between 1887 and 1890. In 1890, he married Florence Digby at St Pancras Church in London and had a son.

Baldry was unable to cope with the added stress caused by his marriage, a new child, and the finicky portrait-painting business. Furthermore, his gnawing sense that, even though he was wildly popular, his art was not of sufficient excellence, led to his suicide. On 29 August 1890, the young artist shot himself at 28 Regent's Park Road in London, then died later that day at St Mark's Crescent. Far from being an impoverished artist, his success as a portrait painter was proven at the inquest where it was stated that he had earned between £3,000 and £4,000 per annum, a very healthy sum at the time. [36] His stylish painting *A Pensive Moment* (1889) demonstrates why Baldry was a sought-after portraitist by London's fashionable elite. An interesting notice of the artist's passing and his emotional state appeared in *The Speaker* which reads:

> The present rage for having one's portrait painted is good for the artists, but not wholly good. The strain as a painter of vogue is becoming terrible. It killed [Frank] Holl, and it seems to have killed Mr. Harry Baldry … He was only 24, yet the strain of his work drove him to complain of 'queer feelings in the head,' of 'the sensation of going mad,' and to play the violoncello sometimes 'as if he were trying to tear the instrument into pieces.' … We have lost then three artists within a very few days, Harry Baldry, Alice Havers, and C. W. Cope R.A.; the two former ones by sad ends enough and the latter full of years. [37]

In addition to his terrible mental distress, Baldry was suffering excruciating pain from tuberculosis. In the days before effective painkillers and medical care, there was only so much suffering a person could endure before death was an altogether preferable solution. We cannot be certain, but at 24 years he may have been a late bloomer just starting to bud and take root.

Harry Leslie Baldry
A Pensive Moment, 1889, oil on board, 61 × 50.7 cm (24 × 20 in)
Cambridge Fine Art

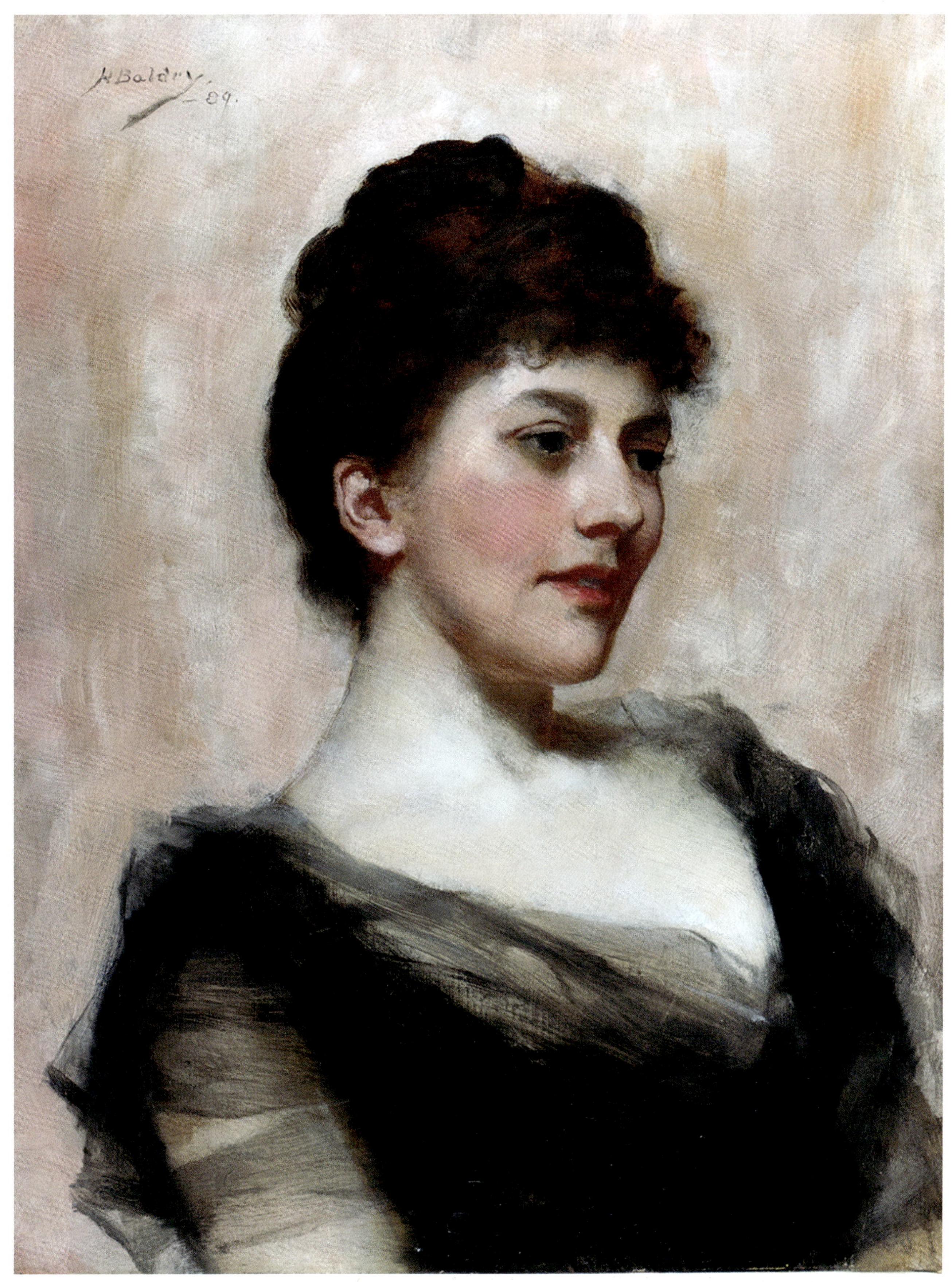

Léon Matthieu COCHEREAU

Montigny-le-Gannelon, 9 Feb 1793 – 30 Aug 1817, Ionian Sea
French, 24 years, 6 months, 22 days

Cochereau was a painter and a student of the celebrated neoclassicist Jacques-Louis David (1748–1825). He was also mentored by his uncle Pierre Prévost (1764–1823) who was a painter of landscapes and panoramic views. By all accounts, Cochereau was a diligent and intelligent student. One story has it that during a three-day Paris festival, his uncle gave him some money to enjoy himself. With forty francs in hand, the young artist purchased a corpse, and for three days meticulously studied and sketched the anatomy.[38] Unfortunately, only a few paintings of Cochereau's oeuvre survive. These include street scenes, portraits, and especially interiors of artist studios and academic model studies. Little known works such as *The Painter, the Model and Her Chaperone* (c.1815) and his large oil, *Lecture Given by Prévost For the Study of Painting Panoramic Views* (Musée des Beaux-Arts de Chartres) demonstrate the quiet 'silent realism' of his oils.

However, as Dr Therese Southgate points out, 'the fame of Léon-Mathieu [sic] Cochereau rests on a single painting.'[39] That painting is *The Interior of David's Studio at Collège des Quatre Nations* (1813). Exhibited at the 1814 Paris Salon, it depicts a live sketching session under the tutelage of the great master and gives viewers a fascinating glimpse into studio life in Paris. The painting was an instant success, finally winning him the respect of his master David and the public at large. A critic for the *Monitor* wrote on 15 January 1815 that the painting, which possessed 'all the qualities one could desire in a genre painting make this work the first of its kind.'[40] Three versions of this painting are known, the most famous being in the Louvre.

Following this success, Cochereau went with his Uncle Prévost to paint a panorama of London, in which he depicted the iconic Westminster Abbey. Just a few years later, in 1817, Cochereau and Prévost took part in an expedition to Palestine organised by Count Forbin. The young artist, who was experiencing signs of dysentery before even leaving France, died of this ailment on the journey, with his uncle and the Count in attendance. According to Forbin, his body was thrown into the sea, 'across from Bizerte, in sight of Athens, near the Isle of Cerigo (Kythira), in the Ionian Sea.' The death was a terrible blow to his uncle, and to French painting. In 1822 a number of his unfinished paintings were shown posthumously at the Paris Salon. From that moment his reputation as an artist was secured; but his greatness always hung in the balance. Due to his short life, it was never resolved.

Léon Matthieu Cochereau
The Studio of Jacques-Louis David, 1814, oil on canvas, 91.1 × 102.9 cm (35⅞ × 40½ in)
Los Angeles County Museum of Art

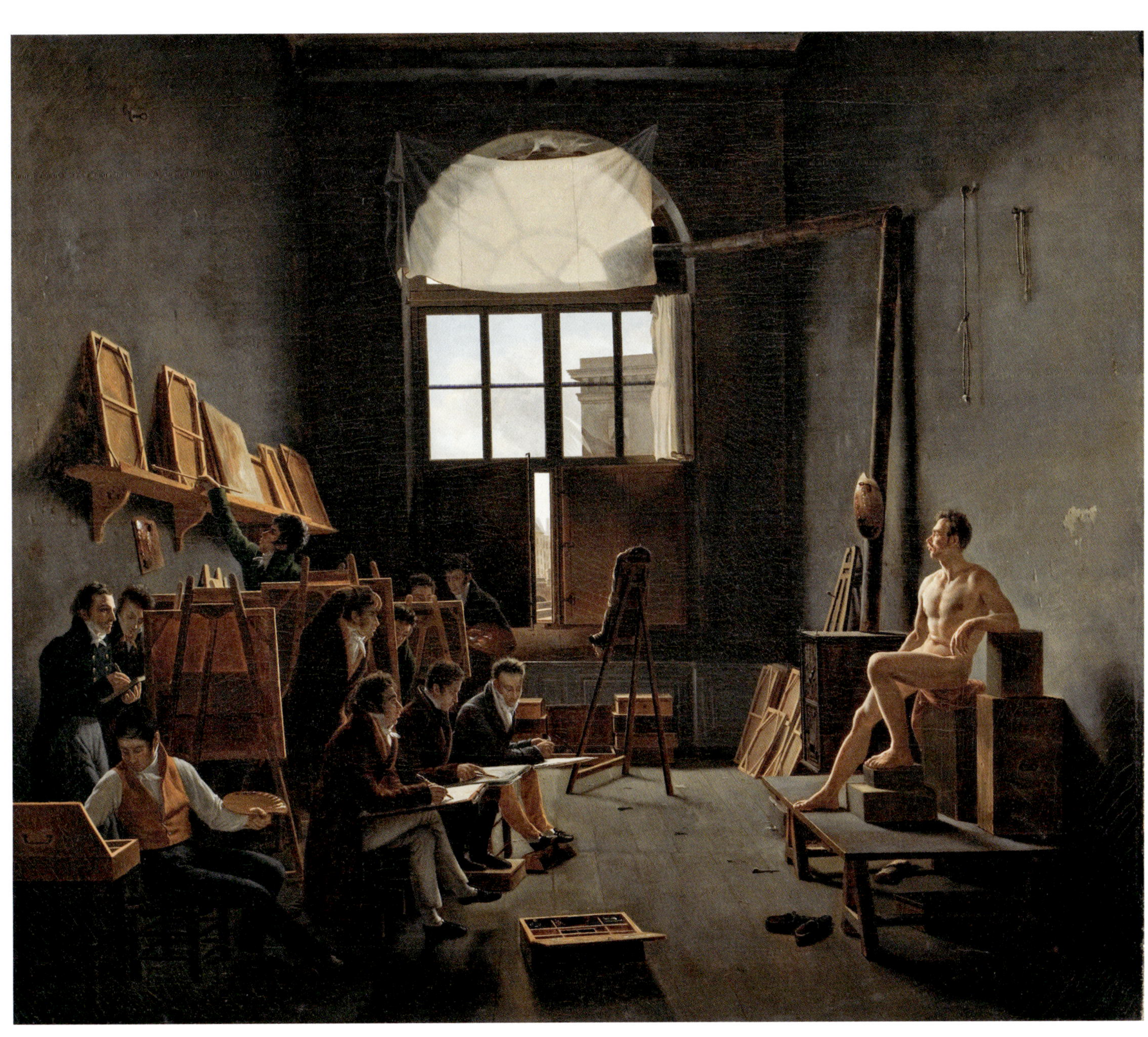

(Charles) Maurice DETMOLD

Putney, 21 Nov 1883 – 9 Apr 1908, Hampstead
British, 24 years, 4 months, 19 days

Maurice was the younger twin brother (by minutes) of the artist Edward Julius Detmold (1883–1957). Both brothers painted watercolours, made woodcuts, and etched illustrations of animals and plants, as well as some religious themes. Maurice shared with his brother, at every stage of artistic development, a parallel career. While youngsters, they studied and drew animals at London Zoo and the Natural History Museum. Being extremely precocious, they both exhibited at the Royal Academy at the age of 14. The noted artist, Edward Burne-Jones even advised them not to attend any art school in order to allow their own aesthetic to blossom.

They were deeply influenced by Japanese art and matured an aesthetic style reflecting natural forms as is seen in Maurice's *Toucan* (c.1899). The brothers often collaborated even to the point of working on the same etching plate and woodcuts. Notably, in 1903 they worked together to illustrate in watercolour Rudyard Kipling's *The Jungle Book*. While Maurice showed equally great ability, his work was less mature because he showed less commitment than his brother. In January of 1905 Edward and Maurice were jointly elected associates of the Royal Society of Painter-Etchers and Engravers. But soon afterwards they resigned, and Maurice ceased to be an active artist. Possibly he realised that his talent was not as significant as his brother Edward's and didn't want to be pulled along on his coat-tails. Having shared so much growing up, the anxiety from their artistic separation must have weighed heavily on Maurice.

Seemingly, out of the blue, while the brothers were just about to leave Hampstead for a holiday in Sussex with their childhood guardian Dr Edward B. Shuldham, Maurice committed suicide by inhaling chloroform. Maurice had pre-arranged with Dr Shuldham to bring the anaesthetic, claiming that he wanted to put down some household cats, but he had probably premeditated it for himself all along. He took his life on 9 April 1908 and was gone at the age of 24, leaving no note to give his reason.

Edward was devastated by the loss but plunged himself into his work and became even more famous. The hypothetical, 'What if Maurice had eventually become ravenously hungry to produce art again, would he have equalled his brother?' cannot be answered. Nevertheless, he would have been wonderfully brilliant in his art. Interestingly, Edward would much later commit suicide himself, with a gunshot wound to his chest because of depression due to failing eyesight.

(Charles) Maurice Detmold
Toucan, c.1899, watercolour and ink, 19.5 × 15 cm (7⅝ × 5⅞ in)
Alamy

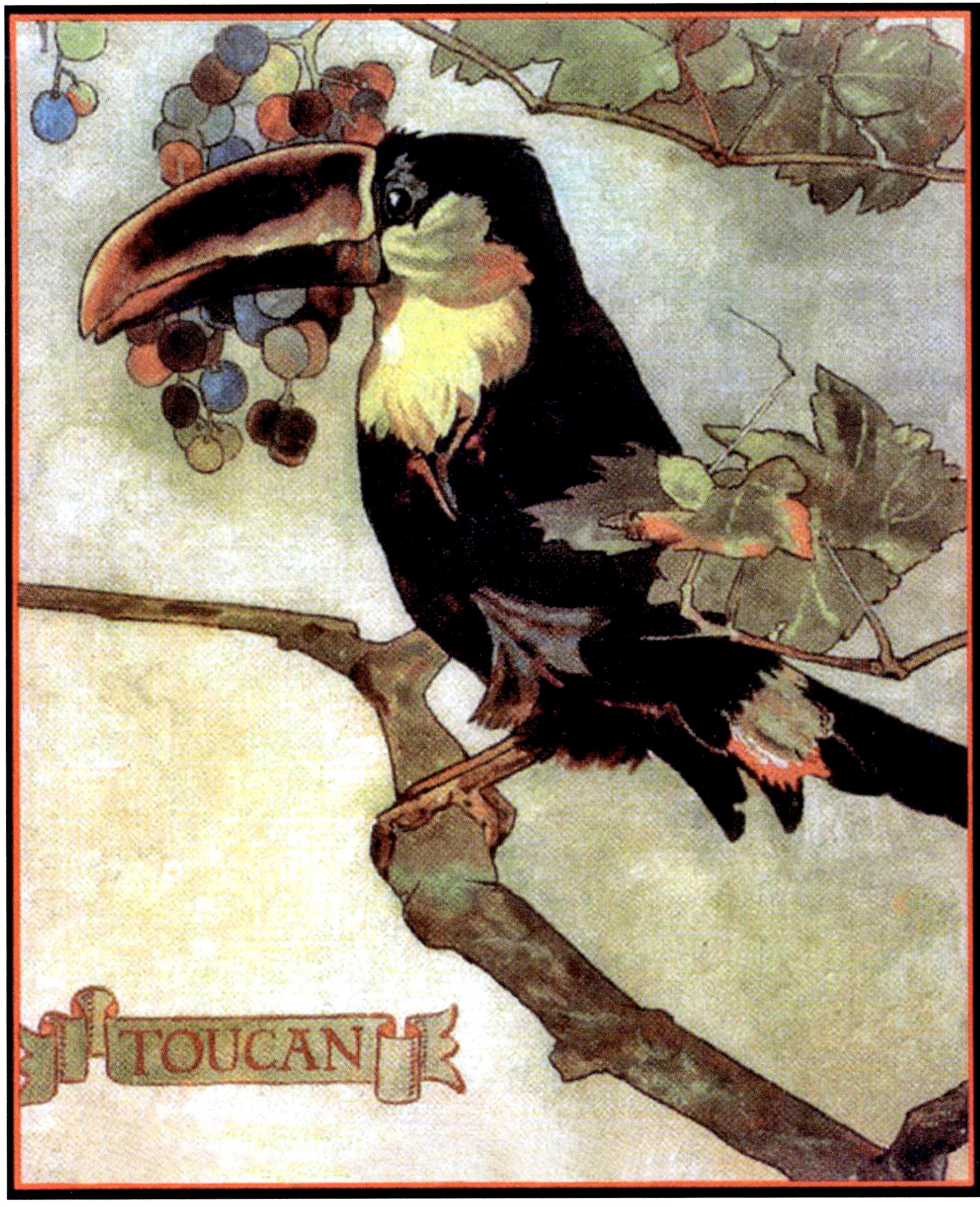

TOUCAN

Jean-Germain DROUAIS

Paris, 25 Nov 1763 – 13 Feb 1788, Rome
French, 24 years, 2 months, 20 days[41]

The mystique of this artist still haunts the pages of art history's unfulfilled promise. Drouais was the son of the outstanding artist François-Hubert Drouais (1727–1775) and grandson of portraitist Hubert Drouais (1699–1767). He received his first lessons from his father and then from the excellent teacher Nicolas-Guy Brenet. In 1782, at the age of 18, Drouais entered the studio of Jacques-Louis David, where he meteorically became David's number one student and an early proponent of neoclassicism.

Drouais had an insatiable work ethic and sometimes would not leave his studio for weeks, however he was also prone to insecurity and over dependence on his teacher. In 1783, while he competed for the Prix de Rome, Drouais grew so anxious he cut his painting in two and took it to David for a critique. David declared it an excellent painting, but Drouais was subsequently disqualified from the competition. However, the next year he won the coveted prize for his Poussin-esque oil, *Woman of Canaan at the Feet of Christ* (1784, Musée du Louvre). In celebration, his fellow students put the 20-year-old artist on their shoulders and triumphantly carried him through the streets of Paris to his mother's house. Later that year, Drouais accompanied David to Rome and Drouais was able to assist his mentor on his masterpiece *Oath of the Horatii* (1784) in Rome.

While in Rome, Drouais was ecstatic about the plethora of ancient art he saw everywhere and the Renaissance painter Raphael. He saw in this master a classical restraint that echoed, to a degree, his own aesthetic proclivities. David returned to Paris the next year, but Drouais remained in Rome and painted several notable works including his dynamic *Naked Warrior, Seated on a Rock Beside His Shield and Plumed Helmet* (c.1786–87) and his famous canvas *Marius at Minturnae* (1786, Musée du Louvre). This painting so moved Wolfgang Goethe that he wrote in his diary *Italian Journey* that in some respects it was superior to David's art. Likewise, the artist Jean-Baptiste Marie Pierre, when he saw *Marius*, predicted that Drouais would even surpass his master.

Unfortunately, this prophecy would never come to pass. Drouais died in Rome at the tender age of 24. Some say he died of cholera or smallpox, and others say malaria. Dr John D. Bandiera of Emory University in Atlanta believes that his constant personal self-neglect and overwork affected his immune system. When Drouais died, David was inconsolable and his fellow students had a monument erected at the Church of Santa Maria in Via Lata, Rome. This prodigy's dramatically truncated career still had considerable influence on his contemporaries. He was venerated by amateurs, critics and artists alike, and nobody more than his mentor, David. This giant of an artist said of him, 'His death has deprived France of a man who was perhaps destined to be mentioned with Raphael.' Bandiera writes of him:

> The belief that the young artist's death had deprived France of a painter with the potential to be another Raphael or Poussin was intrinsic to the Drouais mystique, and the sense of national loss was compounded by the pathetic story of the destruction of a prodigious talent about to come into full bloom.[42]

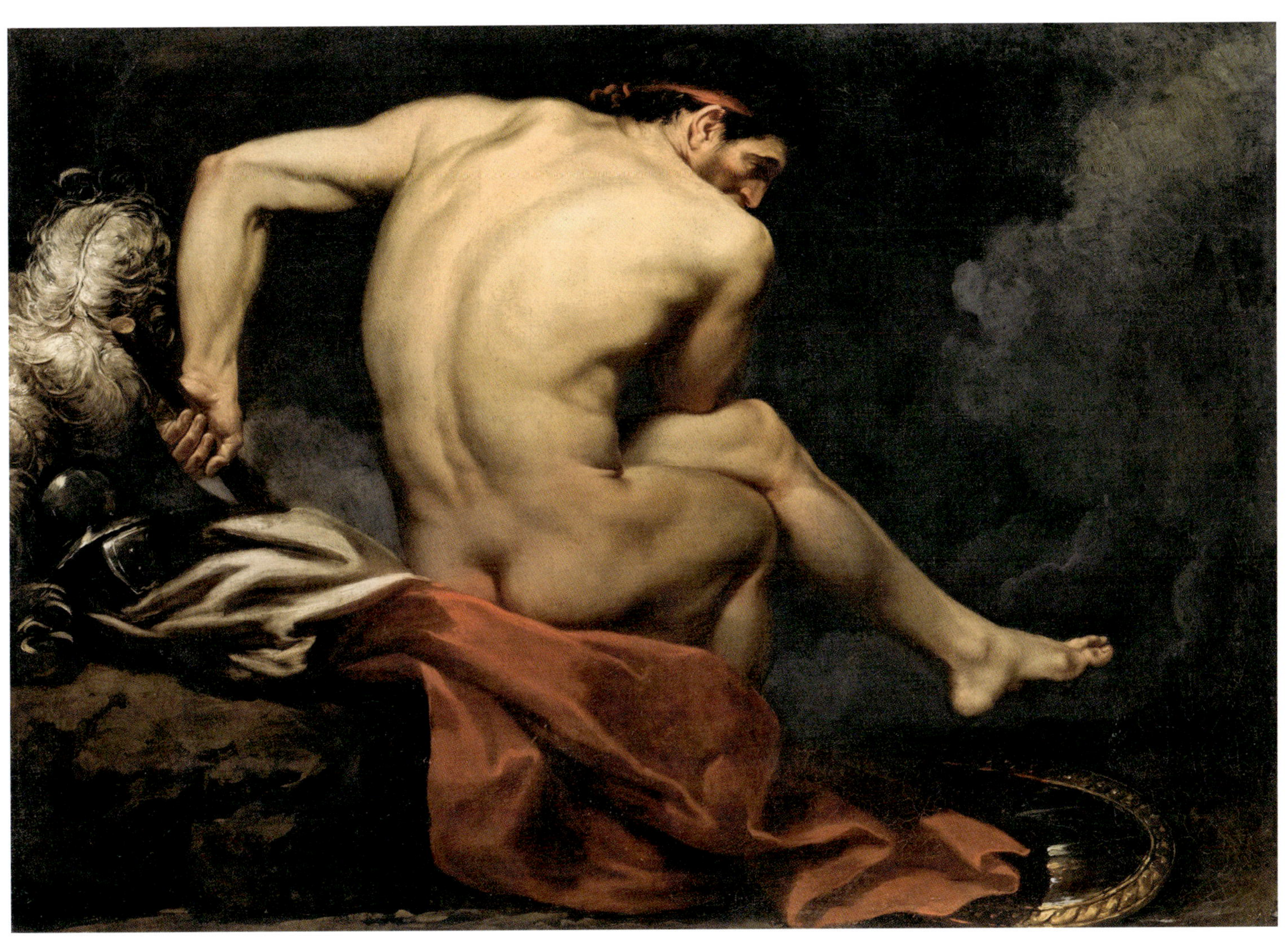

(Johann) Jakob FINK

Schwarzenberg, 23 Nov 1821 – 6 Sep 1846, Rome
Austrian, 24 years, 9 months, 14 days

Johann Fink was born in a village in Bregenzerwald mountain range in the state of Vorarlberg in the Austrian Alps. An idyllic setting for an artist's childhood. He was the only son of a stone mason, Anton Fink. His mother Anna Catharina Thumb was a close relative of the painter Alois Thumb of Bezau. His parents secured an adequate secular education for Johann but also a fine religious one. Fink possessed an early passion for drawing, but often had to do so in secret because his mother saw it as a waste of time. Eventually, he took six weeks of art lessons from an unknown painter in St Gallen, but Fink was largely left to himself to develop his craft.

Although Fink's father wished for his son to become an architect, the young artist was determined to become a painter. At 18 years old, Fink made the mountainous journey to Innsbruck, walking mostly barefoot for three days. There he studied under his father's former teacher, the well-known Nazarene painter, Gebhardt Flatz (1800–1881) also of Vorarlberg. Flatz recognised the young man to be 'very special, yes, a rare developing talent in art.'[43] In 1840, with a grant of 1,500 Dutch guilders from local wealthy families, Fink was able to accompany Flatz to Rome where he was in awe of the artistic treasures he saw there.

Flatz had studied in Vienna with Johann Friedrich Overbeck; his mentor now lived in Rome and Fink became friends with, and was undoubtedly influenced by, this Nazarene master. Fink studied and diligently worked in Rome for six years producing numerous religious works. One of his last endeavours was to produce 12 large drawings portraying the parables of Jesus. Unfortunately, only five were ever completed, but these fine works were highly praised by contemporaries for their originality and technical competence.

While painting an altarpiece commission, Fink suddenly came down with *nervenfieber* (literally, 'nervous fever'). The antiquated medical term *nervenfieber* most often refers to the bacterial infection of typhoid fever. Frequently during the second week of typhoid, the infected individual can enter a state of delirium and become agitated or nervous, thus the origin of the term. This, in all probability, was Fink's fate. He suffered for a fortnight in Rome before he succumbed to the ailment. His beautiful oil painting, *Noli Me Tangere* (1846) vouchsafed the promise of his artistic talent. More than a decade after his death, the famous Italian painter Giovanni Sanguinetti fondly remembered the young painter who 'through his creations awakened in Rome's artistic circles the greatest hope that he would become a first-class master.'[44] Fink certainly would have created many more wise-hearted masterpieces as he advanced in years.

(Johann) Jakob Fink
Noli Me Tangere ('Touch Me Not'), 1846, oil on panel, 76 × 48 cm (29⅞ × 18⅞ in)
Galleria d'Arte Ottocento

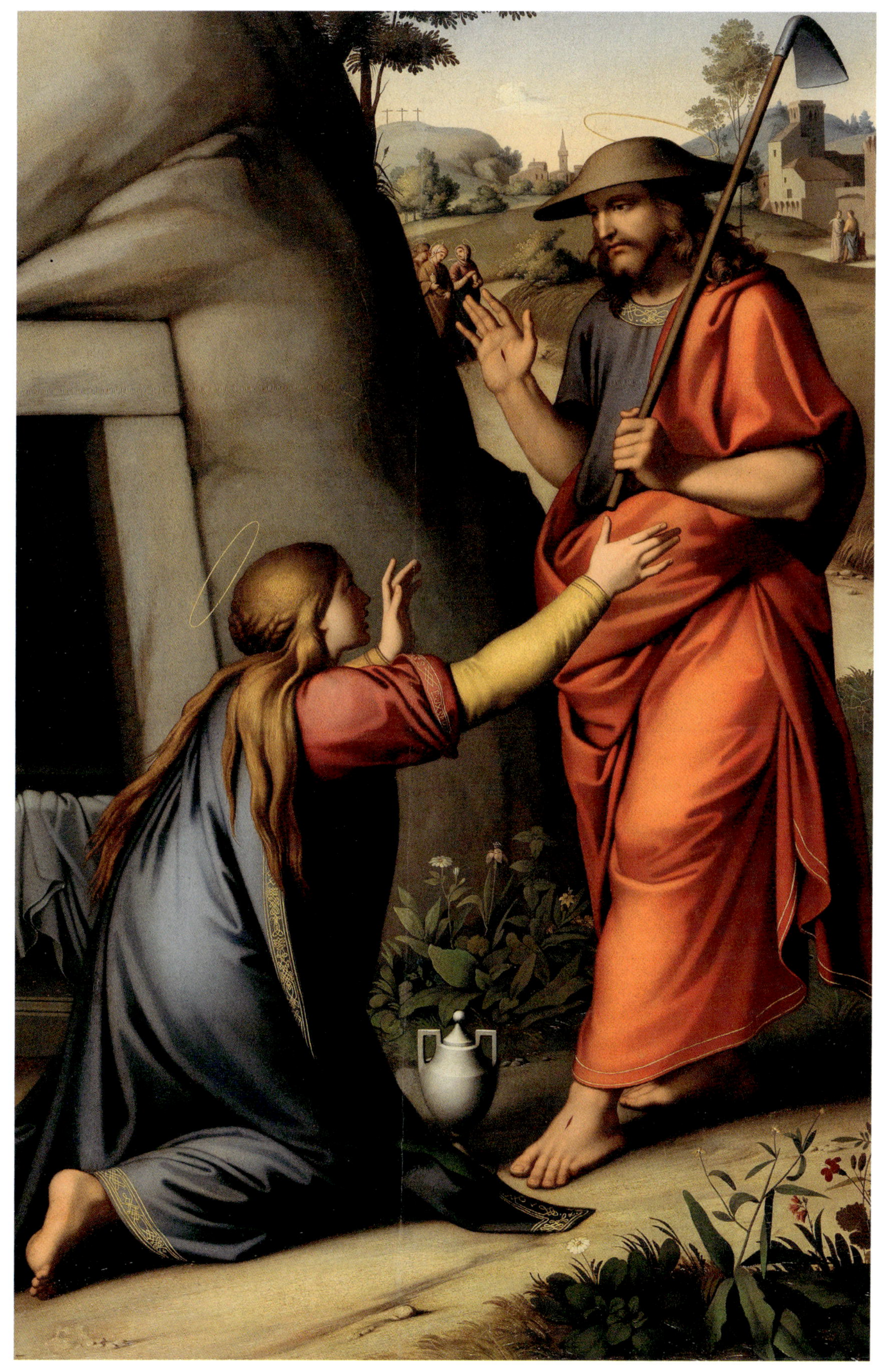

Augustin Alphonse GAUDAR de La VERDINE

Bourges, 18 Aug 1780 – 16 Sep 1804, Siena
French, 24 years, 30 days

Gaudar de La Verdine was the son of the influential nobleman Pierre Gaudart (1736–1800), Lord of La Verdine and Treasurer of France at Bourges. His brother, Pierre Jean François Gaudart de La Verdine (1779–1840), was likewise a painter. Together the brothers studied at the l'École Spéciale de Peinture et de Sculpture (Académie Royale) in Paris under the neoclassicist François-André Vincent (1746–1816). Gaudar de La Verdine was a diligent student and won several awards for his figure drawings in 1796–98.

In 1799, the young painter was awarded the coveted Prix de Rome for his oil *Manlius Torquatus Sentencing His Son to Death* (ENSBA). Following this success, Gaudar exhibited *Cyparissus Mourning His Dying Stag* at the Paris Salon of 1800. Finally, in 1802 he travelled to Italy using the pension that the Prix de Rome provided. Gaudar de La Verdine became a resident at the Académie de France in Rome at the Villa Medici and studied in Italy for two years.[45]

Unfortunately, his success was to be short lived; the promising young artist contracted a disease, probably malaria, which is thought to have claimed the lives of two other Prix de Rome winners around the same time (the musician Albert Androt and the painter Fulchran-Jean Harriet). Gaudar de La Verdine died soon after. A marble plaque was erected in his memory at the Church of San Luigi dei Francesi, Rome.

Many of Gaudar de La Verdine's paintings and drawings have been preserved in French museums (Châteauroux au Musée-Hôtel Bertrand and Musée des Beaux-Arts de Tours) and show his prematurely developed talent. Like his contemporaries, Gaudar de La Verdine worked in a neoclassical mode. Though he was painting classically at the time of his death, he was prone to romantic tendencies. This can be seen in the above-mentioned oil, where a young Cyparissus has tenderly dressed the wound and compassionately embraces the deer. Had he lived longer, he would surely have emerged more fully into his own direction with something beautiful to say.

Augustin Alphonse Gaudar de La Verdine
Manlius Torquatus Sentencing His Son to Death, 1799, oil on canvas, 114 × 146 (44⅞ × 57½ in)
ENSBA, Paris

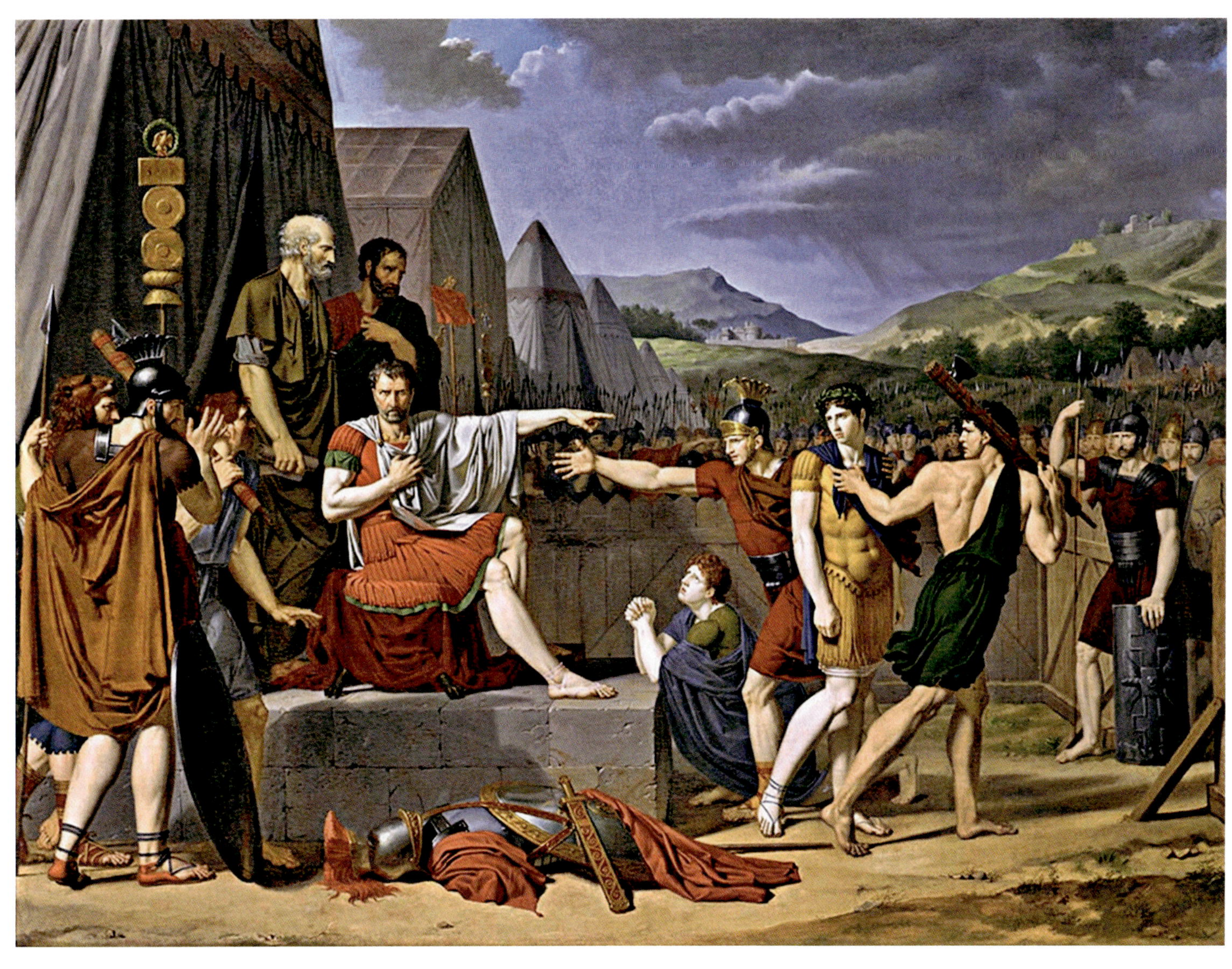

Herman Hugo HAAG

Stuttgart, 15 Oct 1871 – 18 Oct 1895, Salt Lake City, Utah
German/American, 24 years, 4 days

Herman Haag was a talented artist of figurative, religious and landscape themes as a painter and draughtsman. In 1881, Haag and his family converted to the Church of Jesus Christ of Latter-day Saints in Stuttgart. The following year he emigrated from Germany to remote Utah, where his new church was headquartered. Converts from all over the world gathered in this desert wilderness to build a Zion community. Haag was initially a student of Salt Lake City painter James T. Harward (1860–1940). Then at the age of 19, he was called by church leaders to become an 'art missionary'. Haag joined painters John Hafen, Edwin Evans, Lorus Pratt and J.B. Fairbanks in studying at the Académie Julian, Paris in 1891. These five were sent by the church to study French painting so they could return and paint murals in the Salt Lake City Temple, which was nearing completion.

Haag was much younger than his fellow art missionaries, but he progressed quickly and proved his talent. In 1892, he won an award at the Académie Julian for his drawing *John the Baptist Presenting Christ to the Multitude*, and upon his return to Utah he assisted in the temple murals and taught at the University of Utah. Unfortunately, few pieces by Haag exist, due to his poor health. Although he was a strong, robust boy in childhood, he suffered an undiagnosed illness at the age of 12. Confined to bed, the young Haag began to draw to amuse himself, effectively launching his artistic career. When he lacked a model, he drew himself, using a mirror.

Whilst we do not fully know the nature of his disease, it was degenerative and plagued him the rest of his life. In Paris there were days when he could not even walk to the art school. The year before his own death, Haag painted a scene from the Book of Mormon titled *Nephi Obtains the Plates from Laban* (1894). It is a mysterious, foreboding picture, and suggests Haag's own unease about his imminent passing. The artist died in 1895, just days after his 24th birthday. The Salt Lake County death record reports that he died of pyemia (septicaemia) and acute Bright's, a historical term describing a variety of kidney diseases. Haag had something in his art that was compelling. Had he lived, he would have undoubtedly become one of the major artists of the Utah Territory and the entire West.

Herman Hugo Haag
Nephi Obtains the Plates from Laban, 1894, oil on canvas, 119.4 × 91.5 cm (47 × 36 in)
Courtesy of The Church of Jesus Christ of Latter-Day Saints, Museum of History, Salt Lake City, Utah

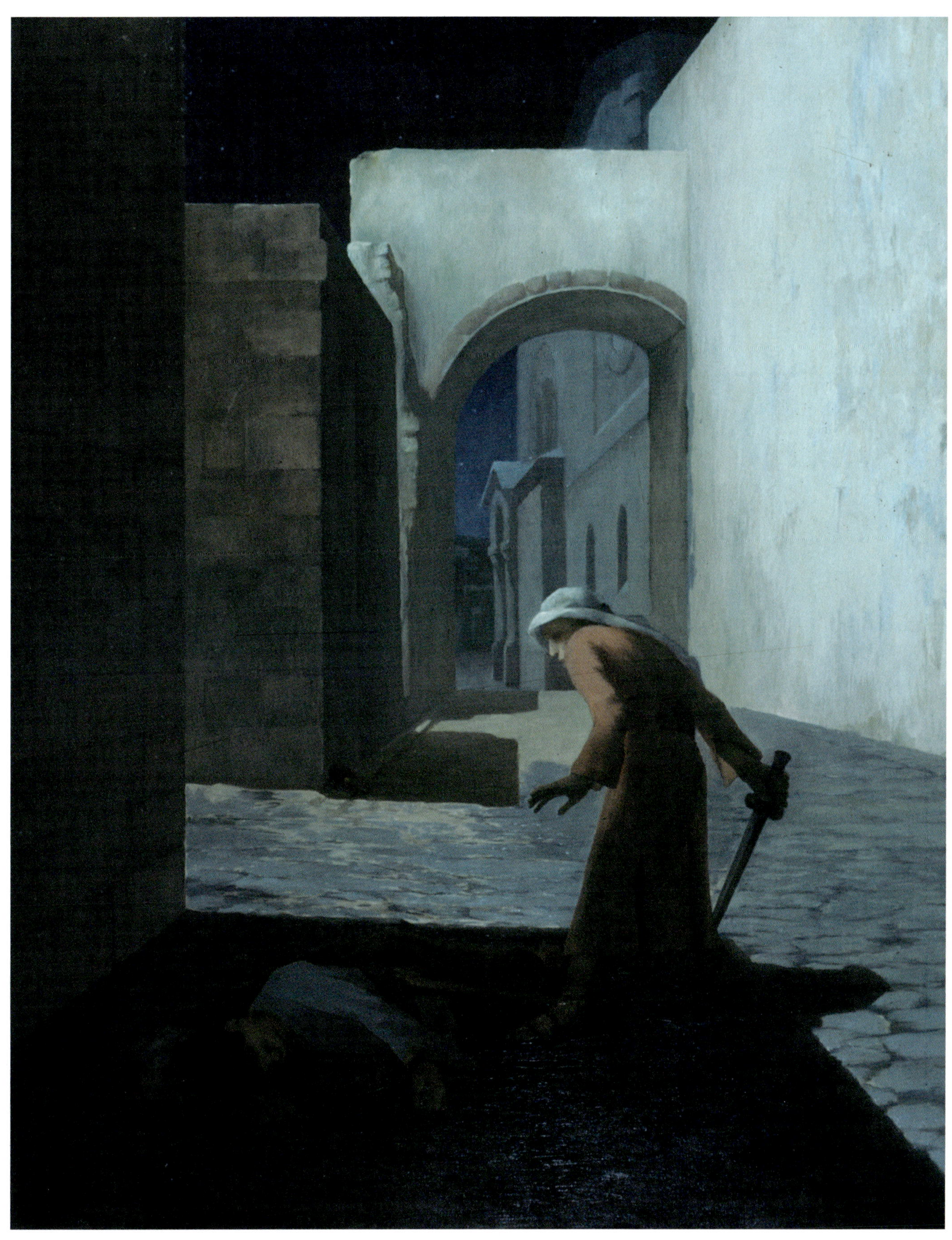

Franz PFORR

Frankfurt am Main, 5 Apr 1788 – 16 Jun 1812, Rome
German, 24 years, 2 months, 12 days

Franz Pforr is frequently remembered as the subject of Friedrich Overbeck's friendship portrait *Der Maler Franz Pforr*. Painted in 1810, the 22-year-old Pforr, dressed in old German costume, gazes out of a gothic arched window. In the background, Overbeck has included Pforr's ideal wife who is both industrious and spiritual as she simultaneously sews and reads from a religious text. In this Nazarene masterpiece, Overbeck depicts Pforr's perfect world, where art and faith intersect in a mediaeval-inspired society. Two years later, Pforr would be dead. He would never marry nor achieve the health and artistic bliss Overbeck wished for him. Instead, Pforr would leave behind only six known paintings and a couple of hundred drawings, but the enormous influence of the artist society he helped to create would be felt throughout Europe.

Pforr was educated in art by his father Johann Georg Pforr (1745–1798) and his uncle, the noted Johann Heinrich 'Goethe' Tischbein the Younger (1751–1829). In 1805 he began studying at the Academy of Fine Arts, Vienna, and since it was the period of the Napoleonic Wars, he volunteered as a guard in the Vienna militia. At the time, the Academy was severely neoclassical. Pforr, who tended towards piety and romanticism, did not feel at home in this environment. He soon had a nervous breakdown and returned to his home in Frankfurt am Main until he was able to get to grips with his delicate mental state. He relied on his Christian faith to restore his mental stability and sense of purpose.

The next year, he resumed his studies in Vienna and gradually began to develop his own personal style. His first large-scale figurative work, *Entry of Emperor Rudolf of Habsburg into Basel, 1273* (1809–10) shows a clarity of vision, flattened perspectives and intentionally awkward figures which reject over-sophistication and retrieve a naïveté and archaic innocence. In 1809, he and five of his fellow students banded together to form the Brotherhood of St Luke (Lukasbundes). These young artists were looking for the lost spirituality in their art, which had been muzzled by stupefying academic methods. They harkened to the more primitive Italian art of Fra Angelico, early Raphael, and northern masters such as Jan van Eyck and Albrecht Dürer.

When war closed the Academy in 1810, the Lukasbundes moved to Rome and lived in the abandoned monastery of Sant' Isidoro del Pincio. Because of their fraternal vows of poverty and their monk-like appearance they were nicknamed the Nazarenes. Pforr's painting *A Shulamite and Mary* (1810–11) is a notable representation of these Nazarene ideals.

Sadly, depression and physical illness constantly overshadowed Pforr's brief life. In October 1811, Pforr travelled to Naples; then, when the tuberculosis became unmanageable, his friends brought him back to Albano, near Rome. It was there that he died in June 1812, aged just 24. Unfortunately, Pforr didn't live long enough to see his art acknowledged, or to see the flowering of the Nazarene Brotherhood, which would gain many followers and influence generations of artists. In many ways, the movement he helped to launch was more important than his small oeuvre. Lethargy fed upon his ill-health and the number of works he produced was miniscule compared to the number of works he sparked.

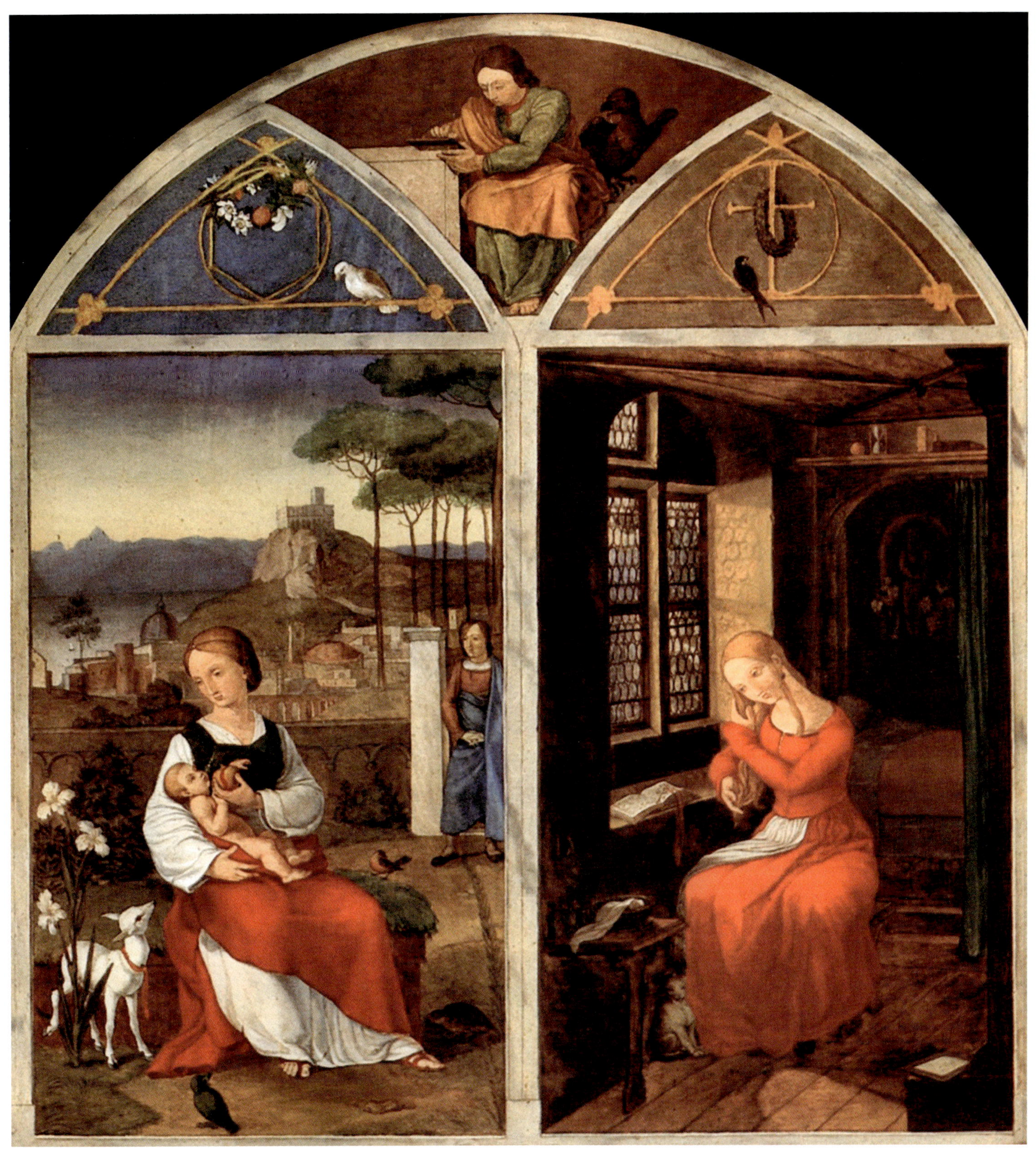

Franz Pforr
A Shulamite and Mary, 1810–11, oil on panel, 34 × 32 cm (13⅜ × 12⅝ in)
Georg Schäfer Museum/Alamy

Jonathan SKELTON

Croydon, c.1735 – 19 Jan 1759, Rome
English, approx. 24 years

Following his premature death, Jonathan Skelton and his art were largely forgotten for 150 years. Only in 1909 when a collection of 84 drawings by him were offered at auction did modern art historians become aware of the young artist who is now considered one of the 'most promising of the early English watercolourists.'[46] The Metropolitan Museum of Art credits Skelton as playing 'a pioneering role in the development of British landscape drawing.'[47] His work anticipated the aesthetic direction of Paul Sandby (1731–1809), who is rightly considered the father of British watercolour.

Little is known of Skelton's early years, but he was a student of George Lambert (c.1700–1765) in the early 1750s. Between 1754 and 1757, he depicted views of the churches and landscapes of Croydon, London, Rochester and Canterbury. By January 1758, Skelton had arrived in Italy, where he was prolific in his depiction of iconic vistas, making him one of the first English watercolourists to visit Rome, and depict Grand Tour subjects. In a series of letters to his patron William Herring (brother of the Archbishop of Canterbury), he writes of his life in Rome and its environs, and enthusiastically writes of his love for Tivoli, 'ye only school where our two most celebrated Landscape Painters Claude and Gasper studied.'

Most of his wash drawings were executed in subtle nuances of grisaille making them all the more precious. This masterful technique can be seen in *The Ponte Molle in the Campagna, Northern Rome* (c.1758). While he did occasionally paint in oil, none of these works is known. Despite his obvious talent and consummate draughtsmanship, Skelton's art did not sell well in his lifetime. Furthermore, fellow English artists in Rome falsely accused him of being a Jacobite, a slander akin to being called a communist in the days of McCarthyism. That was a fatal blow to an already fragile career in the 18th century.

This strain, in addition to living on a near starvation diet, and an illness which modern medicine has diagnosed as chronic duodenal ulcer (or peptic ulcer disease), killed the promising young artist in January 1759. His physical pain in the end was so great that one physician, Dr Jubb, referred to his death as 'a happy release to a very good young man.' It will never be known how Skelton's many experimentations in the medium of oil, watercolour and ink would have developed as he and his art matured. It should be understood that, given a few more years, society would have caught up with his advanced thinking and given him the honour that was his due.

Jonathan Skelton
The Ponte Molle in the Campagna, Northern Rome, c.1758, pen, pencil and wash, 26.7 × 37.5 cm (10½ × 14¾ in)
Christie's London

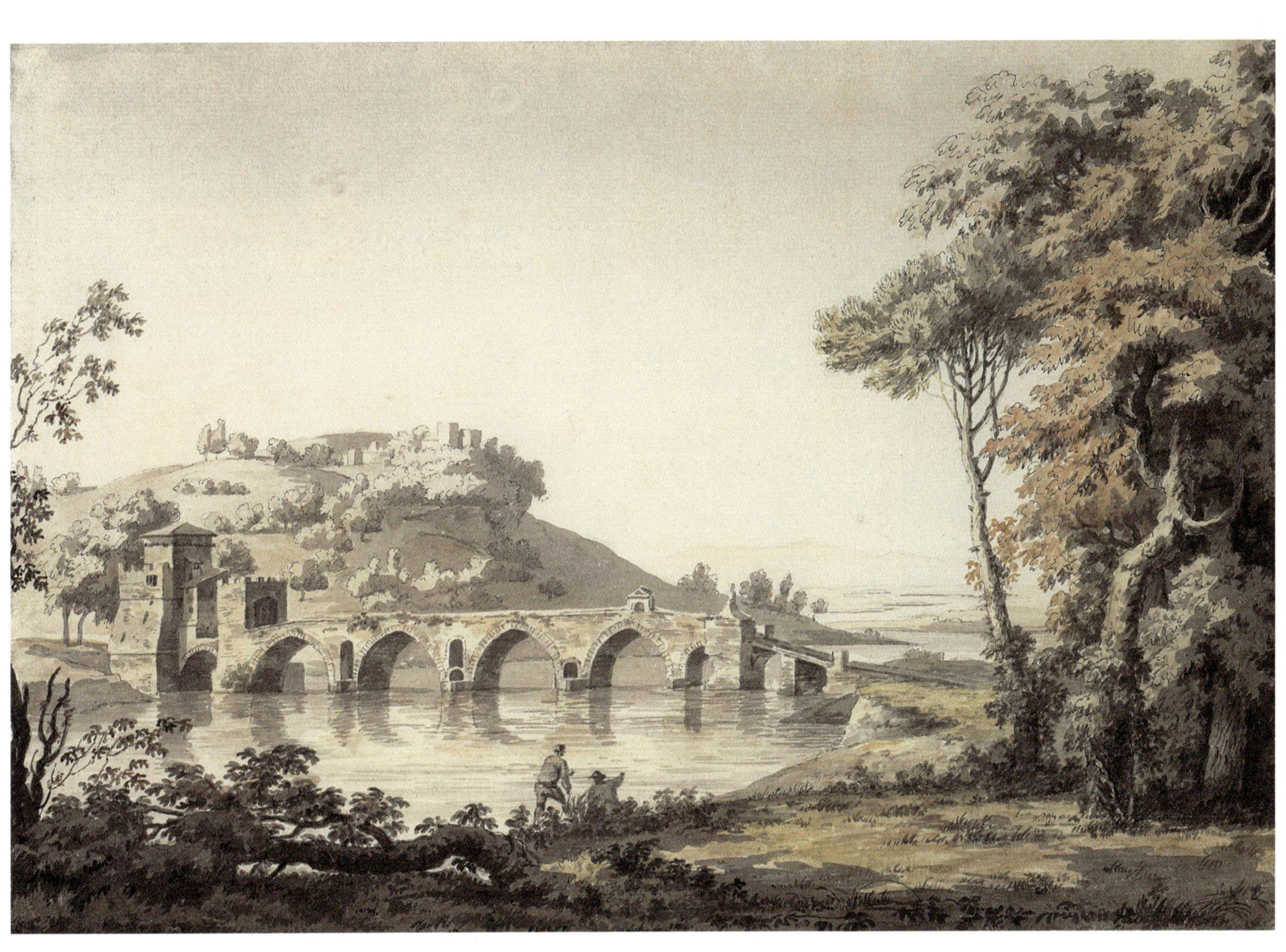

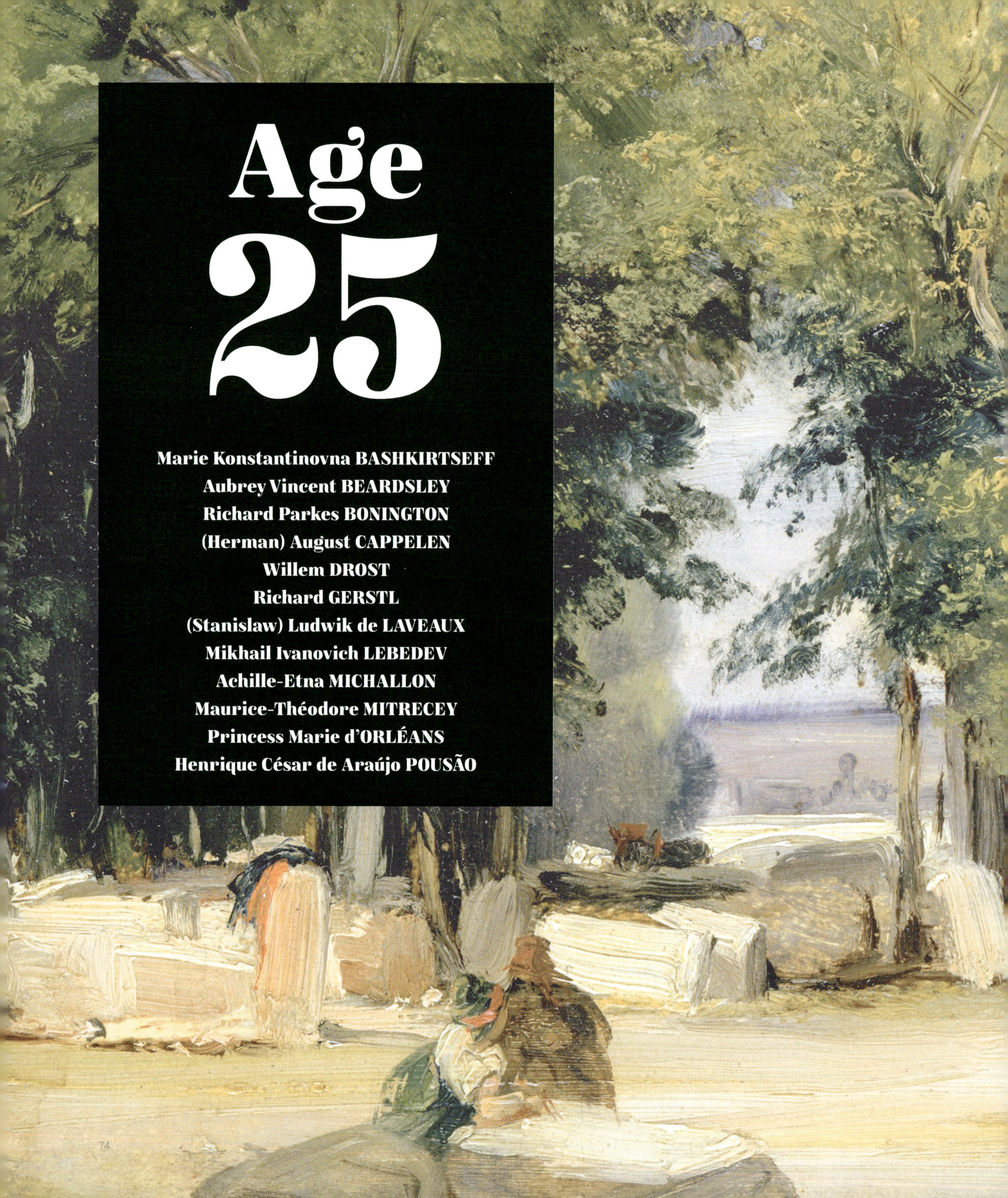

Age
25

Marie Konstantinovna BASHKIRTSEFF
Aubrey Vincent BEARDSLEY
Richard Parkes BONINGTON
(Herman) August CAPPELEN
Willem DROST
Richard GERSTL
(Stanislaw) Ludwik de LAVEAUX
Mikhail Ivanovich LEBEDEV
Achille-Etna MICHALLON
Maurice-Théodore MITRECEY
Princess Marie d'ORLÉANS
Henrique César de Araújo POUSÃO

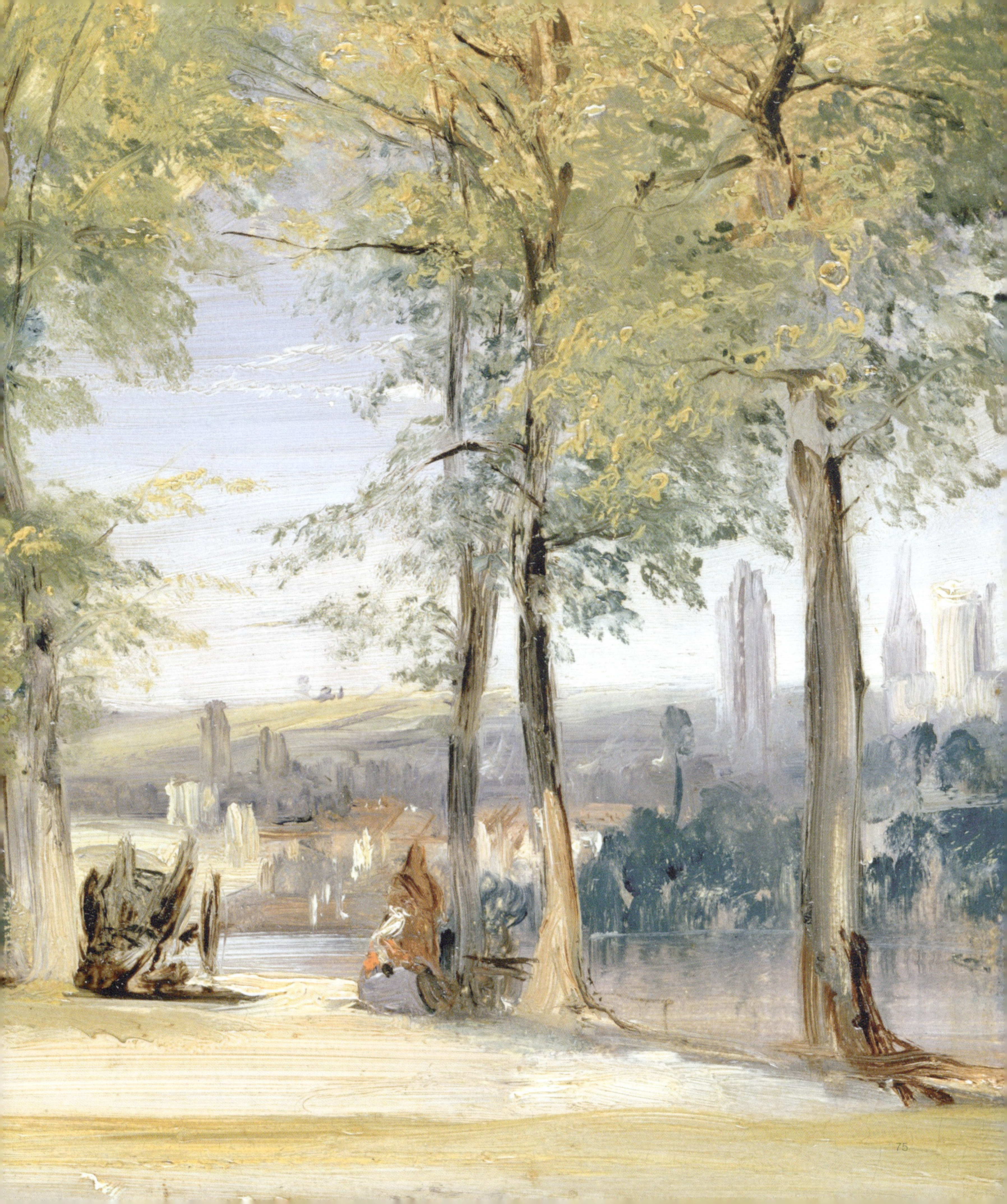

Marie Konstantinovna BASHKIRTSEFF

Gavrontsi near Poltava, 24 Nov 1858 – 31 Oct 1884, Paris
Ukrainian/French, 25 years, 11 months, 8 days[48]

The remarkable life of Marie Bashkirtseff is well documented, thanks to the 20,000 journal pages she penned. These journals were later published to great success as a psychological depiction of a beautiful, wildly talented, ambitious young woman. They detail her intense desire to achieve fame and not, in her own words, 'To die like a dog, like a hundred thousand women whose names are scarcely engraved upon their tombstones.' Her writings rather than her paintings are considered by some to be Bashkirtseff's most enduring legacy. However, given the outstanding quality and originality of the paintings which remain, there is little doubt that she would have left an equally impressive legacy in the visual arts if she had been allotted more time.

Bashkirtseff was born to a wealthy Ukrainian family, who eventually settled in Paris. Musically talented, Bashkirtseff initially considered singing as a career, but she was frequently plagued with chronic laryngitis. This necessitated a change of course, and she dedicated herself fully to becoming an artist of note. 'If my art does not soon bring me fame,' she wrote, 'I shall kill myself and end the whole matter at once.' In 1877, Bashkirtseff enrolled in the famed Académie Julian. Drawn to the art of the realist and naturalist painters, she became close friends with the artist Jules Bastien-Lepage. Exhibiting in four Paris Salons, Bashkirtseff won an honourable mention for a pastel portrait in 1884. In the same year, she also exhibited her most famous painting

A Meeting (Musée d'Orsay, Paris). While it was praised by the press, Bashkirtseff was 'humiliated' that it received no medals, and yet, it was a tremendous final Salon entry.

By 1884, her health was speedily failing. The pulmonary tuberculosis, which she had contracted from a childhood French tutor, had already caused tinnitus and muted her hearing. In 1882, her lungs became greatly affected, and yet her illness did not stop her prodigious work. She had a determined studio discipline as G.H. Perris wrote: 'she was killing herself in the race for fame — working at the studio morning and afternoon, writing and modelling at night at home, and in the intervals rushing about to social functions.'[49] In March 1884 Bashkirtseff wrote, 'I have spent six years, working ten hours a day, to gain what? The knowledge of all I have yet to learn in my art, and a fatal disease!'

Bashkirtseff died 31 October 1884, and her friend Bastien-Lepage died just six weeks later, forever linking the memories of these great painters. Her fitting last words were: 'Life was so beautiful after all.' Hers was a life devoted to beauty. Though prolific, much of her art was destroyed in World War II, leaving around 60 known works today. She was buried in the Passy Cemetery in Paris. Her monument is a grandiose full-sized recreation of her studio which has been declared a French historic monument. It does not, however, relieve the abiding desire to see the glories of the artist's later periods, which can only be imagined.

Marie Konstantinovna Bashkirtseff
A Meeting, 1894, oil on canvas, 193 × 177 cm (76 × 69¾ in)
Musée d'Orsay, Paris

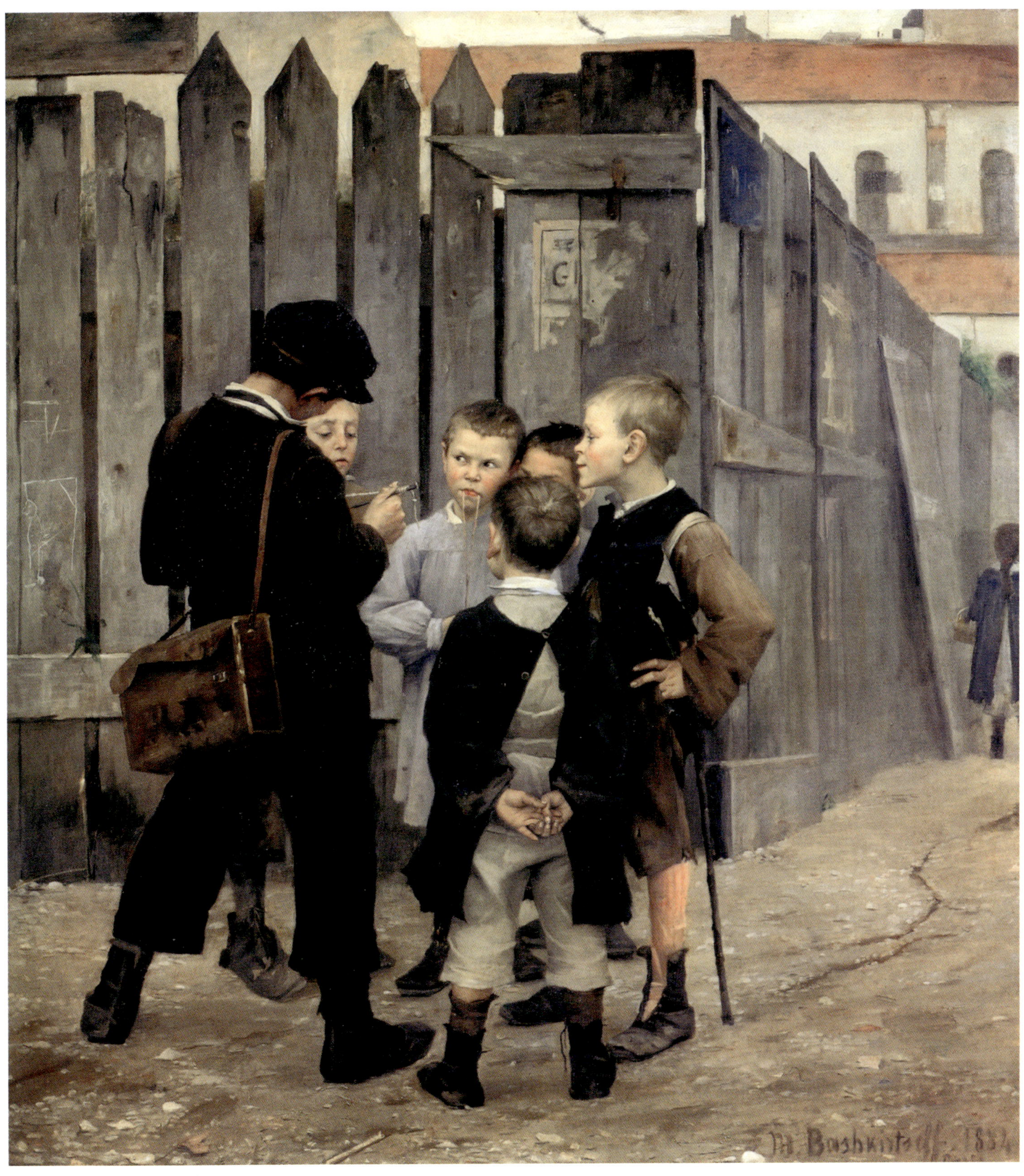M. Bashkirtseff 1884

Aubrey Vincent **BEARDSLEY**

Brighton, 21 Aug 1872 – 16 Mar 1898, Menton
British, 25 years, 6 months, 24 days

From the age of seven, Aubrey Beardsley's days were already numbered. Like his father, and his father's father, Beardsley became infected with the devastating disease of tuberculosis, which would prematurely take his life. Nevertheless, Beardsley's artistic prowess and unique vision would make him arguably 'the most significant figure to emerge in English art in the last decade of the 19th century' despite the brevity of his life.[50] As a teenager Beardsley showed his portfolio to his idol Sir Edward Burne-Jones. The impressed Pre-Raphaelite said, 'I seldom or never advise anyone to take up art as a profession, but in your case I can do nothing else.'[51] He suggested that Beardsley attend evening classes at Westminster School of Art, which he did for several months.

On the merit of his pure genius alone, Beardsley would soon become one of the most influential illustrators of all time. Producing black ink drawings inspired by Japanese ukiyo-e woodblock prints, he became attached to the arts and crafts, symbolist, aesthetic, decadent and art nouveau movements. His mature work was often very dissolute, erotic and grotesque; but always refined and elegant. He had a diabolical wit which won approval from many critics but made him controversial to the public at large. He illustrated a number of books including Thomas Malory's *Le Morte d'Arthur* (1893–4) and Oscar Wilde's play *Salomé* (1894), and was art editor and illustrator for the new quarterly, *The Yellow Book*.

Unfortunately, Beardsley became caught up in the scandal that surrounded Oscar Wilde in 1895, and Beardsley was unjustly fired from his art editor position. Soon after, he began working with a new publisher, Leonard Smithers, and launched the publication *The Savoy*. Under the influence of poet Algernon C. Swinburne, Aubrey moved from aesthetic to the decadent movement with his licentious *Lysistrata* (1896) illustrations. This underscored his pariah status and made him one of the most controversial British artists of his generation.

However, as quickly as Beardsley fell into the bohemian lifestyle, he fell out of it. In March of 1897, after long meditation, Beardsley converted to Roman Catholicism. His new regenerated life was plagued with rapidly collapsing health as attacks of lung haemorrhages intensified. He moved to Menton on the French Riviera. As he lay dying of tuberculosis, his last request to his unscrupulous publisher Leonard Smithers was that he should 'destroy all copies of *Lysistrata* and bad drawings … By all that is holy [burn] all the obscene drawings.'[52] His friend Herbert C. Pollitt and Leonard Smithers ignored Beardsley's request and even published spurious drawings as being by the artist.

The brevity of his life and his 'future that was not-to-be', intersected at the Cosmopolitan Hotel, Menton. He coughed himself to death as he succumbed to tuberculosis, clutching a rosary in his fingers.[53] The underlying question remains: Had he lived, would he have been as great a Christian artist as he had been a profane one?

Aubrey Vincent Beardsley
Salomé, 1893, pen and ink, size unknown
Private collection

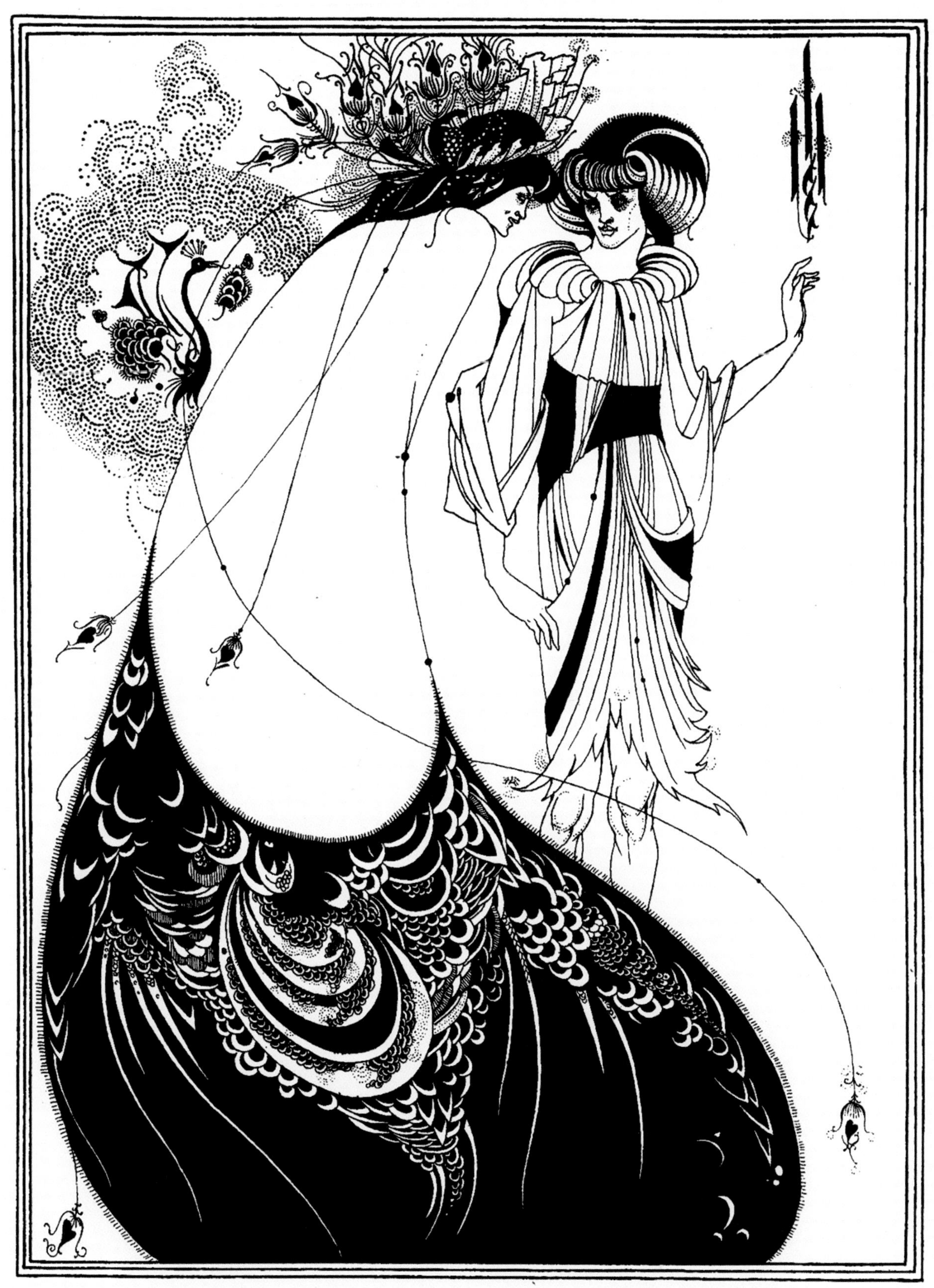

Richard Parkes BONINGTON

Arnold, near Nottingham, 25 Oct 1802 – 23 Sep 1828, London
English/French, 25 years, 10 months, 30 days

Bonington is rightly mentioned in the same breath as legendary painters John Constable and Joseph M.W. Turner. So great was Bonington's contribution to modern landscape painting, he is considered to be, according to the National Gallery, 'one of the most important artists of the early nineteenth century, vital to the understanding of French and British art of the Romantic period.'[54] He is also credited for bringing the English watercolour movement to Europe. These are astounding accomplishments for an artist who lived to be but 25 years.

Bonington was blessed with an early start. Tutored by his father in watercolour painting, he first exhibited at the Liverpool Academy at age 11. At the age of 14 his family moved to Calais, France, and there Bonington became acquainted with the Anglo-French painter Louis Francia. From Francia, he learned the latest English watercolour techniques. Both artists were deeply influenced by the work of Thomas Girtin, an English watercolourist, who coincidentally died young as well. Then, in 1818, Bonington moved to Paris and studied under Antoine-Jean Gros at the École des Beaux-Arts.

Bonington spent a great deal of time travelling the northern French coast and the regions along the Seine, deftly painting the sea, the land, and its rural inhabitants. He exhibited two watercolours from these travels in the Paris Salon of 1822, selling both works. Finally, in late 1823, Bonington began experimenting with oil paints to an equally astonishing effect as his watercolours. His oil study *View near Rouen* (c.1825) demonstrates how quickly he acquired a grasp of this new medium. At the 1824 Paris Salon, he exhibited four oil landscapes to immense praise. Along with Constable, Bonington won a gold medal, taking his place at the forefront of modern romantic painters. His impressive colouration, technical skills and innovations were noted by his many enthusiastic admirers. Similarly, when his pictures were exhibited in London in 1826 and 1828, they too met with great acclaim.

Following his travels to Italy in 1826, Bonington painted Venice as no other had. The young artist was inundated with commissions, and compromised his health by trying to fulfill them. During a sketching tour of the Seine in the summer of 1828, Bonington collapsed from either sunstroke or nervous exhaustion. Furthermore, the artist had tuberculosis and his health began to rapidly deteriorate under its effects. His parents took him to London to receive treatment, but Bonington died just two weeks after his arrival.

Following his death, Bonington's reputation continued to grow and many artists both in England and France imitated his style. One writer noted that 'he exercised an influence out of all proportion to his brief life.'[55] Contemporary art critic, Théophile Gautier asserted, 'With regard to color, the revolution in painting proceeded from Bonington just as the literary revolution proceeded from Shakespeare.' According to biographer Patrick Noon, 'His work, with that of John Constable, would influence the course of French landscape painting for the next decade.'[56]

If Bonington had lived free from the shackles of TB, more extraordinary experimentation, production and influence could have been expected from the artist. Fortunately, a prolific oeuvre comprising some 400 works remains. Eugène Delacroix wrote of his dear friend's precocious abilities: 'Some talents come into the world fully armed and prepared ... Bonnington [sic] had it ... in his hand.'

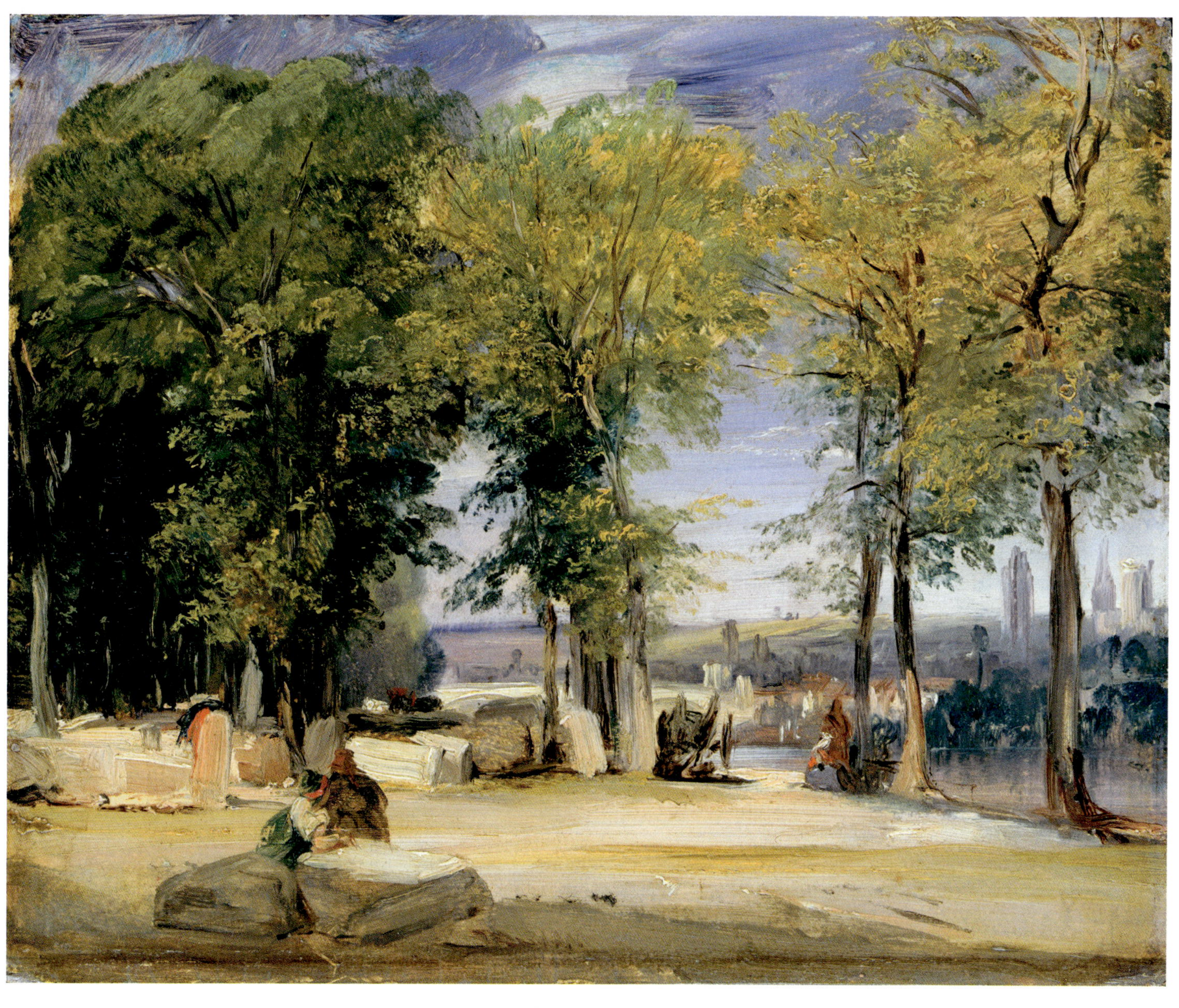

Richard Parkes Bonington
View near Rouen, c.1825, oil on board, 27.9 × 33 cm (11 × 13 in)
Metropolitan Museum of Art, New York, Purchase, Gift of Joanne Toor Cummings, by exchange, 2001

(Herman) August CAPPELEN

Skien, 1 May 1827 – 8 Jul 1852, Düsseldorf
Norwegian, 25 years, 2 months, 8 days[57]

August Cappelen was an important painter of sublime romantic landscapes. His compositions of crags, broken trees, moody lakes and wild rivers from Telemark, Norway display his exceptional talent and early development. Born to a prominent Norwegian family, his first drawing lessons were with his mother who was an avid draughtsman. Following his studies in Skien in 1845, Cappelen resided in Christiania (Oslo) where he befriended and studied under the influential romantic landscape painter Hans Gude (1825–1903). Gude, who had recently returned from Düsseldorf, recognised Cappelen's talents and encouraged him.

Cappelen consequently travelled to Düsseldorf in 1846. There he enrolled at the Kunstakademie, one of Europe's foremost art academies at the time, where he studied with Johann Wilhelm Schirmer until 1850. During the summers, he returned to his residence near Holden, Norway, where he embarked on study trips of the landscape and painted. Despite his brief career, Cappelen is widely considered one of the greatest of the Norwegian Düsseldorf painters.

His most productive period, during which he produced his most important works, was between 1850 and 1852, the two last years of his life. The National Museum in Oslo owns a major collection of more than 150 of his works. These include his impressive oil painting *Waterfall in Lower Telemark* (1852), whose rushing river depicts the powerful grandeur of nature and man's comparative insignificance. *Extinct Primeval Forest* (*Decaying Forest*, 1852), his last known work, found unfinished on Cappelen's easel at his death, has been viewed as the artist's last 'testament and symbol of his destiny' with its sombre mood, toppled trees and decaying beauty.[58]

In spring of 1852, Cappelen became very ill and was unable to work. For some time the artist had suffered intermittently with stomach pains, which affected his art and production. Finally in the summer of 1852, gastric cancer took his life when he was only 25 years old. Cappelen was buried in Düsseldorf, but nearly a century later in 1945, his remains were brought home to the Holla Old Cemetery in Nome, Norway. In 1952, Norwegian sculptor Dyre Vaa created a memorial column with a relief portrait in Cappelen's honour at Holla, a touching tribute signifying that neither the artist nor his art have been forgotten. Indeed, Cappelen's influence on other landscape artists is undisputed, including the painters Morten Müller, Erik Bodom and Lars Hertervig. It is very likely that, had Cappelen lived to full maturity, he would have emerged as one of Europe's most lauded painters of landscape.

(Herman) August Cappelen
Extinct Primeval Forest (Decaying Forest), 1852, oil on canvas, 130.5 × 164 cm (51⅜ × 64½ in)
National Museum of Norway, Oslo

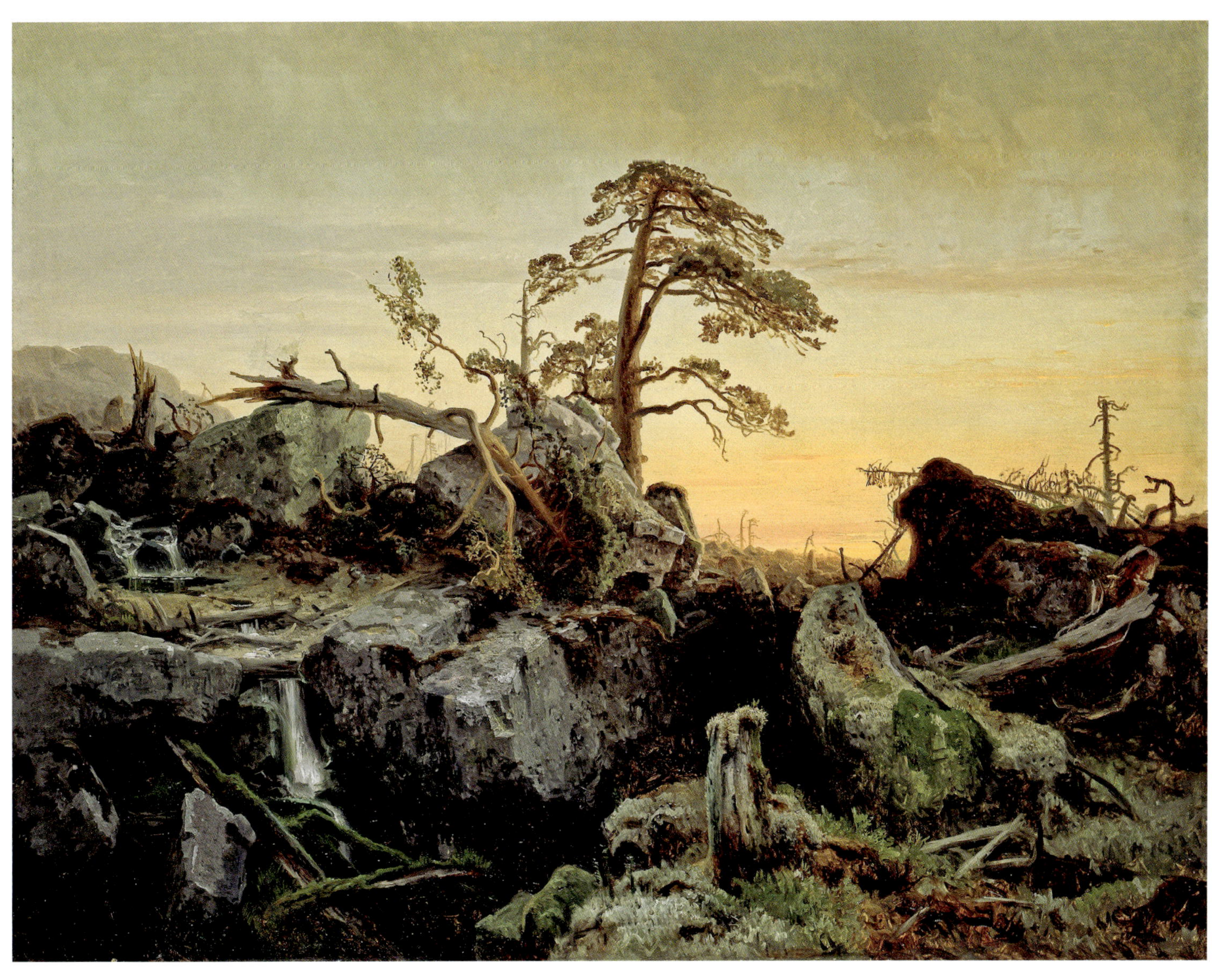

Willem DROST

Amsterdam, baptised 19 Apr 1633 – buried 25 Feb 1659, Venice
Dutch, approx. 25 years, 10 months

Willem Drost was called a 'mysterious man' by art historian Arnold Houbraken (1718), and certainly his life is shrouded in unrecorded history.[59] We know nothing of his training until he became a student and apprentice of Rembrandt (1606–1669) in 1650 at the age of 17. His works, such as *The Vision of Daniel* (1650, Gemaldegalerie Berlin) and *Ruth and Naomi* (1651, Ashmolean), are deeply imbued with the style and philosophical thrust of his master.

His talent was such that several paintings once believed to be by Rembrandt are now considered to be by Drost. One such controversial work is the Frick Museum's painting of *The Polish Rider* (c.1655), squarely ascribed to Rembrandt for hundreds of years but challenged by a number of art historians since the mid–1950s. The present consensus is that the large painting is indeed by Rembrandt with evidence of another hand; Drost being the most widely accepted as that 'other hand'. Drost continued to work in Rembrandt's studio until about 1655, when he departed for Italy.

Drost's notable oil, *Bathsheba with King David's Letter* (1654, Musée du Louvre) has the feel of a northern European artist, but once he travelled south to Italy, his work became softer. His equally fine canvas, *Flora* (c.1657) absorbed the golden influence of the Venetian artist, Titian. This painting was recently rediscovered and sold at Sotheby's New York in January of 2017 for $4,625,000 (£3,596,862). Another painting, *Roman Charity,* also painted in Italy, sold at the same auction house in February 2018 for $1,095,000 (£851,581). These high prices attest to the significance of Drost as one of the most important pupils of Rembrandt.

While in Italy, Drost befriended the German artist Johann Carl Loth (1632–1698) and collaborated with him on a series of paintings. Sadly, following four months of dire illness, Drost died in Venice of fever and pneumonia.[60] He was only 25. Consequently, his known oeuvre is relatively small and attribution has been difficult. It will never be known how Drost would have ultimately developed as an artist. If he had lived to be as old as his master, Rembrandt, would the Italian or northern style have gained dominance in his painting, or would his art have become an innovative hybrid of the two?

Willem Drost
Flora, c.1657, oil on canvas, 99 × 83.8 cm (39 × 33 in)
Sotheby's New York

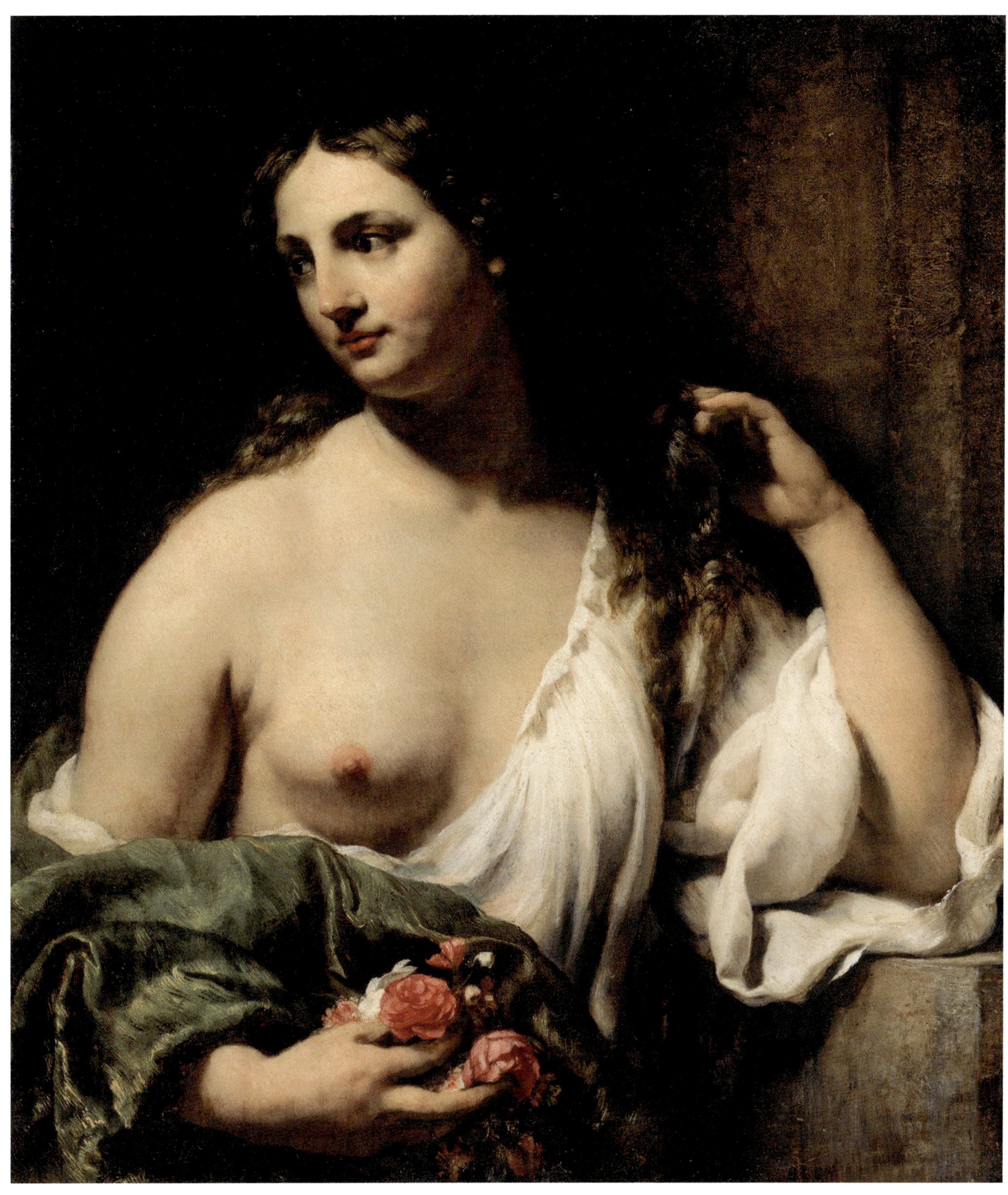

Richard GERSTL

Vienna, 14 Sep 1883 – 4 Nov 1908, Vienna
Austrian, 25 years, 1 months, 22 days

Gerstl never achieved the fame he craved during his lifetime. After his gruesome suicide in 1908, his art was put into storage, only to surface again in 1931 when his brother took two paintings to a dealer to ask if they could be sold or should be disposed of. Soon after, a retrospective exhibition was mounted with some critics calling Gerstl the 'Austrian Van Gogh'. Sadly, the full extent of his genius will never be known since he burned his letters and many of his drawings and artworks while of unsound mind just before his death.

However, the 70 or so remaining drawings and paintings display the artist's intense interest in fauvist portraiture, especially self-portraiture, and his employment of a variety of styles including brushy postimpressionism and pointillism. The spontaneous, abstracted art of his last two years is considered to be 'far in advance of contemporary painting' of his day and to even anticipate German expressionism.[61] Given the paucity of his remaining art, the Classora ranking group, rather surprisingly, rates the artist as 29th of the all-time top 50 artists from Austria.

Ever the outsider, Gerstl kept mostly to himself, except for an intimate circle of friends which included the famous atonal composer Arnold Schoenberg. He entered this circle when Schoenberg threatened suicide in 1907 after a number of musical failures. He was dissuaded by Gerstl, who said, 'You are the greatest living artist that I know.' With this, the composer invited the young painter to join his family for a vacation in the Bavarian Alps. In late July of 1908, he painted a thick blur-of-colour portrait *The Arnold Schönberg Family* (Museum of Modern Art, Vienna).

Living in a flat in the same building as the Schoenbergs, holidaying together and becoming very close, Gerstl and Schoenberg's wife, Mathilde, soon began an ill-fated love affair. Following their discovery in a compromising position by Arnold in 1908, Mathilde left Gerstl and returned to her husband and children. Gerstl was subsequently banished from his group of friends and became depressed and unhinged.

His oeuvre is filled with self-loathing self-portraits. His last known painting, a full-length nude self-portrait against a swirling blue background, is a candid portrayal of an isolated man at odds with the outside world. Finally, on 4 November, the evening of a Schoenberg concert from which Gerstl had been excluded, he took off his clothes, stood on a chair, hanged himself in front of a mirror, and somehow managed to cut himself open with a butcher's knife.[62] Had he lived longer and maintained his lively, original vigour, Gerstl may well have become as well known as another Austrian expressionist – Oskar Kokoschka.

Richard Gerstl
The Arnold Schönberg Family, July 1908, oil on canvas, 88.8 × 109.7 cm (35 × 43¼ in)
Museum of Modern Art, Vienna

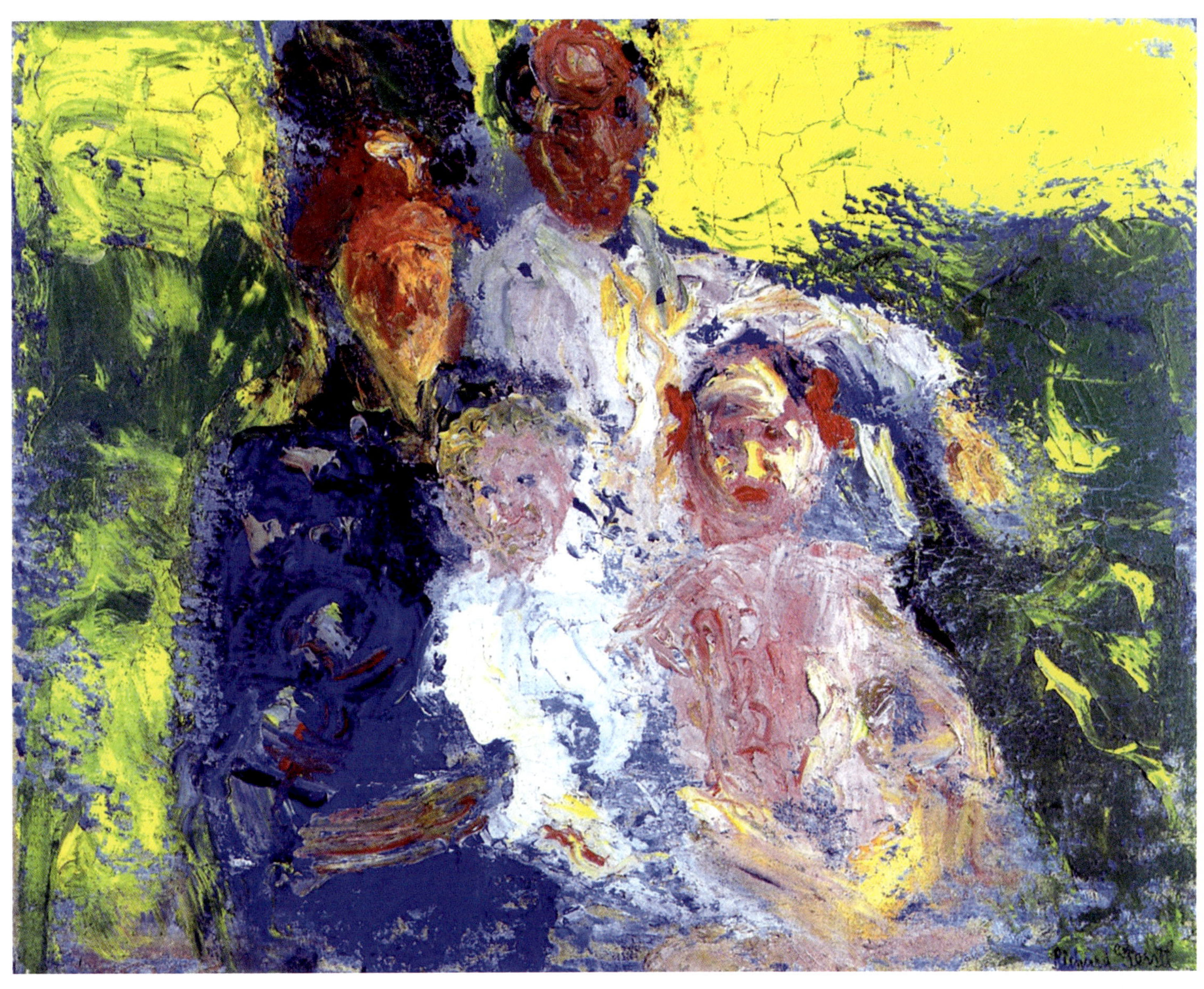

(Stanislaw) Ludwik de LAVEAUX

Jaronowice, 21 Nov 1868 – 5 Apr 1894, Paris
Polish, 25 years, 4 months, 16 days

Ludwik de Laveaux is a highly regarded artist in modern Polish art history. Further immortalised in Stanisław Wyspiański's well-known play *The Wedding* (1901), Laveaux appears in the play as a ghost (Widmo) who visits his real-life ex-fiancé Marysia Pareńska. His spectral character is meant to symbolise romantic love and the spirit of the artist. Laveaux's life does, in fact, read like a bohemian drama. He was neurotic, impulsive, gifted and famous for his love affairs. The most famous being an affair with a count's daughter, Iwona Prośnieńska.

Laveaux was born in Poland to a family of French Protestant descent who had emigrated to Poland because of persecution during the 18th century. He studied at the Kraków Academy of Art (1884–1890) under Józef Mehoffer. His effective canvas from this period, of two young peasant women with baskets in their arms, *To the Town Market* (1889, Lviv National Art Gallery) is imbued with Russian impressionism. Another, very different oil, a more restrained painting from the same year, *Polish Washerwomen* (1889), projects a stark naturalism.

Then Laveaux enrolled for two years at the Academy of Fine Art in Munich under Otto Seitz. Following his studies, he moved to Paris in 1891, but frequently returned to Poland and travelled around Brittany and England. He painted portraits, peasants, landscapes and, most famously, nocturnal Paris street scenes. He was obsessed with the late-night vacant streets with burning lamps. Laveaux was always concerned with the luminous effects of artificial light, lurid colour and blurred silhouettes in an impressionistic and at times expressionistic style.

His oil *Place de L'Opera, Paris* (c.1893) is suffused with half-light punctuated with bright streetlamps while one provocative woman walks towards the viewer. It is late at night and she should not be out alone. Karolina Dzimira-Zarzycha wrote of this period: 'Parisians were surprised that someone named Laveaux barely speaks French. However, the Polish artist did not come to the Seine for a chat. He was in a hurry to paint – he could feel death coming.' [63]

Unhappy with his son's career choices and libertine lifestyle, Laveaux's father ceased funding him in 1891, and the artist lived in poverty which led to declining health. At some point he contracted the dreaded tuberculosis. Laveaux worked so ceaselessly at his art that he almost drowned in a bathtub, too exhausted from his exertions to stay awake. 'Living in misery and the relentless fear of the coming death affected the young artist's psyche; he dreamed of skeletons, he saw a skeleton in his predictions.' [64]

Laveaux was plagued by melancholy and apathy, burdened by nervousness and irritability. In 1894 he was admitted to hospital. His prescribed treatment of 'raw meat and quinine' was unsurprisingly ineffective and he died on 5 April 1894. Each of his various developing styles proved his expansive talent. The direction in which he was headed was modernist expressionism, had he lived and painted longer. If his talent could have been sustained by a healthier body and mind, he would undoubtedly have been placed among the leading artists of the Young Poland period.

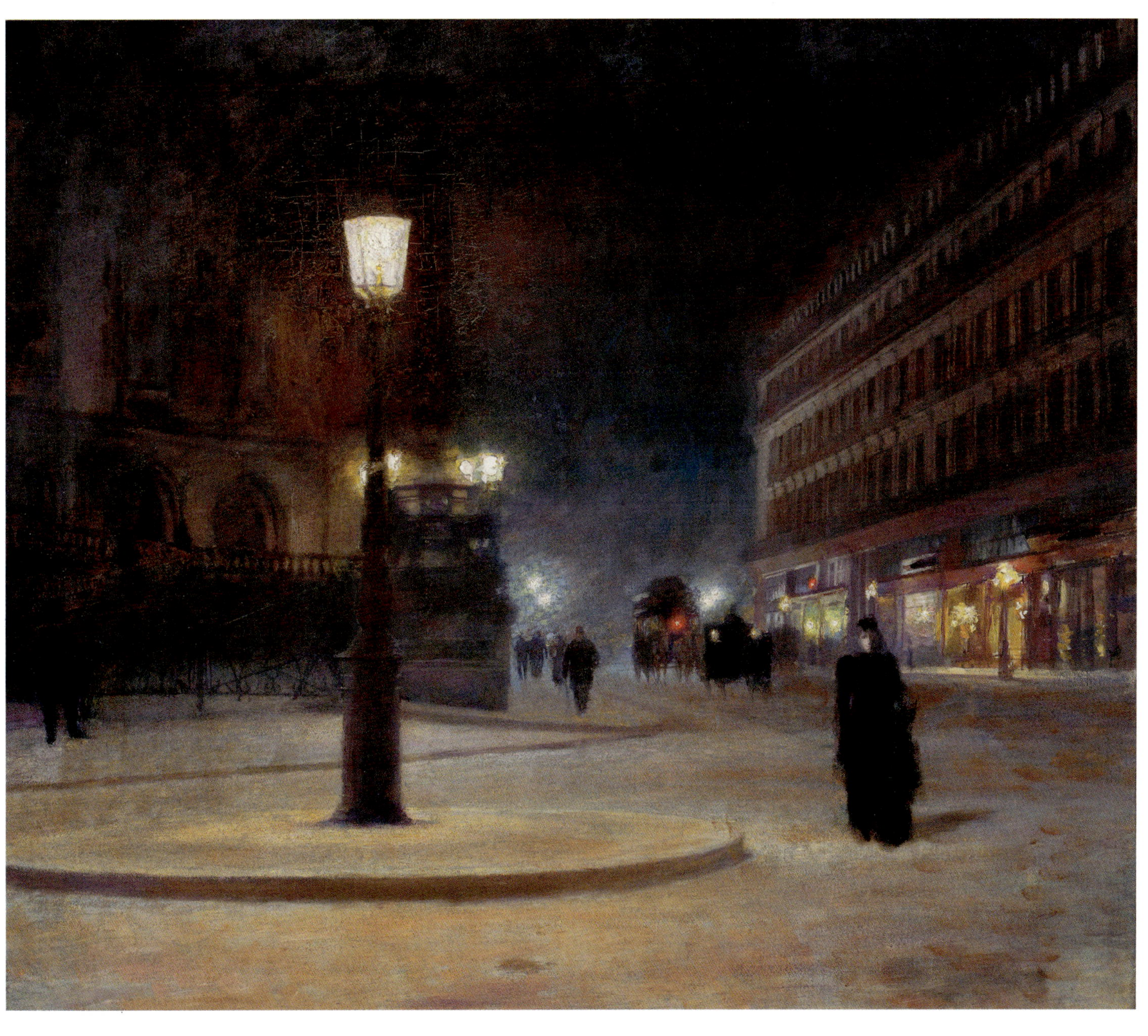

(Stanislaw) Ludwik de Laveaux
Place de L'Opera, Paris, c.1893, oil on canvas, 75 × 84 cm (29½ × 33⅛ in)
National Museum in Warsaw

Mikhail Ivanovich LEBEDEV

Dorpat/Tartu, 4 Nov 1811 – 13 Jul 1837, Naples
Estonian-Russian, 25 years, 8 months, 10 days

The landscape painter Mikhail Lebedev was born into an impoverished serf family. After serfdom was abolished in his region (c.1820s), he attended a nearby school. His early artistic endeavours attracted the attention of Count Fyodor von der Pahlen who sent him to the Academy in St Petersburg on a full Imperial scholarship (1829–1833). There he studied under landscapist Maxim Vorobyov (1787–1855) and progressed quickly. During the four years he was a student at the Academy, Lebedev received two silver medals, and in 1833 he won the school's prestigious gold medal for his painting *View of Lake Ladoga*. The painting was purchased by Emperor Nicholas I in exchange for a diamond ring, which the artist sold and gave the proceeds to his poor family in Dorpat.

He was also awarded the title of 'Artist' and a fourteenth civil service rank (a title in the Russian Civil Service Table of Ranks which outlined a system of promotion based on personal ability rather than hereditary right). With effort and regular participation in exhibitions, Lebedev could have risen to the title of 'Academician' and earned a tenth civil service rank. This would have been a great honour for a young artist who had been born under the lowest of circumstances, but unfortunately, it was never to be.

Lebedev's gold medal earned the young painter a pension to study abroad at the expense of the Academy. He travelled to Italy in 1834 and lived among the large Russian artist colony there. In Italy, Lebedev painted the environs of Rome, Sorrento, Capri and Naples. His 1836 canvases, *Ariccia near Rome* (State Tretyakov Gallery, Moscow) and *Albano near Rome* (Samara Regional Art Museum) prove his exquisite handling of mood, composition and medium. His landscape paintings effectively utilise the device of dark foliage with sunny spots as contrast.

Regrettably, he visited Naples in May of 1837 at the beginning of a cholera epidemic and pathetically died, along with 20,000 other victims, from this disease a few months later. When the great painter Karl Bryullov heard of his death, he exclaimed, 'What losses in one year: Pushkin and Marlinsky as poets and Lebedev, whom Russia could be proud of as the best landscape painter in Europe.' While his art is greatly admired and hangs in Russia's most prominent museums, he did not show the genius of F.A. Vasilyev or Achille-Etna Michallon, who similarly died in their twenties. Sometimes prodigies are late bloomers in their own way. While he quickly found a certain representational 'aptness', perhaps his expressive power would have more slowly revealed itself in deep maturity. That is, if he had worked prodigiously and lived much longer.

Mikhail Ivanovich Lebedev
Ariccia near Rome, 1836, oil on canvas, 55 × 45 cm (21⅝ × 17¾ in)
State Tretyakov Gallery, Moscow

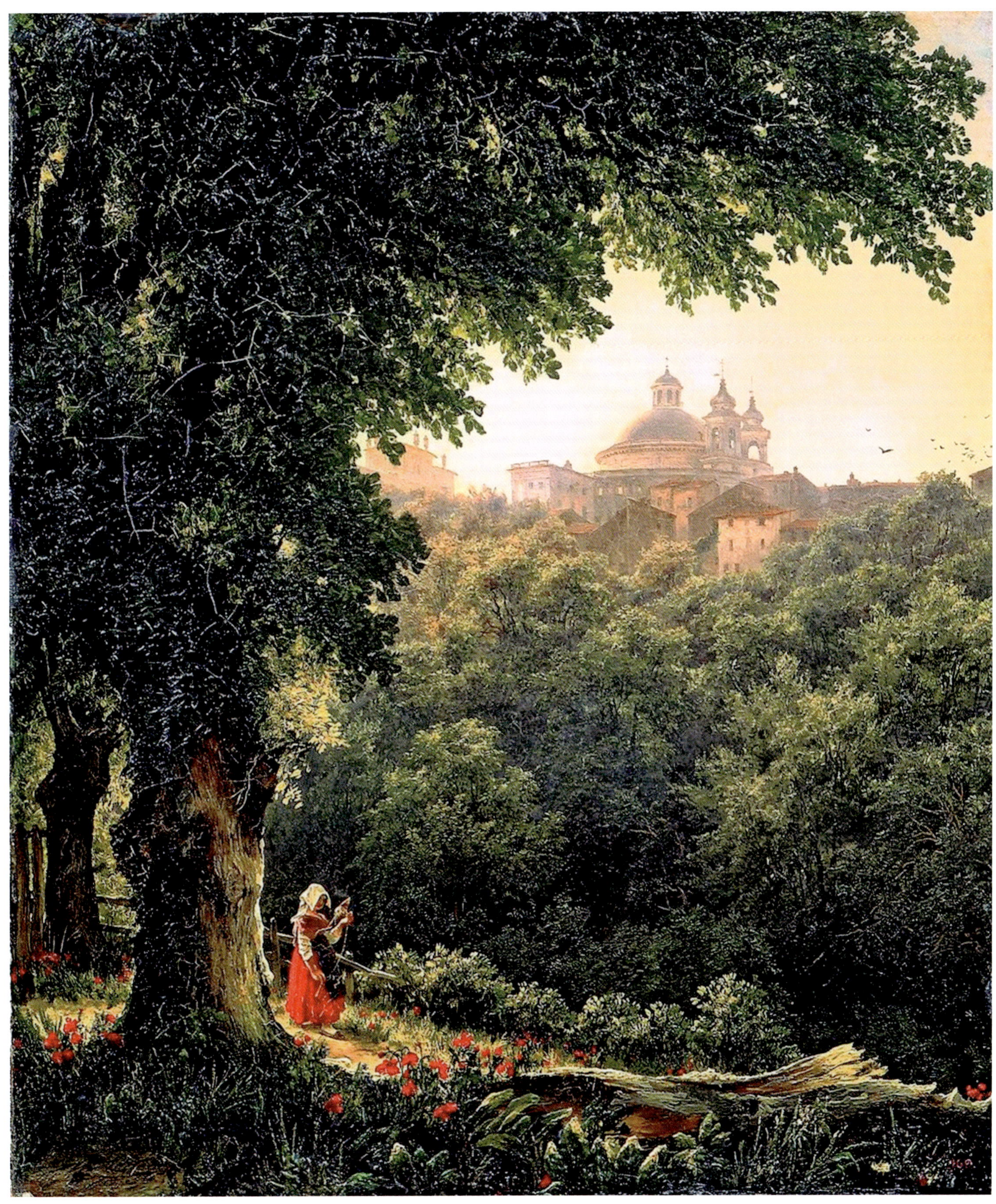

Achille-Etna MICHALLON

Paris, 22 Oct 1796 – 24 Sep 1822, Paris
French, 25 years, 11 months, 3 days

Like his father, Michallon was blessed with an abundance of talent but very little time. His father, the sculptor Claude Michallon (1751–1799), died early at 48 years when his son was just an infant. Michallon was raised in the art communities at the Louvre and the Sorbonne, and from an incredibly early age studied at Jacques-Louis David's studio in Paris. No works from this early date are known, but reports note that Michallon was very precocious. Starting in 1808, until 1812, Michallon received financial help from Prince Nicolai Yusupov of St Petersburg, Russia, after the prince saw his art in David's studio and was impressed by the 12-year-old's talent. Later, other illustrious patrons followed suit, such as the Duchess de Berry and the Comte de L'Espine.

Michallon's first Paris Salon entries came in 1812 when he was but 15, with two works of art, winning a second-class medal. When his mother died in 1813, Michallon was raised and mentored by his uncle, the sculptor Guillaume Francin (1741–1830). He also studied with Pierre-Henri de Valenciennes (1750–1819), and later with Jean-Victor Bertin (1767–1842). The first inkling of greatness came in 1816 when he painted a modest-sized canvas, *The Oak and the Reed* (Fitzwilliam Museum, Cambridge) after La Fontaine's book of the same title. The sublime and the terrible forces of nature break the mighty oak but only sway the flexible reed with Michallon pictorialising this fable.

Then, in 1817, Michallon won the inaugural Prix de Rome for historical landscape painting with his *Democritus and the People of Abdere* (ENSBA, Paris). The following year he left for Rome at the same time as his friend, Léon Cogniet. While in Italy he painted *The Death of Roland* (Salon 1819, Louvre). His major oil, *Marmore Falls, near Terni* (c.1820) is beautiful with its languid sense of harmony. During these years he painted numerous oil sketches on location, a painting method he and Valenciennes pioneered. After studying throughout Italy, including Sicily, he returned to France in 1821. Upon his arrival in Paris he opened his own studio which was frequented by Jean-Baptiste-Camille Corot. One of his last major paintings was *Philoctetes on the Island of Lemnos* (1822, Musée Fabre), which was exhibited to acclaim.

Michallon was adept at depicting atmospheric effects and time of day, and took his place in the evolution of plein-air painting. A classical romanticist, his paintings expressed the changeableness of nature and the sublime, which were his forté even though it seems occasionally contrived. A certain melancholic violence of passion and dramatisation of nature foreshadow his new approach. Tragically, Michallon died suddenly of pneumonia in Paris at 25 years of age. It was said of him that his death ended the 'brief career of perhaps the most promising landscape painter of his generation.' [65] His myriad en plein-air oil studies attest that he had a searching eye and a penetrating soul, and vouchsafed a brilliant future which was so suddenly taken from him and the world.

Achille-Etna Michallon
The Oak and the Reed, 1816, oil on canvas, 43.5 × 53.5 cm (17⅛ × 21 in)
© Fitzwilliam Museum, Cambridge

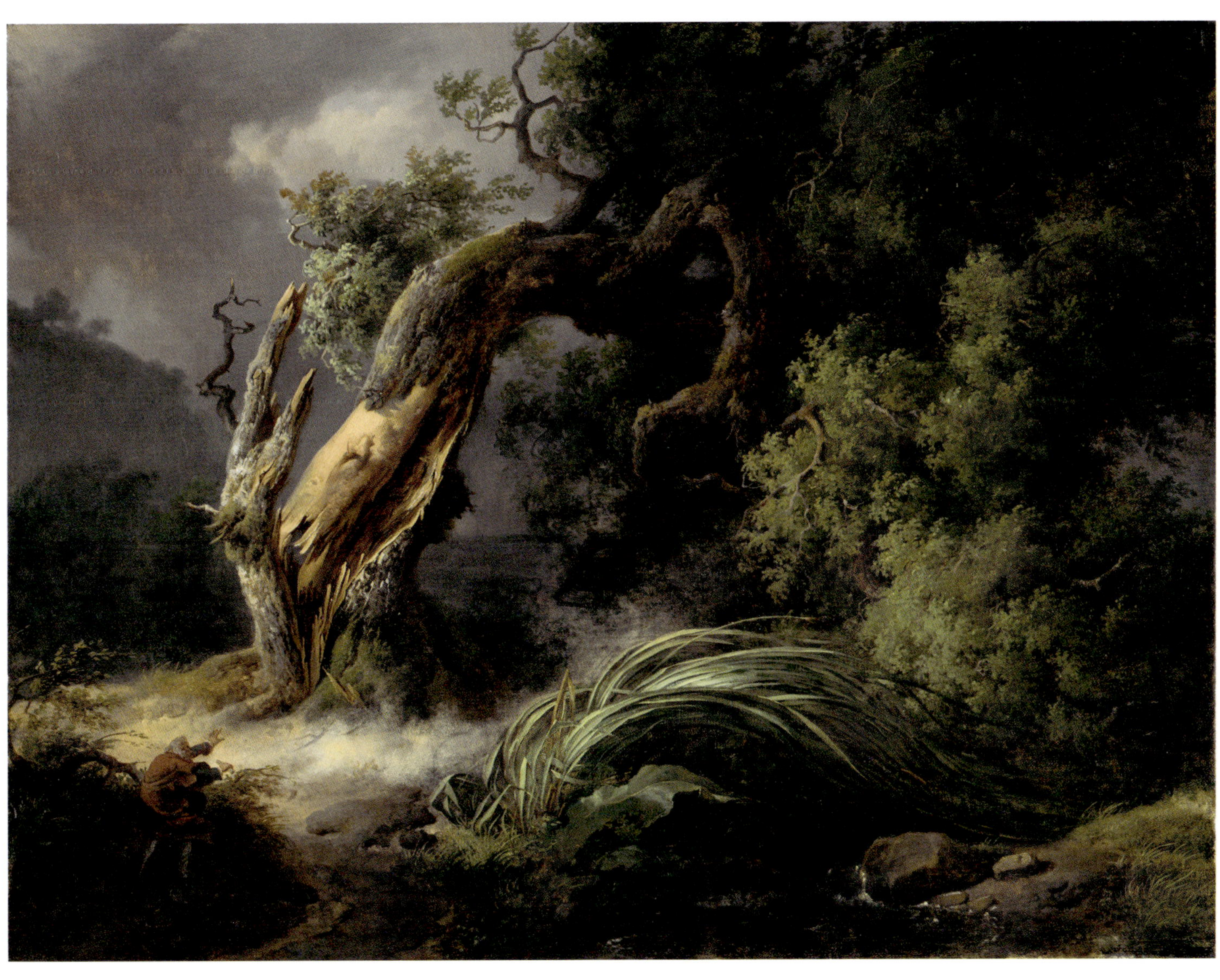

Maurice-Théodore MITRECEY

Paris, 2 Jan 1869 – 20 Jan 1894, Florence
French, 25 years, 19 days

Mitrecey was a gifted 19th-century academic figurative and narrative painter. He lived at No. 2 rue Mandar in Paris with his parents Alphonse François Mitrecey (1840–1871) and Angélique Chennevière (1846–1871), who were artificial-flower manufacturers. They were tragically killed in 1871 leaving as orphans the two-year-old Maurice and new baby André. The young sons were raised either by other members of the family or in an orphanage. Unlike so many in this book, he had no known artistic heritage to fire his passion for the arts. Nevertheless, he was somehow proficient enough to be accepted at 19 into France's most prestigious art academy.

He entered the École des Beaux-Arts de Paris in 1888 and studied in the workshops of the noted academic artists, Eugène Thirion, Jules Lefebvre and Tony Robert-Fleury. These artists thought so much of the orphaned Mitrecey that they claimed themselves his 'foster fathers' and him their 'high son'. That same year he participated in a sketching contest with studies for his tempestuous oil, *Jesus Soothing the Storm* (1888–91, ENSBA). He entered the same contest in 1891 with a standing nude male figure, then again in 1893 with a half-length figure. While talented, he failed to win the Prix de Rome competition with his minor masterpiece, *Job and His Friends* (1892, ENSBA).

The following year, Mitrecey entered the Paris Salon with a portrait of a woman (1893), his first and only work exhibited there. That year, he also won the École des Beaux-Arts Leprince Prize for painting, and more importantly he finally won the coveted Prix de Rome with his *Samson Turning the Mill Wheel* (1893) now in the École Nationale Supérieure des Beaux-Arts (ENSBA). From his three major narrative oils one can see an artist who expressed himself with power and technical brilliance. This award provided the young artist with funds to study in Rome, the aspiration of almost every artist at the time.

Most tragically, after his triumph, he died just outside Florence on the road to the French Academy's Villa Medici in Rome. Following a bathe in the frigid Arno River and while having fun with his friends, he became ill and very suddenly died. His funeral address states that a 'cruel illness took possession of him in a few days' and 'in the midst of implacable pains' he succumbed. [66] Not even the illustrious doctors could save him, underscoring the fragility of life in a time of rudimentary medicine. A large, emotional funeral mourned his loss at the Badia Fiorentina Church in Florence. Unlike so many of the forgettable names who were winners or near winners of the Prix de Rome, Mitrecey had the talent and ambition to become a great artist. His hypotheticals were boundless.

Maurice-Théodore Mitrecey
Samson Turning the Mill Wheel, 1893, oil on canvas, 113 × 145 cm (44½ × 57 in)
ENSBA, Paris

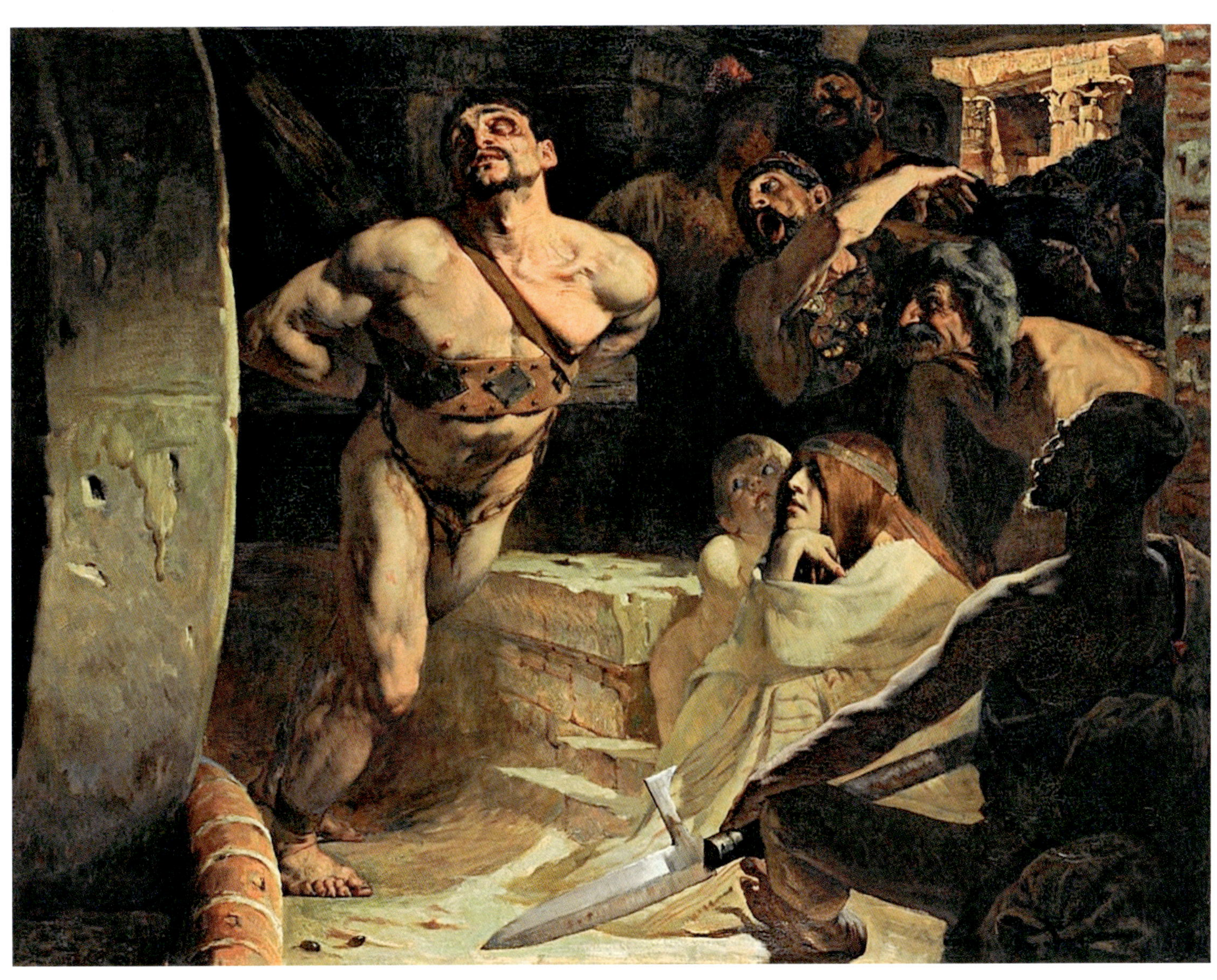

Princess Marie d'ORLÉANS

Palermo, 12 Apr 1813 – 6 Jan 1839, Pisa
Italian/French, 25 years, 8 months, 26 days

Marie d'Orléans was known by many names during her short life: Mademoiselle de Valois, Princess Marie of Orléans, Duchess of Württemberg and, most memorably, Artist Romantique. She was the third child of Louis-Philippe, King of France, and his wife Maria Amalia, daughter of King Ferdinand I of Naples. She was thoroughly educated at her father's insistence and began drawing lessons under the tutelage of the renowned Dutch master Ary Scheffer (1795–1858), when she was only 12 years old. [67] Although she was not initially very dedicated to her artistic studies, Scheffer encouraged her to pursue sculpture and there she found a medium to which to devote herself. In 1838, Scheffer painted a portrait of d'Orléans sitting in her studio, moulding tool in hand (*Princess Marie d'Orléans in her Studio*, oil on canvas).

D'Orléans was given a studio at the Tuileries Palace and there she completed several notable sculptures including *Joan of Arc Crying at the Sight of a Wounded Englishman* (1834, Musée des Beaux-Arts de Lyon; cast in Musée de Grenoble), and *Joan of Arc in Prayer* (c.1835) – a work which was exhibited with great success at the 1837 Salon. Her work did not lack for energy or earnestness for she lunged in spurts into her projects. The princess was described as a lively character with great energy, interested in both parties and politics. Her marriage in 1837 to Prince Alexander of Württemberg was, of course, a politically arranged one. In January 1838, a fire destroyed her workshop and she caught a cold escaping into the chilly night. That year she also gave birth to her only child, Duke Phillip. Weakened by her ordeals and ill with pulmonary tuberculosis, Marie left for Pisa with the hope that the warm Italian climate would assist her recovery.

However, she died, aged just 25 on 6 January 1839. According to her teacher, Ary Scheffer, Marie 'dreamed of an elevated life as an artist, and of exercising a profound influence over the arts in France.' [68] Her oeuvre, while small, has not been forgotten. Her enduring legacy left one writer to comment in 1860:

> Cut off in the morning of life, endowed as she was with gifts of every kind and a heart which throbbed with the truest love of her country, she left a sort of saint-like luminous track behind her at her too early departure. [69]

In 2008, an exhibition of her work was held at the Louvre in Paris titled *Marie d'Orléans 1813–1839, Princesse et artiste romantique*, securing her memory to this day.

Princess Marie d'Orléans
Joan of Arc, 1837, cast in bronze 1840s, 50.8 cm (20 in) high
Courtesy of Clark Art Institute, Williamstown, MA

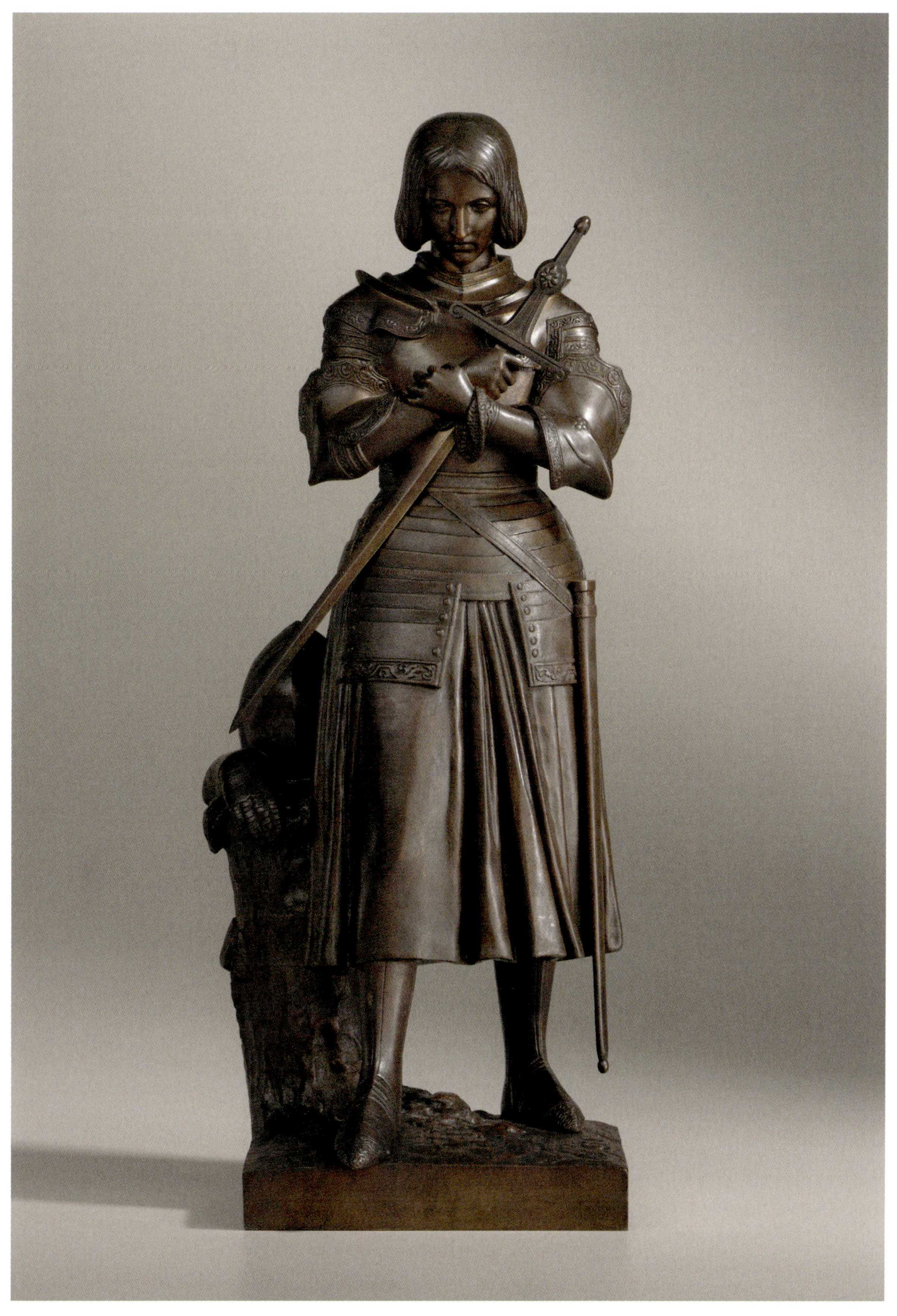

Henrique César de Araújo POUSÃO

Vila Viçosa, 1 Jan 1859 – 20 Mar 1884, Vila Viçosa
Portuguese, 25 years, 2 months, 20 days

Broad strokes, bold colours and brilliant light; these were the artistic concerns of the naturalist painter Henrique Pousão. His originality and mastery of plein-air painting placed him at the forefront of the first generation of Portuguese naturalist painters. Born the son of a court judge, Pousão was the grandson and great-grandson of painters. Consequently, his talent was recognised early and he was sent to Porto to study with António José da Costa (1840–1929) at just 12 years of age. He subsequently enrolled at the Fine Arts Academy of Porto, aged 13, and graduated with distinction in 1879. Around this time, his friend João Marques de Oliveira introduced him to plein-air painting, forever changing the young painter's artistic trajectory.

Securing a scholarship to study abroad in 1881, Pousão travelled to Paris with fellow student José Júlio de Souza Pinto and entered the École des Beaux-Arts under Adolphe Yvon and Alexandre Cabanel. Unfortunately, his poor health (acute bronchitis and tuberculosis) interfered with his studies and doctors recommended he leave Paris for southern France. Hoping that a warmer climate would help, he sought treatment in Marseille, then settled in Rome in 1882.

Deeply influenced by the Macchiaioli, and French and Spanish naturalist painting, Pousão began to innovate and develop his own stark naturalism. Inspired by the bright and crystal-clear atmosphere of the Mediterranean, he painted the landscape, people and buildings with a confident and modern sensibility. One outstanding oil by the artist, *White Houses of Capri* (1882, Museu Nacional de Soares Dos Reis, Porto) reveals the artist's strong understanding of composition, colour and light. Unfortunately, Pousão's health continued to dissipate. Feeling worse, he moved to Naples and then the Isle of Capri, painting as he went, at times on wooden panels no larger than a postcard. It was in Capri that his best work was created, and his landscape painting continued to evolve and, as one writer notes, 'exceed the aesthetic concerns of the painting of his time.'[70] Unfortunately, Pousão was never able 'to develop the modernity that he appeared to understand intuitively.'[71]

Early in 1884, fearing the end was near, he returned to his home in Portugal. Shortly thereafter, surrounded by family, Pousão passed away from pulmonary tuberculosis, the disease that had also claimed the life of his mother two decades earlier. Henrique was a prolific painter during his short life and his father gave his oeuvre to the Academy in Porto. He was a painter of such quality that it was written by his friend Pinto: 'he perfected the sense of light and the dimension of color, which he knew how to express like no other artist of his generation.' Pousão's efforts would indeed have a significant impact on contemporary Portuguese painters, who would themselves pick up the banner of naturalism.

Henrique César de Araújo Pousão
White Houses of Capri, 1882, oil on canvas, 70 × 140 cm (27½ × 55⅛ in)
National Museum Soares dos Reis, Porto, Portugal

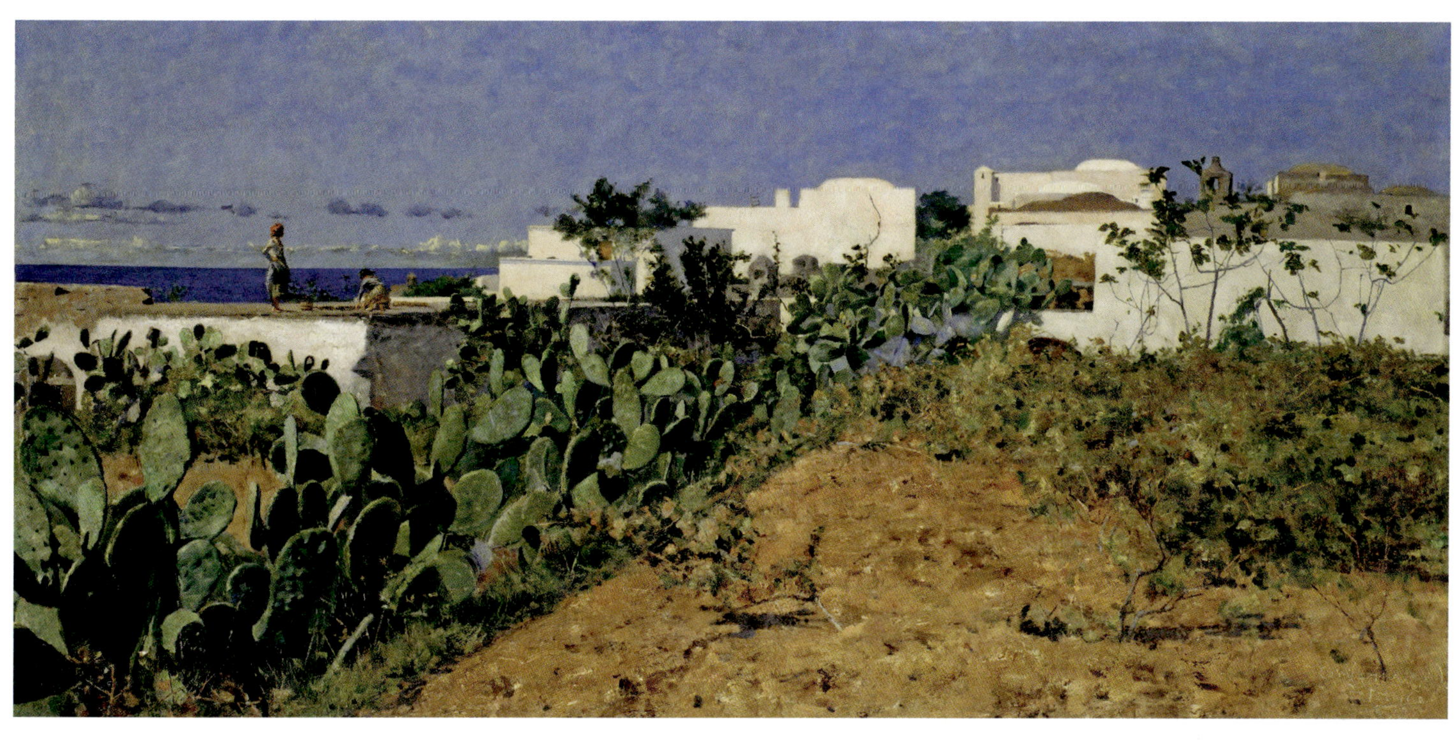

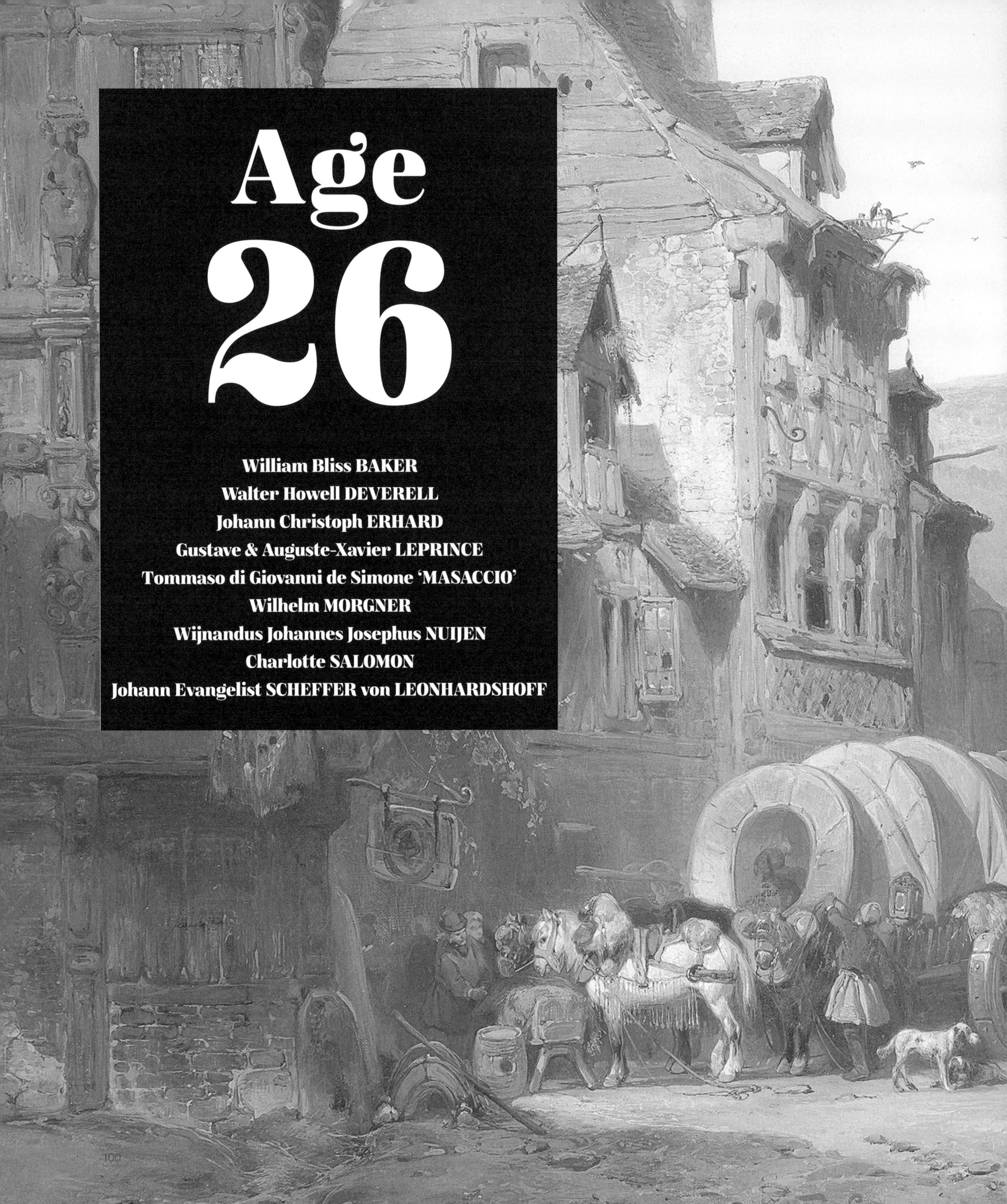

Age
26

William Bliss BAKER
Walter Howell DEVERELL
Johann Christoph ERHARD
Gustave & Auguste-Xavier LEPRINCE
Tommaso di Giovanni de Simone 'MASACCIO'
Wilhelm MORGNER
Wijnandus Johannes Josephus NUIJEN
Charlotte SALOMON
Johann Evangelist SCHEFFER von LEONHARDSHOFF

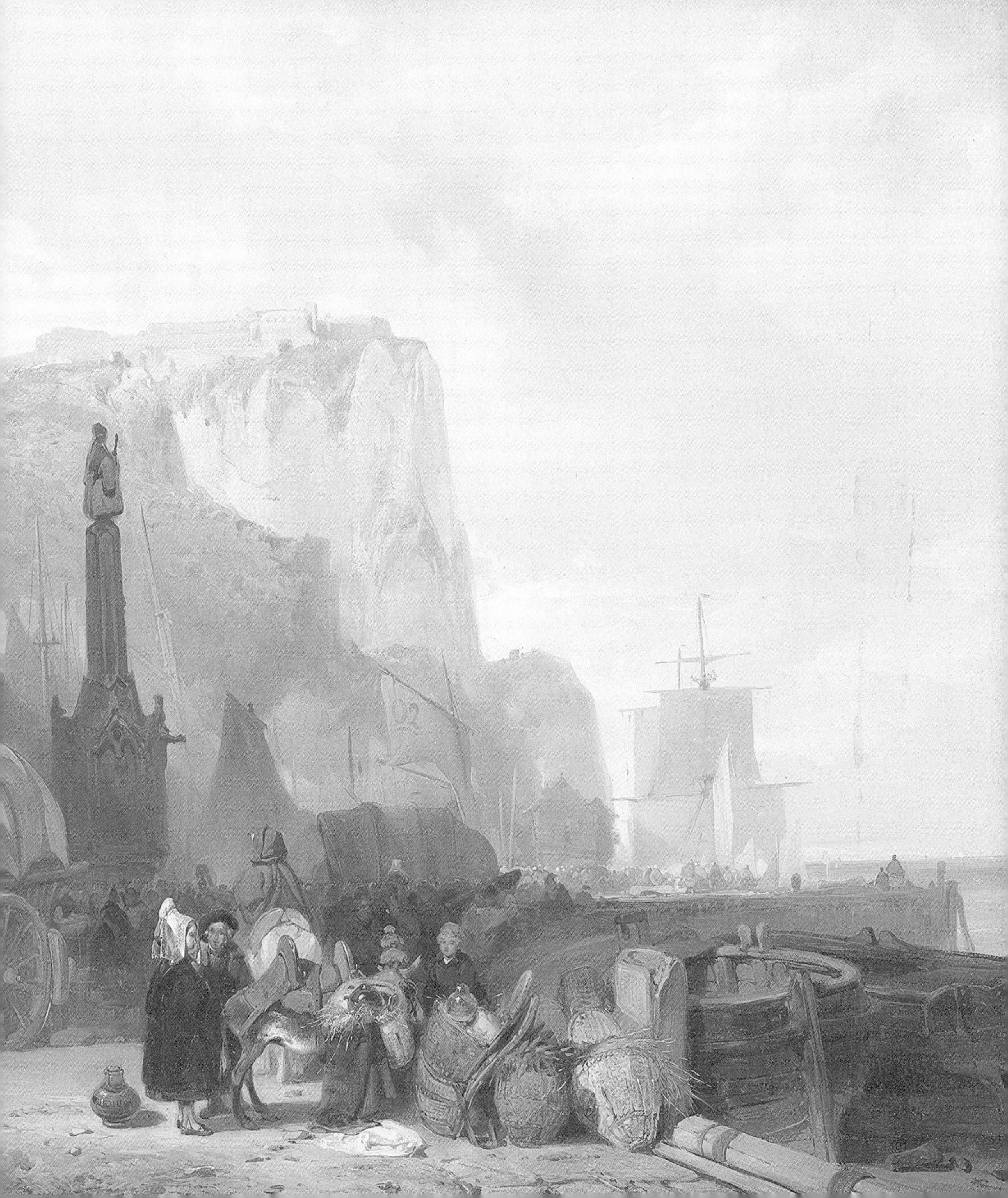

William Bliss BAKER

New York City, 27 Nov 1859 – 20 Nov 1886, Hoosick Falls, New York
American, 26 years, 11 months, 25 days

Baker was a late Hudson River School landscape painter who trained at the National Academy of Design from 1876 to 1880. There he studied with the marine painter Mauritz F.H. de Haas and the famous landscapist Albert Bierstadt. From his summer studio called 'The Castle' on Ballston Lake, a spa just north of Albany in upstate New York, and his New York City studio in the Knickerbocker Building, Baker was very prolific. During his short life he managed to paint 130 pictures which were sold from his estate by the American Art Association in 1887. Most of these were studies as well as finished works of exquisite and sophisticated quality.

In 1879 he took the Elliott Prize medal at the National Academy of Design (NAD) competition and then in the spring of 1885 he was awarded the prestigious Hallgarten Prize at the NAD Exhibition for his painting *Woodland Brook*. His artistic career was certainly on the rise. His masterpiece, *Fallen Monarchs* (1886) was painted in the year of his death, and is now in the collection of Brigham Young University Museum of Art. Those used to European manicured forest floors will be taken-aback by the mass of debris and decaying logs lying everywhere. It is truly primitive and wild.

Alfred Trumble's book, *Representative Works of Contemporary American Artists* published in 1887 gives ample praise to the picture, selecting it as one of the 30 greatest works by contemporary American painters. Writing in Victorian prose, Trumble says of the marshy forest painting:

> Stealing down through the tangle of thicket, half buried and lost here and there under the mantle the passing year shakes down upon it, come the ghost of the stream whose moisture brings life to the overarching boughs, and feeds the branching rootlets with the sap they must send shooting up to the loftiest tendrils that shiver under the sky. Prone in their majesty the departed monarchs lie along it, as imploring the vitality it can no longer give to them.[72]

Baker died at his father's farm at Hoosick Falls, New York of spinal injuries following an ice-skating accident.[73] He fell and fractured one of the lower vertebrae of his spine. *Harper's Weekly* wrote of his last month: 'During the earlier month of his long illness he suffered excruciating pain, and to-the-last was never free from suffering, more or less acute. His mind remained absolutely unclouded until within an hour or two of the close, which he awaited with calm and unflinching courage.'[74] The *New York Times* reported of his death, that it 'deprived America of one of its most promising artists.' The *New York Evening Post* commiserated that, 'His untimely death will be deeply regretted by all who take an intelligent interest in American artistic progress.'

William Bliss Baker
Fallen Monarchs, 1886, oil on canvas, 76.2 × 101.2 cm (30 × 39⅞ in)
Courtesy of Brigham Young University Museum of Art, Gift of Thomas E. Robinson

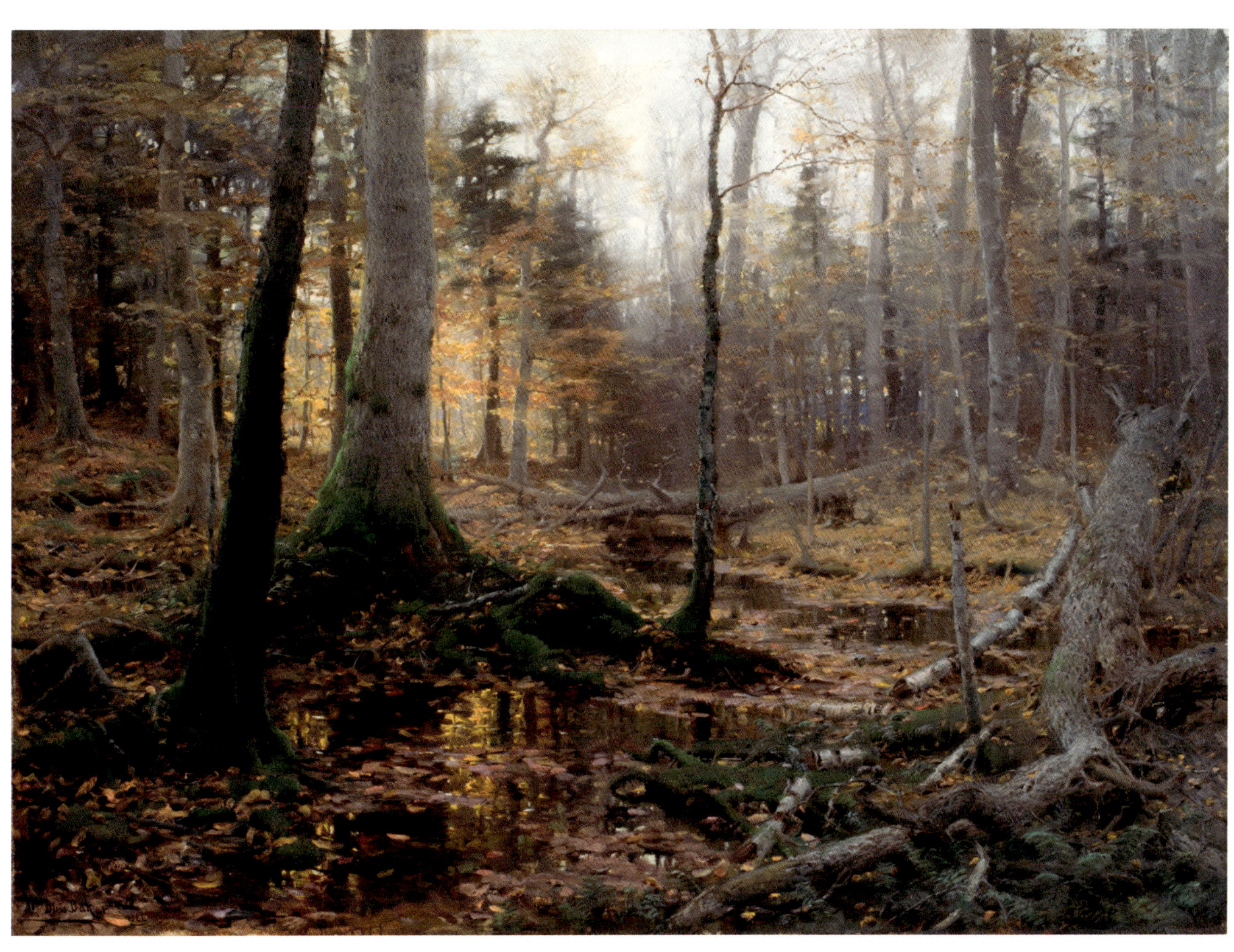

Walter Howell DEVERELL

Charlottesville, Virginia, 1 Oct 1827 – 2 Feb 1854, London
British, 26 years, 4 months, 2 days

Walter Deverell's art career had but limited critical and commercial success in his lifetime. He produced just 20 works in oil and was largely forgotten after his death. However, Deverell's contribution to the early days of the Pre-Raphaelite Brotherhood (PRB) is now widely recognised. He was the Brotherhood's 'unofficial' member and was remembered by William Michael Rossetti as the 'pet' of the whole circle. This devotee of PRB principles and aesthetics was talented, handsome and, unfortunately, terminally ill.

Deverell was born of an English family in Virginia and moved to London as an infant. He first studied at Sass's Drawing Academy (1844) where he met Dante G. Rossetti. The pair became fast friends and later shared a studio together. Deverell then enrolled at the Royal Academy Schools in 1846 and came to know the other soon to be Pre-Raphaelites, John Everett Millais and William Holman Hunt. In 1848, the same year he became a teacher at the Government School of Design, Deverell joined a sketching club called the Cyclographic Society, a precursor to the Pre-Raphaelite Brotherhood.

Unfortunately, Deverell was not there that fateful evening in September 1848 when the Pre-Raphaelite Brotherhood was formed. A couple of years later, in January 1851, he was intended to take James Collinson's membership seat in the Brotherhood, but that meeting never materialised, perhaps due to Deverell's poor health. Nevertheless, Deverell became fully engaged with the society – serving as a model for several of their most important paintings, and writing for and distributing their journal *The Germ*. His own paintings imitated their style and subject matter.

Walter was notable for discovering the PRB's star model, Elizabeth Siddal. Siddal's first appearance in a Pre-Raphaelite painting was as Viola in Deverell's Shakespearian *Twelfth Night: Act II, Scene IV* (1849–50). Siddal may have had feelings for the handsome and charming Deverell, or vice versa, but in the end she chose his healthier (at least physically healthier) friend Dante Gabriel Rossetti.

By 1853, Deverell's health had begun to seriously deteriorate. His illness was called Bright's disease, a form of chronic kidney nephritis. His father's death in June 1853 placed the pressure of providing for his siblings on his shoulders. Furthermore, his long commute to Marlborough House, where the Government School of Design was housed, from his home in Kew, took its toll on his health. By the autumn of 1853, unable to go on, he was obliged to give up teaching.

Unable to afford their home in Kew any longer, the family moved to Chelsea. In his final months, Deverell became interested in modern social subjects, as seen in the unfinished painting *Irish Vagrants*. It would have been of great interest to see how this new genre would have developed within his oeuvre, but, unfortunately, Deverell passed away, aged just 26. His friend William Michael Rossetti wrote a touching tribute in the *Spectator*, lamenting that he was 'A genius cut short, a life unaccomplished.'[75]

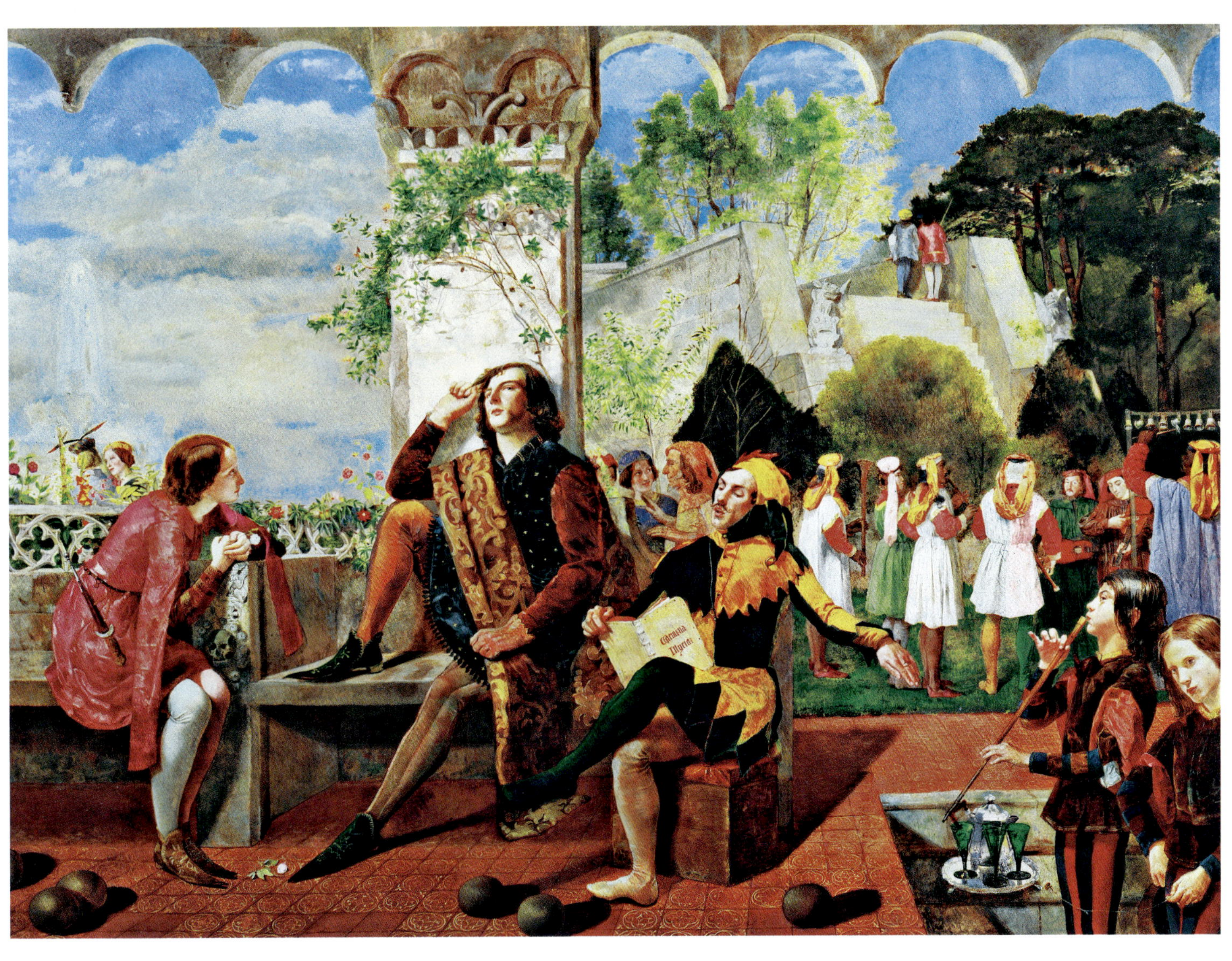

Walter Howell Deverell
Twelfth Night: Act II, Scene IV, 1849–50, oil on canvas, 101.6 × 132.1 cm (40 × 52 in)
John H. Schaeffer AO Collection / Christie's Images

Johann Christoph ERHARD

Nuremberg, 21 Feb 1795 – 20 Jan 1822, Rome
German, 26 years, 11 months

Erhard's talent in drawing was recognised young. From age 10 he studied at the Städtische Zeichenschule in Nuremberg, and was then apprenticed under the engraver Ambrosius Gabler. Erhard's works include etchings, drawings and watercolours. While Erhard depicted genre scenes, and Napoleonic War troops, his first love was landscape, to which he displayed a romantic devotion as seen in *Im Höllenthal* (1818, etching) and *Rock Cliffs above a Stream* (c.1818, graphite, National Gallery of Art).

Between 1816 and 1819 he lived in Vienna, making several notable sketching trips to Schneeberg, Salzburg and Berchtesgaden with artist friends. Erhard's charming watercolour, *The Artist Travelling in the Mountains with His Resting Friend – Johann Adam Klein* (1817, Kunsthalle Bremen) recalls one such artistic outing, where Erhard is sketching and his friend Johann Adam Klein rests near him. The twin beech trees beside them are thought to 'symbolize their early bond of friendship.'[76] However, despite the travel and comradery with fellow artists, by 1818 Erhard's emotional and mental health was waning. He exhibited signs of depression, dissatisfaction with his art, and abdominal complaints.

Perhaps to ease his melancholy, his friends encouraged him to travel to Rome with them, which he did in October 1819. For several months Erhard was very productive, depicting landscapes of the great city and its environs. However, during the heat of the Italian summer his health began again to decline. He became withdrawn, depressed and even experienced hallucinations. In one such instance, he thought he saw the devil in the form of a shepherd while sketching at Ponte Salario.[77] Just before Christmas in 1820, Erhard tried to commit suicide by drinking caustic soda. He received treatment from the personal physician of Crown Prince Ludwig of Bavaria and was nursed by a friend's wife.

Finally, in the summer of 1821, he was able to resume his work on a painting trip to Olevano Romano. Unfortunately, his recovery was short lived. On 18 January 1822, he placed a pistol in his mouth and shot his throat. He was taken to hospital where he died two days later, but not before his Catholic friends had him emergency baptised and his last rites read. Many of his works were published posthumously and gained notice by younger artists such as Ludwig Richter, who were greatly influenced by them. Scholarship of the late 20th and early 21st centuries has placed him among the best German illustrators of his generation.[78]

Johann Christoph Erhard
The Artist Travelling in the Mountains with His Resting Friend – Johann Adam Klein,
1817, watercolour, pen and black ink over pencil, 12.8 × 18.4 cm (5 × 7¼ in)
Kunsthalle Bremen

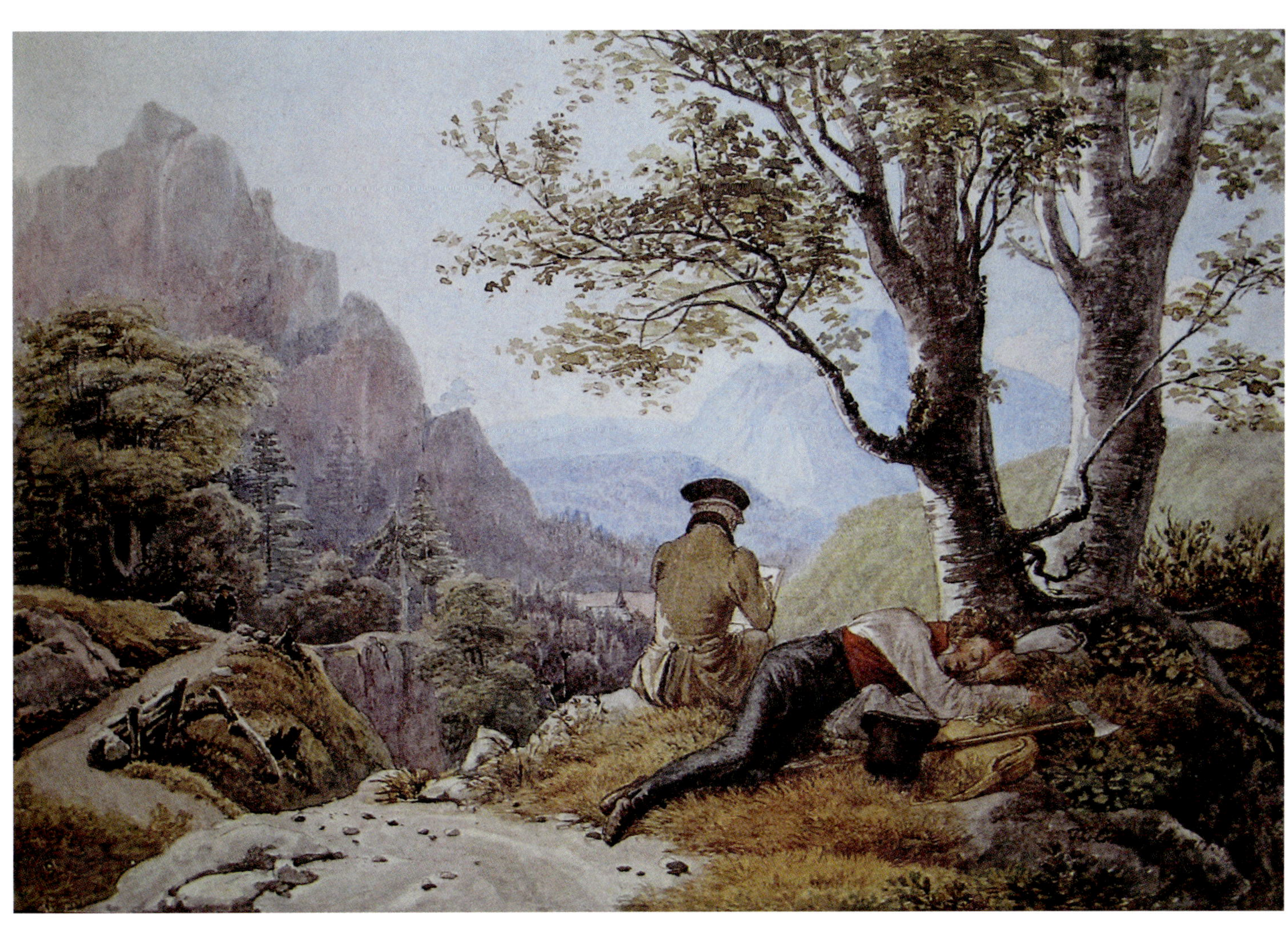

Gustave & Auguste-Xavier LEPRINCE

Paris, 5 Jun 1810 – early 1837, Paris(?)
French, approx. 26 years

Paris, 28 Aug 1799 – 26 Dec 1826, Nice
French, 27 years, 3 months, 29 days

Longevity was not a gift for the Leprince brothers. Auguste-Xavier, Robert Léopold (1800–1847) and Gustave Leprince were the talented sons and pupils of the painter and lithographer Anne-Pierre Leprince. The brothers appear to have been very close, with the elder brothers mentoring the much younger Gustave. At one point, the brothers lived together at La Childebert Studio, No. 9 rue Childebert, Paris, and their paintings of French rural landscapes reflect their influence upon one another.

While their similarities in life abound, so did their deaths, with all three living truncated lives. Most notably, Gustave and Auguste-Xavier died at the tender ages of 26 and 27, while Robert Léopold died at 47. Gustave followed in the style of his brothers and became a proficient landscape painter. His fine oils *View of the Graville Priory* and *View of the Environs of Fontainebleau* (Musée de la Chartreuse de Douai), demonstrate his skill. However, he was not as productive nor did he attain nearly the same level of greatness as his brother Auguste-Xavier.

Auguste-Xavier proved to be a master of multiple artistic genres and mediums. He worked in oil and watercolour, and pursued lithography as well. He painted portraits, figurative genre, street scenes, bucolic landscapes, and even caricature. His style and subject were consistent with a number of other contemporary artists, including Louis-Léopold Boilly (1761–1845), Nicolas Antoine Taunay (1755–1830), Jean-Louis Demarne (1752–1829) and his dear friend Eugène Isabey (1803–1886). Leprince was also heavily influenced by the brilliant plein-air landscape painter Richard Parkes

Bonington (1802–1828) who likewise died in his twenties.

Auguste-Xavier successfully exhibited at multiple Salons de Paris, winning a medal in 1819. His works attracted the patronage of the Duchess de Berry, and today his paintings hang in many notable museums and collections. His oils *Loading Livestock aboard 'Le Passenger' in the Port of Honfleur* (1823, Musée du Louvre) and *View of the Graville Priory* (c.1825) show he was an outstanding talent. He was prolific and not only showed promise but produced results as well. He would have risen to a higher second tier of artists, and was better, some say, than the masterful Boilly at the same age.

It is not known how Auguste-Xavier died, although it is likely that his failing health caused him to abandon Paris for the warmer climate of southern France. This suggests that the infectious lung disease of tuberculosis may have been the culprit. If so, it is conceivable that his brothers were susceptible and also suffered and died from the same condition. They all had lived in close proximity and may well have contracted the illness from each other. Tuberculosis potentially takes years to show its effects, and, if survived in the first round, often recurs later.

The disease was perhaps responsible for Gustave's early death and the reason that Robert Léopold retired to Chartres as a young man, only to die at the age of 47. With Robert Léopold's death a decade after Gustave's, this dynasty of artists came to a mournful close. Had they lived in good health, they would have been the subjects of a distinctive chapter in art history.

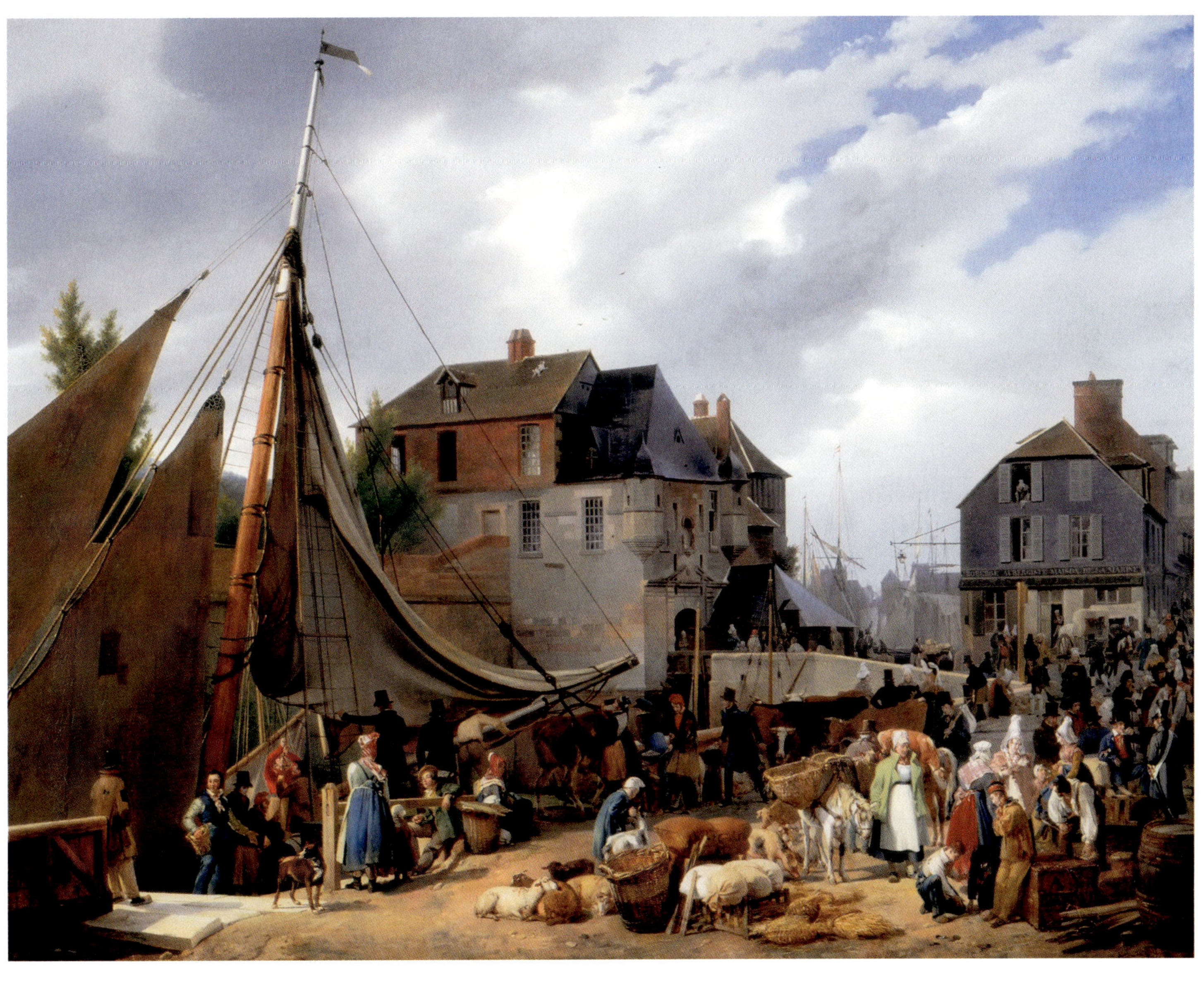

Auguste-Xavier Leprince
Loading Livestock aboard 'Le Passenger' in the Port of Honfleur, 1823, oil on canvas, 130 × 160 cm (51¼ × 63 in)
Musée du Louvre

Tommaso di Giovanni de Simone 'MASACCIO'

San Giovanni Valdarno, Republic of Florence, 21 Dec 1401 – summer 1428, Rome
Italian, approx. 26 years, 8 months

Undoubtedly the most famous and influential artist to die in his twenties; Masaccio was the first great Italian painter of the Quattrocento. As the most superlative artist discussed in this book, his is the most lamented loss. Masaccio's art not only profoundly impacted the artists of the early Renaissance (Filippo Lippi, Fra Angelico, Andrea del Castagno and Piero della Francesca), but also those of the High Renaissance (Leonardo da Vinci, Michelangelo and Raphael) and, consequently, 'the entire subsequent course of Western painting.'[79]

Giorgio Vasari considered Masaccio to be the best painter of his generation because of his natural realism and wrote that 'all the most celebrated' sculptors and painters of Florence studied his frescos in order 'to learn and to grasp the precepts and the rules for good work.' A remarkable distinction considering Masaccio's oeuvre is relatively small and his career exceptionally brief – just six years.

Masaccio transformed the direction of Italian art and, for the first time, presented it in a more rational, natural and humanist way. He was one of the first to use and master linear perspective and dramatic chiaroscuro as he moved away from the International Gothic style and co-founded the Renaissance. His weighty figures are lifelike, seemingly occupying three-dimensional space, and employing foreshortening. Although he painted altarpieces, he was essentially a fresco muralist and could work in larger scale. He studied the art of Giotto and was friends with Brunelleschi and Donatello. *The Tribute Money* (1425, wall fresco) in the Brancacci Chapel, Santa Maria del Carmine in Florence is one of Western art's supreme masterpieces.

It is remarkable that this young artist could make such a splash in art history without us knowing anything about his life before age 20. We don't know where or with whom he apprenticed. He only appears on the art history register when he joined the Florentine Arte dei Medici e Speziali (Guild of Doctors and Apothecaries, to which painters also belonged) on 7 January 1422. His first known work, *San Giovenale Triptych*, was dated 23 April 1422, and from there he rapidly progressed. Masaccio collaborated for a time with the artist Masolino da Panicale, and worked chiefly in Florence, Pisa and Rome until his premature death. His affectionate nickname, Tommaso, meaning clumsy or messy Tom, was given to him because, according to Vasari, he was an 'absent-minded and careless person' who cared about nothing but art.

In 1428, Masaccio left Florence for Rome to avoid his creditors, and unfortunately, like so many artists before and after him, met his untimely death there. His passing was sudden and unexpected, leaving his altarpiece for the Basilica of Santa Maria Maggiore unfinished. According to legend he was poisoned by a jealous rival painter, although some suspect he might have died of the plague. Upon hearing of his death, the artist Filippo Brunelleschi exclaimed, 'We have suffered a very great loss in Masaccio.' His death precluded what promised to be one of the greatest careers in all art history. Now known only to artists and art historians, his name undoubtedly would have eclipsed all but the top 10 artists in history. But it was not to be.

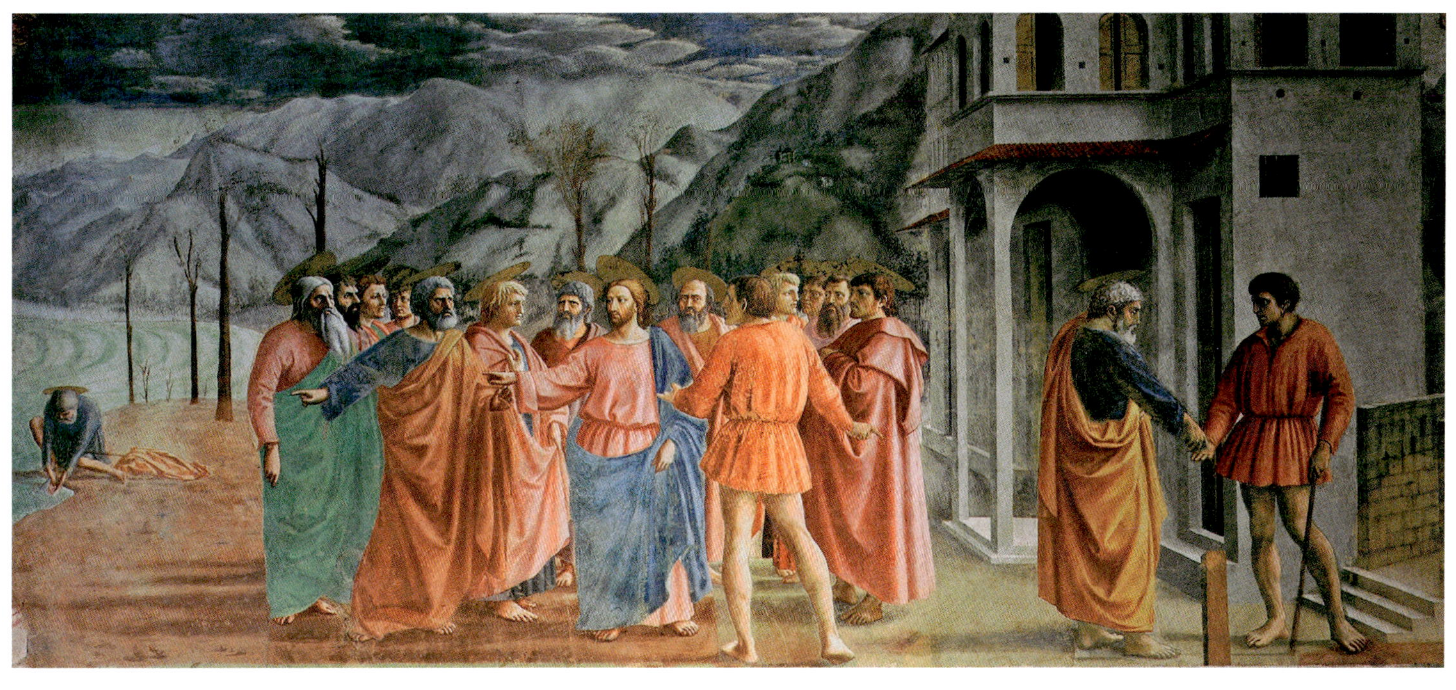

Masaccio
The Tribute Money, 1425, wall fresco, 247 × 597 cm (97¼ × 235 in)
Brancacci Chapel, Florence

Wilhelm MORGNER

Soest, 27 Jan 1891 – 16 Aug 1917, Langemarck
German, 26 years, 6 months, 21 days

World War I ended the prolific career of one of Westphalia's leading expressionists and pioneers of abstraction. Wilhelm Morgner was handsome (like a young Charlie Sheen), hardworking, gifted and hugely successful. He began drawing in 1895, aged four, and as a boy his paint box was his most prized possession. His mother wanted her son to become a Protestant minister, not an artist, and sent the young Morgner to Soest Archigymnasium to study. However, after the 16-year-old attempted to run away to pursue art in America (only making it as far as Amsterdam), his mother relented. Religious subject matter, however, would play a major role in his art until the end of his life.

In 1908, he studied in Worpswede with the expressionist painter, Georg Tappert (1880–1957), who acted as a mentor to the young Morgner. The next year, Morgner returned to his hometown of Soest where he established a studio and mounted his first exhibition. Morgner produced at a rapid pace and often on a large scale, many of his canvases measuring more than a square metre (11 square feet). In just nine years, Morgner created around 234 oils and 2,000 drawings and etchings.

He developed his own personal style but drew heavily on inspiration from old masters such as Rembrandt, and modern masters such as Jean-François Millet, Vincent van Gogh, Georges Seurat, Paul Signac and Robert Delaunay. His neo-impressionist paintings, such as *Potato Harvest* (1910, Wilhelm-Morgner-Haus), are characterised by energetic square brushstrokes in a mosaic fashion, or lines, waves and dots, employing bright pure colours. Morgner participated in many important exhibitions such as the New Secession and Jury Free exhibitions in Berlin, der Blaue Reiter in Munich and the Sonderbund in Cologne. His art attracted the admiration of famed artists Franz Marc and Wassily Kandinsky, and gained further notice in artistic publications including *Die Aktion* and *Der Sturm*. Morgner had every hope of continued success and experimentation, but first he had to report for his year of mandatory military service in the autumn of 1913. Unfortunately, before that year was up, World War I had begun, and Morgner was enlisted for the duration. War permanently ended the artist's easel-based painting career, but he was still able to pursue drawing and watercolour painting on a smaller scale.

Morgner proved to be an excellent soldier. He earned an Iron Cross (second class) and was promoted to Corporal and then Sergeant. At one point he served as a military war artist in Bulgaria and Serbia, before returning to the fighting on the Eastern Front. In 1917, he was moved to the Western Front and there participated in the Battle of Langemarck. The battle was a great blow to the German army and to German art. In the gory conflict, Morgner was killed by British soldiers while resisting capture.

Initially he was reported as missing, but it soon became evident that he was probably interred in the mass burial, called the 'Comrade Grave', of some 25,000 German soldiers. His last work, a Crucifixion carved into a tin plate, was a foreboding symbol of death. His art, positive as it is, was declared 'degenerate' by the Nazis and eight pieces were shown in the 1938 exhibition of degenerate art in Berlin. However, today Morgner is widely revered. A museum in Soest is named in his honour, and The Wilhelm Morgner Prize is awarded to winning artists every three years.

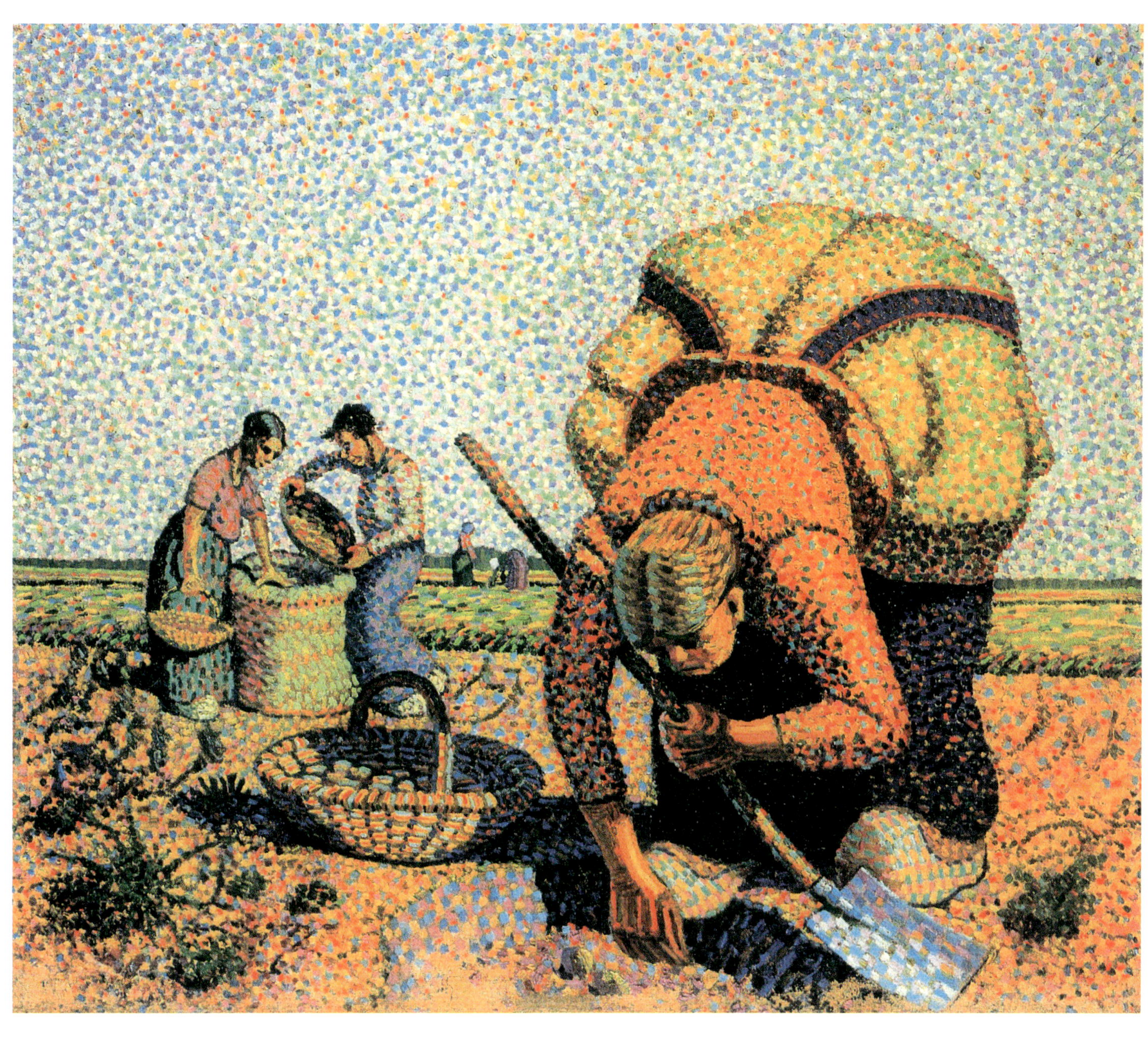

Wilhelm Morgner
Potato Harvest, 1910, oil on canvas, 145 × 162.5 cm (57 × 64 in)
Wilhelm-Morgner-Haus, Soest, Germany

Wijnandus Johannes Josephus NUIJEN

The Hague, 4 Mar 1813 – 2 Jun 1839, The Hague
Dutch, 26 years, 2 months, 30 days

Born the son of a humble baker, Nuijen would become a mainstay of Dutch art during his short life. Nuijen's artistic career began at the age of 12 when he was first apprenticed to the noted Dutch romantic landscape painter Andreas Schelfhout (1787–1870), who later became his father-in-law. He then took the opportunity to study under Bartholomeus Johannes van Hove (1790–1880) at the 's-Gravenhaagsche Teken Academie in The Hague from 1827 to 1829. When only 16 years old, Nuijen was awarded the gold medal by the Felix Meritis Society in Amsterdam for *Landschap met Hoeve* (1829). Though young, this first official success established Nuijen as a respected landscape painter.

After his studies Nuijen travelled to Germany, Belgium and France, spending a great deal of time along France's northern coasts. There, he fell under the spell of Richard Parkes Bonington (1802–1828) and Eugène Isabey (1803–1886). Later, the influence of other French romantic landscape painters such as Théodore Gudin (1802–1880) and Eugène Lepoittevin (1806–1870), whose work he saw during his visit to Paris in 1833, was seminal.

Following his travels, Nuijen's interpretation of subject, colour and style developed quickly, and he was revolutionary in his approach to colour and brushwork. He incorporated aspects of 'foreign' romanticism in his style, which allowed for more personal originality, drama and imagination. This was very unlike the Dutch painting of his day. Nuijen painted picturesque villages and enlivened harbour scenes, rural landscapes and seascapes, inspired by what he had learned in France. His magnificent oil *Figures by a Harbour Inn – Normandy* (1836) demonstrates his success in this genre.

In 1836, Nuijen became a member of the Koninklijke Akademie in Amsterdam. King William II of the Netherlands greatly admired his art and bought four of his oils. As a thoroughly romantic Dutch painter, Nuijen was not always appreciated by critics. He was, however, highly regarded in the art community. He taught and influenced numerous painters including Johannes Bosboom, Charles Leickert and Charles Rochussen. Nuijen produced prolifically and, upon his death, his estate included around 150 paintings, in addition to numerous drawings. Many of his paintings are now in museum collections including the Rijksmuseum in Amsterdam.

The cause of his death, less than a year after his marriage, is unknown. Nevertheless, the grief of his passing was significant, with a funeral procession of more than 100 people accompanying his casket to the Catholic cemetery. At his graveside a choir of 20 singers performed a burial song. His artist friends did not forget him. They raised funds for a memorial and, three years later, the stone was unveiled at a grand ceremony, with all who attended praising the painter whose art had gained even more fame following his death. With great feeling the poet Isaac Marcus Calisch inscribed on Nuijen's tomb: 'The Genius called Nuyen; he shortly lived. His dust is in this grave, but his name defies death.' Indeed, he died a propitious painter of the new Dutch school.

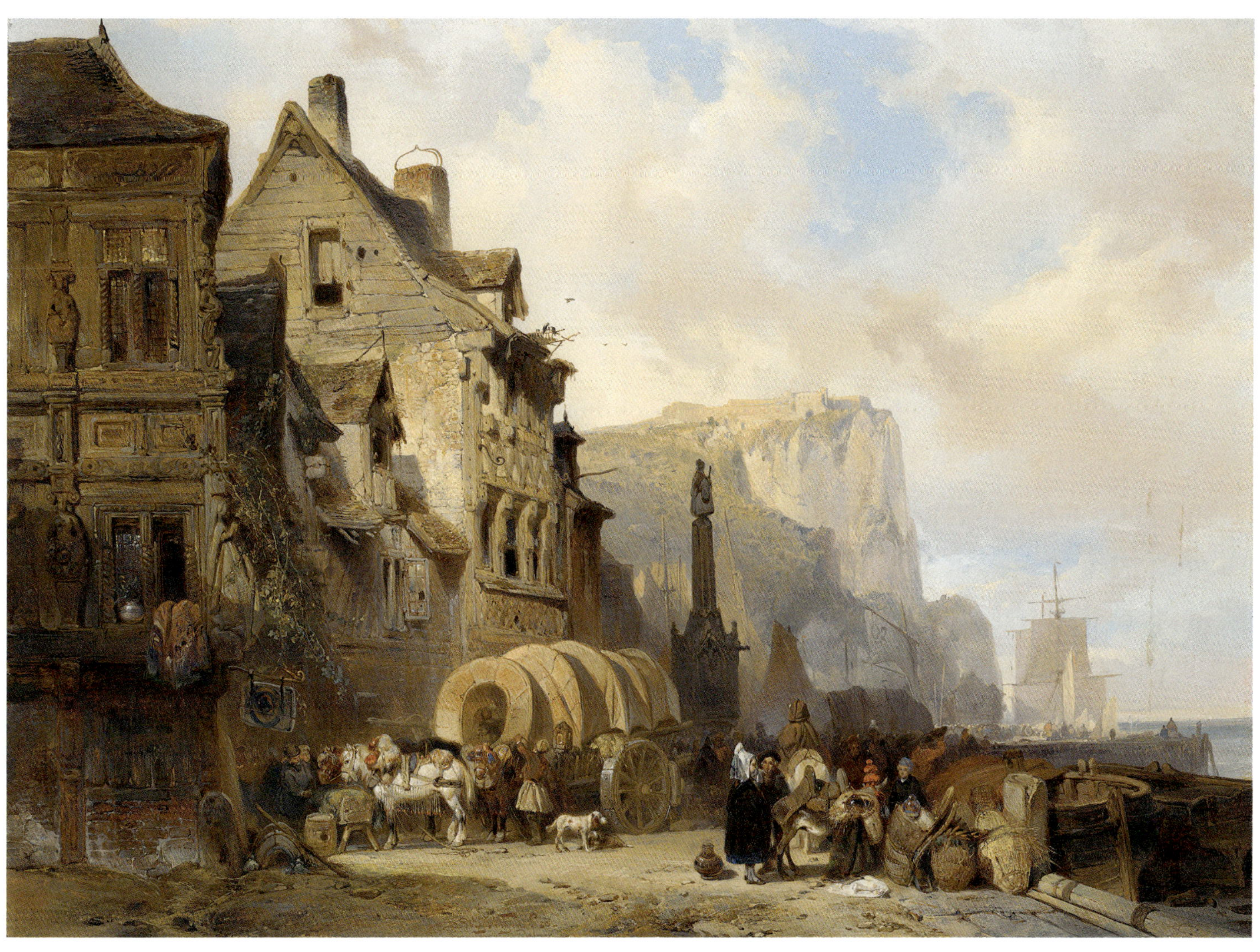

Wijnandus Johannes Josephus Nuijen
Figures by a Harbour Inn – Normandy, 1836, oil on canvas, 65.5 × 87 cm (25¾ × 34¼ in)
Christie's London

Charlotte SALOMON

Berlin, 16 Apr 1917 – 10 Oct 1943, Auschwitz
German, 26 years, 5 months, 25 days

The heart-rending life, art and death of Charlotte Salomon has served as rich material for plays, a novel, a documentary, a film and even a ballet-opera. Interestingly, Salomon herself saw her life as a dramatic work. In the midst of the chaos of war, the young refugee artist painted her own singspiel (operetta) titled, *Life? Or Theatre?* (1940–42). This autobiographical gouache series of nearly 800 works weaves fact and fantasy in recounting her and her family's story from World War I through the rise of Nazism in painting and text. The work was produced at a critical juncture in Salomon's life, when she wondered 'whether to take her own life or to undertake something eccentric and mad.' Fortunately, *Life?* was the answer. Since the 1960s, *Life? Or Theatre?* has been exhibited and published to great acclaim, with one reviewer calling the work 'one of the most fascinating and indefinable artworks of the 20th century.'[80]

Salomon was born during World War I to an educated Jewish family. Her mother committed suicide when Salomon was just nine years old, a fact that was hidden from the young girl. Later, she would learn that many of her relatives had likewise taken their own lives, a family trait that would haunt her. Exceptionally gifted at drawing, in 1936 Salomon was admitted to the State Art Academy in Berlin which allowed only 1.5 per cent of the student body to be Jewish.

Kristallnacht in 1938 marked the end of the family's peace. Her father was sent to a concentration camp for a time and Salomon went to live with her grandparents in Villefranche on the French Riviera. Far from being a haven, during her time there she personally witnessed her grandmother committing suicide by jumping from a window, as her mother had done. Furthermore, evidence suggests that her grandfather may have sexually abused her.

The Vichy government also sent Charlotte to Gurs internment camp in May 1940, but she was released later that summer. In 1941 Salomon was living apart from her grandfather, but in 1942 they were forced to live together again until her grandfather's death in February 1943. A recently discovered letter states that she poisoned him with a drug-laced omelette, although whether Salomon's confession is true or imaginary is unknown. For a time, Salomon was safe in the Italian-occupied French Riviera since the Italians were not deporting Jews.

Salomon worked and painted prolifically and in June 1943 even married another German-speaking Jewish refugee, Alexander Nagler. However, when the Nazis finally occupied the Riviera in September 1943, Salomon and her husband were quickly arrested and transported. Arriving at Auschwitz concentration camp on 10 October 1943, the five-month pregnant Salomon was gassed soon after her arrival, as was the custom with pregnant women. Although her life was short and full of struggle, Salomon's art exemplifies the victory of the human spirit. Curator Mirjam Knotter aptly notes that Salomon was 'An extraordinarily brilliant artist, creating work under conditions where you couldn't think anyone could create anything.'[81]

Charlotte Salomon
Untitled from *Life? Or Theatre?*, 1940–42, gouache on paper, 32.5 × 25 cm (12¾ × 9⅞ in)
Collection Joods Historisch Museum, Amsterdam

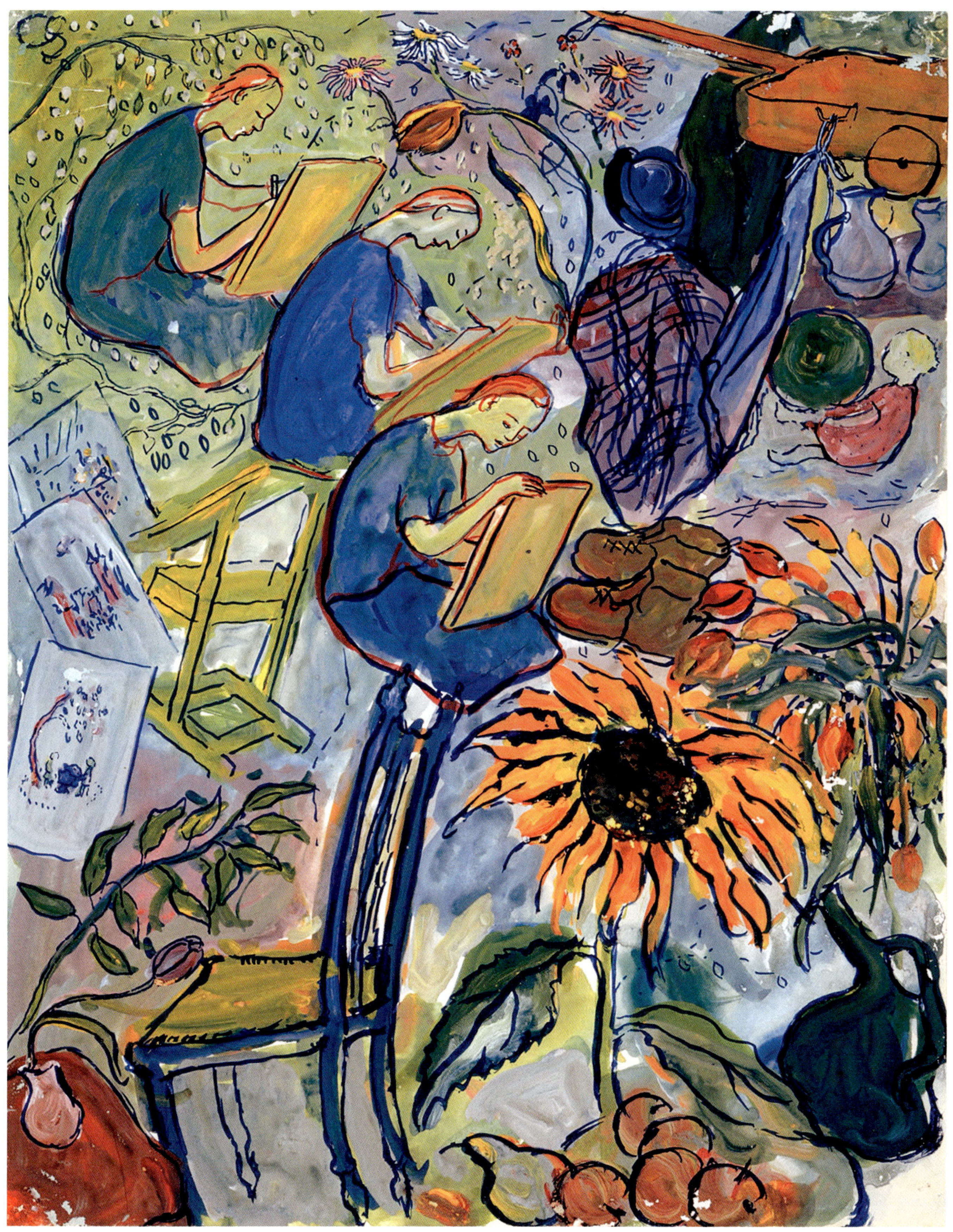

Johann Evangelist SCHEFFER von LEONHARDSHOFF

Vienna, 30 Oct 1795 – 12 Jan 1822, Vienna
Austrian, 26 years, 2 months, 14 days

Scheffer's talent and tenacity distinguished him as a significant representative of Romanticism. Though his oeuvre is small, it is notable, with several paintings in important museums and collections. Scheffer came from a noble but impoverished family and was therefore permitted to pursue a career in the arts. At age 16, he began his studies at the Academy of Fine Arts in Vienna. There, he became enthralled by the art of the rebel romanticists, The Nazarenes, and moved away from the academic style towards a more archaic manner of expression. Ultimately, he looked to Raphael as his artistic role model and avidly studied and copied his works. This earned Scheffer the nickname of 'Raffaelino' (little Raphael).

In 1812, the 17-year-old Scheffer took a trip that changed the course of his life. He travelled to Venice for his sister's marriage, and then journeyed to the Renaissance city of Ferrara where he contracted pulmonary tuberculosis, an incurable ailment that led to his premature death. Fortunately, on his return trip to Vienna, he met his future patron Prince-Archbishop Franz von Salm-Reifferscheidt, who was astounded by the teenager's talent. From 1814 to 1816, the Prince-Archbishop funded Scheffer's extended stay in Rome and Italy.

In Rome, Scheffer became close friends with Nazarene master Friedrich Overbeck. Eventually, Scheffer was officially admitted as a member of the Lukasbund (Nazarene Brotherhood), and he happily lived and worked alongside these legendary artists. Additionally, he had the honour of painting a portrait of Pope Pius VII, earning himself a knighthood in the Supreme Order of Christ. Unfortunately, his idyllic time in Rome was short lived. Failing lungs and a financial crisis drove the artist back to Austria in 1816, where the Prince-Archbishop appointed him as court painter. As his illness became more severe, he was nursed back to health by a friend's wife, Cäcilia Bontzak. Inconveniently, the artist fell deeply in love with Cäcilia, and painted several works in her honour. Momentarily recovered, he emerged to paint *Votivbild Vargemont* and *Cäcilia Playing the Organ*, which established his reputation.

His last visit to Rome was in 1820–21, when he engaged mainly in religious themes. *The Virgin Mary in Hortus Conclusus* (1820) shows the charm and reverence of his devotional paintings. He also diligently finished his masterpiece *Death of Saint Cecilia* (Belvedere, Vienna). Though a depiction of a dying saint, it has been interpreted as a sorrowful tribute to Cäcilia Bontzak's final rejection and his own imminent death. Returning to Vienna in 1821, Scheffer died a short time later. One writer notes, 'J Scheffer von Leonhardshoff is one of the artists to whom an early death cut off a promising career and brought undeserved oblivion. With a longer life, his name would have rightly shone with those of Overbeck and Cornelius.' [82]

Johann Evangelist Scheffer von Leonhardshoff
The Virgin Mary in Hortus Conclusus, 1820, oil on panel, 34.5 × 27 cm (13⅜ × 10⅝ in)
Private collection

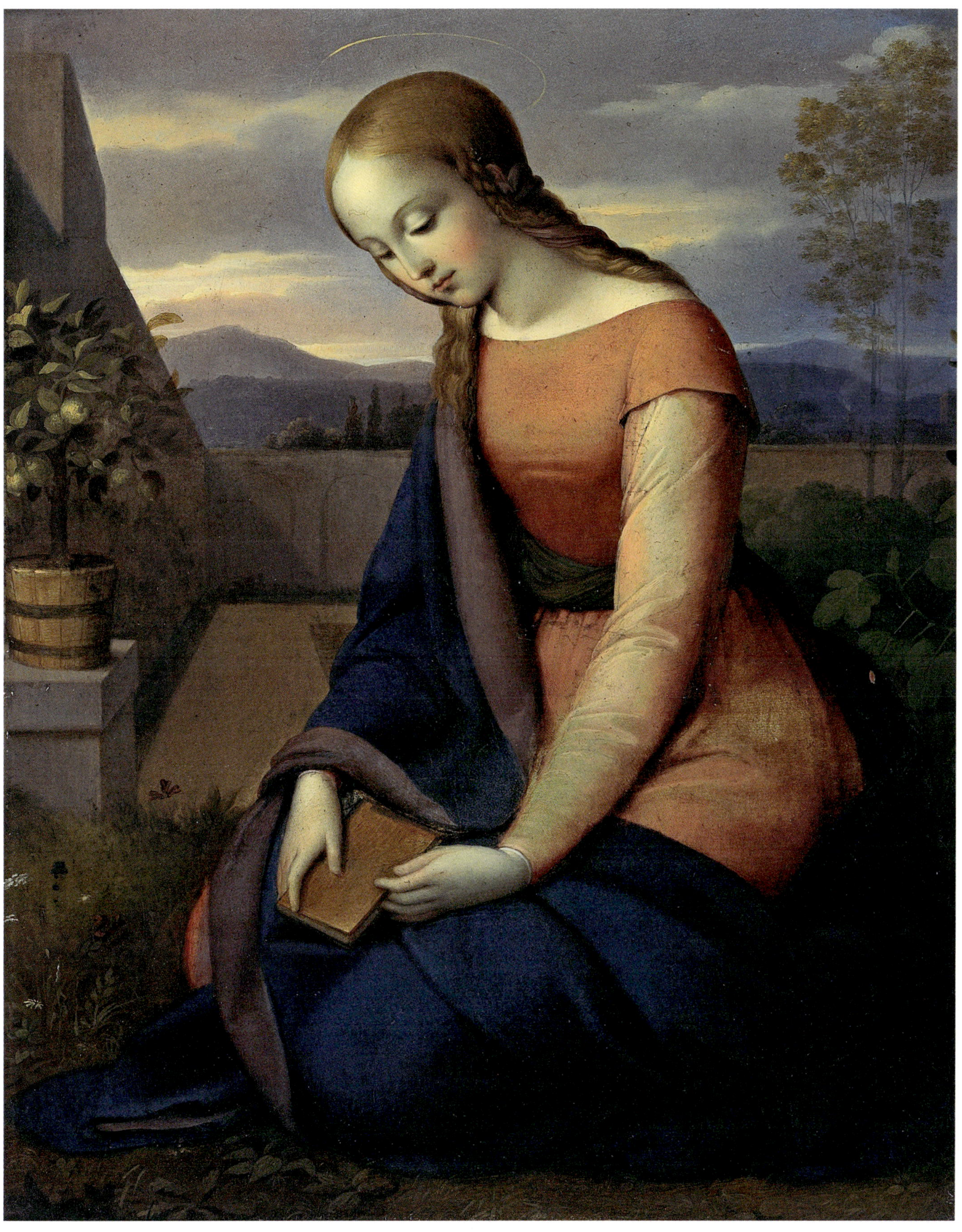

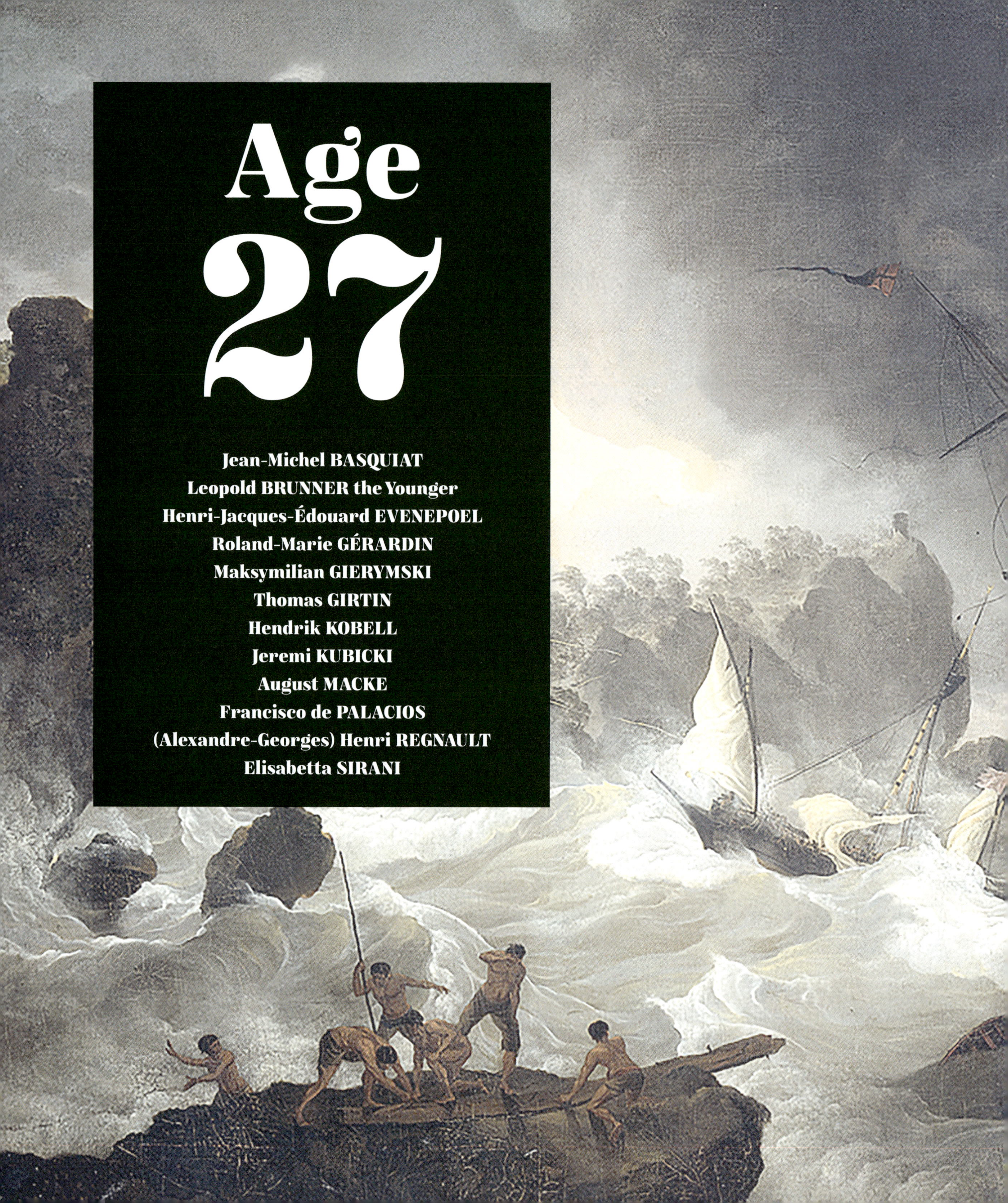
Age
27

Jean-Michel BASQUIAT
Leopold BRUNNER the Younger
Henri-Jacques-Édouard EVENEPOEL
Roland-Marie GÉRARDIN
Maksymilian GIERYMSKI
Thomas GIRTIN
Hendrik KOBELL
Jeremi KUBICKI
August MACKE
Francisco de PALACIOS
(Alexandre-Georges) Henri REGNAULT
Elisabetta SIRANI

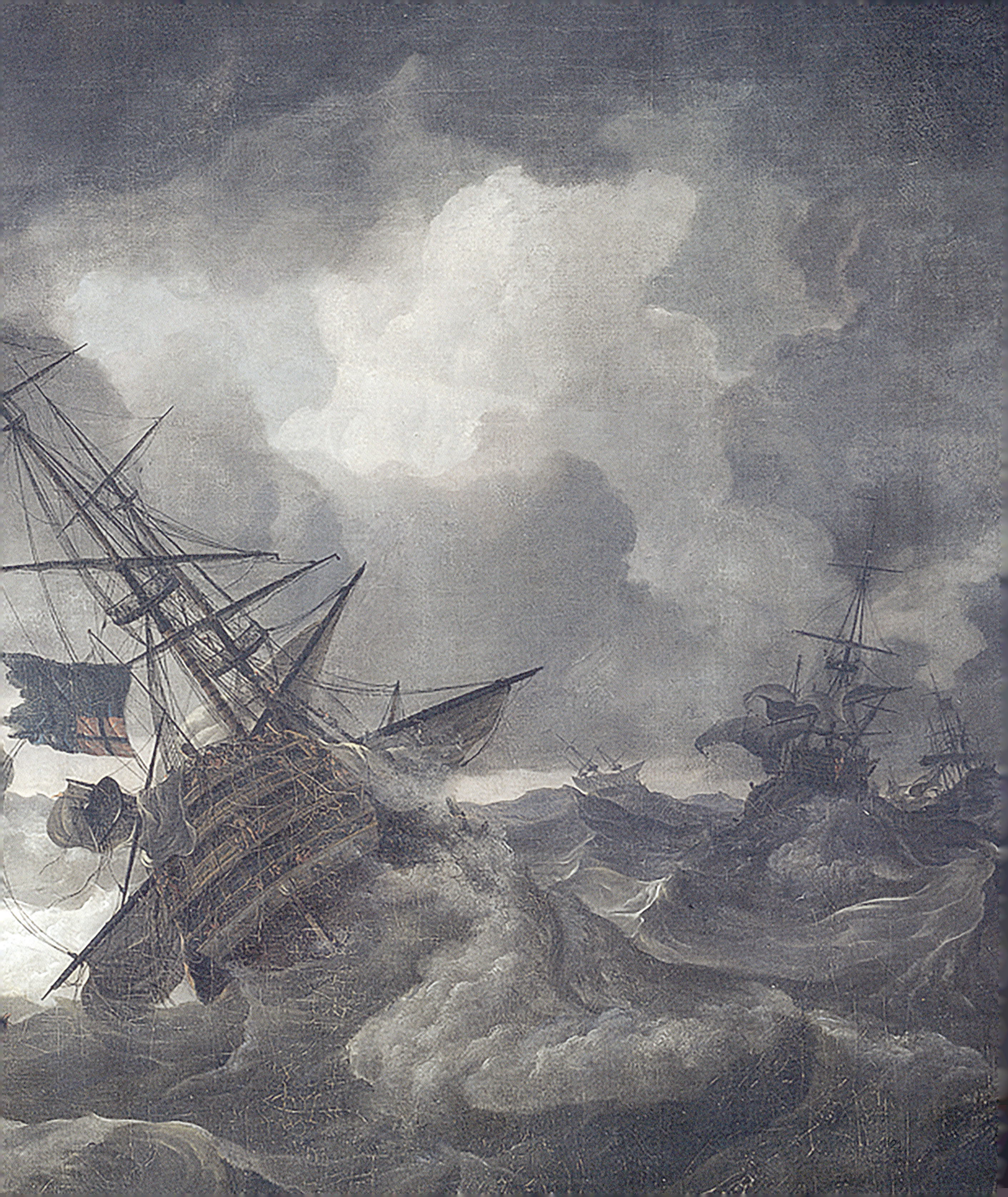

Jean-Michel BASQUIAT

Brooklyn, New York, 22 Dec 1960 – 12 Apr 1988, New York City
American, 27 years, 3 months, 22 days

Jean-Michel Basquiat's career was short and meteoric. His art, in contrast, has made a lasting and significant impact on the contemporary art world. Born in Brooklyn, Basquiat was of Haitian and Puerto-Rican descent. As a child and teenager he was intelligent and rebellious, always drawing and frequenting art museums, but never attended art school. Basquiat first came to the attention of the art community in 1977 through his graffiti art, signed with the logo SAMO©. In 1980, he participated in his first exhibition 'The Times Square Show', but painting remained a challenge since Basquiat lacked the funds for a studio space and for buying basic art materials. Instead, he would draw on anything that he could find, including doors, and tables and windows.

In late 1980, his art captured the notice of collectors and he began producing prolifically. His style is described as neo-expressionistic. Moving away from the minimalist-abstraction of previous decades, Basquiat's art is primarily centred on the human (skeletal) figure within a riot of colour and line. His paintings often tell a story in an original way, frequently employing words directly on his canvases. By 1981 he was exhibiting in New York and internationally, and his solo shows would frequently sell out. Unfortunately, Basquiat was reckless with his new-found wealth – buying drugs, throwing parties, and famously painting in expensive Armani suits. He also had a string of girlfriends including the singer Madonna before her rise to fame. It was during these years (1981 to 1983) that Basquiat is considered to have produced his best work.

In 1984, Basquiat began an artistic collaboration with Andy Warhol, an artist he had long idolised, and a deep friendship ensued. Unfortunately, their 1985 exhibition, featuring their 16 collaboration paintings, was poorly received. In response, Basquiat and Warhol had a falling out. Even though they never reconciled, Warhol's death in February 1987 was a blow to Basquiat. He became more and more reclusive as his heroin addiction began to spiral out of control. His last exhibition in 1988 contained the painting *Riding with Death*, a sombre foreboding of his own death just months away.

Aged just 27 years old, Basquiat overdosed on heroin in his studio, giving him membership in the famed '27 Club' – a list of popular artists, actors and musicians who, by coincidence, died when just 27 years old. Nevertheless, Basquiat left an impressive legacy, having produced around 1,500 drawings and 600 paintings, and his art has ongoing appeal amongst cosmopolitans. In 2017, Basquiat's painting of a skull, *Untitled* (1982), sold for $110.5 million (£86.5 million), setting a new record for any American artist at auction. While his art prices are well documented, Sotheby's accurately observes that 'The influence of Basquiat's complex aesthetic on subsequent generations of artists remains incalculable.'[83]

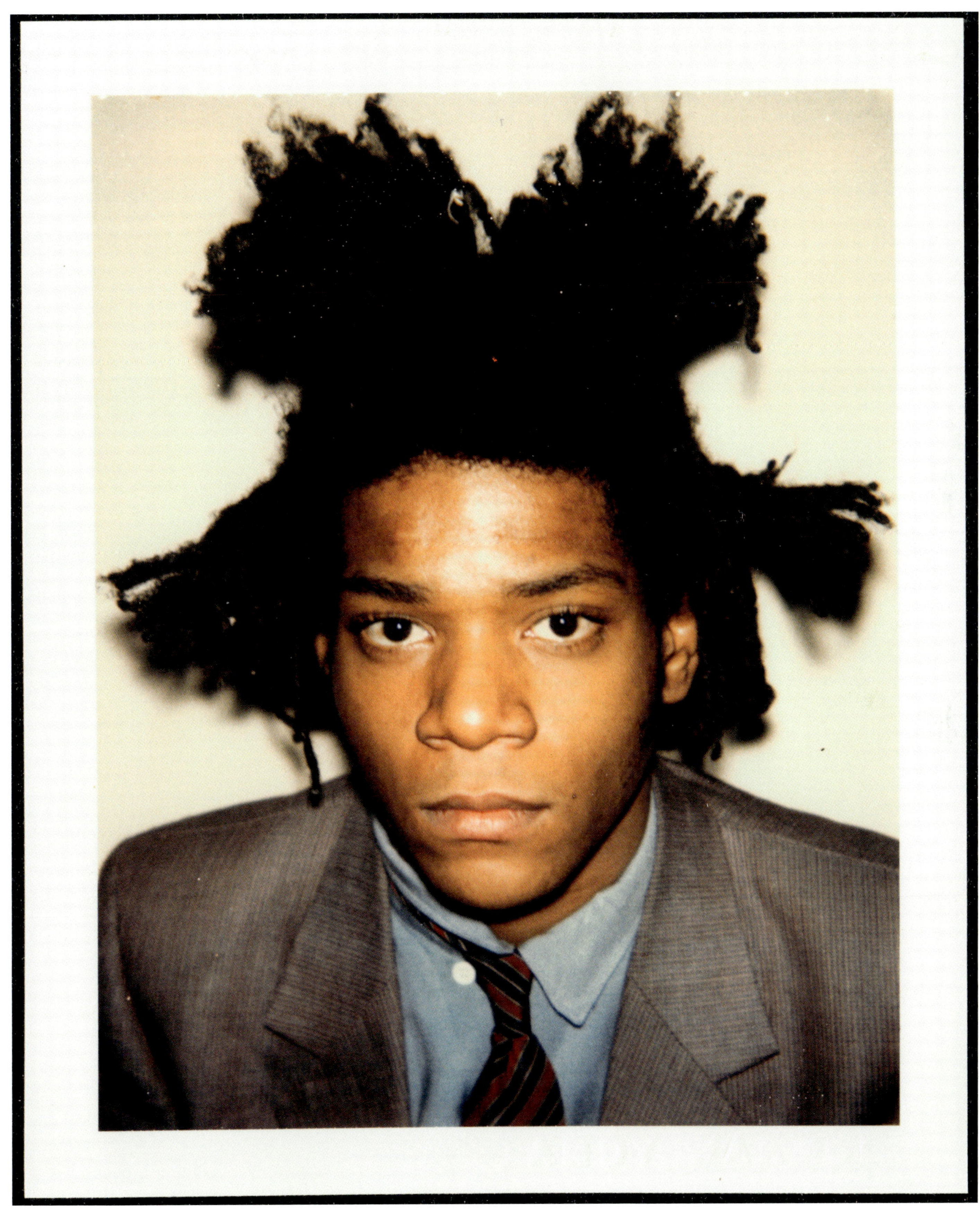

Leopold BRUNNER the Younger

Vienna, 14 Sep 1822 – 24 Dec 1849, Vienna
Austrian, 27 years, 3 months, 11 days

Leopold Brunner was tutored in art by his illustrious father, the court painter to King Ferdinand of Austria, Leopold Brunner the Elder (1788–1866). The elder Brunner was a fine landscape, figure and floral-botanical painter, mostly in watercolour, and encouraged his sons in the arts. Leopold Brunner's younger brother, Josef Brunner of Vienna (1826–1893), likewise became a professional artist, mostly of landscapes and city views. In 1840, Leopold enrolled at the Vienna Academy of Fine Arts, studying with Josef Feid and specialising in the depiction of animals. He also carefully studied the lithographic prints made after the animal and figure paintings of the alpine painter Friedrich Gauermann (1807–1862). Gauermann's romantic art would greatly influence the young painter.

At the Academy, Brunner developed strong friendships with his fellow students. One such student companion, August Xaver Carl von Pettenkofer (1822–1889), painted the young idealistic Brunner's portrait at 18, and signed it 'friend and fellow schoolboy' in 1840. Then, five years later, another friend, Georg Decker (1818–1894), painted *The Artist Leopold Brunner the Younger* (c.1844, Kunsthistorisches Museum, Vienna) in profile. In this portrait, Brunner is handsome, bright eyed and appears the picture of health.

There are no hints of any underlying illness that might have caused his unfortunate early death.

Most of Brunner's extant work depicts rustic farm animals – horses, cows, sheep and goats. He was, however, not a livestock artist per se, rather he often included poignant rural figures who live in harmony with these gentle animals. One such is his lithograph *The Sick Horse* (1843) in which the concerned figures surround the horse, discussing possible cures. The Belvedere Galerie in Vienna owns his delightful *Boy and Girl with Sheep and Goats* (1849). In this canvas, we see a young shepherd and shepherdess with their animal charges as they take an intimate moment to converse on a bridge.

Perhaps his most advanced painting is *Girl with Goat* (1849, Kunsthistorisches Museum, Vienna), painted the year of his death. Coupled with the works above, we see an artist just coming into his own. Dying at the age of 27, Brunner was not a young prodigy, nor a 'late bloomer', but rather he followed the regular development of most artists of his day. For Brunner, time just ran out. It is not known how his life came to an end, but it is sad because he was a solid fine artist who had much to say regarding the symbiosis of people and animals.

Leopold Brunner the Younger
Girl with Goat, 1849, oil on canvas, 52 × 62.1 cm (20½ × 24½ in)
Kunsthistorisches Museum, Vienna

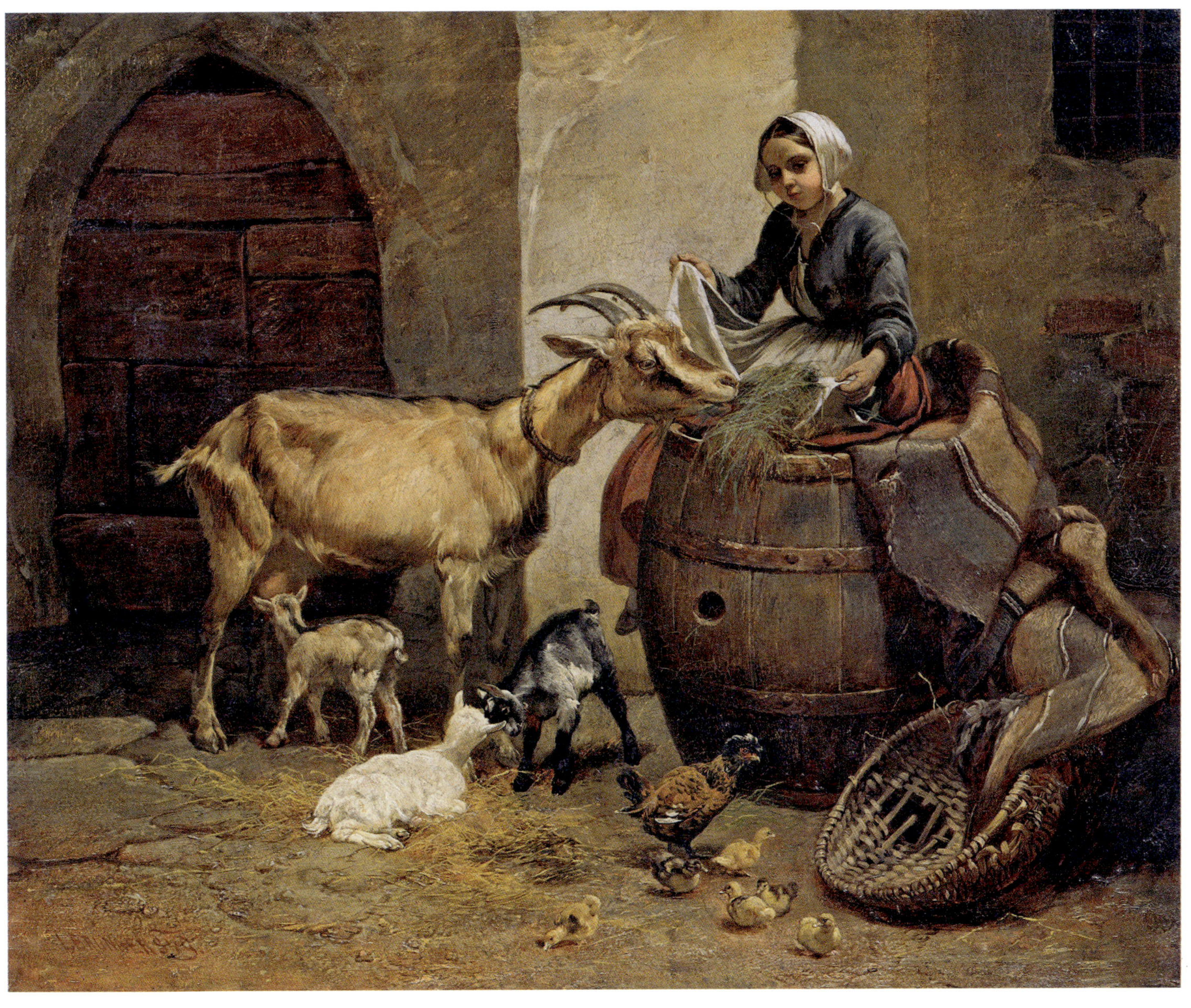

Henri-Jacques-Édouard EVENEPOEL

Nice, 3 Oct 1872 – 27 Dec 1899, Paris
Belgian, 27 years, 2 months, 25 days

Though Belgian, Henri Evenepoel was born in Nice, France. His mother's health was failing, and the balmy climate of the French Riviera was intended to cure her ailments, but she still died, leaving behind her young son. Tragically, a similar tale would unfold a generation later. However, when Evenepoel died he also left behind a tantalisingly incomplete oeuvre that hinted at spectacular future success. Evenepoel studied at the Académie Royale des Beaux-Arts in Brussels and then the École des Beaux-Arts in Paris. This was followed by four years at the atelier of Gustave Moreau where the master took much interest in the budding artist. There he made important connections with early modernists: Matisse, Rouault and Toulouse-Lautrec. While in Paris he lived with his encouraging cousin Louise van Mattemburgh, her husband Michel de Mey and their two children. Evenepoel became known for his poster and illustration commissions. In paint, he depicted Paris street scenes, interiors, and especially portraits of family and friends. He was also an avid photographer.

In 1894, Evenepoel exhibited for the first time at the Salon des Artistes Français, with a portrait of his married cousin Louise de Mey. This was followed by successful submissions to the Salon du Champ-de-Mars, where he exhibited annually for the rest of his life. *At the Moulin Rouge* (1897) explores the energy and excitement of Parisian life. Being abstract and representational, the work is a synthesis of colliding sensitivities.

Evenepoel's personal life was no less eventful. Evenepoel and Louise fell in love and began an illicit romantic relationship, which ultimately destroyed her marriage and led to the birth of a son, Charles. His affection for his son is evident in the charming portrait *Charles au Jersey Rayé* (1898). It was therefore difficult for Evenepoel to leave his young family in October 1897, when the damp Paris climate necessitated a six-month sojourn in Algeria to improve his failing health.

While the artist's early work was sombre in palette, after his stay in Alegria it became bolder in colour, light and decisiveness. For this reason, and his association with Matisse, some scholars inaccurately view Evenepoel's art as a precursor of fauvism. However, unlike the fauves, he exalted in silhouette and aesthetic beauty. By 1899, the artist had begun to experience critical and financial success. His *Spaniard in Paris* (1899) sold for a thousand francs to the Museum of Fine Arts in Ghent. Furthermore, with Louise's divorce finalised, he hoped to soon marry her and recognise his son. Sadly, this was not to be.

Evenepoel died suddenly of typhoid in Paris. We can only speculate where his career would have taken him. Perhaps he would have pursued fauvism, or more likely, his style would have continued to develop in a more realist fashion. Either way, his remaining body of work is highly valued today. His biographer, Francis Hyslop insightfully wrote, 'Evenepoel's realism was usually refined, delicate, and poetic ... In spite of his painfully short career, Evenepoel left a substantial body of fine pictures that possess a durable value.'[84]

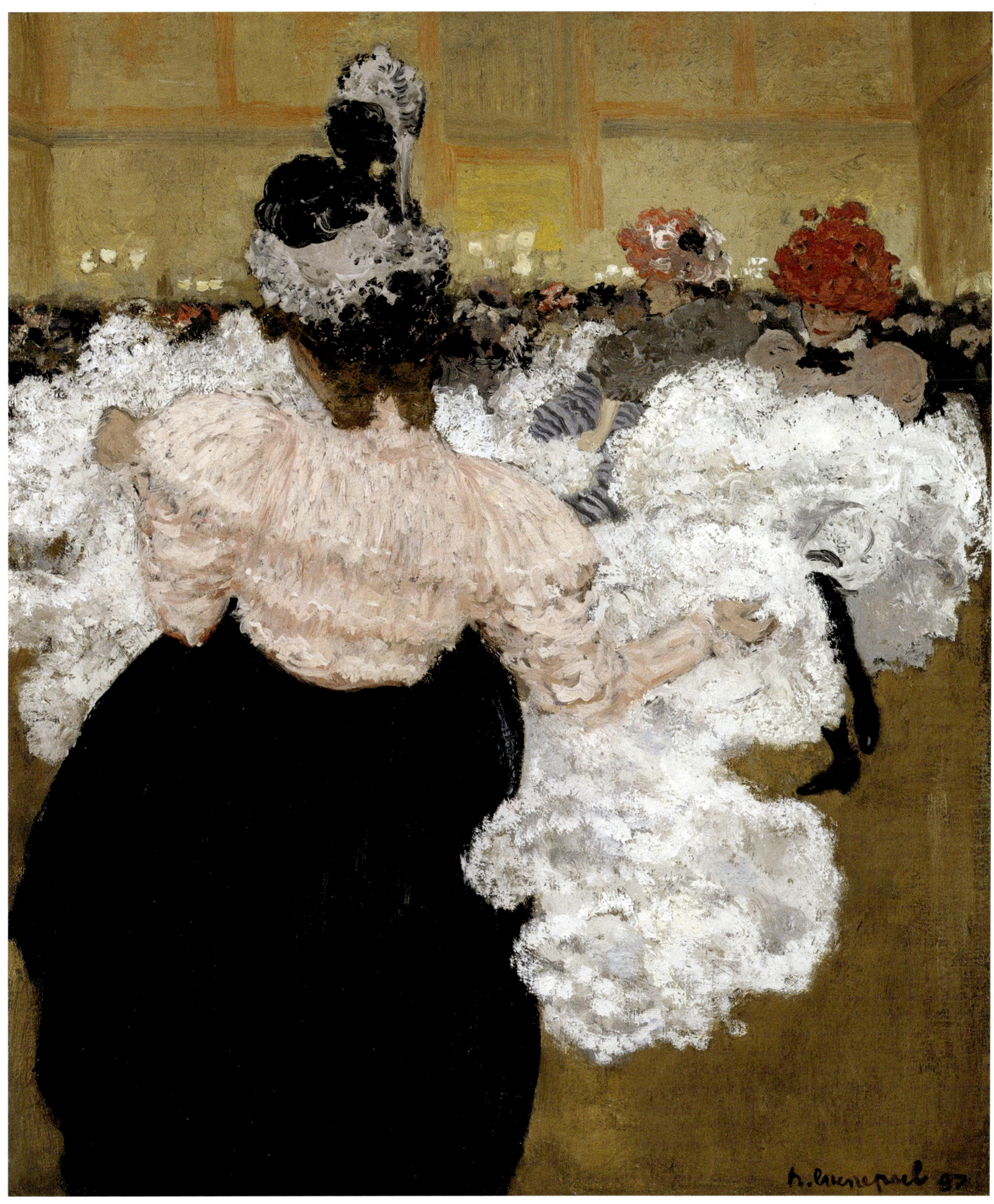

Roland-Marie GÉRARDIN

Paris, 18 Nov 1907 – 21 Feb 1935, Rome
French, 27 years, 3 months, 4 days

As a young artist, Roland-Marie Gérardin was gifted and driven, but he tragically died just as fame began to present itself. Initially, Gérardin studied at the École des Arts Décoratifs. Then in 1926, he entered the illustrious École des Beaux-Arts in Paris and studied with Louis Roger, Pierre Laurens and Paul Albert Laurens. At just 20 years old, he began exhibiting at the Salon des Artistes Français. Eager to prove himself, the young artist was driven to win the illustrious scholarship award to study in Rome – the Prix de Rome. Unfortunately, his first attempt at the prize, in 1928 with the subject Concert Champêtre, failed.

Nevertheless, his major painting *Repas de Paysans* (Peasants' Meal) was successfully exhibited at the Palais des Beaux-Arts, Brussels in 1929. The painting depicts a group of peasants lazily picnicking by a river on a blanket covered with mostly eaten food. Painted at only 22 in the style of the day, its thickly pigmented brushwork and strongly designed figures point to his aesthetic direction. Restless, this was not where he would remain aesthetically.

He continued to experience success until, in 1930, he won a distinguished award for Tête d'expression with his oil *Vigilance of a Segovian Shepherd* (1930, ENSBA). Gérardin was at first chagrined and then euphoric to receive Second prize or 'runner-up' in the Prix de Rome competition of 1930 for his oil, *Geneviève de Brabant*. This bitter-sweet achievement was augmented in 1930 and 1931 with two silver medals at the Salon des Artistes Français. Though the award was initially elusive, Gérardin persevered and finally won the Prix de Rome with his forceful oil, *Susanna and the Two Elders* (1933, ENSBA).

Gérardin left for Rome immediately, and after less than two years at the French Academy's Villa Medici in Rome he died from an aggressive pancreatic cancer at the age of 27 years; just one more artist to die in the Eternal City. However, his passing did not go unnoticed. Just a few months later the École des Beaux-Arts mounted a retrospective honouring his work and life. Then, in 1936, a fellow 1933 Prix de Rome (music) winner, Robert Planel, created a musical composition in Gérardin's memory titled 'Our Father in Heaven'. Amazingly, Gérardin's atelier seems to have stayed intact for many years, for its contents were not dispersed until an auction in 1999.

In his short but successful career, Gérardin produced many large, brightly coloured and substantial paintings. He painted many nudes, such as the outdoor allegorical *Femme Alanguies* and Parisian nightclub subjects. He chose to depict women in his work quite lustily and sometimes in a ribald manner. Against this decadent backdrop, he painted a number of religious pictures, causing one to wonder what they meant in his oeuvre. Unfortunately, precious little is known about his personal life and personality.

Roland-Marie Gérardin
Peasants' Meal, 1929, oil on canvas, 185 × 200 cm (72⅞ × 78¾ in)
Yves Bresson/Musée d'Art Moderne et Contemporain – Sainte Étienne Métropole

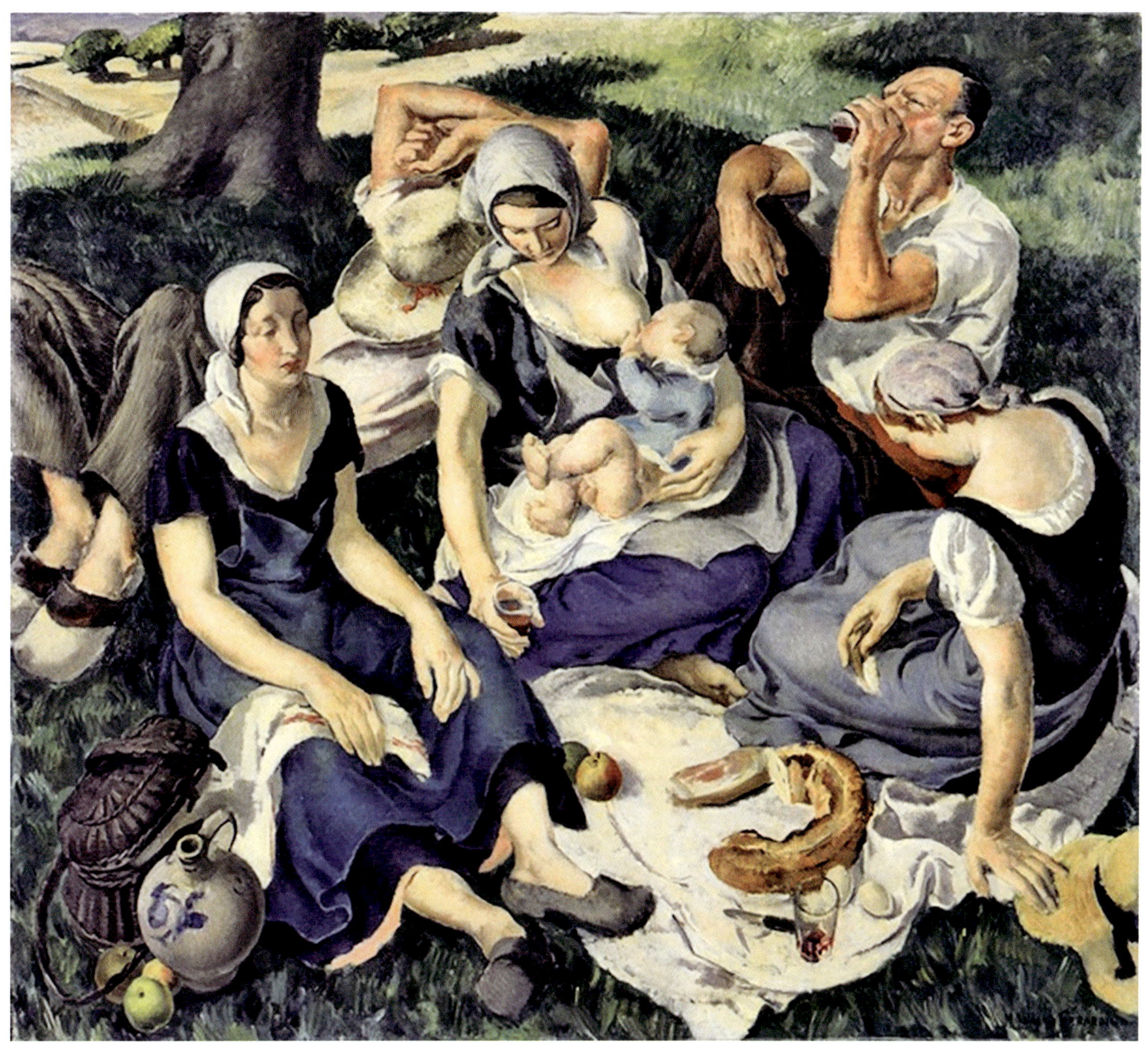

Maksymilian GIERYMSKI

Warsaw, 9 Oct 1846 – 16 Sep 1874, Bad Reichenhall
Polish, 27 years, 11 months, 8 days

This rather tragic figure was a painter and watercolourist, and older brother of the famed artist Aleksander Gierymski. Maksymilian was indelibly scarred for life by the genocidal events of the January Uprising in 1863. As a youth of only 17, Gierymski participated with the insurgents against the brutal Russian partition and occupation of Poland. He spent nearly a year fighting in the Lublin and Kielce regions, witnessing the grim realities of war and the hopeless odds in which his countrymen fought. He somehow survived the conflict and avoided subsequent punishment from the Russians. However, the experience 'branded his psyche with permanent sadness and melancholy.'[85] This sombre tone permeated his later canvases.

Finding art education in Warsaw after the Uprising lacking, Gierymski largely taught himself art with some help from another artist, Juliusz Kossak. Then, in 1867, he was given a government scholarship to study at the Munich Academy of Fine Art under history painters Józef Brandt and Karl von Piloty. Gierymski also entered the studio of battle painter Franz Adam in Munich. At last, Gierymski received the longed-for formal training, and he progressed rapidly, reaching artistic maturity by the youthful age of 23.

Gierymski was a military painter, but not in the usual sense. He did not exalt in grand assaults, pitched battles, or manoeuvres. His military pictures depicted tired and toilsome figures, exhausted soldiers often in disarray, scattered about usually in blustery weather and in the dim dusk as in *Polish Militiamen* (1873). He also painted hunting scenes and genre paintings of mundane villages. His tonal atmospheric landscapes came mostly during the summers of 1870–72, when he vacationed in Poland.

While his lyrical realist style received great critical and popular approval in Munich, Gierymski's art was not immediately appreciated in more conservative Poland. He persevered and participated in numerous exhibitions with great success, earning medals and commissions, and even selling work to Emperor Franz Joseph of Austria. In 1874 he was elected a member of the Royal Academy of the Arts in Berlin.

Sadly, in 1872 he became ill with tuberculosis, following a trip to Poznań. Gierymski travelled to Merano and Bad Reichenhall to receive treatment, but to no avail. In 1873, his brother Aleksander travelled with him to Rome in the hope that the drier climate would ease Maksymilian's consumptive symptoms and he could live and work there. However, he returned to Munich and Bad Reichenhall during the summer of 1874. When his health became so poor that he could no longer paint, he wrote about art.

Gierymski died in September 1874, just a month before his 28th birthday. Despite his early death, Gierymski was a prolific painter and a strong representative for the Polish school of painting, eventually inspiring many young artists and critics after him.

Maksymilian Gierymski
Polish Militiamen, 1873, oil on canvas mounted on panel, 48 × 80 cm (18⅞ × 31½ in)
Private collection

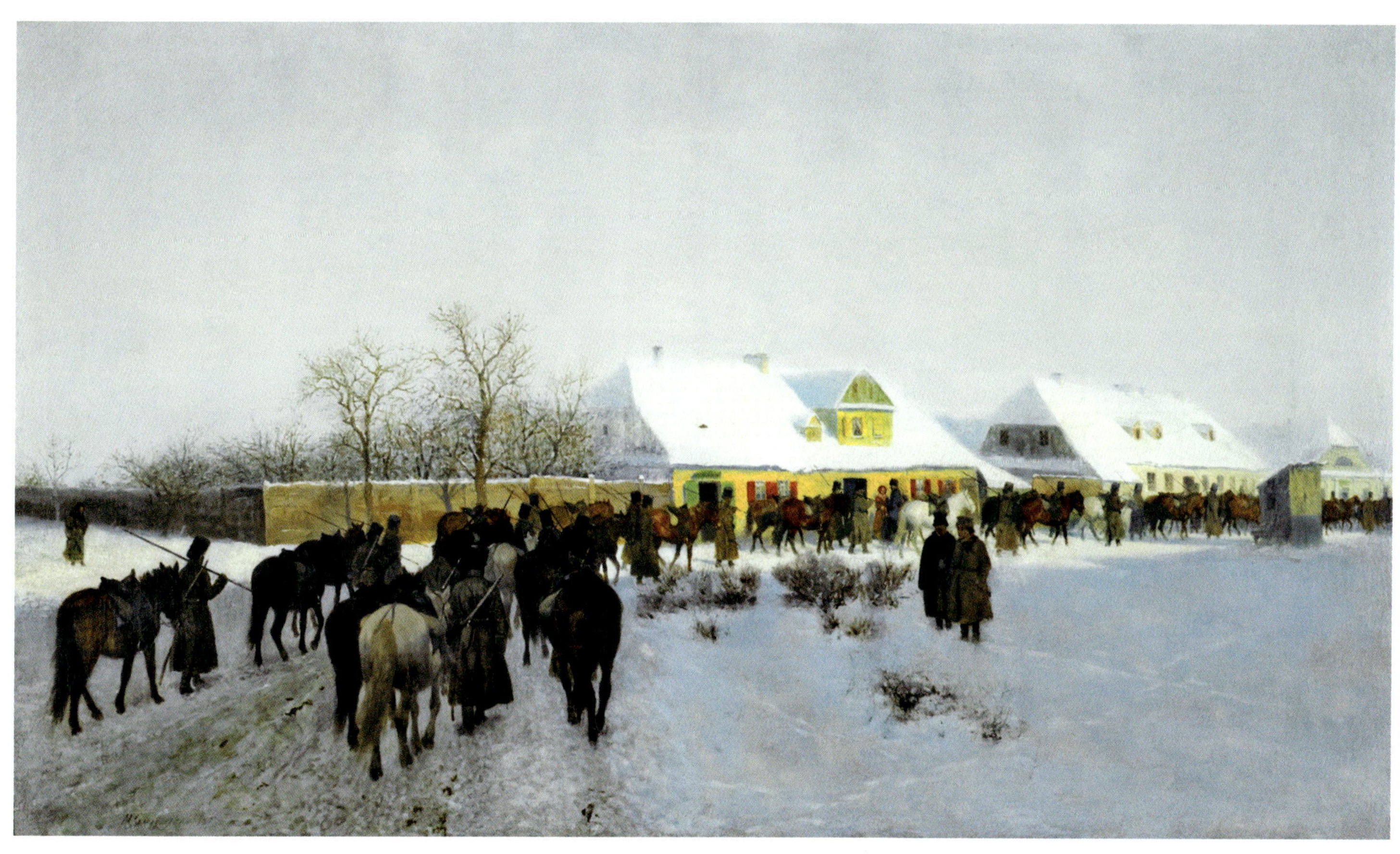

Thomas GIRTIN

London, 18 Feb 1775 – 9 Nov 1802, London
British, 27 years, 8 months, 23 days

In a career of just over ten years, Girtin forever elevated the status of watercolour from being a 'drawing' to a 'painting' medium. What was once considered a medium for amateurs, printmakers or draughtsmen, became a highly regarded art form under Girtin's able hand. Born the son of a brushmaker, Girtin was apprenticed to the topographical watercolour painter Edward Dayes at the age of 13. There, he learned traditional watercolour techniques. One of his tasks as an apprentice was to make watercolours after the sketches of other artists. This proved helpful, for once he became an independent artist, he worked beside J.M.W. Turner making copies after the works of John Robert Cozens amongst others. Girtin would, however, prove to be far more than just a copyist.

His later work displays not only a mastery of the medium but a proclivity for experimentation and originality which became progressively better throughout his career. He infused watercolour with a fresh boldness, an expanded colour palette, and atmospheric effects, as seen in *Durham Cathedral and Castle* (c.1800, J. Paul Getty Museum Collection). These romantic qualities went far beyond topographical pictures.

Highly regarded in his day, Girtin exhibited frequently at the Royal Academy and was able to charge higher prices than watercolours usually fetched. He undertook many sketching tours throughout England and North Wales, even travelling to Paris in 1801–1802 despite his declining health. Shortly before his death, Girtin completed a major 33-metre (36-yard) panorama of the city of London, titled *Eidometropolis*. Well received, it was a mammoth task for one so ill.

Girtin, who had little patience for his illness, reportedly said to his doctor, 'I don't care what you do to me, if you will only put me in such a way that I can continue to make drawings.' He was newly married and had every hope for a long and successful career. Unfortunately, this was not to be. In late 1802, Girtin died in his studio from what appears to have been an asthma attack, although he might also have had tuberculosis or, according to some contemporaries, an 'ossification of the heart.'

His dear friend and landscape painting rival J.M.W. Turner later said of Girtin: 'Had poor Tom lived, I would have starved.' Indeed, art historian Matthew Plampin notes that, 'Among his peers, Girtin was really the only one who could hold a candle to Turner. At the Royal Academy, while Turner was admired in competitions, Girtin was often declared the winner.'[86] His death brought to an end one of the brightest lights in British art history. Fortunately, his work would prove to be very influential to rising young artists, including the incredibly important and also short-lived, Richard Parkes Bonington. Today, Girtin's watercolours are found in major museums and collections around the world.

Thomas Girtin
Durham Cathedral and Castle, c.1800, watercolour, 37.5 × 48.9 cm (14¾ × 19¼ in)
J. Paul Getty Museum/Alamy Stock Photo

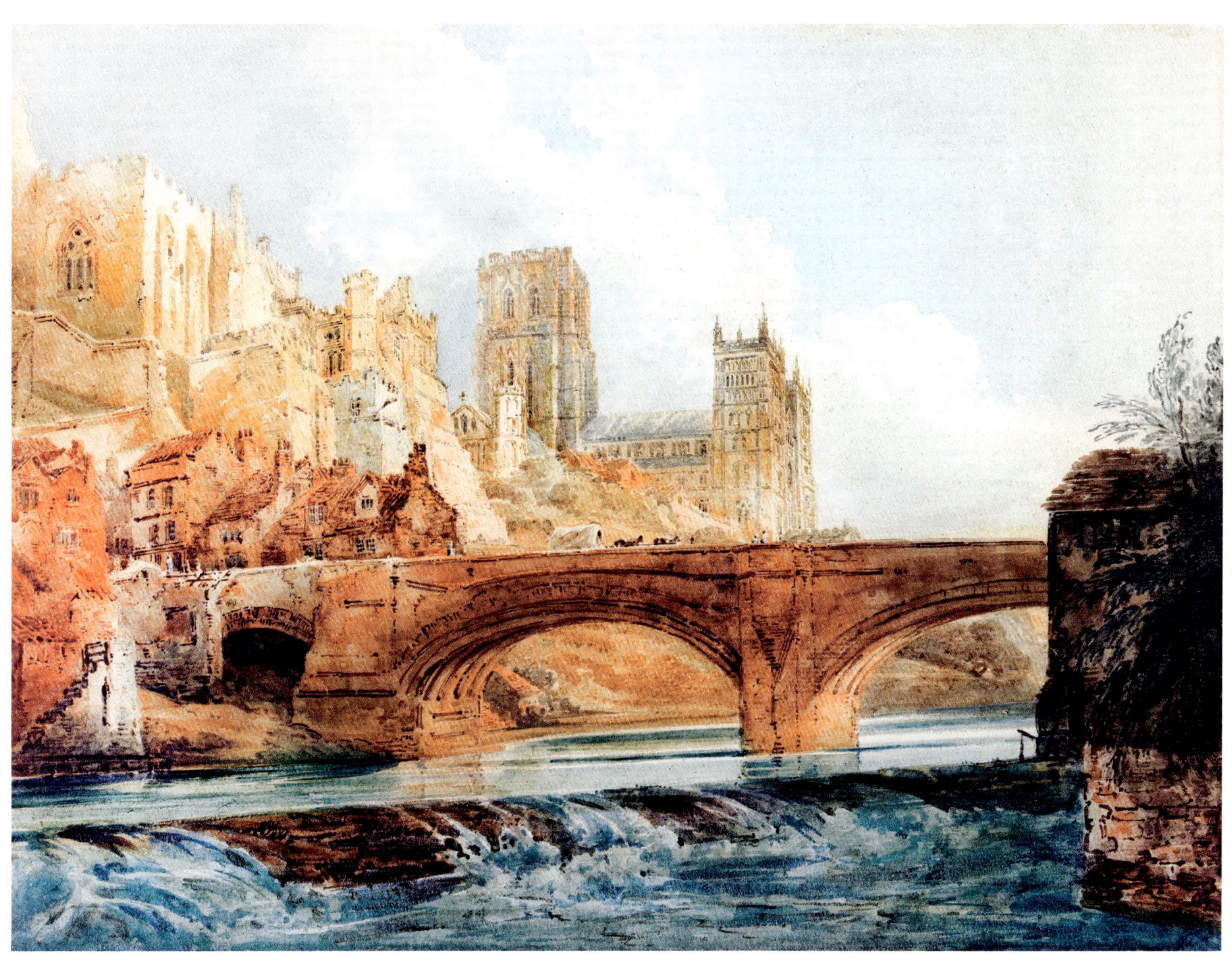

Hendrik KOBELL

Delfshaven-Rotterdam, 13 Sep 1751 – 3 Aug 1779, Delfshaven-Rotterdam
Dutch, 27 years, 10 months, 22 days

Hendrik Kobell was a marine and landscape painter, etcher and watercolourist of note. Art was his family's business. Hendrik had a brother Jan Kobell I (1756–1833) who was an art engraver, and Hendrik became the father of the important artist, Jan Baptist Kobell II (1778–1814). Just to complicate matters, his uncle Jan Kobell had two sons (Hendrik's cousins) Ferdinand Kobell (1740–1799) and Franz Kobell (1749–1822), both outstanding German landscape painters. Hendrik was also the uncle of painter Jan Kobell III (1800–1838), and this barely touches the complexities of the Kobell-family artistic dynasty.

Hendrik's father was a pottery merchant and as a youth Hendrik was trained to be a pottery merchant as well. This early exposure to the pottery business may have instigated his need for decoration and later fine art. Though not a professional, his father taught the rudiments of drawing to his sons as a part of their general education. By the later 1760s Hendrik had become fascinated by ships and spent time in Rotterdam harbour, as well as in and around the city, making drawings and watercolours of the rivers and the landscape.

In 1770, when he was 19, his father arranged for his son to travel to London on a business trip. Instead, Hendrik spent much of his time drawing the commercial ships and military galleons he saw there. After this trip, he returned home to the northern Netherlands in 1771 with the determination to study art. His father relented and Hendrik soon left the pottery business to study at the Stadstekenacademie in Amsterdam for two years.

Hendrik's success at art school led to his being elected a member of the prestigious art society Hierdoor tot Hoger which translates as 'Thus to the Heights'. He travelled to Paris in 1772 and in that same year finally settled back in Rotterdam, where he helped set up a drawing academy similar to that in Amsterdam. In 1774, Hendrik married and settled comfortably into a professional career. He became best known for his action-packed marine pictures of precarious ships in stormy weather and navel engagements. His marvellous oil, *Shipwreck* (1775, Rijksmuseum) gives testimony that his art possessed cinematic drama. He seems to have deliberately related his work to the Dutch Golden Age 17th-century marine-painting tradition of artists such as Willem van de Velde and Ludolf Backhuysen, while using 18th-century ships and rigging to keep his work contemporary.

Just as his carefully planned and orderly life was finding success, Hendrik's wife died and he followed shortly thereafter, dying of an unknown cause. Unfortunately, Hendrik's death left his infant son, Jan, to be raised in an orphanage in Utrecht, but remarkably the boy became an internationally known landscape and animal artist in his own right. Jan's own career was, likewise, tragically cut short when he died in an insane asylum at the age of 35. Fortunately, Hendrik left a sizeable oeuvre consisting of about 20 etching plates, hundreds of drawings and 40-50 paintings. Michael Bryan wrote of him: 'His touch is bold and spirited; his colouring somewhat too green and his water vapory, but he shows taste and judgment in the selection and management of his subject.'[87] High praise for one who left the scene all too soon.

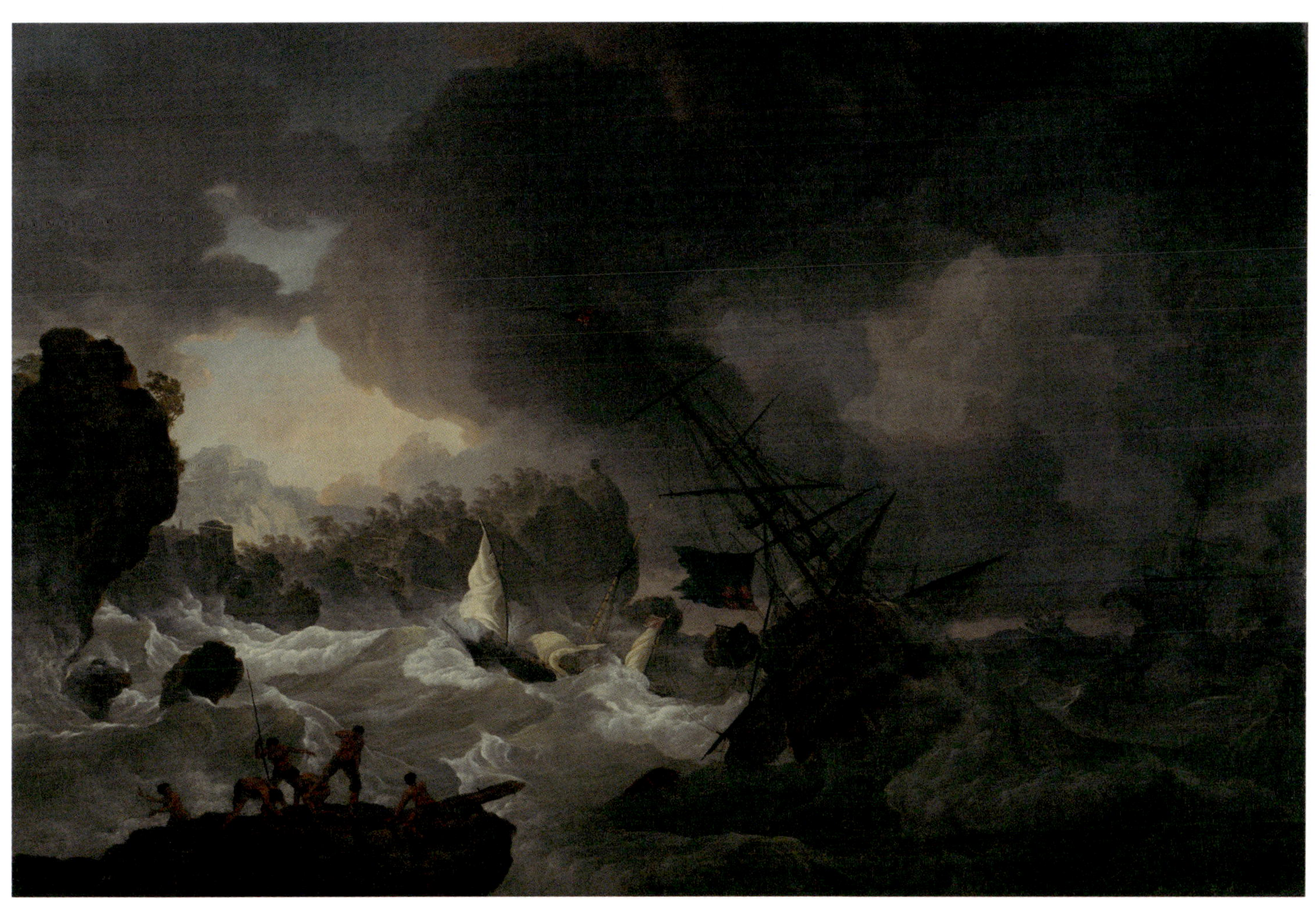

Hendrik Kobell
Shipwreck, 1775, oil on canvas, 93.5 × 135 cm (36¾ × 53⅛ in)
Rijksmuseum, Amsterdam

Jeremi KUBICKI

Łodź, 6 Apr 1911 – 6 Dec 1938, Warsaw
Polish, 27 years, 8 months, 1 day

Kubicki was a Polish artist of the interwar period (1918–39). He studied at the Academy of Fine Art in Warsaw (1929–35) under L. Pękalski and T. Pruszkowski. Joining with Pruszkowski and other Academy students, he became a member of the Bractwo św. Łukasza (Brotherhood of Saint Luke). Taking their cues from the Nazarene movement (also known as the Brotherhood of Saint Luke), they worked together like a mediaeval guild and were dedicated to historical and religious themes in art. While Kubicki developed his own distinct style, he worked with the Brotherhood for many years.

Like the famed Polish painter Tamara de Lempicka, Kubicki painted pictures for commercial institutions (including Polish ocean liners) and decorative paintings for the Wedel chocolate shop in Warsaw and the Panneaux Polish Spa. Interestingly, he also competed in two Summer Olympics art competitions in Los Angeles (1932) and Berlin (1936). His masterpiece *Cyclists* (1935, National Museum in Warsaw) was painted for the Berlin Olympics, and captures well the energy of the sport with its curving lines and rhythmic 'dashed' brush strokes. Unfortunately, though deserving, he won no medals at either Olympics art competition. Mostly, Kubicki painted undulating landscapes featuring people taking part in activities. In 1937, he won a major award at an exhibition in Paris.

Together with his friends in the Brotherhood, he created decorations for the Paris 1937 Exposition Internationale, and later helped again to paint seven historical compositions intended for the Polish Pavilion for the 1939 New York World's Fair. Professionally, Kubicki appeared to be fully employed, but the artist had experienced a major personal setback. In 1934, he had married Anna Henneberg. She was herself an artist, and a sports aviator as well. Tragically, she died of tuberculosis just two years later, in 1936.

Before the World's Fair project was completed, Kubicki unexpectedly shot himself in the temple and died. While it might have been accidental, it was probably intentional, but for no definite reason. Was his wife's premature passing two years previously the catalyst for his own death, or was there another contributing factor? Adding insult to injury, almost his entire output was destroyed during World War II, making it difficult to fully assess Kubicki's potential. However, Polish art historian M. Wallis wrote of him that his art had 'the charm of a fantastic fairy tale and at the same time something decadent and almost perverse. [He was a] great original talent.'[88]

Jeremi Kubicki
Cyclists, 1935, oil on canvas, 121.5 × 148 cm (47⅞ × 58¼ in)
National Museum in Warsaw/Alamy

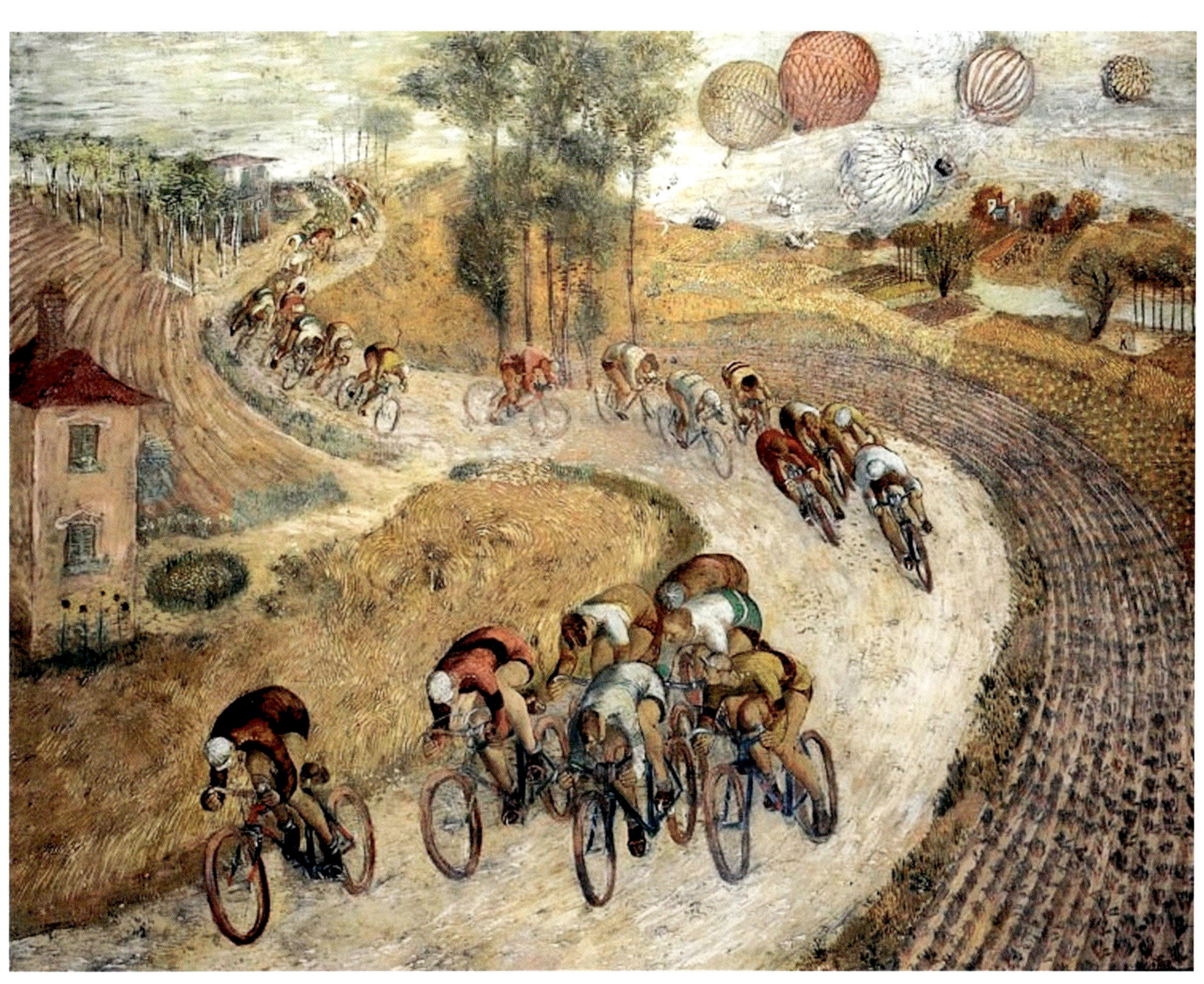

August MACKE

Meschede, 3 Jan 1887 – 26 Sep 1914, battlefield in Champagne, France
German, 27 years, 8 months, 24 days

In contrast to many artists who died in their twenties, Macke's personality and art can be described as colourful, happy and full of joie de vivre. While he is considered a German expressionist, his art does not partake of the angst or negativity for which that movement has become known. Instead, his landscapes, still-lifes, portraits and genre paintings are serene, almost paradisiacal. Macke's father was an amateur artist, and his passion for art spread to his son. Macke's art education included just two years' study at the Dusseldorf Academy of Art (1904–1906), evening classes from Fritz Helmuth Ehmcke (1905), and several months in the studio of Lovis Corinth (1908).

However, it was Macke's travels and contact with other artists that had the greatest impact on his art. In Paris, he experienced with awe the work of the French impressionists and post-impressionists. Because of Matisse, Macke brightened his palette and broadened his stroke. Likewise, his friendships with Franz Marc, Wassily Kandinsky, Robert Delaunay and Paul Klee profoundly influenced his style, and he joined with them in becoming a founding member of the highly important art movement, Der Blaue Reiter. The coalescing of these influences is evident in such works as *Four Girls* (1912–13), with its simplified, flattened forms and bold colours. Prolific, Macke's oeuvre includes nearly 600 paintings, 600 watercolours and more than 9,000 drawings, moving through a range of styles – impressionism, fauvism, cubism, orphism and abstraction.

In the spring of 1914, just months before his death, he travelled to Tunisia, where he produced some of his most memorable works. His style was still evolving and maturing, making the tragedy of his death all the more poignant. That year he was conscripted into the army, forcing him to leave behind his beloved wife and young children. His last painting, titled *Farewell*, with its mournful browns and blacks, contrasts starkly with his usual optimistic style, and perhaps reflects the artist's own despair at leaving his family and art for the grisly World War I.

Macke was killed in combat during the second month of the Great War, dying at the front in Champagne, France. His dear friend, the artist Franz Marc, mourned Macke's loss when he said, 'In war we are all equal, but among a thousand good men, a bullet hit an irreplaceable one … We painters know well that with the loss of his harmony, the colour in German art will become many shades paler' and one might add 'darker'. Like Marc, who also died in World War I (in 1916), Macke's influence on later avant-garde German painting is incalculable.

August Macke
Four Girls, 1912–13, oil on canvas, 105 × 81 cm (41⅜ × 31⅞ in)
Museum Kunstpalast, Dusseldorf

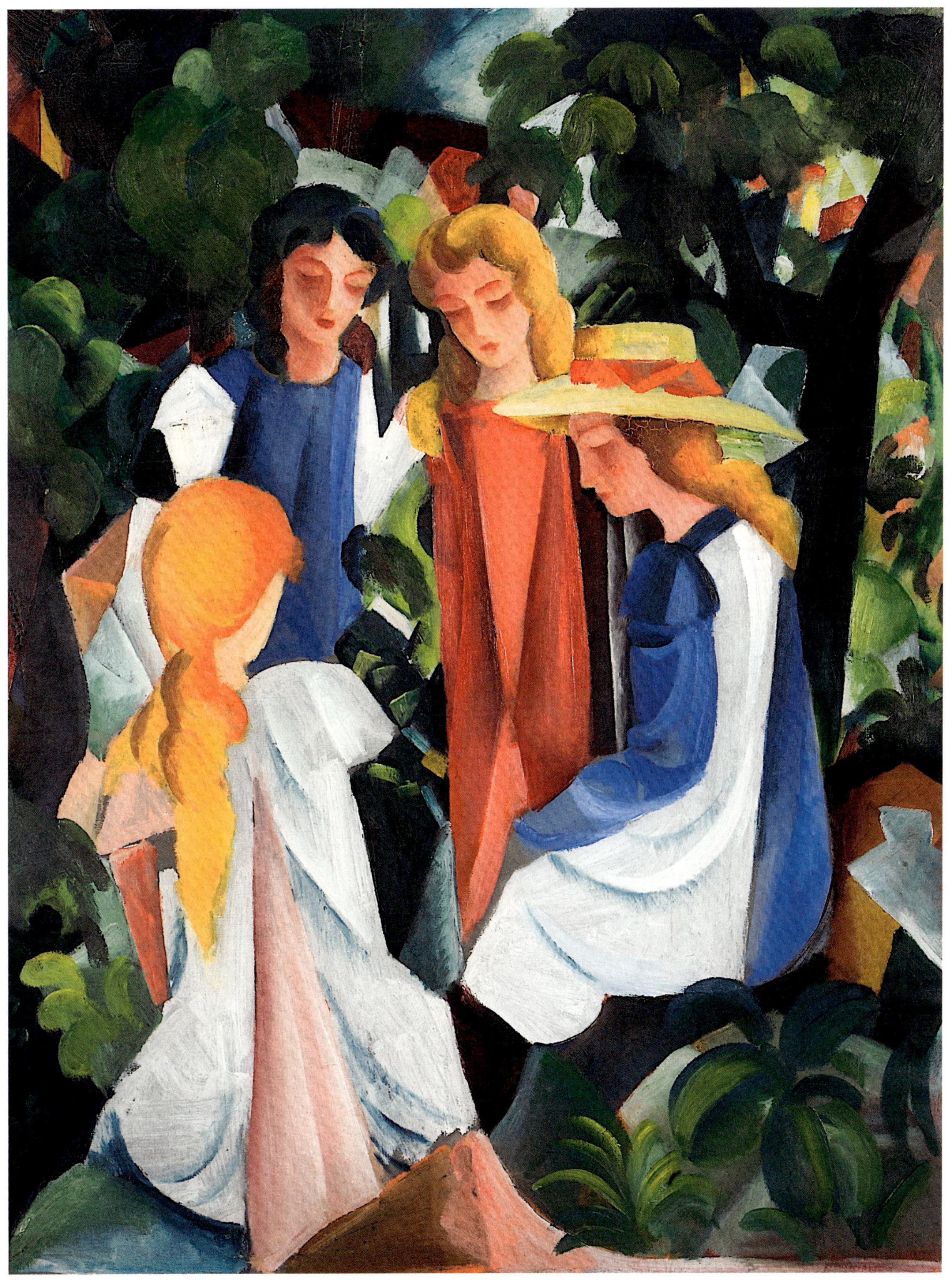

Francisco de PALACIOS

c.1622/25 – 27 Jan 1652 , Madrid
Spanish, approx. 27 years

For centuries, Francisco de Palacios has been considered a minor figure in Spanish baroque art, with only a handful of still-lifes and religious paintings to his name. While art historical scholarship on this artist still leaves many questions, recent examinations of primary resources and critical art connoisseurship have vastly changed opinion on the painter and his body of work. Errors, which have persisted for centuries are now being overturned by recent scholars.[89]

The eminent, but not infallible, art writer Antonio Palomino (1655–1726) was the first to incorrectly state that Palacios died in 1676 around the age of 36 years old, making his birthdate around 1640.[90] However, Palacios's marriage certificate of 10 January 1646, clearly states that 'both spouses are under twenty-five but over twenty', placing Palacios's birth squarely between 1622 and 1625. According to Palomino, Palacios received pictorial training from Diego Velázquez (1599–1660), one of the greatest artists of all time. He was, at the very least, a protégé of this master.

The circumstances of Palacios's marriage are most interesting in that he married well above his rank to Josefa Bergés, the daughter of the painter and art dealer Francisco Bergés and his wealthy wife Felipa de Mendoza. Her dowry was a hefty 6,000 reales in cash, jewellery and household items. The couple were later blessed with two children, Francisco and Catalina. That his father-in-law was an art dealer who appreciated his art was a significant advantage in the Madrid art world.

Palacios was a very capable table-top food and flowers still-life, landscape, allegorical and portrait artist. Two of his best still-lifes found their way into the Austrian collection of the Earl of Harrach. Another work has recently come to light on the art market. *Still-Life of Silver and Gold Plate with Fruit, Pastry, and Other Objects and Vessels on Table*, painted in c.1649, displays a complexity in the treatment of pantry items, with a muted palette.

Though the number of known paintings by Palacios is small, his large canvases *St Onofre* and *St Francis of Assisi* hang today in the Convent Calatravas en Moralzarzal (Madrid). Furthermore, a drawing by the artist titled *The Annunciation* is in the collection of the Prado Museum. Other works have recently been attributed to Palacios as well. The most prominent of these reattributions being *The Knight's Dream* (1650, Real Academia de Bellas Artes de San Fernando). This masterpiece of the Spanish 17th century, which has long been assigned to the artist Antonio de Pereda, has been reattributed to Palacios by art historian Pérez Sánchez. Time will tell if this attribution sticks, for it may have been a collaboration painting. However, it hints at a bright future for Palacios's reputation.

Near the end of his life, in December 1651, while he was seriously ill (and perhaps in delirium), Palacios ordered (at great expense) 505 masses to be said for his soul, 100 masses for his parents and one for the canonisation of the Blessed Maria de la Cabeza. He died a month later, already a celebrated artist. We do not know what caused his death, but perhaps the illness took his mind before it took his body. Had he lived in good health, Palacios could have become a major figure in the pantheon of Spanish 17th-century art. Nearly 400 years after his death, Palacios is an artist on the rise again.

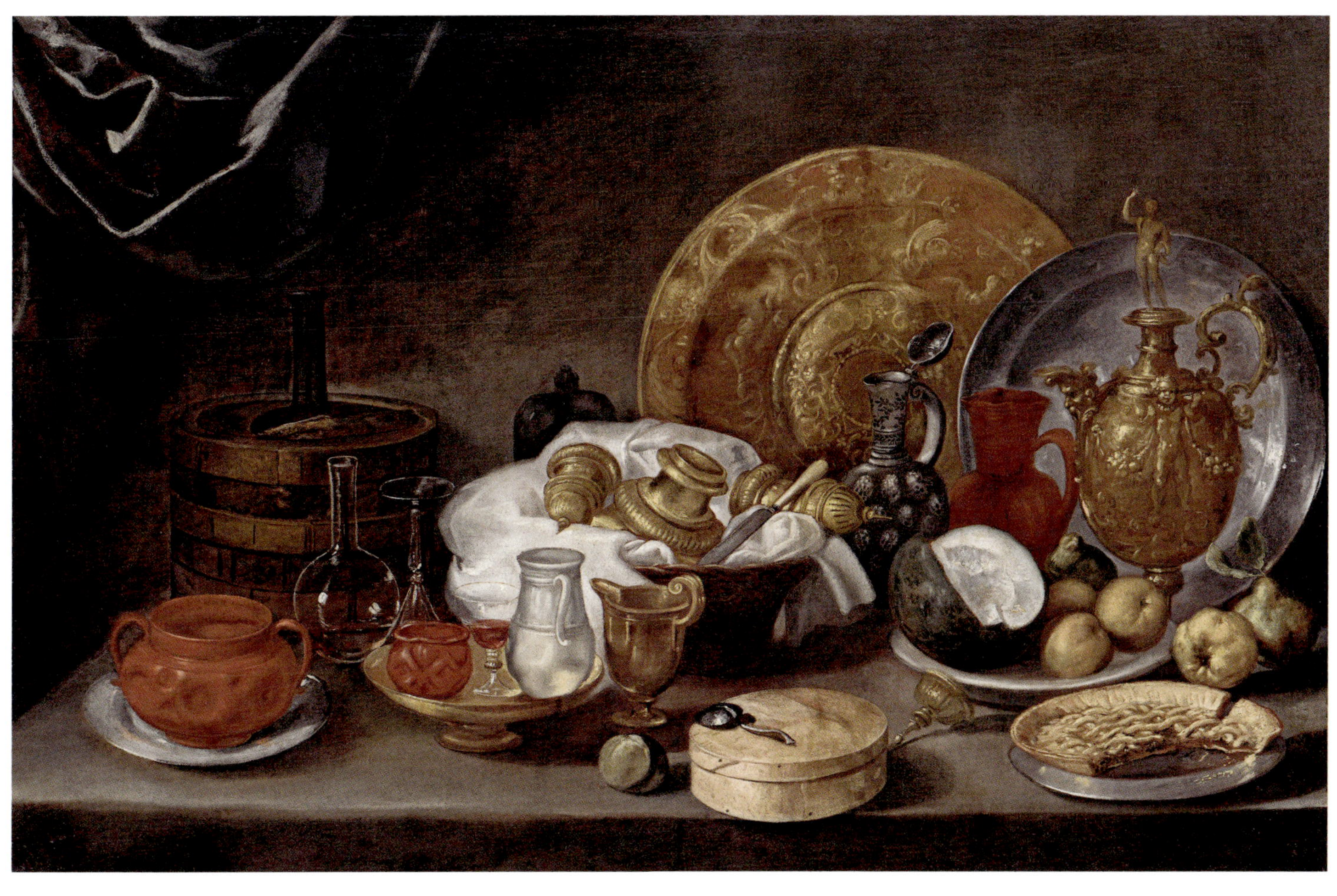

Francisco de Palacios
Still-Life of Silver and Gold Plate with Fruit, Pastry, and Other Objects and Vessels on Table, c.1649, oil on canvas, 105 × 169 cm (41⅜ × 66½ in)
Colnaghi, London

(Alexandre-Georges) Henri REGNAULT

Paris, 31 Oct 1843 – 19 Jan 1871, battlefield of Buzenval, France
French, 27 years, 2 months, 20 days

This heroic artist was the son of the notable chemist and physicist Henri Victor Regnault (1810–1878). Recognising his son's potential, he sent the 17-year-old to the École des Beaux-Arts where he studied with Antoine Montfort, Louis Lamothe and the celebrated Alexandre Cabanel. Henri Regnault was brilliant and decidedly ambitious. In 1863, he competed for the Prix de Rome, but was beaten. Finally, in 1866, Regnault carried off the Prix de Rome convincingly with his *Thetis Bringing the Arms Forged by Vulcan to Achilles*. The following year he departed for Rome, but the antiquities there did not interest him so much as the influence of the modern Hispano-Italian school with its emphasis on visual and material properties. In 1868, he sent back to Paris his required Salon entry, the equestrian masterpiece, *Automedon with the Horses of Achilles* (Museum of Fine Arts, Boston).

Attracted to the drama of the Spanish Revolution, Regnault toured Spain and filled his sketch-books with the sites he found there. After witnessing the revolutionary general passing on horseback to the cheers of jubilant crowds, the artist painted the striking portrait *Juan Prim* (1868, Musée d'Orsay, Paris). Returning to Rome, he prepared two submissions for the 1870 Paris Salon – *Judith* and the instantly famous *Salome* (Metropolitan Museum of Art, New York). The exotic vision, *Salome*, created the 'Art sensation and success of the season'. Though condemned by some critics, one exhibition-goer noted that the painting 'possessed a peculiar fascination which was difficult to analyze or to define', and crowds thronged before it. [91]

Regnault visited Morocco and then, in the summer of 1870, settled in Tangier. There, he bought a property and built a large studio in which to paint his massive paintings. One such painting was his fascinatingly gory Orientalist painting, *Execution without Trial under the Moorish Kings of Granada* (1870, Musée d'Orsay, Paris). There is every reason to believe that Regnault would have produced many more vibrant masterpieces. Art journalist Lucy Hooper wrote, 'Though his fame was swiftly acquired, it was founded on an enduring basis.' Unfortunately, Hooper continues, 'The career of Henri Regnault was as exceptionally brilliant as it was brief.' [92]

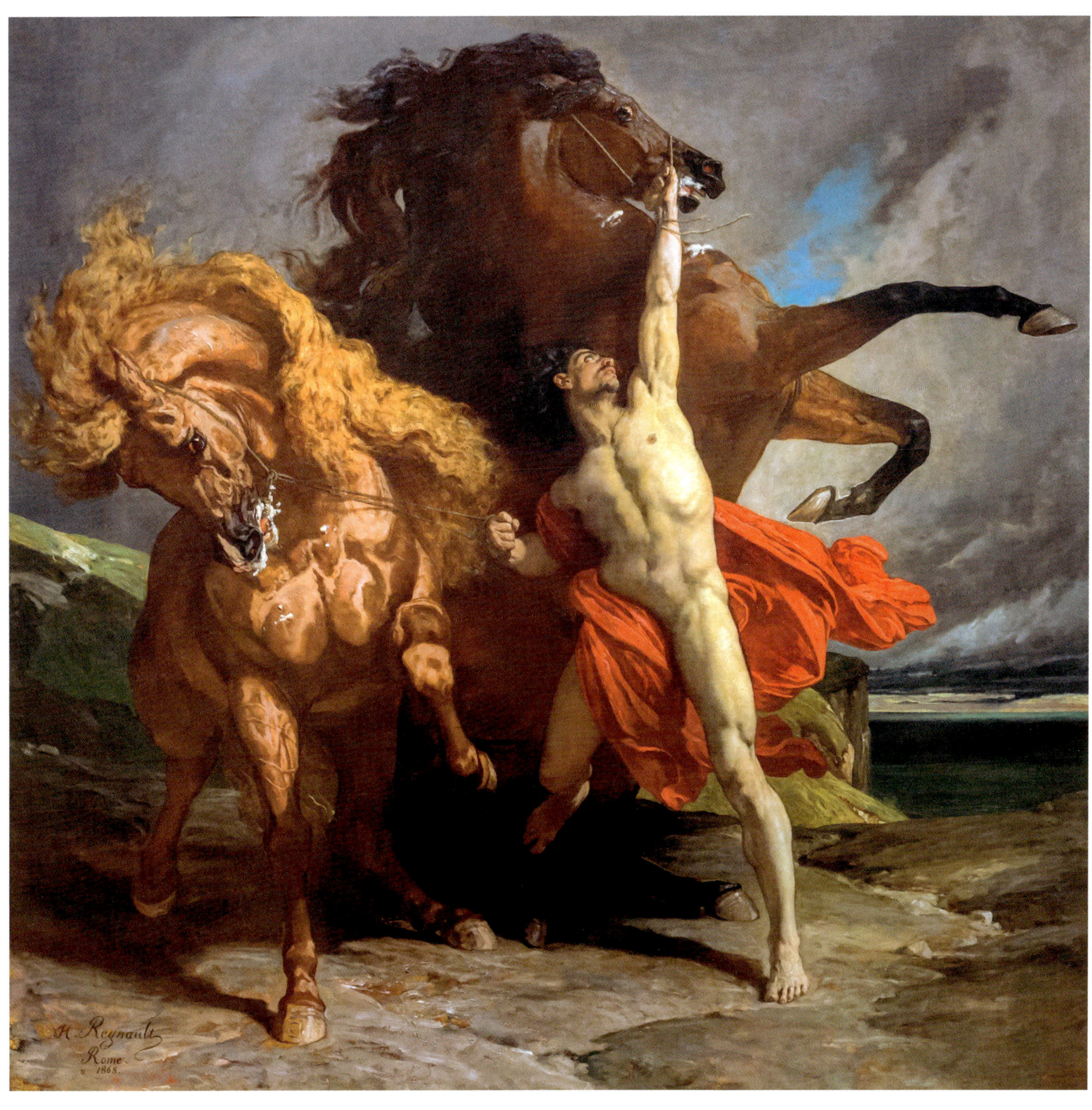

H. Regnault
Rome
1868.

When the Franco-Prussian War began in autumn of 1870, Henri Regnault immediately left Tangier for Paris. Expecting to return soon, he left an unfinished painting in his studio.

Arriving in Paris in September, Regnault and his friend, the artist Georges Clairin, joined the ranks of the National Guard. Prix de Rome winners were exempted from military duty, but Regnault wished to defend Paris. Seven miles west of Paris, during the Battle of Buzenval, the two friends were separated. A general retreat was sounded and Clairin left the field, but not Regnault. One report said that he stayed back to fire his last bullet because he was a sniper (Franc-tireur). He fell with a Prussian bullet to his left temple. The painter Carolus-Duran, after seeing the body of Regnault, painted his tragic oil study, *Henri Regnault Dead on the Battlefield* (Palais des Beaux-Arts de Lille). Another eyewitness, an American volunteer who was on the battlefield digging graves, stated that Regnault's fiancé was there:

> We saw out there, the young lady who was soon to have married Henri Regnault. She was looking for his body among the dead and found it during the day. The memory of that sweet, brave girl in that awful scene has lent a pathos to the story of his life and death which I do not get out of the writers and painters who have since dwelt so much and so lovingly upon the subject. [93]

This academic romantic-realist painter of absolute genius was widely mourned. The acclaimed history painter Ernest Meissonier called Henri Regnault the 'future of French art' and the greatest artist of his generation in his funeral oration on 27 January, the day before France surrendered to Prussia. Meissonier's 1884 oil, *The Siege of Paris*, features Regnault as the fallen hero against the personification of Paris at the centre of the painting. His composer friend, Camille Saint-Saëns dedicated his *Marche Héroique* (1871) to the dead painter. Regnault paid the ultimate price for Paris, but given the quality of his art, and the future treasures he was yet to paint, one wishes he hadn't. Indeed, his death was too heavy a loss from this needless conflict, and France was less for the war and for Regnault's death.

Henri Regnault
Salome, 1870, oil on canvas, 160 × 102.9 cm (63 × 40½ in)
Metropolitan Museum of Art , Gift of George F. Baker, 1916

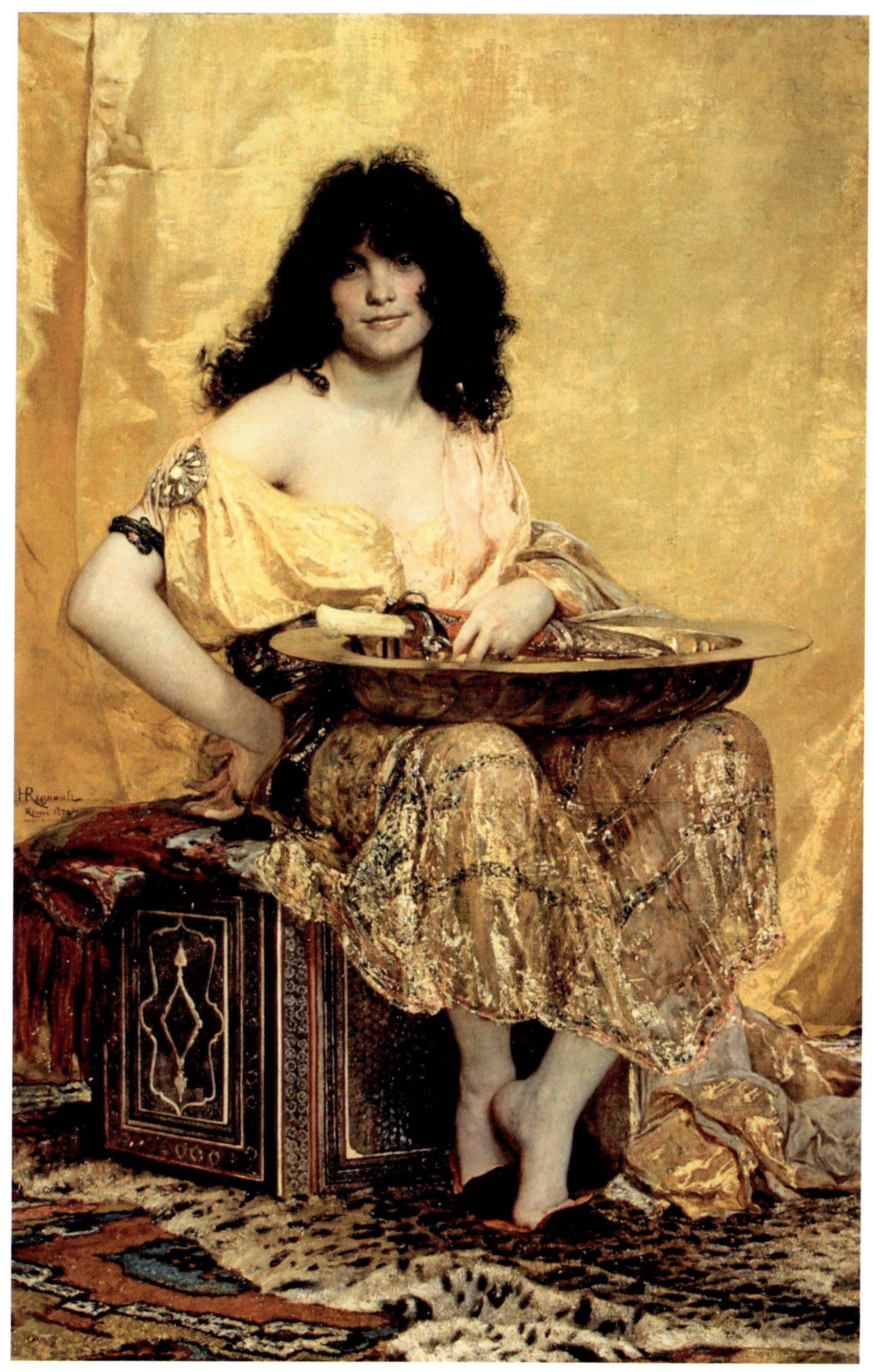

Elisabetta SIRANI

Bologna, 8 Jan 1638 – 28 Aug 1665, Bologna
Italian, 27 years, 7 months, 21 days [94]

Elisabetta was a baroque painter of the Bolognese School and the daughter-student of the artist Giovanni Andrea Sirani (1610–1670), who had studied under the famous Guido Reni. He was initially hesitant to tutor her in art, but was persuaded by Carlo Cesare Malvasia, a family friend and writer on the Bolognese School of Painters. Elisabetta quickly mastered the craft, and some scholars believe she overshadowed her father. She is most noted for her religious, historical, allegorical and portrait paintings, which have an elegant, compelling dynamism. This is made obvious when compared to the earlier Bolognese female artist Lavinia Fontana, whose work is more timid. After Artemisia Gentileschi, Sirani was probably the strongest female artist of her time in Europe.

When her father became incapacitated by gout in 1654, Sirani ran the family studio and workshop at age 16. Between student fees and painting commissions she was able to support her parents, siblings, the studio and herself, entirely through her art. She was a prolific artist, known for the rapidity of her painting metre. At the time of her early death she had prodigiously painted more than 200 pictures, for which she achieved great fame. Because of her gracious personality, artistic talent and ability to satisfactorily complete commissions, a cult blossomed around her and she was humorously called the reincarnation of Guido Reni. Laura Ragg wrote of her in glowing terms: 'She has so much self-assurance, and so little self-consciousness, that their [visitors to the studio] presence is no embarrassment to her.' [95]

Sirani established an art school which, like Bologna itself, was progressive. She schooled her two sisters (Barbara and Anna Maria) and at least 12 other women as well as a number of men, in painting. Her atelier was certainly the first to encourage professionally directed females towards painting careers, not just finishing-school drawing classes. Because the school was unique in her day, it was possibly Sirani's single most significant contribution to the art of the baroque period.

Her oil *Ten Thousand Crucified Martyrs* scandalously depicting male nudity as a lady artist, also contributed to enlarging the range of artistic expression to which a woman could aspire. Her painting *Judith*

Elisabetta Sirani
Allegory of Painting (Self-Portrait), 1658, oil on canvas, size unknown
Pushkin State Museum of Fine Arts, Moscow/Alamy

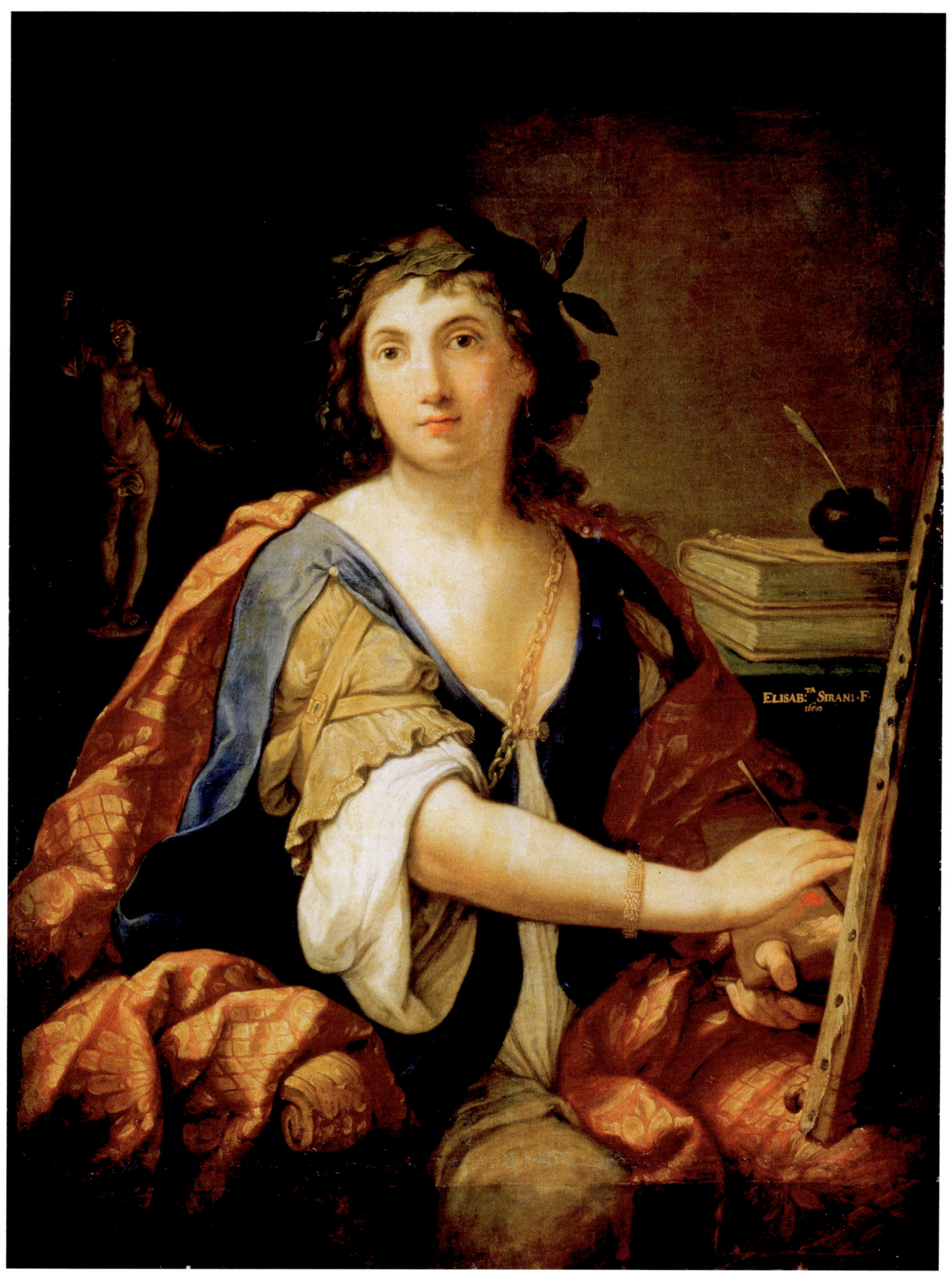

ELISAB.TA SIRANI ·F·
1660

with the Head of Holofernes attests to her being a significant artist in her own right. Sirani's prices at auction also validate her art historical significance: *Portia Wounding Her Thigh* (1664) sold in 2008 for $505,000 (£390,000), and *Finding of Moses* (date unknown) sold for $216,200 (£167,000) in 2018 at the Dorotheum in Vienna. Recently, the National Museum of Women in the Arts in Washington, D.C. acquired her laudatory *Virgin and Child* (1663).

The circumstances of her early death are mysterious. In the spring of 1665, Sirani grew depressed and became underweight with an undiagnosed stomach ailment that triggered her sudden demise in August of that year. The city of Bologna mourned her death with a large, elaborate public funeral. One official wrote, 'She is mourned by all. The ladies especially those whose portraits she flattered, cannot hold their peace about it. Indeed, it is a great misfortune to lose so great an artist in so strange a manner.' In eulogy, the artist was honoured as 'the glory of the female sex, the gem of Italy, the sun of Europe'.[96]

Bereft, her father's mind became entangled in conspiracy theories surrounding her death. He blamed her maid, charging her with poisoning his daughter's meals out of jealousy. The court exiled and then acquitted the maid. More theories abounded. For example, Sirani never married and Carlo Malvasia believed that it was not poisoning, but love sickness and her father (who had run off any suitors) that were to blame for her early death: '[This] vivacious and spirited woman, concealing to the highest degree her craving for a perhaps coveted husband denied to her by her father.'

Remaining suspicious, local authorities finally had the young artist's remains exhumed, and an autopsy revealed that she died of a perforated stomach – the combined effect of stress, exhaustion and gastric ulcers. Others felt that her demanding father was culpable for her death from a stomach ulcer due to overwork and unrelenting responsibility. More recent opinion blames her death on the natural onset of peritonitis.[97] In recognition of her significant contribution to art and by the consent of her many admirers, Sirani was laid to rest beside the artist Guido Reni in the Basilica of San Domenico, Bologna.

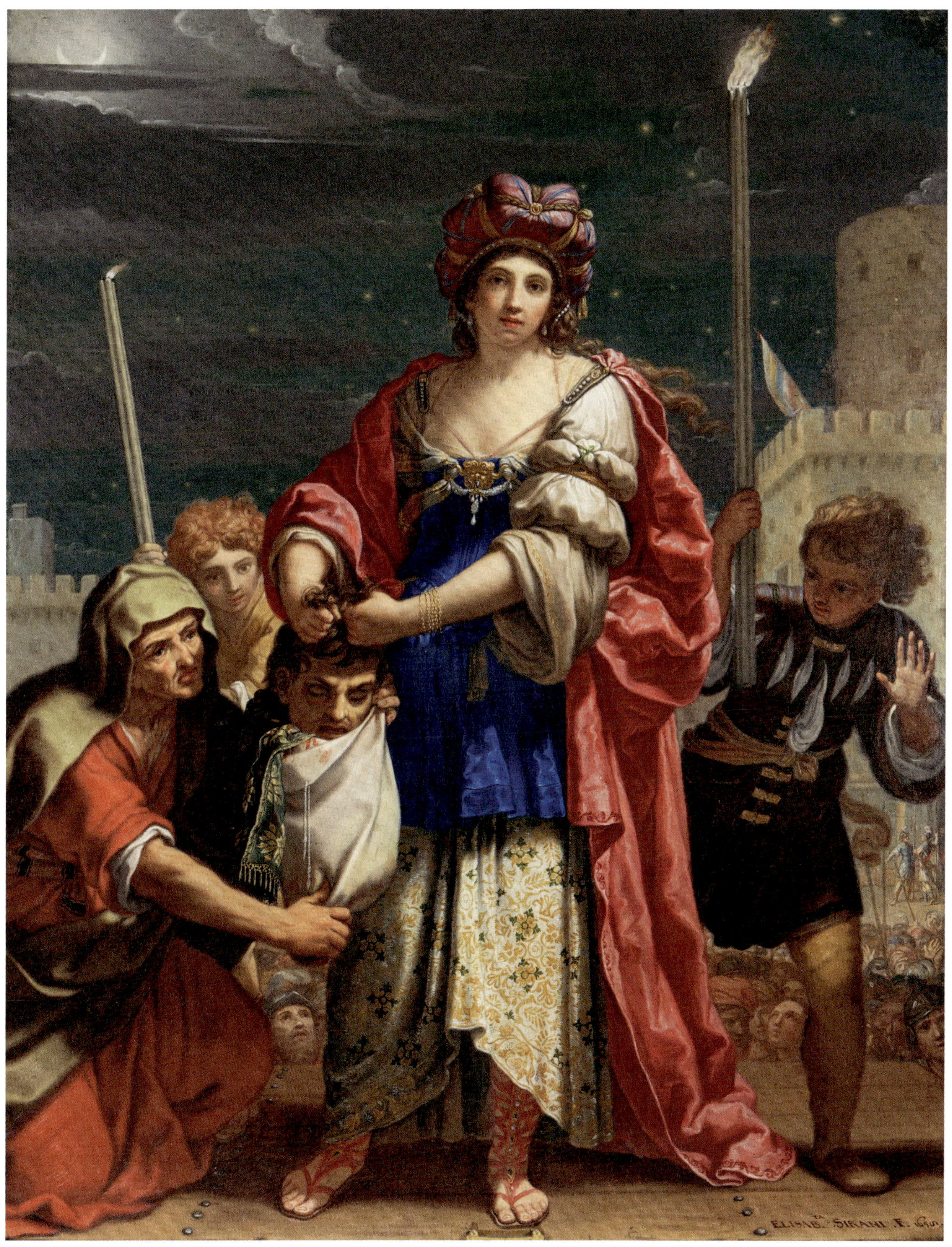

Age
28

Lucia ANGUISSOLA

(Jean) Frédéric BAZILLE

Wilhelm Ferdinand BENDZ

Bartolomeo BISCAINO

Pauline BOTY

Arnoldo CORRODI

Ilse D'HOLLANDER

Thomas FOSTER, ARHA

Eva FRANKFURTHER

Brian HATTON

(Johann) August HEINRICH

Laurent 'Gaston' JACQUOT-DEFRANCE

Ernst KLIMT

Dean Allan MILLMAN

Isack Jansz. van OSTADE

Petr Stipanovich PETROVSKY

Paulus Pietersz POTTER

Hugh RAMSAY

Peter RINDISBACHER

Antonio SANT'ELIA

Egon SCHIELE

Amrita SHER-GIL

Geertgen tot SINT JANS

Bob THOMPSON

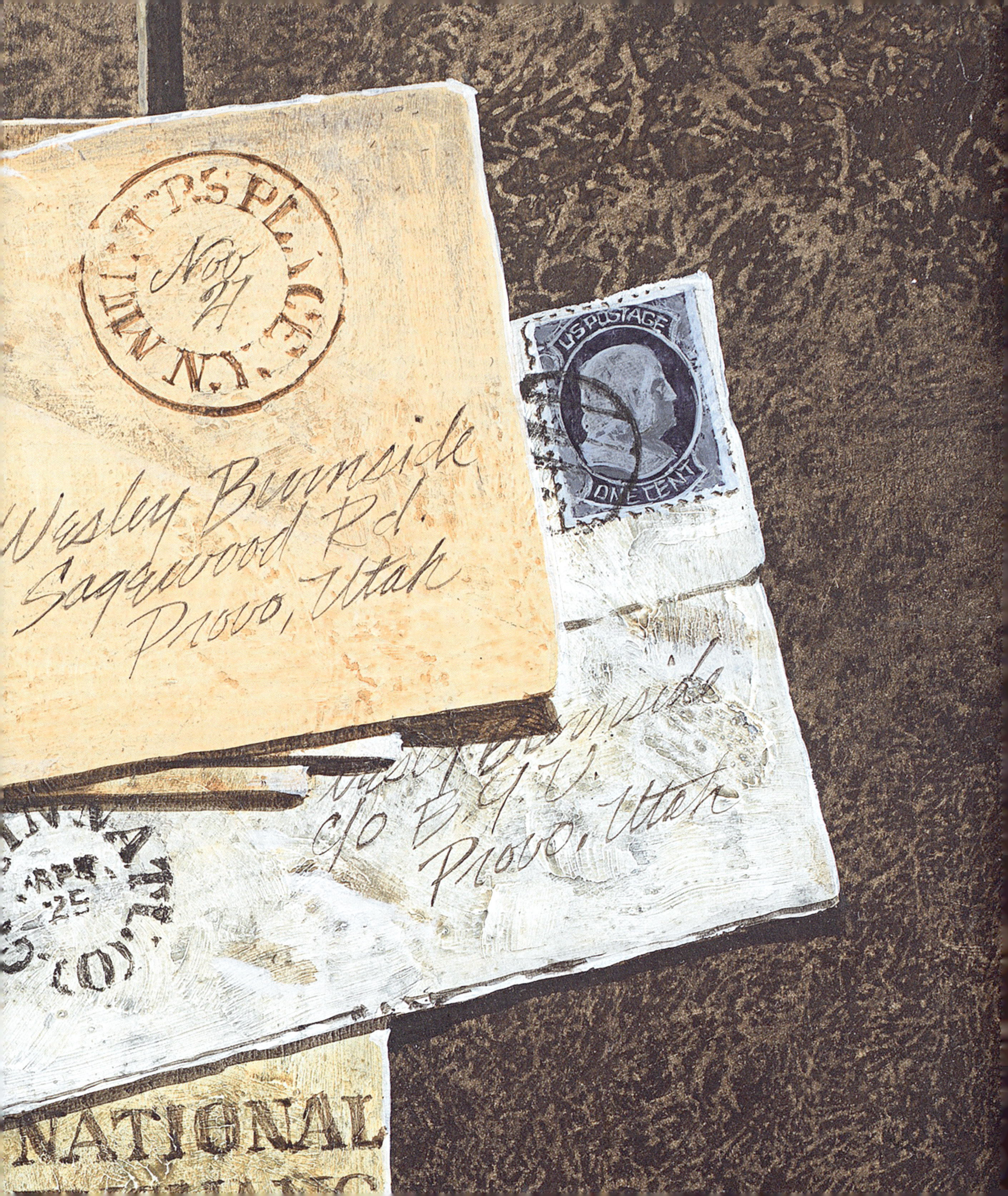
U.S. MILL'T P.S PEACE
Nov
27
N.Y.
US POSTAGE
ONE CENT
Wesley Burnside
Sagewood Rd.
Provo, Utah
Wesley Burnside
c/o B.Y.U.
Provo, Utah
NATI TL
APR
25
COL
NATIONAL

Lucia ANGUISSOLA

Cremona, c.1537 – 1565, Cremona
Italian, approx. 28 years [98]

Lucia Anguissola was the third of six sisters and one brother from a noble Cremona family in Lombardy. The father, Amilcare, believed in the ideas of Baldassare Castiglione – that education was as important to young women as it was to men. Therefore, all the Anguissola children received a well-rounded education and were encouraged in several arts. Remarkably, five of the sisters became painters, the eldest two, Sofonisba and Elena, even completed professional art apprenticeships; a very unconventional education for females during the Italian Renaissance.

While three of the sisters abandoned art careers upon their marriage and admission to a convent, Sofonisba and Lucia pursued painting for the rest of their lives. While Lucia died desperately young at about 28 years, Sofonisba lived to be 93 years old and gained immense international fame during her lifetime. Her paintings are in the collections of some of the world's foremost museums.

Lucia was trained by Sofonisba along with her less-talented sisters Europa and Anna Maria. Like her elder sister, Lucia specialised in portraiture. She may have been introverted because little else is known about her personally, while her elder sister was noted for her social skills. In contrast to Sofonisba's numerous surviving works, Lucia's meagre oeuvre amounts to just a handful of signed paintings. However, the talent evidenced in her small body of work led the 17th-century art historian Filippo Baldinucci (1624–1696) to state that if Lucia had not died so young, she had the potential to have 'become a better artist than even Sofonisba.' [99] Additionally, Sofonisba expert Dr Marie Kusche is of the opinion that Lucia's short-lived artistic career 'was as promising as that of Sofonisba herself.' [100]

When the famed artist and art writer Giorgio Vasari (1511–1574) visited the Anguissola family in 1566, Lucia had died the year before, but he praised her portrait *Pietro Manna, Physician from Cremona*. This painting now hangs in the Prado Museum in Madrid. There are no details on how Lucia died, history's pages are closed and those details are unforthcoming. If Lucia had lived, it is possible that she would have enjoyed a modicum of the same fame and royal patronage as Sofonisba. However, Lucia's paintings *Virgin and Child* and *Self-Portrait* (1557) in the Castello Sforzesco in Milan, though fine, do not elicit any great confidence that Baldinucci was correct.

Lucia Anguissola
Self-Portrait, 1557, oil on panel, 28 × 20 cm (11 × 7⅞ in)
Castello Sforzesco, Milan

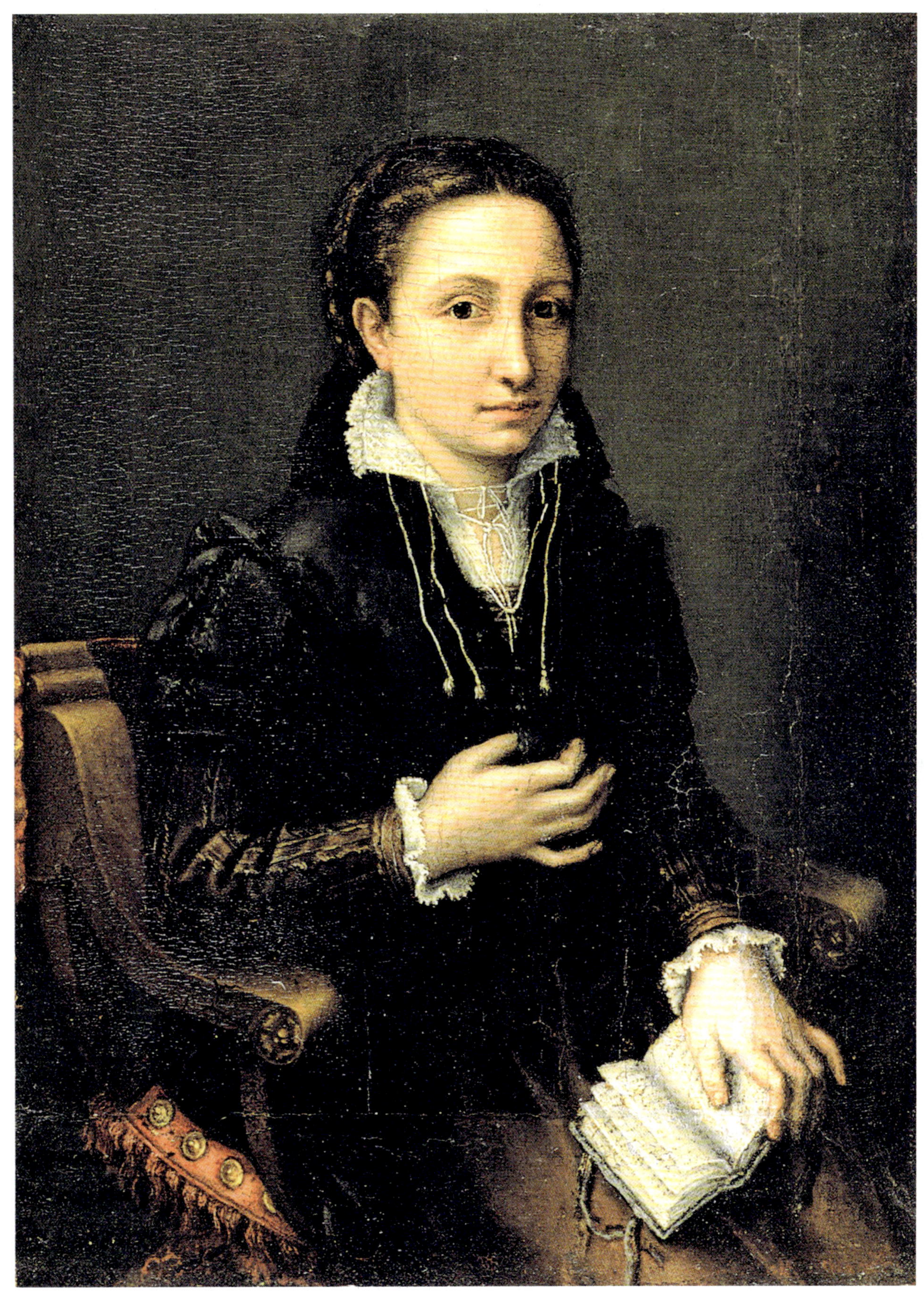

(Jean) Frédéric BAZILLE

Montpellier, 6 Dec 1841 – 28 Nov 1870, battlefield, Beaune-la-Rolande, France
French, 28 years, 11 months, 23 days

Born of wealthy parents in South West France, Bazille became interested in art after seeing a work by romantic artist Eugène Delacroix (1798–1863). His family, however, insisted that he pursue a career in medicine. Moving to Paris in 1862 he studied medicine, but he also enrolled in art classes at the studio of Swiss artist Charles Gleyre (1806–1874). There, by happenstance, he met and became close friends with Claude Monet (1840–1926), Pierre-Auguste Renior (1841–1919) and Alfred Sisley (1839–1899).

After Bazille failed his medical-studies exam in 1864, his family finally permitted him to take up painting full-time and even supported him financially. He worked closely with other French impressionist artists and offered his studio and art supplies to the more needy of them. The artist's oeuvre includes landscapes, nudes, studio interiors and portraits, but he is best known for his paintings of figures in plein-air such as *Family Reunion* (1867). Bazille frequently exhibited at the Paris Salon, however his painting *Bathers (Summer Scene)* received a mixed reception at the 1870 Salon, which the artist found discouraging.

Perhaps with a desire to prove himself after this disappointment, Bazille enlisted in the Zouave regiment in August 1870, just a month after the outbreak of the Franco-Prussian War. His friends Monet and Renior tried, in vain, to talk him out of it. His best friend, the musician Edmond Maître, called him 'stark raving mad'.[101] Bazille, however, persisted and was first sent to Algeria for training before returning to France for the Battle of Beaune-la-Rolande.

Bazille does not appear to have had a death wish, for on the eve of battle he is reported to have said, 'I have no intention of being killed, there's too much I still want to do with my life.' Nevertheless, when his officer was injured, he took command and led an assault. The artist was hit twice and died on the battlefield just a week before his 29th birthday. His grieving father travelled to the battlefield and recovered his riddled body. Bazille was buried in the Protestant cemetery of Montpellier where a beautiful monument still stands today in his honour.

His death must have been considered a waste by his artist friends because Renior bitterly recalled that 'He had not died romantically, galloping over a Delacroix battlefield; but pitifully, during the retreat, on a muddy road at Beaune la Rolande.'[102] Though he died several years before the impressionists' first exhibition in 1874, it is widely believed that if Bazille had lived he would have become one of the greatest of the first-line French impressionist painters. In fact his marvellous canvas still-life *Pots de Fleurs* of 1866 sold for $5,328,000 (£4,111,000) at Sotheby's New York in May 2004. His delightfully sensitive touch, observation and the vibrant use of colour with the new coal-tar pigments advocates for the eternal glory of his work; but death dreadfully rationed the size of that oeuvre.

Frédéric Bazille
Family Reunion (also known as *Family Portraits*), 1867, oil on canvas, 152 × 230 cm (59⅞ × 90½ in)
Musée d'Orsay, Paris

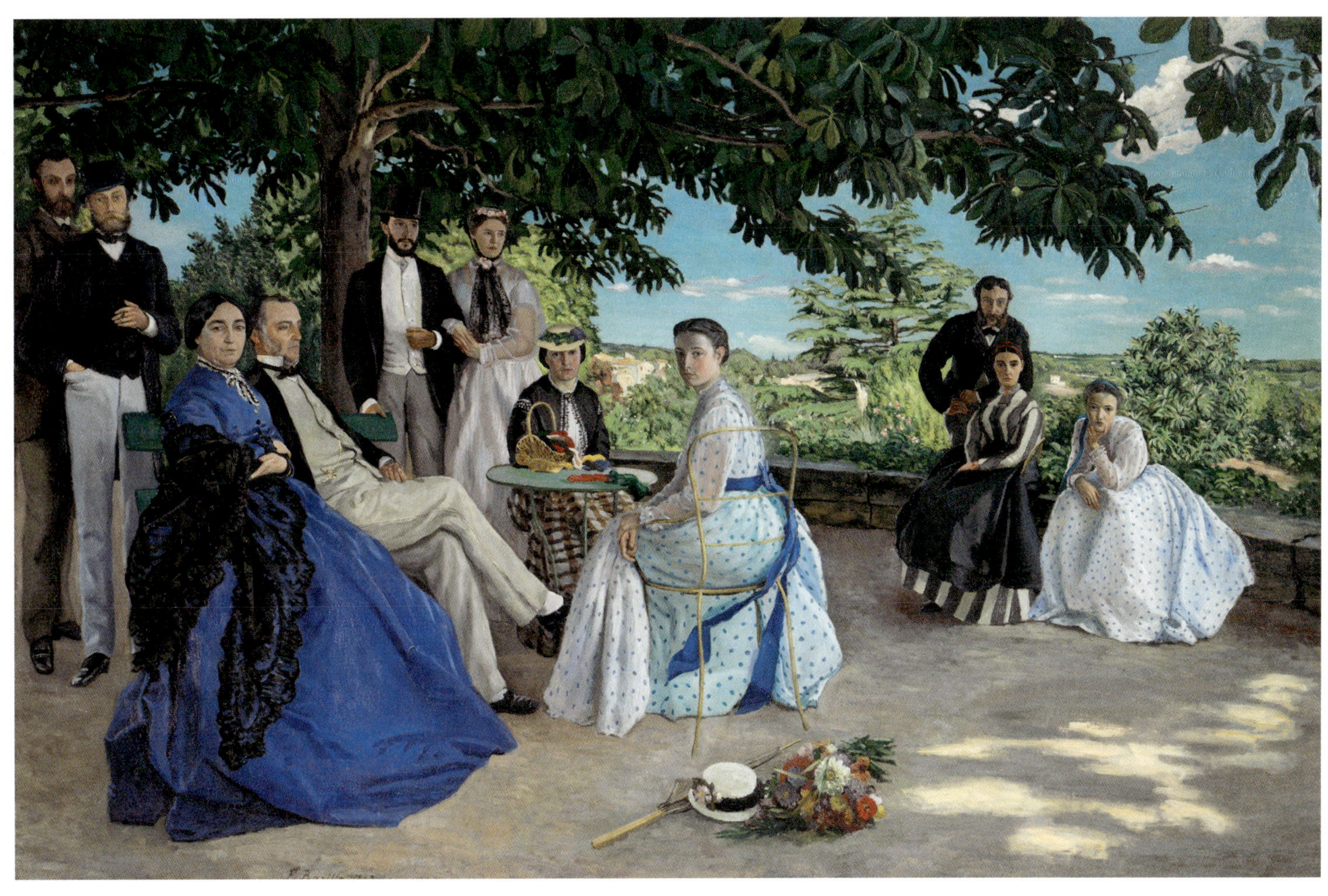

Wilhelm Ferdinand BENDZ

Odense, 20 Mar 1804 – 14 Nov 1832, Vicenza
Danish, 28 years, 7 months, 26 days

Wilhelm Bendz is considered one of the great talents of the Danish Golden Age. Born in Odense on the island of Funen, his father was a prominent country judge. He enrolled at the Royal Danish Academy of Fine Arts in Copenhagen (1820–25) where he studied under the most significant Danish artist of his day, Christopher Wilhelm Eckersberg (1783–1853). Bendz soon became one of his best students and acquired the nickname 'Excellent Bendz' from his teacher.[103] In 1825 he made an unsuccessful attempt to win the gold medal in history painting, which was considered the most prestigious genre at the time.

Because of this failure, he began to specialise in genre and portrait painting, at which he excelled. More importantly, he painted contemporary pictures often of his fellow art students in class and in their daily activities. Danish art began to flourish at this time, and Bendz was one of the talented young artists who ushered in this new Golden Age. Bendz's depictions of this new group of artists show them to be not just craftsmen but important members of the intellectual community of Denmark.

After graduation, Bendz contributed to the annual exhibitions at Charlottenburg in 1826, 1827 and 1828. Three of these paintings were acquired by the Danish Royal Painting Collection, including *The Life Class at the Royal Academy of Fine Arts* (1826) and the fascinating oil *A Young Artist Examining a Sketch in a Mirror* (1826), in which Bendz gives the viewer insight into the working methods of an artist. In late 1830, he received a travel scholarship which enabled him to visit southern Europe. After shorter trips to Dresden and Berlin, he journeyed to Munich in 1831. This city was becoming a vibrant artistic centre and Bendz stayed there for about a year because of the 'art scene' and a commission from King Ludwig. He painted the mountain landscape of Bavaria and completed his most important work from this time, a group portrait titled *Artists in the Evening at Finck's Coffee House in Munich* (1832).

Then, in the autumn of 1832, Bendz continued his journey towards Rome with two artist friends. The group crossed the Alps to Trieste and then sailed to Venice – a strenuous journey. Though Bendz felt ill with severe abdominal pains in Venice, they continued travelling towards Rome on foot, passing through Padua and finally Vicenza. Upon arrival, Bendz immediately went to bed, and though he was under a doctor's care, he died within days. The cause of death has been variously reported, but typhoid fever seems the likely culprit.[104] Bendz never made it to Rome, though one wonders what salient effect his study of antiquity and the Renaissance would have had on his art. Bendz left a small oeuvre on account of his academically demanding technique, ambitious pictures, and short life. He certainly was one of the brightest stars of Denmark's most successful artistic generation, and his death was a serious loss to the Danish school of painting.

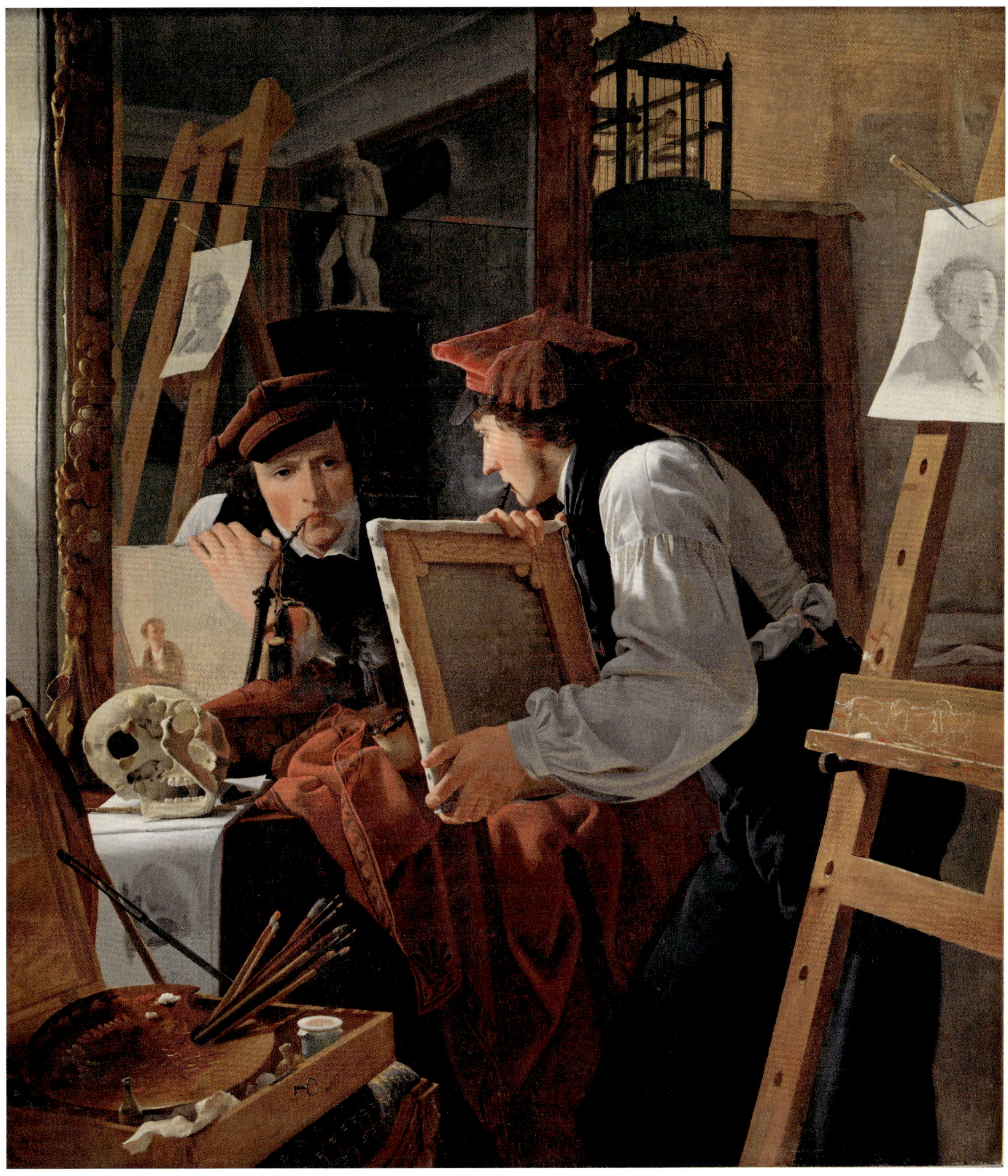

Bartolomeo BISCAINO

Genoa, baptised 14 Apr 1629 – 1657, Genoa [105]
Italian, approx. 28 years

Bartolomeo Biscaino was the son and pupil of the baroque artist Giovanni Andrea Biscaino (1605–1657) in Genoa, Italy. Giovanni was considered only a 'mediocre landscape painter'. [106] However, his early artistic instruction effectively jump-started Bartolomeo's career and allowed him to produce a fair number of fine works before his early death. In about 1650, Bartolomeo began his studies under the noted Ligurian painter, Valerio Castello (1624–1659) where his work took on the essence of sfumato (smokiness). This year also marks the earliest known work by the artist, *St Ferrando in the Act of Imploring the Virgin* (c.1650, Museo di Sant' Agostino, Genoa). Although *St Ferrando* is an immature work, Biscaino soon developed a more vivid style of nuanced colour and light.

Biscaino was greatly inspired by Rubens, Parmigianino and Pellegro Piola. In his many drawings and 40 known etchings, one can also detect the influence of Genoan artist Giovanni Benedetto Castiglione (1609–1664). Indeed, Biscaino's graphic work is what he is best known for today. The British Museum owns a large collection of his prints and the J. Paul Getty Museum houses his sweeping baroque drawing *Mystic Marriage of Saint Catherine* (c.1655). This excellent chalk and gouache work demonstrates the artist's mastery of composition and expression, and use of light.

The attribution of Biscaino's oil paintings has proven troublesome. What were thought to be his three greatest paintings in the Dresden Gemäldegalerie are now reattributed to his teacher Valerio Castello. Fortunately, canvases from private collections and institutions occasionally appear on the art market, giving a rare glimpse of his talent. His oil *The Flight into Egypt* (Chiswick Collection) has a grace and vitality which is the hallmark of the best artists. Had he lived, Biscaino's star would have beamed much brighter in the constellation of artistic talents.

Just as Biscaino was achieving a personal style, his career was cut short by the plague. This catastrophe menaced Genoa, beginning in July 1656 with the deaths of 10,000 souls and the following year with 70,000 more. Only 14,000 inhabitants of Genoa were spared. Both Biscaino and his father fell victim to its grip, one right after the other in quick succession. Biscaino's artist friend and fellow pupil of Castello, Giovanni Paolo Cervetto (c.1630–1657), likewise fell victim to the plague. Unlike many other early deaths of talented artists where the loss is lamented with great grieving, Biscaino's death was just one among thousands and hardly noted by recorders who were stricken down themselves. He is buried in a nameless mass grave, the day of his death forgotten.

Bartolomeo Biscaino
Mystic Marriage of Saint Catherine, c.1655, red chalk and white gouache, 28.9 × 39.8 cm (11⅜ × 15⅝ in)
J. Paul Getty Museum, Los Angeles, Digital image courtesy of the Getty's Open Content Program

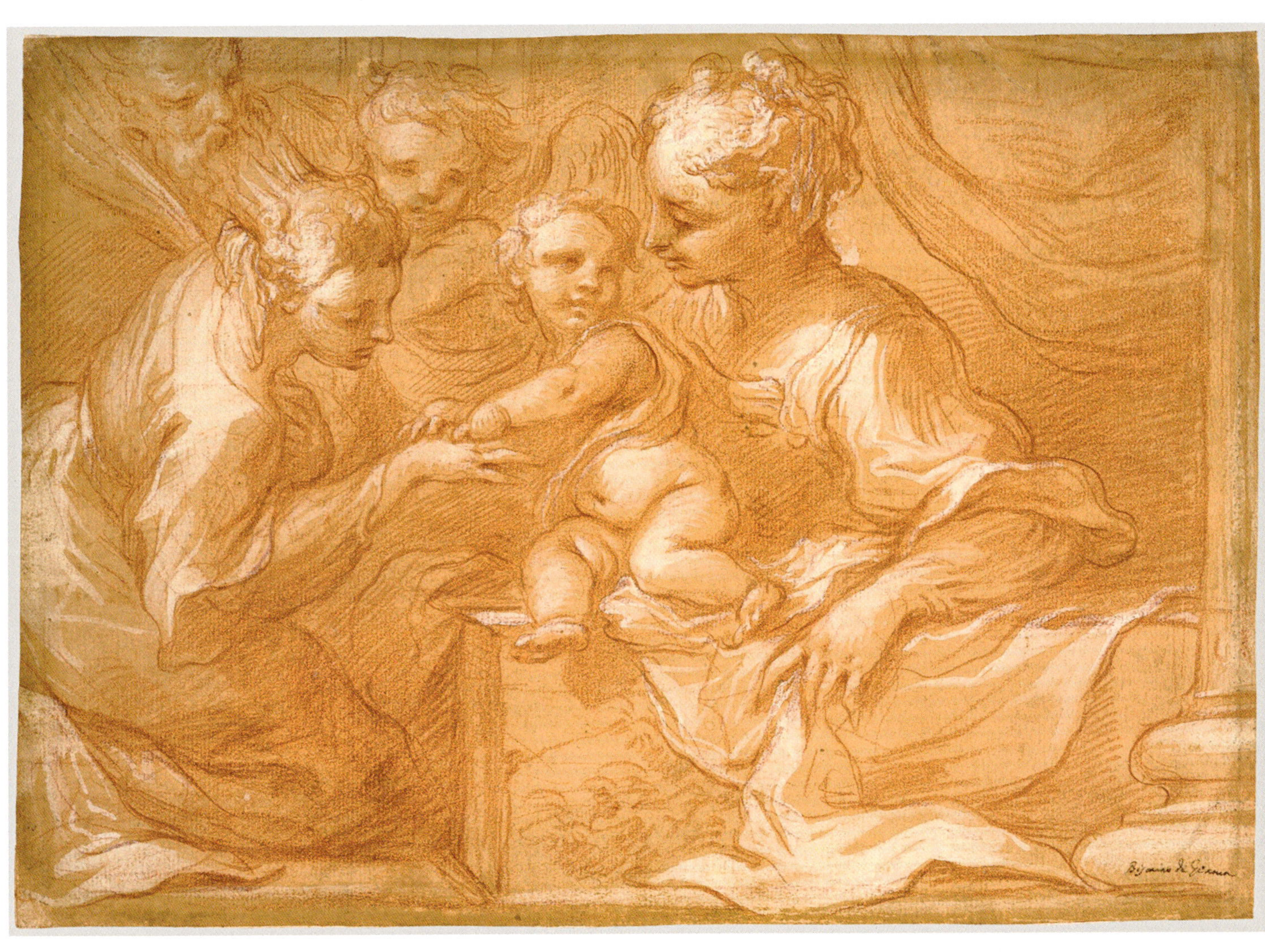

Pauline BOTY

Carshalton, 6 Mar 1938 – 1 Jul 1966, London
British, 28 years, 3 months, 26 days

Boty was one of the founders of the British pop art movement, and the movement's only serious female painter. She made paintings and collages that displayed a confident femininity and sexuality. Through her 'rebellious' art she critiqued the 'man's world' and became a second-wave feminist icon. In 1963, she declared on The Public Ear radio programme, 'A revolution is on the way … All over the country, young girls are starting, shouting and shaking, and if they terrify you, they mean to, and they are beginning to impress the world.'

How did she come about? Boty studied at the Wimbledon School of Art, where she was called the 'Wimbledon Bardot' because of her stunning good looks, personality and blonde hair. Then she attended the Royal College of Art in London. By 1960 Boty had begun to develop her own style of pop art, somewhat reminiscent of James Rosenquist, and in 1961 she exhibited at her first pop group show. She was also featured in Ken Russell's film *Pop Goes the Easel* (1962) alongside pop art legends Peter Blake, Peter Phillips and Derek Boshier. That same year, Boty painted *Colour Her Gone*, of the recently deceased Marilyn Monroe. However, painting was not her only interest. Boty was a radio presenter and performed in numerous plays and minor television roles. In April of 1965 she had a bit part in the film, *Alfie* starring Michael Caine.

Boty married left-wing actor and writer Clive Goodwin in 1963 after a 10-day romance, because he was the very first man she had met who 'really liked women'. A year and a half later she became pregnant.

During a prenatal examination, a tumour was discovered and she was diagnosed with cancer. She refused an abortion or to undertake the much-needed chemotherapy, fearing her baby might be harmed. She did this brave act knowing she would not survive herself. A baby girl, named Katy 'Boty' Goodwin was born in February 1966 and the artist died five months later.

Because of her short life and competing acting career, the body of her work is not large. Art being such a jealous master, her many interests compromised the depth she might have otherwise attained. Had she lived, who knows what may have lay ahead artistically for her. She certainly would not have become forgotten, but would have obtained colossus status with her self-perpetuating iconic stature. For nearly 30 years, Boty's paintings were stored in a barn on her brother's farm and were nearly thrown away a number of times.

Her reassessment began with the 1993 Barbican exhibition *The Sixties Art Scene in London* that proved her significance to the British pop movement. *Time Out* stated: 'Boty's paintings shower with critical blows the macho stance of Pop.'[107] Hers was not the only early death to plague the family. Twelve years later her husband Clive died of a brain haemorrhage. Tragedy struck again in 1995 when their daughter Boty died of a heroin overdose. She was only 29 years old. It is said that bad luck always comes in threes, and such was the case for the unfortunate Boty/Goodwin family.

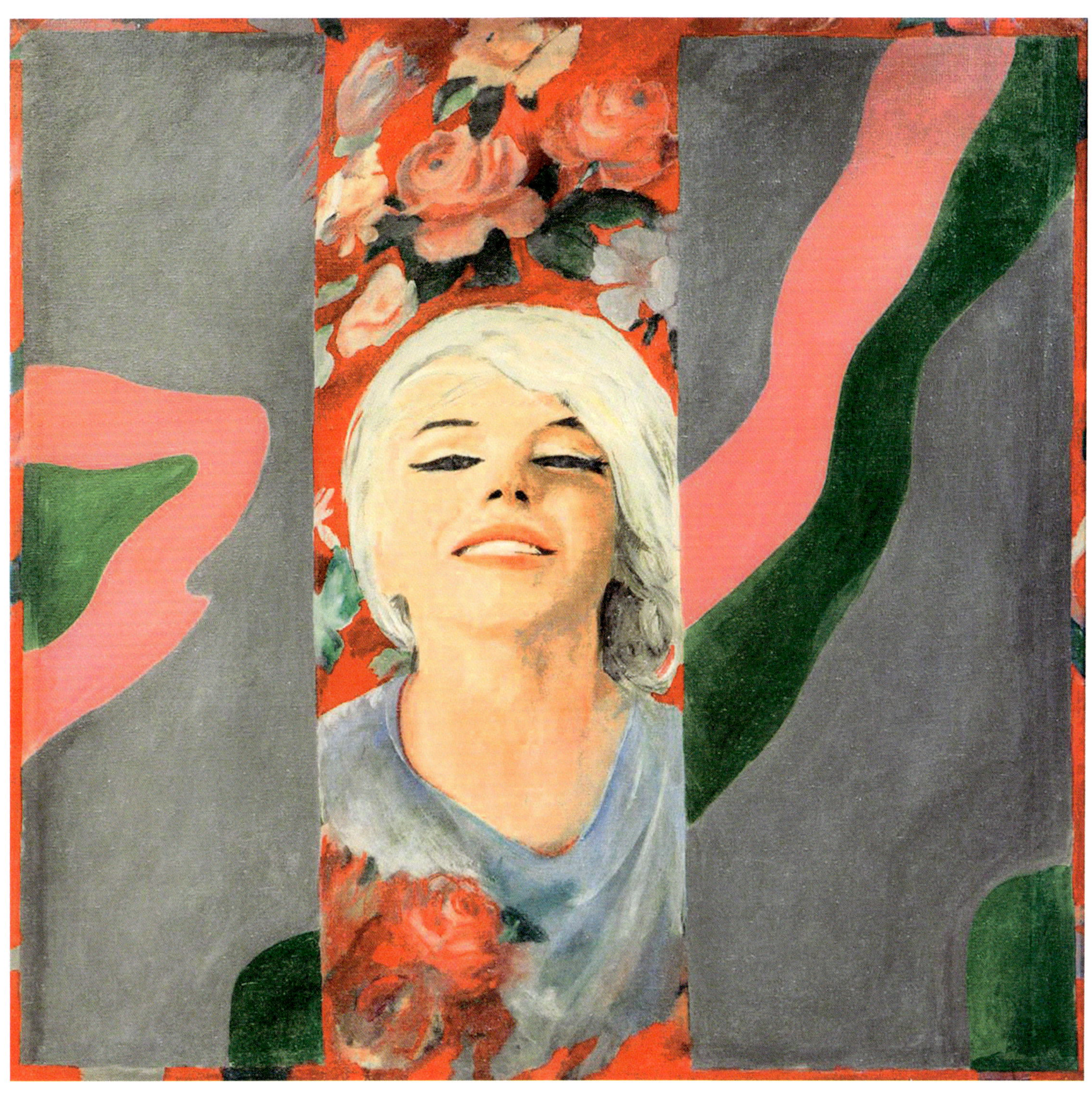

Arnoldo CORRODI

Rome, 12 Jan 1846 – 7 May 1874, Rome
Italian, 28 years, 3 months, 26 days

Arnoldo Corrodi was the youngest son of the Swiss-Italian watercolourist Salomon Corrodi (1810–1892) and younger brother of the famous painter Hermann David Salomon Corrodi (1844–1905). The brothers were best friends and nearly inseparable. They first studied with their father, who was a professor at the Academy of St Luke in Rome. In 1860, the 14-year-old Arnoldo and his brother went on a study trip to Geneva and stayed there for several years, studying under Alexander Calame and Alfred van Muyden. At some point Arnoldo also attended the studio of history painter August Weckesser in Rome. For several dizzying years, the Corrodi brothers travelled together, most notably to Paris where, in 1872, Arnoldo exhibited a genre painting at the Paris Salon, *Children Collecting Flowers.*

Like his father, Arnoldo was a figurative and landscape painter, and like Hermann, he was a landscape and Orientalist painter. Inspired by the Spanish painter Mariano Fortuny, Arnoldo also created many lavish costume and history paintings, but his oeuvre subtly gravitated towards the rural genre and intimate painting. In Rome, Arnoldo and Hermann shared a studio. Arnoldo was a productive painter and pursued engraving as well. Unfortunately, it will never be possible to fully assess his abilities because in 1892 a fire at Hermann's studio destroyed much of the brother's art. It can be said, however, that Arnoldo was an excellent artist, although, because of his truncated career, Hermann must be considered the greater of the two brothers.

In 1874, life was moving forward well for both brothers, when a figurative thunder-bolt struck. *The Magazine of Art* explains that 'Arnold [sic] Corrodi was seized with cerebral inflammation and died suddenly in 1874. It is difficult to exaggerate the effects of the blow upon the surviving brother.'[108] Hermann was devastated and stopped painting for almost two years.

The cessation of Arnoldo's life halted the stream of his sensitive Italian domestic life scenes. Each was touched with just the right amount of pathos, giving every canvas meaning. Implacable death intervening with artistic endeavour had no right to take him so soon. Being prolific assuaged the bite of his early death, allowing his hand to be seen assiduously at work on many canvases. The year before he died, Arnoldo painted a joyous fancy dress Venetian scene, *Gondola Ride* (1873, Basel Kunstmuseum) in which the artist shows off his joie de vivre. His work has increased in appreciation to this day, and the best word to define this Italian's work is 'Italianate'.

Arnoldo Corrodi
Gondola Ride, 1873, oil on panel, 41 × 61 cm (16⅛ × 24 in)
Alamy

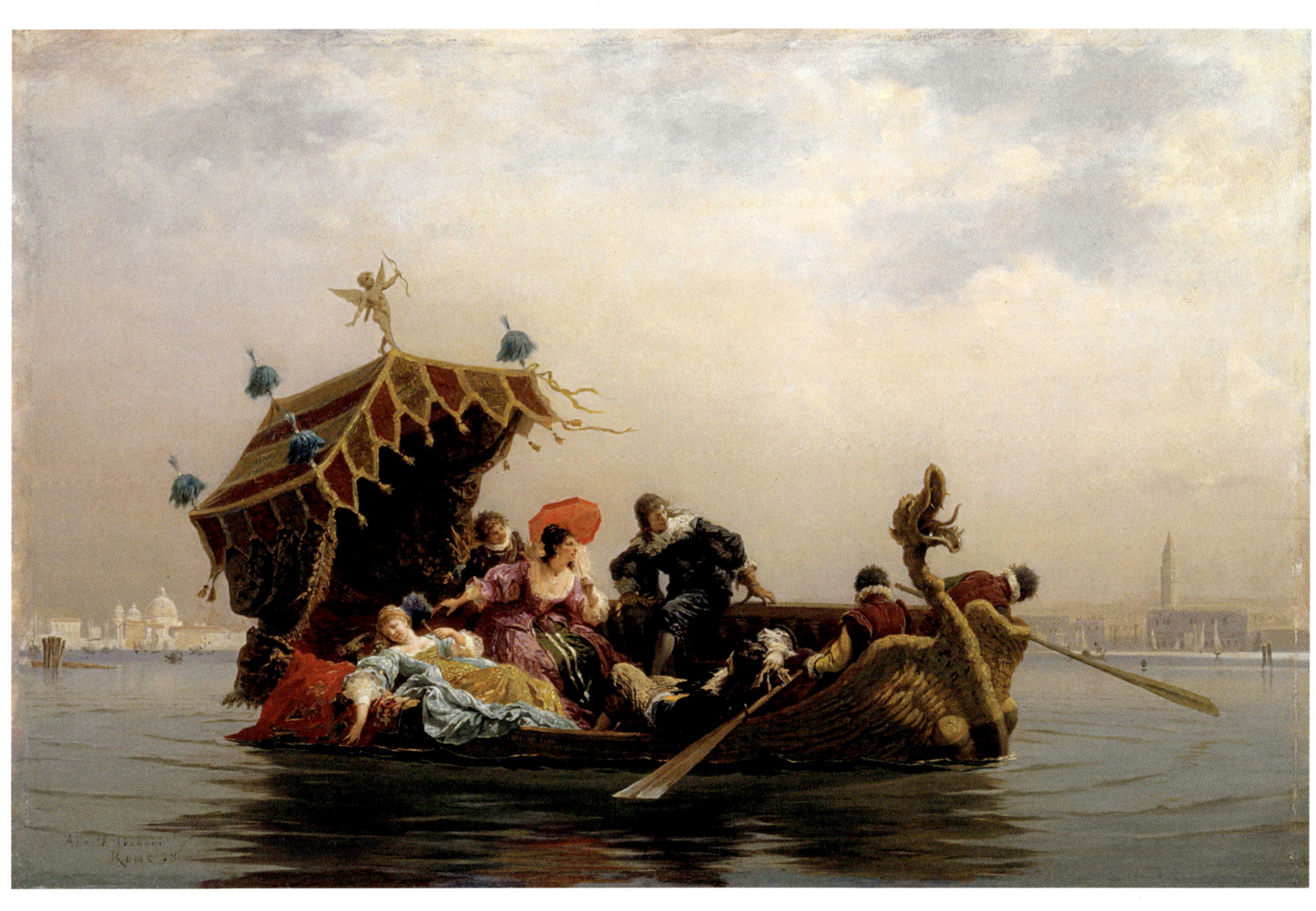

Ilse D'HOLLANDER

Sint-Niklaas, 18 May 1968 – 30 Jan 1997, Paulatem
Belgian, 28 years, 8 months, 13 days

Before her early death, D'Hollander would bicycle the fields of the Zwalm lowlands and the hilly Ardennes of Belgium, internalising the perception of the natural landscape. Flemish vistas, like the illustrated photograph, contributed to her aesthetic sense and are often referenced in her landscapes and abstract works. Following her art studies at the St Lucas Beeldende Kunst in Ghent, D'Hollander wrote her only existing artist's statement:

> A painting comes into being when ideas and the act of painting coincide. When referring to ideas, it implies that as a painter, I am not facing my canvas as a neutral being but as an active being who is investing into the art of painting.

Sometimes D'Hollander's abstract impressionist canvases and works on paper were small in scale, while at other times they were large and sweeping. She was influenced by Nicolas de Staël and by her friend and mentor Raoul de Keyser. Her expressive and deceptively economical paintings possess the subtle tonal essences of 'soft-edge' art. The linear parts of her painterly canvases have a decided hesitancy as she drags the brush across its surface. David Nash wrote of her work: 'Floating color fields in soft earthy shades evoke feelings of calm and tranquility.'[109]

During the last eight years of D'Hollander's life (1989–1997), her confidence and searching spirit seem to have become more focused and riveted, resulting in more than 500 paintings. Then, just as she was achieving aesthetic and critical acclaim, she unexpectedly ended her own life. Art critic for the *Observer*, Laura Cumming writes, 'Ilse D'Hollander was so young when she died that almost the first response to her work might be a kind of shocked sorrow to think of such brilliance so abruptly extinguished.'[110] Indeed, her tragic suicide imbues her art with a certain mystique and gravitas.

For more than a decade her oeuvre was stored at a friend's farm, then slowly it began to resurface and a renewal of interest brought her to public attention. Although she only had one show at an art café in Kelken during her lifetime, New York and London sales galleries have promoted her work through several solo and group exhibitions. Though numerous articles have been published analysing her art, none has described her death or the reasons behind it. The life of an artist confronting a bare canvas, with nowhere to hide, and insisting on being 'significant' is daunting at any age. But paintings such as *Untitled* (c.1997, oil on paper) with its brilliant zinc yellow thrown against grisaille softer colours, prove she still had it in her; or was it her quintessential 'last painting'?

Wouter Pattyn
Belgian landscape, windmill in field, photograph
Alamy

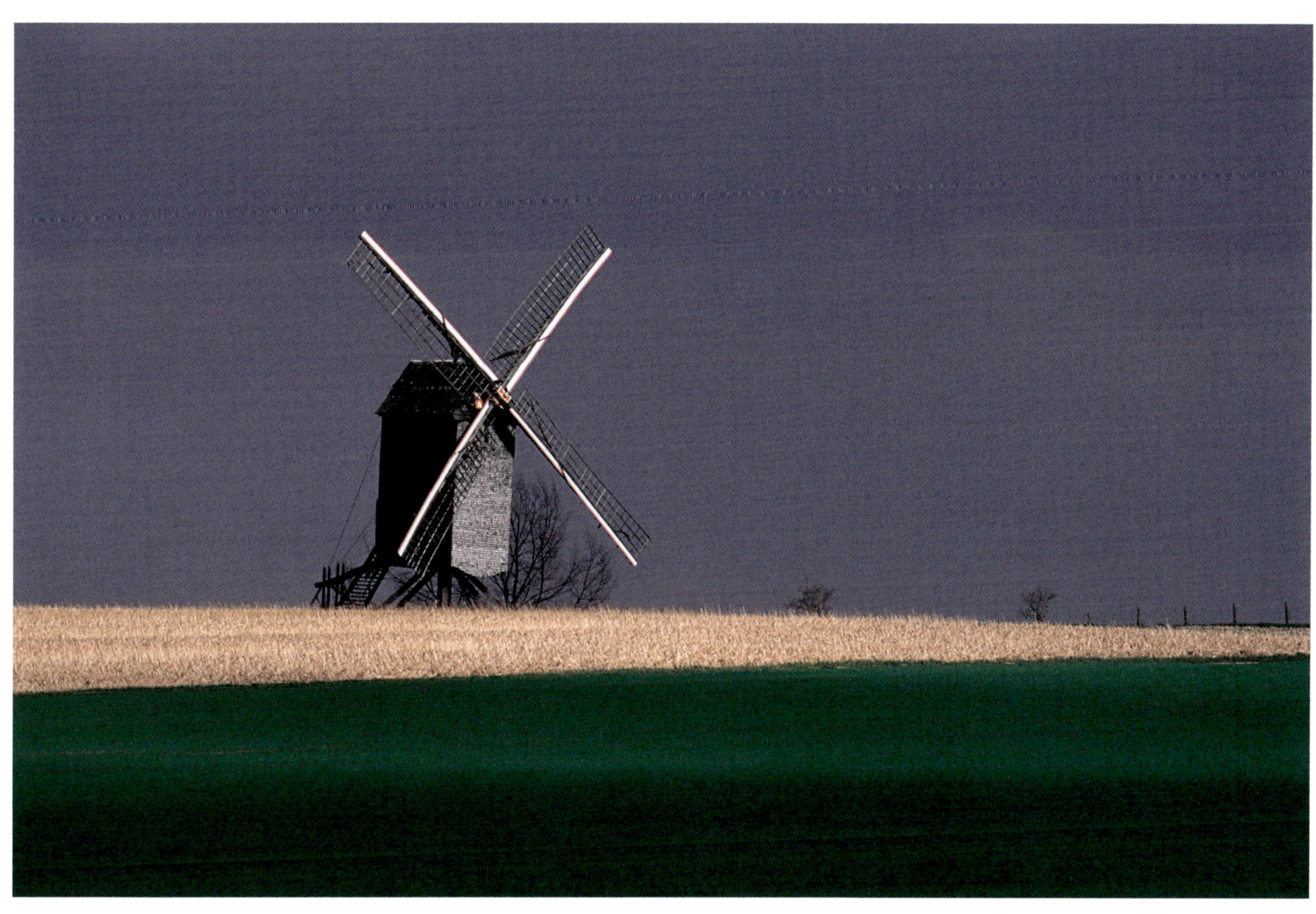

Thomas **FOSTER,** ARHA

Birr, County Offaly, 1798 – 28 Feb 1826, London
Irish, approx. 28 years

Supposedly the illegitimate son of Irish nobility, Foster was born in County Offaly, Ireland. His good looks, winning wit and exceptional talent promised a truly illustrious career. Showing an early gift for drawing, at the age of 13 Foster became the pupil of Robert Lucius West at the Royal Dublin Society's Art School. Aged 16, he sent three entries to the exhibition at the Hibernian Society of Arts and was awarded a cash prize of £34 2s. 6d., a princely sum in 1815.[111]

The ambitious young artist left Ireland in 1818 to study at the Royal Academy Schools in London. From 1819 to 1826, he exhibited regularly at the Academy's Summer Exhibitions. One notable entry was his *Portrait of Thomas Elrington, Provost of Trinity College* (1820), which was thereafter exhibited in Dublin. His talent attracted the patronage of the Right Hon. John Wilson Croker and through him Foster made friends with the leading portrait painter of the day, Sir Thomas Lawrence.

Foster painted, in the fashion of his day, an excellent portrait, *Sir Henry Rowley Bishop the Noted Composer* (c.1821), and Samuel Wm Reynolds made a quality mezzotint after this work. His remarkable ability to portray likenesses, and his pleasing personality, made him a successful society painter. When the Royal Hibernian Academy in Dublin was founded in 1823, Foster became one of its 10 associates and was by far the youngest. Foster was brilliantly orchestrating his career, and by all accounts his reputation was considered to be on the rise, but all was not

right. An entry in *A Dictionary of Irish Artists* elaborates:

> He was advancing rapidly in his profession, but his love of society, in which his agreeable manners and conversation made him popular, interfered with his art. According to Northcote he was good- looking, good-natured, and a wit. [Yet] His end was melancholy.[112]

Foster killed himself with a pistol in a Piccadilly hotel on 28 February 1826. The letter he left stated that his friends had deserted him for no reason and that he was tired of life, but the contributing factors appear to be far more complex than that. The previous year, his benefactor, John Wilson Croker, commissioned him to paint a large canvas of *Louis XVIII Receiving the Garter at Carlton House*, and after making many studies for it, Foster became dejected over the results.

At the same time, it is believed by some that Foster fell in love with the actress Anna Maria Tree of whom he painted a portrait. Ms Tree, however, had married the wealthy James Bradshaw in the summer of 1825, after her own earlier suicide attempt. The difficulties of a complex work of art coupled with a hopeless amorous attachment, and some unknown fracas with friends, conspired to destroy a life and career that was going places. Now he is lost to the world, but it is hoped that this book's small entry might revive the remembrance of this young talent.

Samuel Wm Reynolds
Portrait of Henry Rowley Bishop, Composer (1786–1855),
1822, mezzotint by Samuel Wm Reynolds after Foster's oil on canvas, 50.8 × 35.7 cm (20 × 14 in)
Private collection

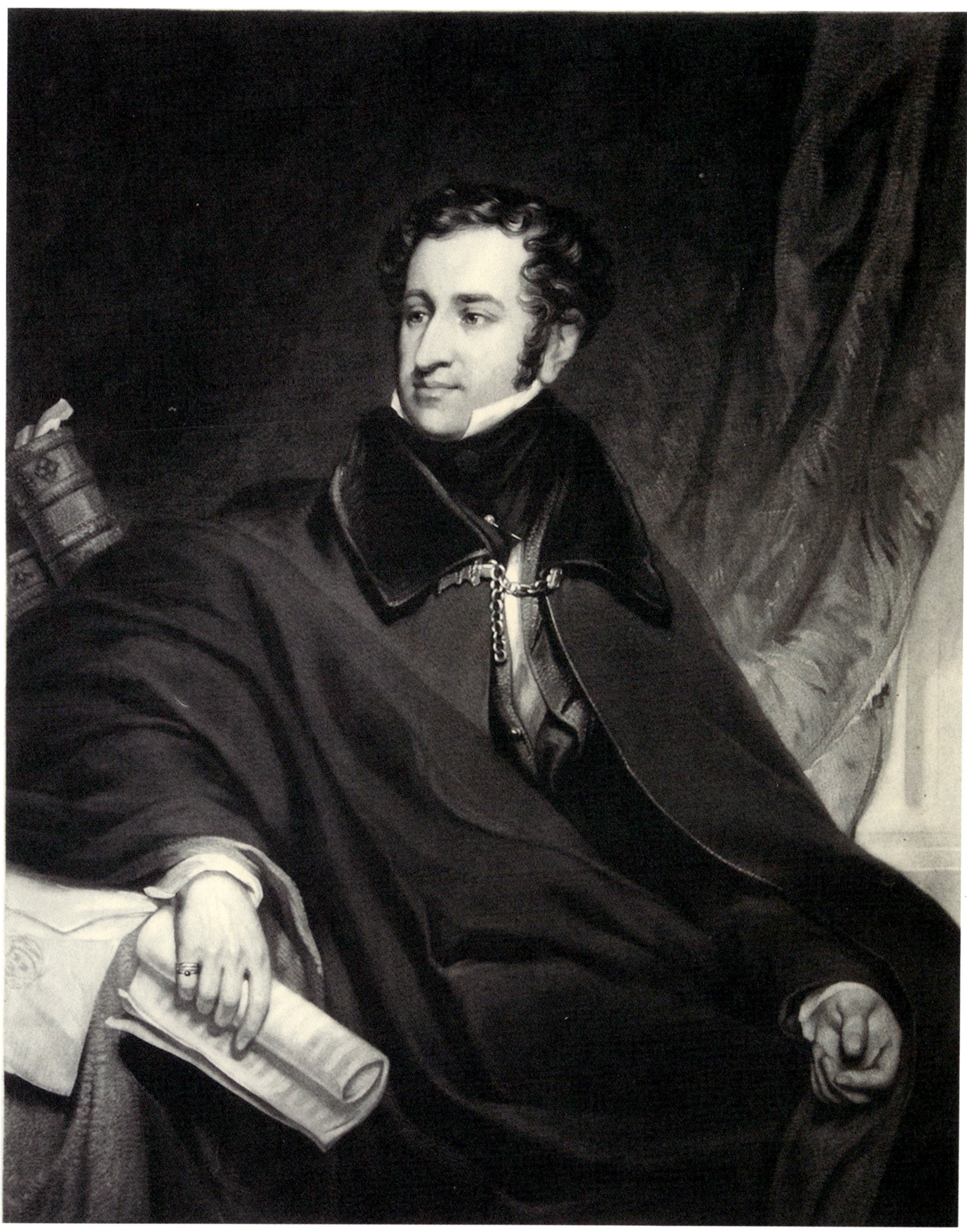

Eva FRANKFURTHER

Berlin, 10 Feb 1930 – Jan 1959, London
German/British, approx. 28 years, 10 months

Frankfurther's turbulent childhood, defined by upheaval and displacement, would play out to be a motivating force in the young artist's life, art and sudden death. Born to an educated Jewish family in Berlin, she lost her mother to cancer when she was just 18 months old. Her father – a successful businessman – remarried several years later but the family was soon in very real danger with the rise of Nazism in Germany. Frankfurther and her two siblings were sent by Kindertransport to a boarding school in England in April of 1939. Her father and stepmother followed in August 1939, on one of the last planes out of Germany. Reunited, the family eventually settled in London, but Eva and her elder sister were sent away again, this time to Hertfordshire for four years, as child evacuees from the London bombings of World War II.

In 1946, Frankfurther enrolled at St Martin's School of Art, where she studied for six years. Always carrying a sketch-book, she sketched everywhere she went, creating hundreds of life studies. With inspirations ranging from Rembrandt to Käthe Kollwitz and German expressionism, her art developed into a figurative expressionist style with loose brushwork and dry paint, focusing on people and their lives. Upon completion of her studies, Frankfurther shunned the mainstream London art scene and instead settled in a damp basement apartment in Whitechapel, working apart from other artists. Determinedly independent, Frankfurther worked nights as a dish-washer and counter-hand at Lyon's Corner House, and later as a labourer at a sugar refinery. During the day, she painted.

Passionate about people, especially those who, like herself, had been displaced, she depicted the residents of London's East End with its colourful Jewish and immigrant population. Her compelling portraits and intimate genre pictures are at times rather glum but reveal a tender sensitivity as in *Couple with Infant* (1956). They also give a historical view into 1950s London. Sarah MacDougall explains, 'this body of Frankfurther's work has a documentary value recording the changing face of a new multicultural Britain.'[113]

Unfortunately, Frankfurther was prone to frequent excessive mood swings. She was very self-critical and would occasionally destroy her art in frustration. Longing for brighter skies, she travelled to Italy, Greece and Israel for eight months. Unfortunately, returning to the grey London climate was too much for her and she became depressed again. Feeling uncertain about her artistic future, she applied to study social work at the London School of Economics, but in the end quietly committed suicide in January 1959. Frankfurther produced an impressive 200 oil paintings (all on paper), some etchings and hundreds of drawings. The Ben Uri Gallery explains her legacy: 'Despite the brevity of her artistic career, she left behind an important body of work based above all on compassion for the dignity of ordinary working people of all races and communities.'[114]

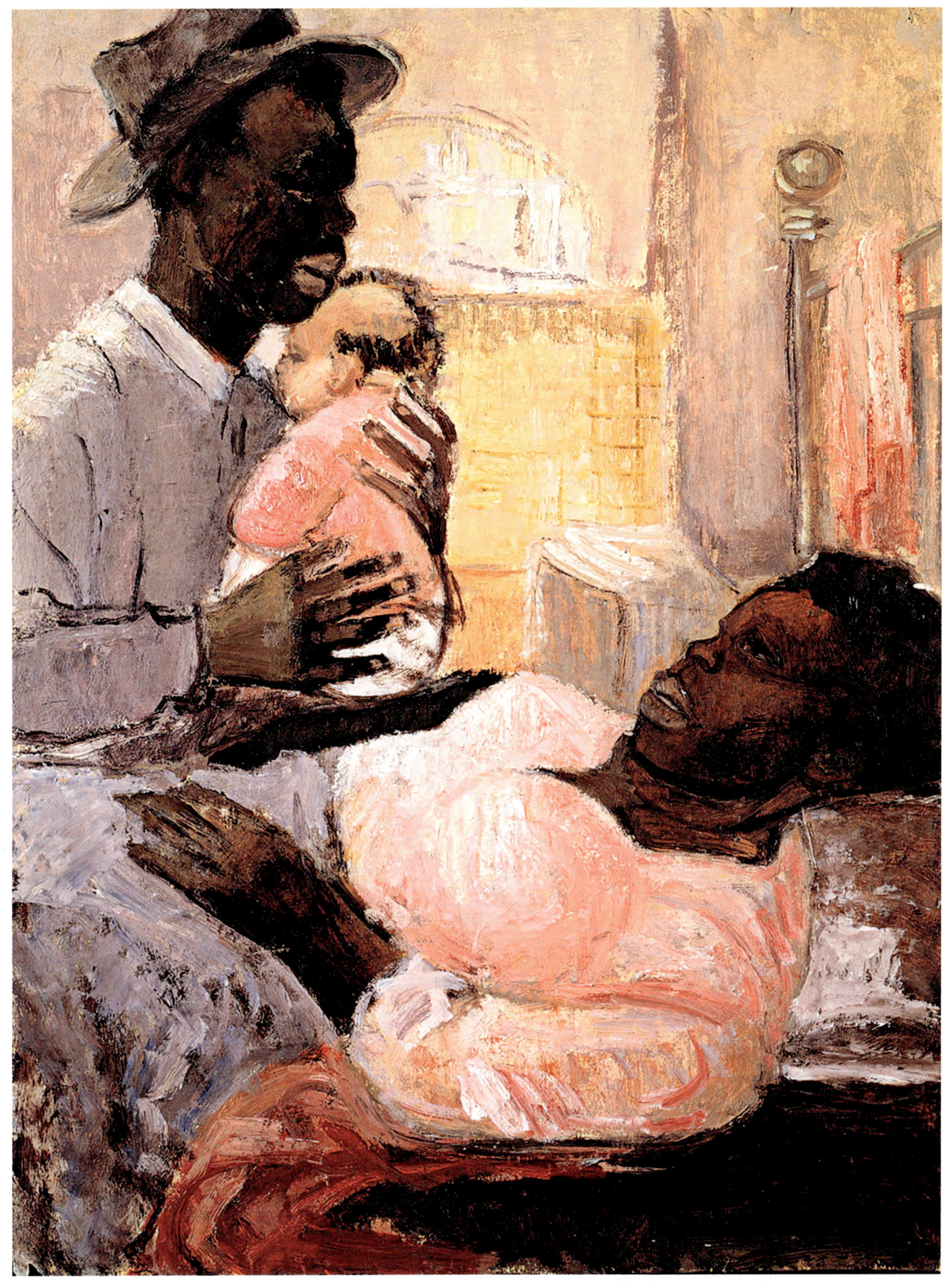

Brian HATTON

Whitecross, Hereford, 12 Aug 1887 – 23 Apr 1916, Oghratina, Egypt
British, 28 years, 8 months, 12 days

The remarkably diverse artist Brian Hatton displayed his proclivity towards art at a very young age. When he was just eight years old, he won his first medal at the Royal Drawing Society, and at the age of 11 he was awarded the 'Gold Star'. He attracted the notice of the famed painter George Frederic Watts, who took an interest in him and became his mentor. From 1906 to 1908, Hatton studied at the esteemed Hospitalfield Art School in Arbroath, Scotland under the Scottish portrait and figurative painter George Harcourt (1868–1947). Then, in 1908, Hatton settled for a time in London until a remarkable opportunity presented itself. Hatton was selected to join the expedition of noted Egyptologist William Flinders Petrie to Quma, Memphis and Athribis in Egypt. There he painted many fine oil studies, not returning to England until May 1909.

By late 1910 Hatton had become a student at the Académie Julian in Paris, where he was able to immerse himself in the fine arts. Then Hatton rented a studio in South Kensington, London in January of 1912 and there began his professional career as a portrait painter. Much of his work had heretofore been country and rural life, with animals, farm hands, landscape and imaginative work from literature. He had always made drawings and painted portraits of his dear sisters Ailsa and Marjorie, but now he embarked on a portrait career against stiff London competition. Hatton met with success, even winning commissions from the British royal family, among other illustrious individuals. However, by 1914, with war on the horizon, commissions vanished.

World War I broke out at the end of July 1914 and just a month later, Hatton volunteered. He joined the Queen's Own Worcestershire Hussars, with the Yeomanry Regiment of the British Army. Because of his asthma and his earlier travels, he was assigned to fight in Egypt, but before shipping out, Hatton hastily married his sweetheart Lydia Bidmead. Sadly, Lydia would be widowed less than two years later, when Hatton was killed in action during the Battle of Katia just east of Suez, on Easter Sunday, 23 April 1916. His body was not found for months, but he was eventually identified by the photograph of Lydia and the postcard addressed to her that he carried in his wallet.

Hatton left a wife, a daughter and a budding art career. One writer later noted of him: 'Had he not belonged to the lost generation who fought in World War I, Brian may have become known as a talented artist.'[115] Instead, Hatton's reputation lingered in obscurity for decades. His masterful drawing *Civilisation* (1914), with its brutal depiction of the callous nature of war, reveals the depth of his talent. In 1926, Walter Shaw Sparrow wrote an article on the painter titled 'Brian Hatton: young painter of genius killed in the war', in which he makes the insightful observation that 'Brian had the rarest of all things – true genius.'[116]

Brian Hatton
Civilisation – Study, 1914, charcoal drawing, size unknown
Hereford Museum and Art Gallery

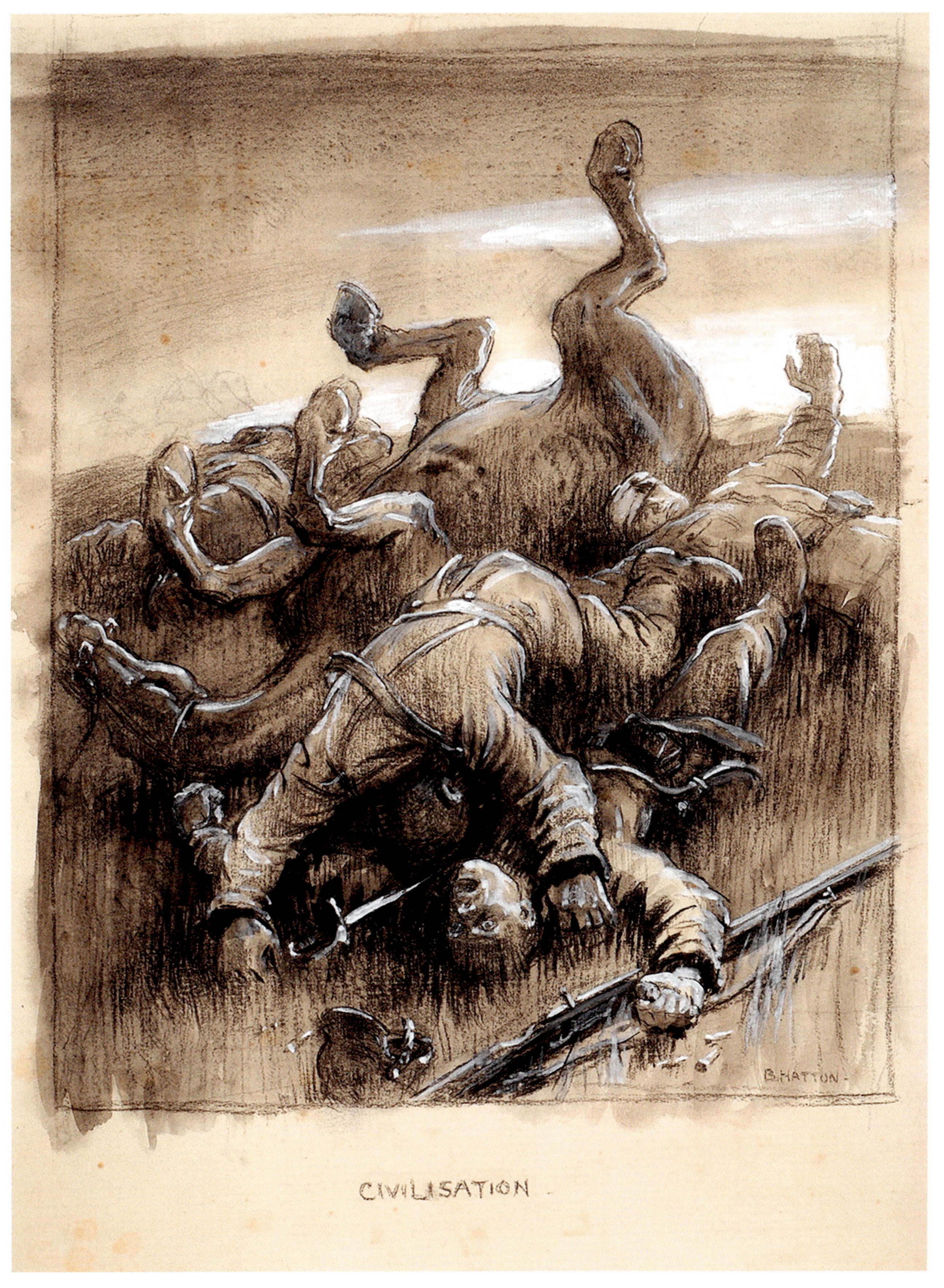

CIVILISATION
B.HATTON

(Johann) August HEINRICH

Dresden, 17 Aug 1794 – 27 Sep 1822, Innsbruck
German, 28 years, 1 months, 11 days

Heinrich's already short life was further troubled by protracted poor health and poverty, leading to a relatively small oeuvre. There are only about 110 known works by the artist including drawings, watercolours and a handful of oil paintings. Bombing during World War II further diminished his extant works, but what remains reveals a unique landscape artist who worked in a style apart from his time. Born the eldest son of a poor tailor, Heinrich studied at the Dresden and Vienna academies. When lung disease forced him to return home in 1818 to be nursed by his sister, he became friends with and a pupil of the great romantic artist Caspar David Friedrich. The famous painting by Friedrich titled *Two Men Contemplating the Moon* (1819) is thought to represent the young Heinrich and the elder Friedrich together.

Like Friedrich, Heinrich was a passionate devotee of nature. However, his art leans slightly towards the mundane rather than the sublime. Heinrich chose to depict in exacting detail the more minor beauties of nature such as the foliage at the edge of a forest or a clump of fir trees. A master of pencil and watercolour, Heinrich came to oil painting late in his career. In 1820, while on an art excursion to the spectacular rock formations at Utterwalder Valley in Saxon Switzerland, the artist recognised that only in oil painting could he 'imitate precisely the hues and tonalities found in nature.'[117] The canvas *Rock Canyon in Utterwalder Valley in Saxon Switzerland* (1820) is one of Heinrich's very first oil paintings, and depicts in extraordinary detail the light, colours, foliage and weathered stone of the canyon.

Unfortunately, Heinrich completed very few oils despite his competency in the medium – a tragic result of his limited funds and brevity of life. Eventually, Heinrich secured himself a stipend to study art in Italy, but he never reached his destination. Instead, he died of consumption (or a similar pulmonary disease) at the Golden Lion Inn at Innsbruck, Austria, while on the road to Italy for the first time. Sadly, he never fully realised the precious 'future promise' he surely would have achieved.[118]

(Johann) August Heinrich
Rock Canyon in Utterwalder Valley in Saxon Switzerland, 1820, oil on canvas, 52 × 42 cm (20½ × 16½ in)
Osterreichische Galerie Belvedere, Vienna

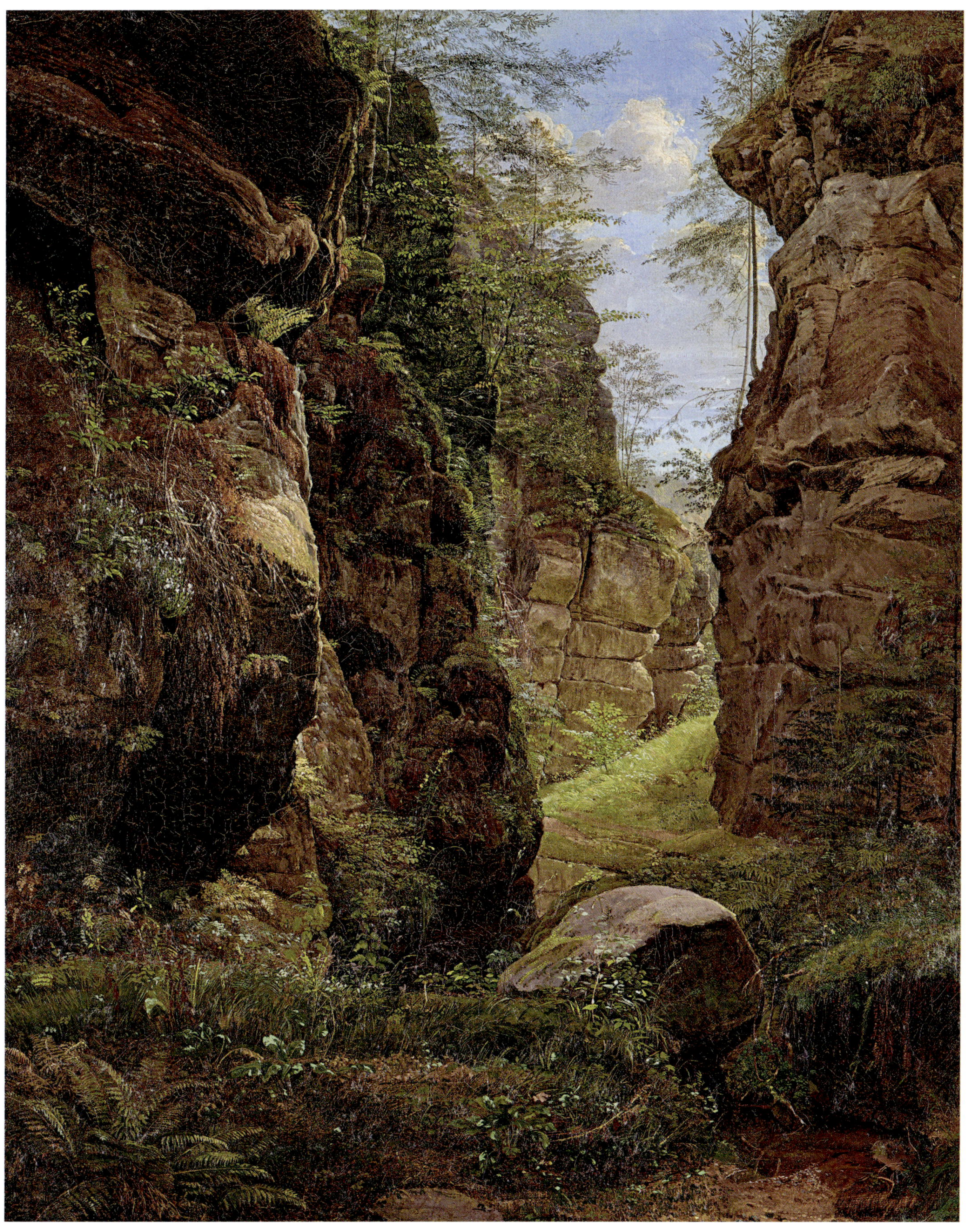

Laurent 'Gaston' JACQUOT-DEFRANCE

Le Perthus, 22 Apr 1874 – 19 May 1902, Rome
French, 28 years, 28 days

Jacquot-Defrance came from a Lorraine family and first distinguished himself as an outstanding student of the Nancy École des Beaux-Arts where he was a student of Jules Larcher (1849–1920). In 1894 he was accorded a municipal stipend and became a 'Pupil of the City of Nancy' at the famous École des Beaux-Arts in Paris, France's leading art academy. There, he first worked under William A. Bouguereau and Gabriel Ferrier, then with Léon Bonnat and Albert Maignan, the latter being the most influential. Maignan's guidance can be seen in Defrance's last painting, found on his easel at his death, *A Nun with Her Students* (1901, unfinished) with its academic impressionism, rich pigmentation, loose brush and saturated colours.

In 1897 he competed for the École's Prix de Rome without success. He again entered the competition in 1899 and took Prix Chenavard (third place) with his oil *Hercules between Vice and Virtue*. He also won a Medal Third Class at the Salon de Paris of 1899. The following year, he painted *Rachel and Jacob at the Well* (1900), which won another Medal Third Class at the Paris Salon. Improving slightly, the 1901 Paris Salon awarded him a Medal Second Class for *Les Boeufs*.

Then, finally, Jacquot-Defrance triumphed with his excellent painting *Christ Heals the Paraplegic in the Shade of an Olive Grove* (1901, ENSBA), winning the 1901 premier scholarship prize – the Grand Prix de Rome. 'This time,' his biography notes, 'his work surpassed without dispute those of his competitors, and was unanimously ratified by the public and the judgment of the Institute and teachers from the École.' [119] Most importantly, this provided the artist with the necessary funding to live and study in Rome.

His success was tragically short-lived. Jacquot-Defrance died after just a few months at the French Academy's Villa Medici in Rome. An inordinate number of Prix de Rome winners died in Italy; the causes are rarely mentioned. We can only guess what the 'coalition of evil forces from nature' described in Jacquot-Defrance's obituary could have been. [120] (He was replaced the next year by the 1902 Prix de Rome winner – Victor Guétin.) However, his death was widely commemorated. One mourner lamented, 'Jacquot-Defrance was already an artist of talent, honesty, personality. He had become a master who would have honoured French art, because he had the mark of great minds: never satisfied with his effort, it seemed to him that the ideal retreated as we saw it getting closer.' [121]

A bronze bust by Henri Bouchard (the 1901 Prix de Rome winner for sculpture) was erected in Jacquot-Defrance's memory in the Saint-Louis-des-Français church in Rome. The noted sculptor Eugène Guillaume, then director of the Académie de France in Rome, gave a speech at his funeral in Lorraine, and a street was named in his honour – Rue Jacquot de France – in the town of Laxou, in the suburbs of Nancy. Though the artist is little known today, his contemporaries knew he was going to amount to something.

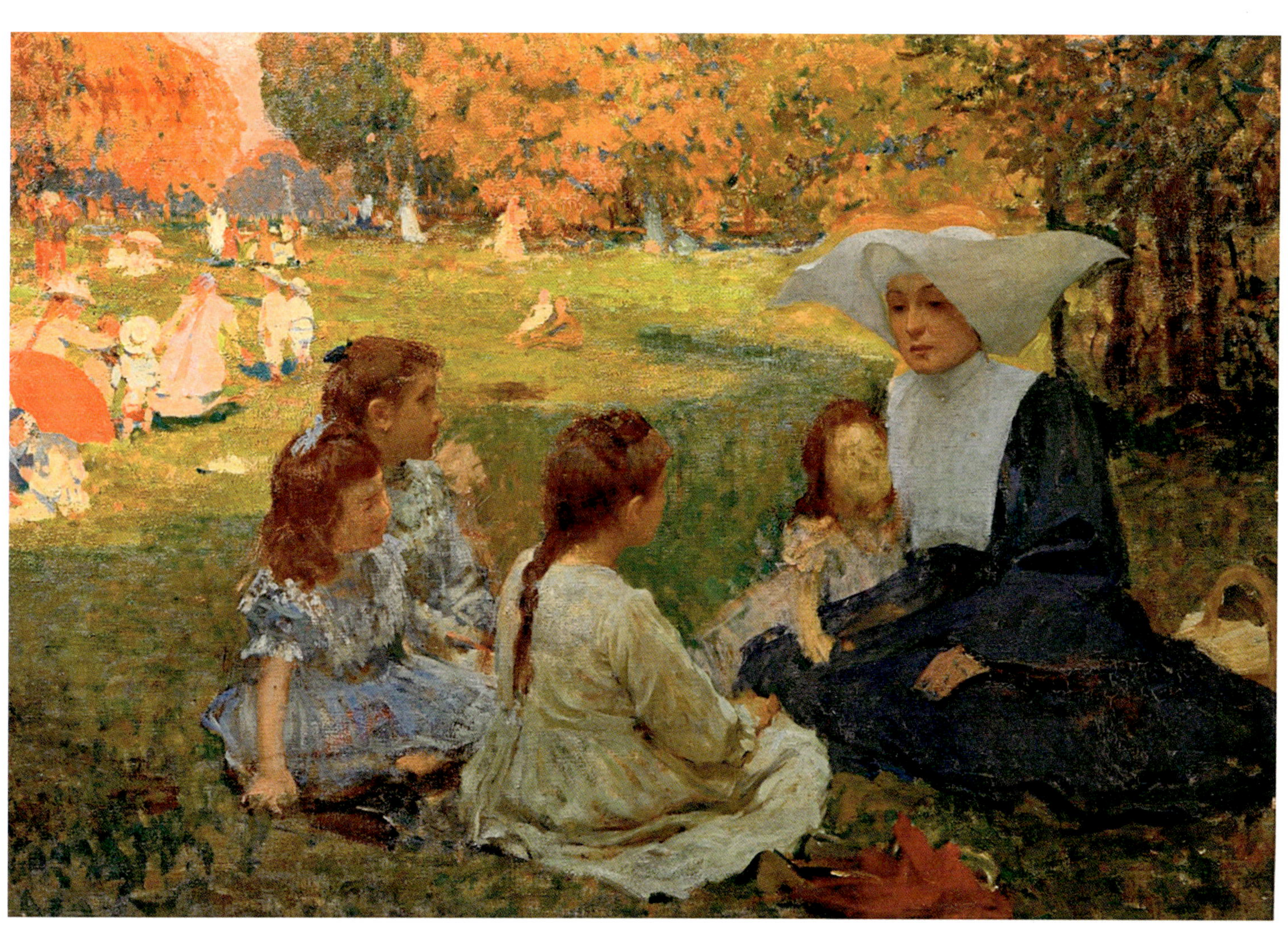

Laurent Jacquot-Defrance
A Nun with Her Students, 1901, oil on canvas, 61 × 81 cm (24 × 31⅞ in), unfinished at death
Drouot Auctions, Paris

Ernst KLIMT

Vienna, 3 Jan 1864 – 9 Dec 1892, Vienna
Austrian, 28 years, 11 months, 7 days

Commonly known only for being the younger brother of Gustav Klimt (1862–1918), Ernst Klimt was a gifted artist in his own right. Ernst's early death ended a prolific career in a profession which, as it did for his brother, may have taken any number of unexpected paths. Son of the gold engraver Ernst Klimt Sr, Ernst studied with his brother at the Vienna Kunstgewerbeschule. Around 1881, the brothers and their friend Franz Masch (1861–1947) began the Jugendstil company of artists – a business through which they received commissions including curtain designs and mural paintings for theatres. The most famous of these was the frescoes for the staircase and ceiling at the magnificent beaux-arts Burgtheater in Vienna (1886–88). Ernst also completed numerous historical and costume paintings and portraits.

In 1891, Ernst married Helene Flöge and had a daughter the following year. Sadly, the couple had been married just 15 months when Ernst died suddenly of pericarditis (inflammation of the tissue around the heart). Ernst's father also died that year, leaving Gustav to take financial responsibility for both families. Gustav became the guardian of Ernst's daughter Helene and also completed Ernst's unfinished paintings. The death of his brother had a profound effect on Gustav and an artistic crisis ensued. From that point, Gustav's style began to depart from the conventions of academic art in which he and his brother worked, towards a more symbolic and personal style.

Had Ernst lived, it is uncertain which artistic direction his own art would have taken or the influence he would have exerted on his brother Gustav. However, it may well have changed the man who became the founding president of the Vienna Secession. Ernst was a slightly more romantic painter than Gustav, as seen in his canvas *Francesca de Rimini and Paolo* (c.1890). Though younger than Gustav, Ernst seemed more 'fixed' in this approach to fine art. Perhaps he would have been a more academic version of his elder brother as one of his last paintings, *Pan and Psyche* (1892) suggests.

Ernst Klimt
Francesca de Rimini and Paolo, c.1890, oil on canvas, 125 × 95 cm (49¼ × 37⅜ in)
Österreichische Galerie Belvedere, Vienna

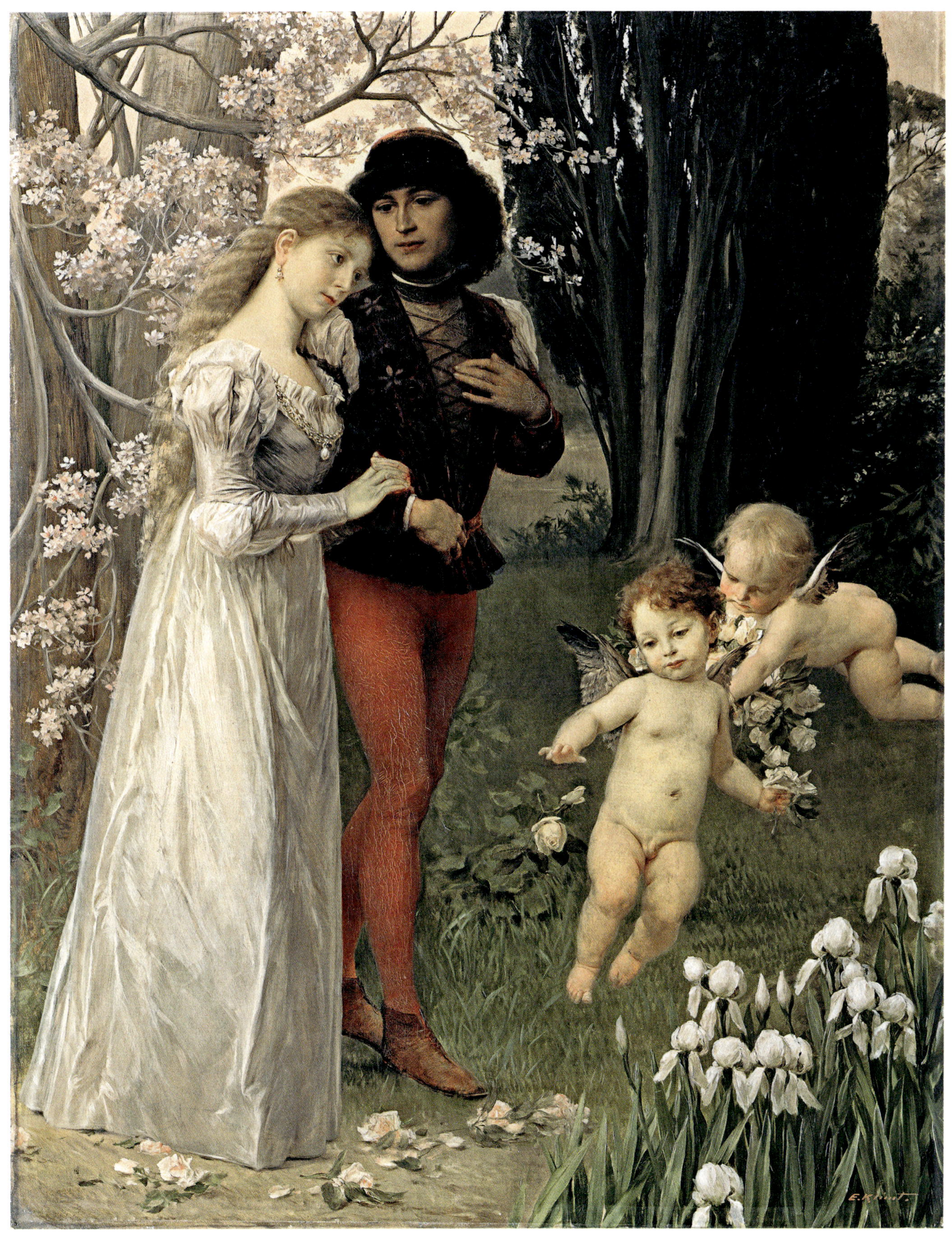

Dean Allan MILLMAN

North Adams, Massachusetts, 28 Nov 1948 – 24 Jan 1977, Provo, Utah
American, 28 years, 1 month, 28 days

Dean Allan Millman was born in North Adams, Massachusetts, but he lived most of his life in the American West. From a young age, he possessed the confidence and drive to believe that anything was within his grasp. His biographer writes that 'From the time he could hold a pencil this young man never stopped drawing.'[122] When only 13 years old he made national headlines when he rode his bike more than 2,600 miles from Sunset, Utah to New York City and then to Williamstown, Massachusetts.

As a teenager in Utah, Millman was already known for his art and he was asked to paint a large mural for his high school's graduation. He studied art at Brigham Young University (BYU) in Provo, Utah, and took a class from Professor Glen Turner who growled to his obstinate student: 'Dean, you cannot use acrylic in this watercolour class!' But Millman used acrylic so thinly that Turner thought it was watercolour and gave him a top grade. Being a little wild, hippie and anti-war pacifist, he didn't fit in well at conservative BYU and dropped out before graduating because 'He wanted to prove to the world that his success was due solely to his own talent and not to academic aptitude.'[123]

Dean possessed magnificent artistic ability, blending the styles of Andrew Wyeth and BYU watercolour professor Robert Marshall. He used watercolour, gouache and acrylic to produce visions of rural America in landscape and still-life reminiscent of the artist Kenneth Riley. His trompe-l'oeil painting *In Homage to Dr Wesley M. Burnside* (1971) is a memorial to BYU art history professor Wesley Burnside whom Dean credits for having 'discovered' him. Burnside introduced Dean to the wiley art dealer Dewey Moore of Lamplighter Gallery in Salt Lake City. Millman successfully exhibited there, making Moore rich and Millman famous.

Vern Swanson, a dear friend and roommate of Millman's, remembers well: 'Dean was intelligent, dogmatic, and had a wry humour and puckish personality. He was only 21 in early 1970 when I first met him. Dean being so young seemed indifferent to his immense artistic talent for design, narrative and touch. It all came so easily to him. He would goof-off until he ran out of money; then would quickly paint another show and have it framed within a month. His two shows a year would sell out to eager collectors who couldn't get enough of his brilliant though youthful art. Then, with the money he would enjoy himself and not paint until he was poor again.'

Then, one month in 1974, at the height of his productivity, he began to feel ill with something that the doctors were unable to diagnose. While living in Vermont in December of 1975, he was finally diagnosed with a rare form of leukaemia. Too unwell to work, he ceased to produce art and 12 months later, in January 1977, he died at the age of 28. Ever the optimist, in September 1976 he married his tender girlfriend Carolyn ('Carrie') just months before his death – both knowing that the end was near. As the phrase goes: 'The brightest star always burns out first.'

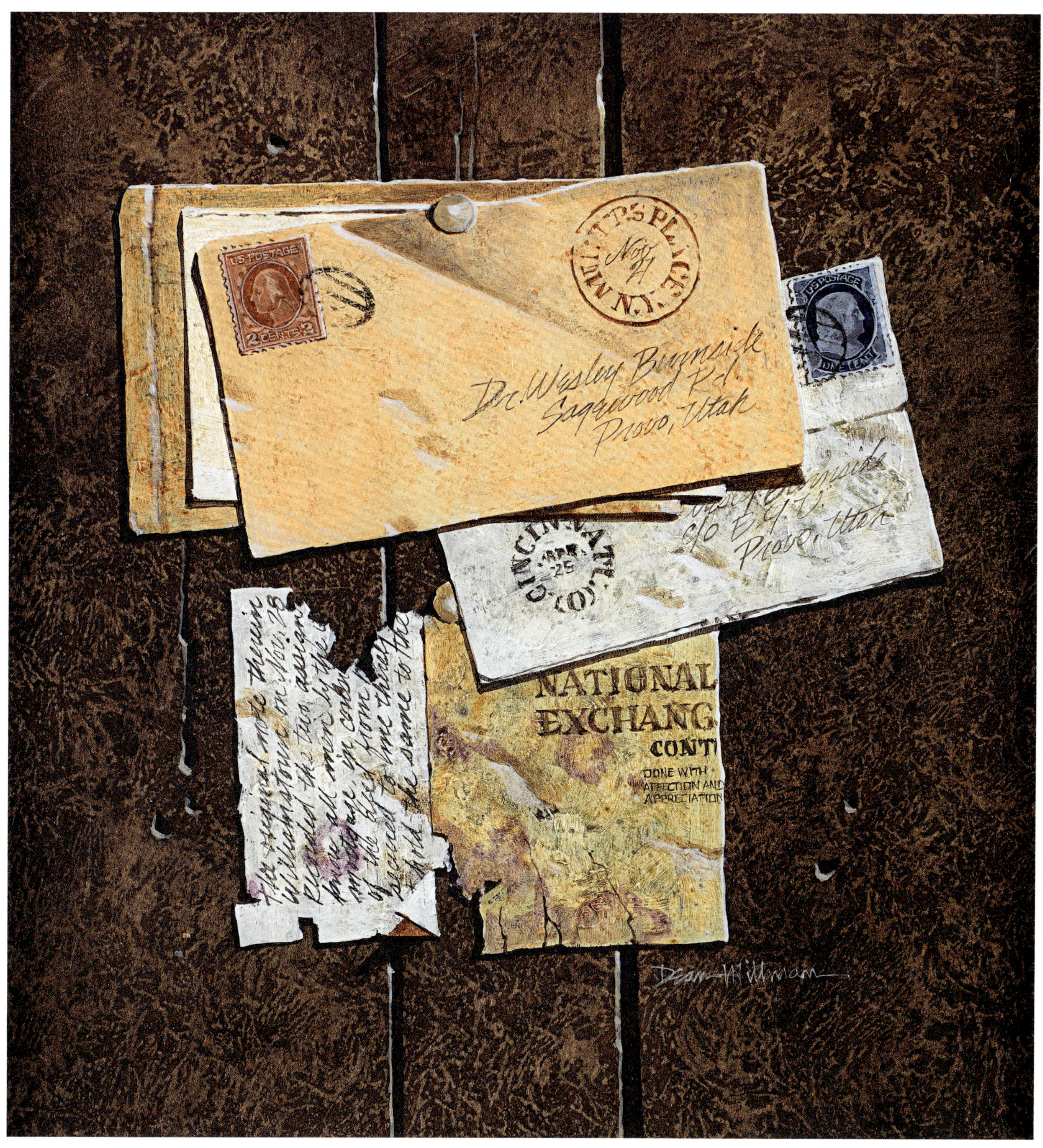

Dean Allan Millman
In Homage to Dr Wesley M. Burnside, 1971, acrylic on board, size unknown
©Millman Estate c/o Lynn Millman-Weidinger, Courtesy of Springville Museum of Art, Utah, Gift from Tony Christensen, Anthony's Fine Art and Antiques

Isack Jansz. van OSTADE

Haarlem, baptised 2 Jun 1621 – buried 16 Oct 1649, Haarlem
Dutch, approx. 28 years, 4 months

Isack van Ostade was the eighth and youngest child of Jan Hendrick Ostade, a linen weaver from the hamlet of Ostade near Eindhoven. Isack was also the younger brother of the noted artist Adriaen Jansz. van Ostade (1610–1685). Though the brothers were born in Haarlem, they both took on the name 'van Ostade' after their ancestral home. Isack studied under his brother until the age of 20, when he began his own professional career. He may also have studied with the landscape painter Salomon van Ruysdael, increasing the depth of his education.

Isack was first inspired by Rembrandt, but under the influence of his brother began to paint more along his lines, namely interiors, genre and landscapes. In 1643 Isack was admitted into the Haarlem Guild of St Luke, and he soon began to develop a style of his own. He painted, in a positive manner, village high streets, roadside inns, frozen canals, and interesting peasant genre. Often, his art, like that of Philips Wouwerman, included a white horse for interest.

In quick succession, Isack lost several family members. His mother died in 1640, his father in 1641, and Adriaen's wife in 1642. It appears that Isack also was not in the best of health. It is postulated that after 1643, Isaac abandoned Haarlem, near the coast, for Eindhoven in south central Holland for a time to benefit his health. There, he created his rustic ink and wash drawing *View of Eindhoven from the Northeast* (1645), now in the J. Paul Getty Museum. He certainly returned home before his death and was buried in Haarlem on 16 October 1649.

Isack's work has a sunny but mellow disposition. His best work may have been his winter scenes. The vibrant, bustling nature and excellent handling of paint and colour in these scenes are evident in his *Frozen Canal with Horse-Drawn Sledge near a Cottage and Bridge* (c.1646). His works are highly valued today and can be found in leading museums such as the Louvre in Paris, National Gallery of Art in Washington, D.C., and the Hermitage in St Petersburg. In his paintings and many drawings there is a refined grace and searching quality to his work, but he simply did not live long enough to bring his art to perfection.

An examination of his more famous brother's work painted before his 29th birthday, shows that Isack's art was equally as good at that age. Had he lived, Isack could very well have been as successful as Adriaen. Nevertheless, his influence on contemporary Dutch painting is considered substantial. In a career of just seven years, Isack van Ostade was one of the lights of the Dutch Golden Age, but he flickered out with just over 100 known finished paintings and many studies predicting a brilliant future.

Isack van Ostade
Frozen Canal with Horse-Drawn Sledge near a Cottage and Bridge, c.1646, oil on panel, 37.2 × 33.8 cm (14⅝ × 13¼ in)
Sotheby's London

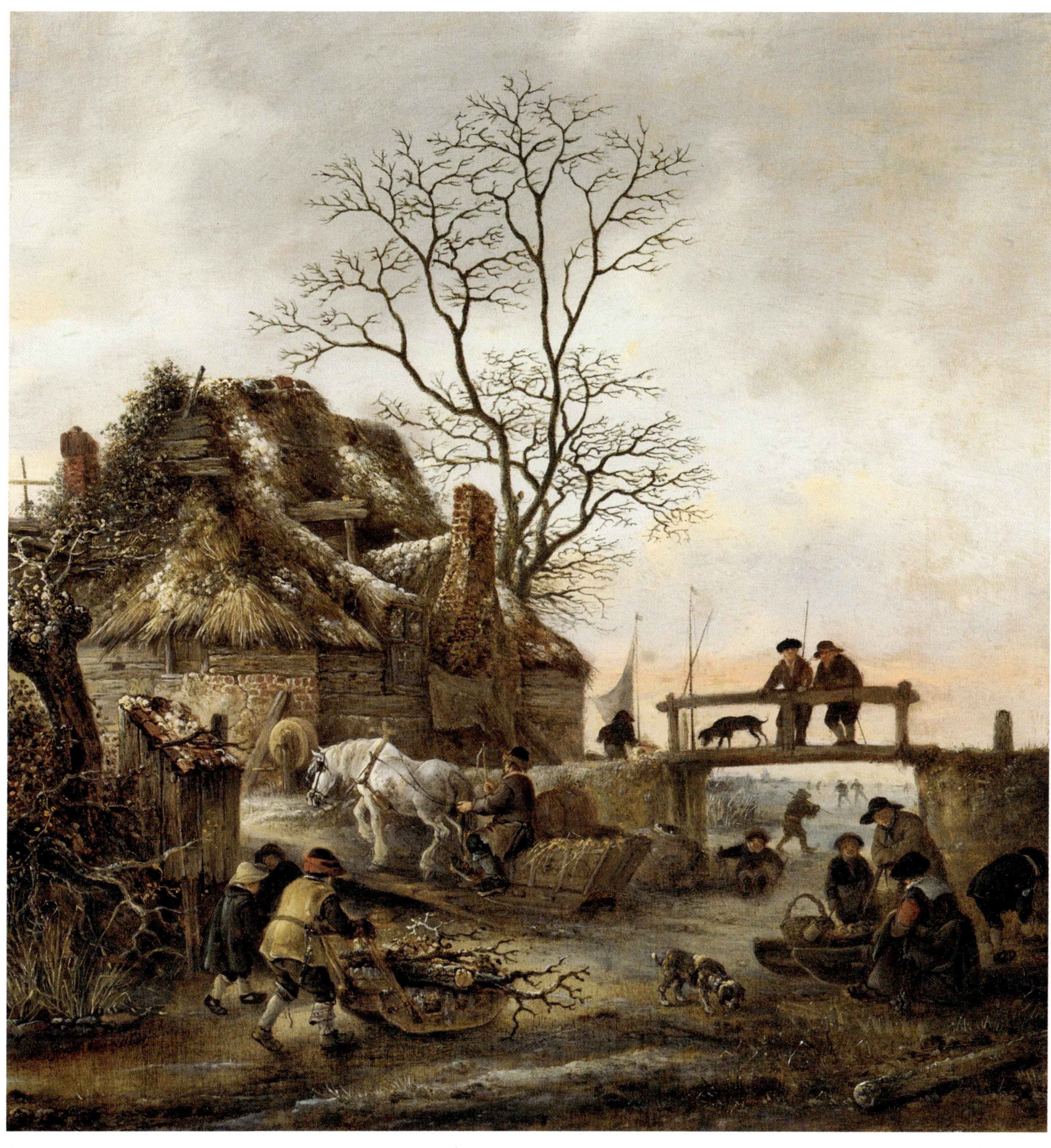

Petr Stipanovich PETROVSKY

Oranienbaum, 1814 – 11 Jun 1842, Rome
Russian, approx. 28 years

The short-lived Russian artist Petr Petrovsky was a determined and talented painter of religious scenes. When Petrovsky's father died, the task of providing for the family fell on the 16-year-old artist's shoulders. He was given a position in the State Paper Procurement Department, but art was his true passion. Simultaneously working and studying, he attended drawing classes at the Academy of Fine Arts from 1831.

Since his day job did not give him the opportunity to fully immerse in his artistic studies, in 1837 the Society for the Encouragement of the Arts, provided him with a pension to study full-time at the Academy in St Petersburg. At the Academy, he studied first under Professor Fyodor A. Bruni, and then the famous Karl Pavlovich Bryullov (1799–1852). Bruni was known for his ability to fuse neoclassicism with romantic tendencies, and his influence can be seen in Petrovsky's art.

Surrendering himself completely to the study of art, he still managed to provide for his mother and sisters by fulfilling art orders given to him by the Society. This new focus allowed the young Petrovsky to progress at astounding speed, and he began exhibiting with great success. He received a second-place medal for his drawing from life, and in 1838, he received a silver medal for his painting *John the Baptist*. Just the next year, Petrovsky won the gold medal and was awarded the title of 'Artist' for his impressive oil *The Appearance of an Angel to the Shepherds* (1839, Cherepovets Museum of Art). Other notable paintings include a commissioned work for the Nicholas Military Cathedral at Kiev Fortress and his emotional *Hagar and Ishmael in the Desert* (1841).

The oil *Hagar and Ishmael* was an instant hit and won the artist a substantial cash prize. Furthermore, Petrovsky's gold medal allowed him to apply for a funded study-trip to Europe. With the success of *Hagar and Ishmael,* and the recommendation of the Society for the Encouragement of the Arts, Petrovsky was awarded the travel scholarship by the Academy of Fine Arts, and in 1841 he departed for the Russian Academy in Rome. The *Russian Biographical Dictionary* explains: 'The artist gladly took advantage of the long-awaited opportunity to travel to Italy, but overwork and deprivation completely tore at his strength.'[124] The unfortunate artist had only recently reached Rome when he died from tuberculosis. He departed this world at the youthful age of 28, just as his hard-fought career was rapidly ascending.

Petr Stipanovich Petrovsky
Hagar and Ishmael in the Desert, 1841, oil on canvas, 100 × 118 cm (39⅜ × 46½ in)
State Tretyakov Gallery, Moscow

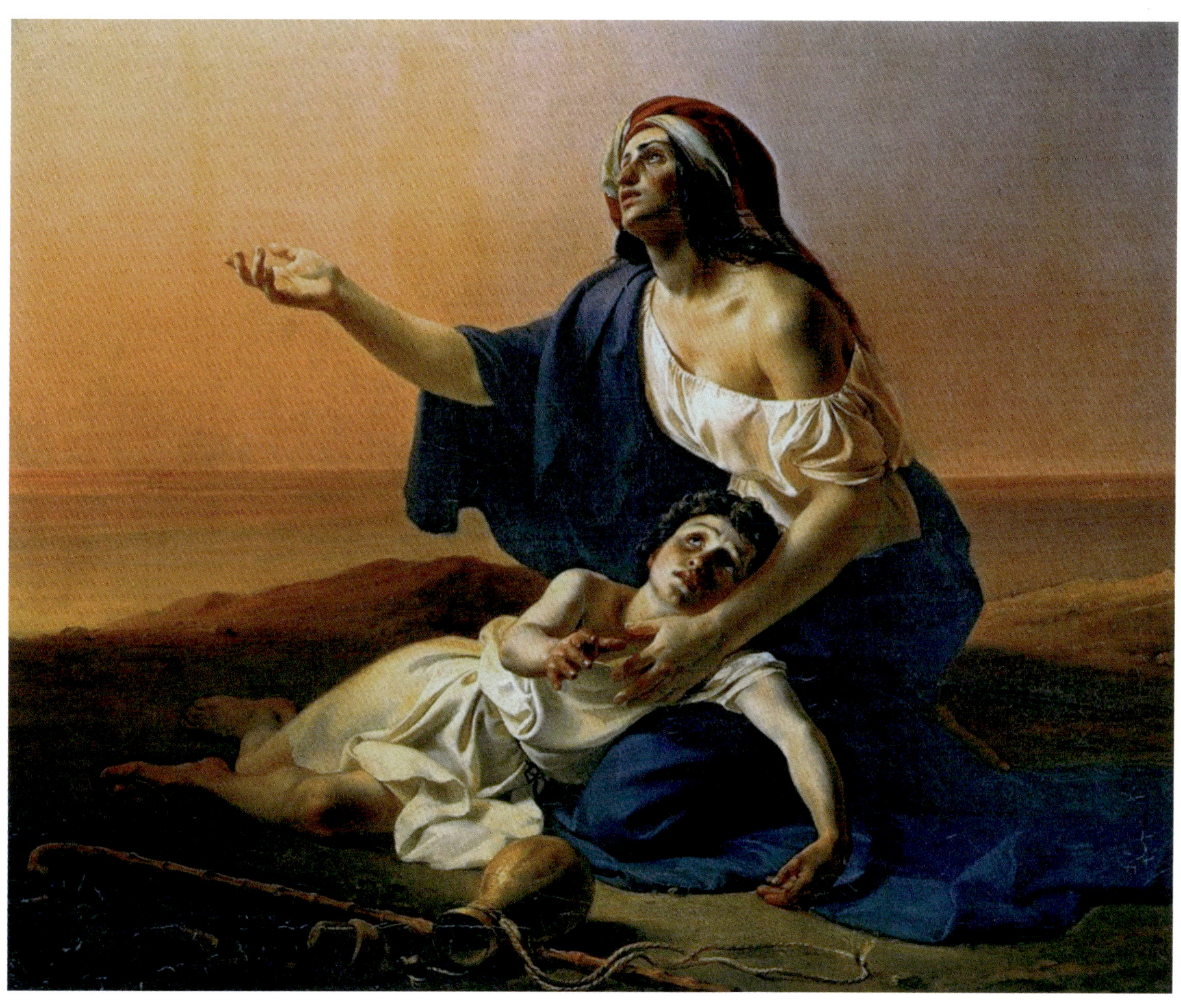

Paulus Pietersz POTTER

Enkhuizen, baptised 20 Nov 1625 – buried 17 Jan 1654, Amsterdam
Dutch, approx. 28 years, 1 month

One of the leading animal painters of the Dutch Golden Age, Paulus Potter profoundly altered the perception of how animals were portrayed in Western art. Potter's father, Pieter Symonsz. Potter (c.1600–1652), was a gifted painter himself, but his career has long been overshadowed by the brilliance of his son's. Nevertheless, he gave his son his first art lessons, though later, Paulus would study under Claes Moeyaert (c.1590–1655) in Amsterdam. Paulus was very precocious, and his earliest picture is dated 1640, when he was only 15 years old. In 1642, he was registered as a student of the important artist Jacob de Wet (1610–c.1675).

By 1649, Paulus had moved to The Hague and until 1652 rented a house from the landscape painter Jan van Goyen. In 1650 he married Adriana Balcken Eynde, the daughter of the city architect, and his father-in-law introduced him to The Hague's elite. This garnered many commissions for his paintings of farm animals, mostly depicting cows, steers, horses and sheep painted in realistic terms. Despite his radically new approach, there was a ready market for his paintings.

One scholar observed: 'He is said to have wandered the Dutch countryside with sketchbook in hand, equally sensitive to how farm animals behave at different times of day and to light's vicissitudes from morning to dusk.'[125] His life-sized masterpiece *The Bull* (1647), painted when he was only 21 years old, is a portrait of a steer with a man as a background figure. Even though it portrayed a smelly farmyard with flies swarming around the bull's back, and a storm threatening in the distance, it was very popular. Its 'living image' of farm life made cattle painting de rigueur in Holland for the next three centuries.

The Potters moved back to Amsterdam in May of 1652. The move was precipitated by the encouragement of Dr Nicolaes Tulp, who had recognised Rembrandt's genius 20 years earlier. Dr Tulp acted as Potter's mentor, and perhaps personal physician. It may have been Dr Tulp who diagnosed Paulus's illness of consumption (tuberculosis), and wanted him in Amsterdam so he could treat his condition.

The noted portraitist Bartholomeus van der Helst painted Paulus's likeness shortly before the latter's death in 1654. He depicted the cow-painter in full finery and in the bloom of health, probably not in the miserable condition that he was. Timothy Cole wrote of this portrait: 'It seems very remarkable that this should portray a likeness of a man wasted with consumption at death's door. But it is not more remarkable than his life, which was one of prodigious labour, and wonderful perseverance.'[126]

Paulus Potter's health failed rapidly and he died from tuberculosis induced by overwork. A. Wheelock Jr noted: 'From very early in his career, he accorded animals an extremely important position in his compositions and was one of the first artists to depict them as subjects in their own right.'[127]

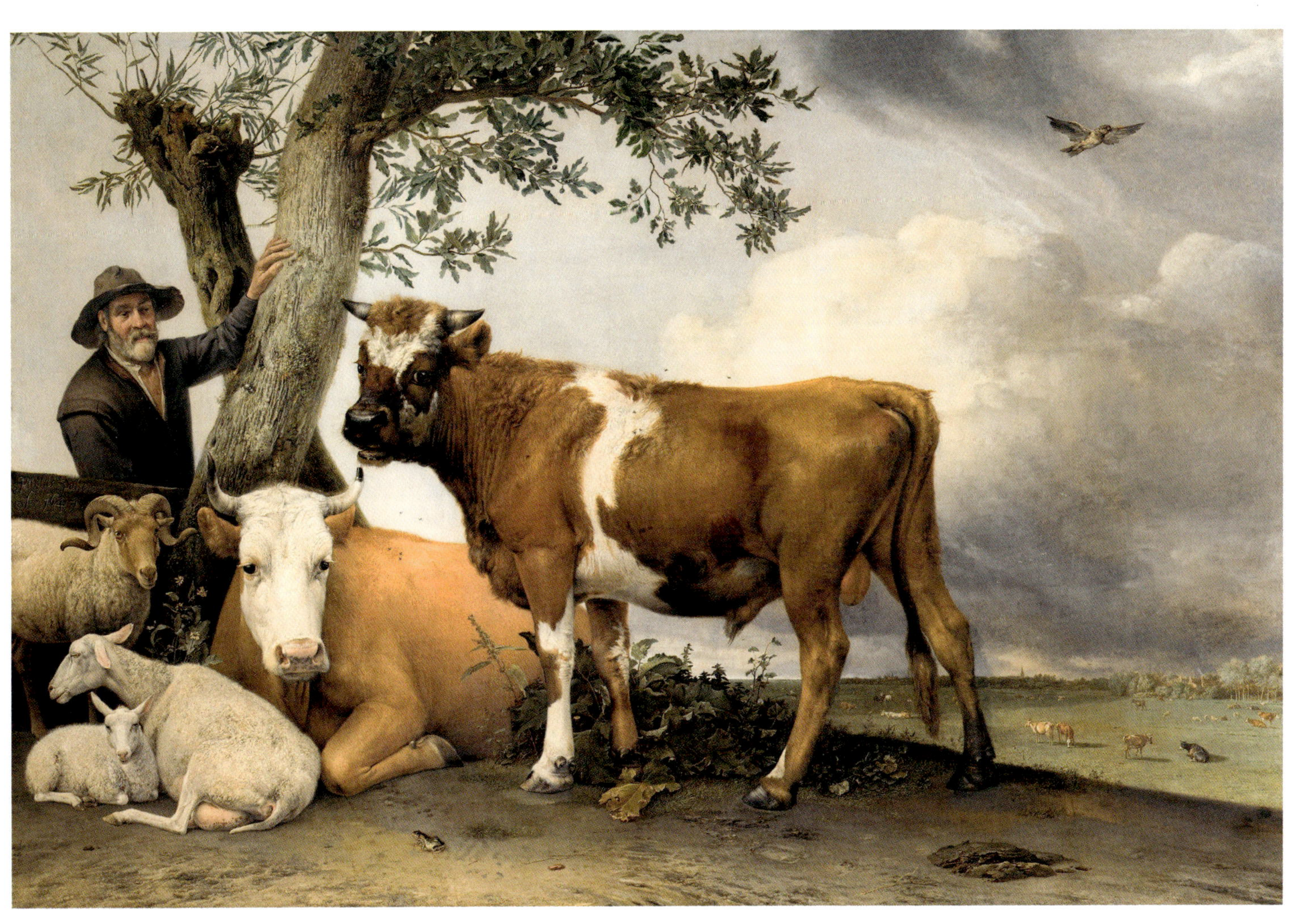

Paulus Pietersz Potter
The Bull, 1647, oil on canvas, 235.5 × 339 cm (92¾ × 133½ in)
Mauritshuis, The Hague

Hugh RAMSAY

Glasgow, 25 May 1877 – 5 Mar 1906, Melbourne
Australian, 28 years, 9 months, 9 days

Despite his abbreviated career, Hugh Ramsay is still considered one of Australia's most significant portrait painters, and his paintings hang today in Australia's foremost museums. Ramsay was the sixth son of the successful Scottish-born businessman John Ramsay. The pious family moved to Australia in 1878 and established themselves in Essendon, near Melbourne. At the age of 16, Ramsay entered the National Gallery of Victoria Art School where he studied under Bernard Hall and Frederick McCubbin. Through Hall, Ramsay learned to admire the work of Velázquez, Whistler and Manet.

Determined to study in Europe, Ramsay raised the funds himself and left his family and fiancée for Paris in September 1900, where he enrolled in the Académie Colarossi. In April 1902, Ramsay had four pictures accepted into the Salon of the Société Nationale des Beaux-Arts. This success and an introduction led to a commission from the famous soprano, Nellie Melba, then at the height of her fame. She invited him to London to paint her portrait, and while there, Ramsay saw John Singer Sargent's work at the Royal Academy and was profoundly impressed.

Ramsay seemed on the cusp of success, but within weeks of his arrival in England doctors diagnosed him with tuberculosis. Two years of overwork, poor diet and unsanitary living conditions had made him susceptible to the illness which, at the time, had no known cure. Ramsay returned to the warmer climate of Australia in the hope that it would ease his symptoms and return him to health.

On returning to Australia in 1902, and despite doctor's orders to rest, Ramsay continued to work with renewed vigour and breadth of style. Facing imminent death, he undoubtedly wished to leave a legacy of the greatness that was his. Amazingly, he painted some of his finest works during this period, such as *The Lady with a Fan* (1904) of his fiancée Lischen Muller, and *The Sisters* (1904) of his own angelic sisters. Ramsay was best known for these elegant fashionable portraits, in which he demonstrated a keen and sensitive insight into the characters of his sitters. His technical ability was precocious, and his subtle use of colour and rejection of trivial detail gave gravitas to his work. In his weakened condition, he broke off his hopeless engagement to Lischen, knowing that the end was near. His sister Jessie nursed him, but his health continued to fail and he died at 28.

As one of Australia's most gifted painters, Ramsay was known as an 'artist's artist'. His biographer P. Fullerton aptly notes: 'His career spanned scarcely a decade; he was, however, prolific, accomplished and mature beyond his years.'[128] The eulogies have continued for over a century. In 1929, Arthur Streeton wrote: 'His death is the greatest loss Australian art has suffered; if he had lived it is difficult to imagine what would have been the limit of his unusual powers.' Then in 1943, during the War, George Bell testified to his unforgettable talent: 'How he would have reveled in the problems of today and what heights he would have achieved! That he died before achieving his full stature as an artist is not only a personal tragedy; it is a national calamity.'[129]

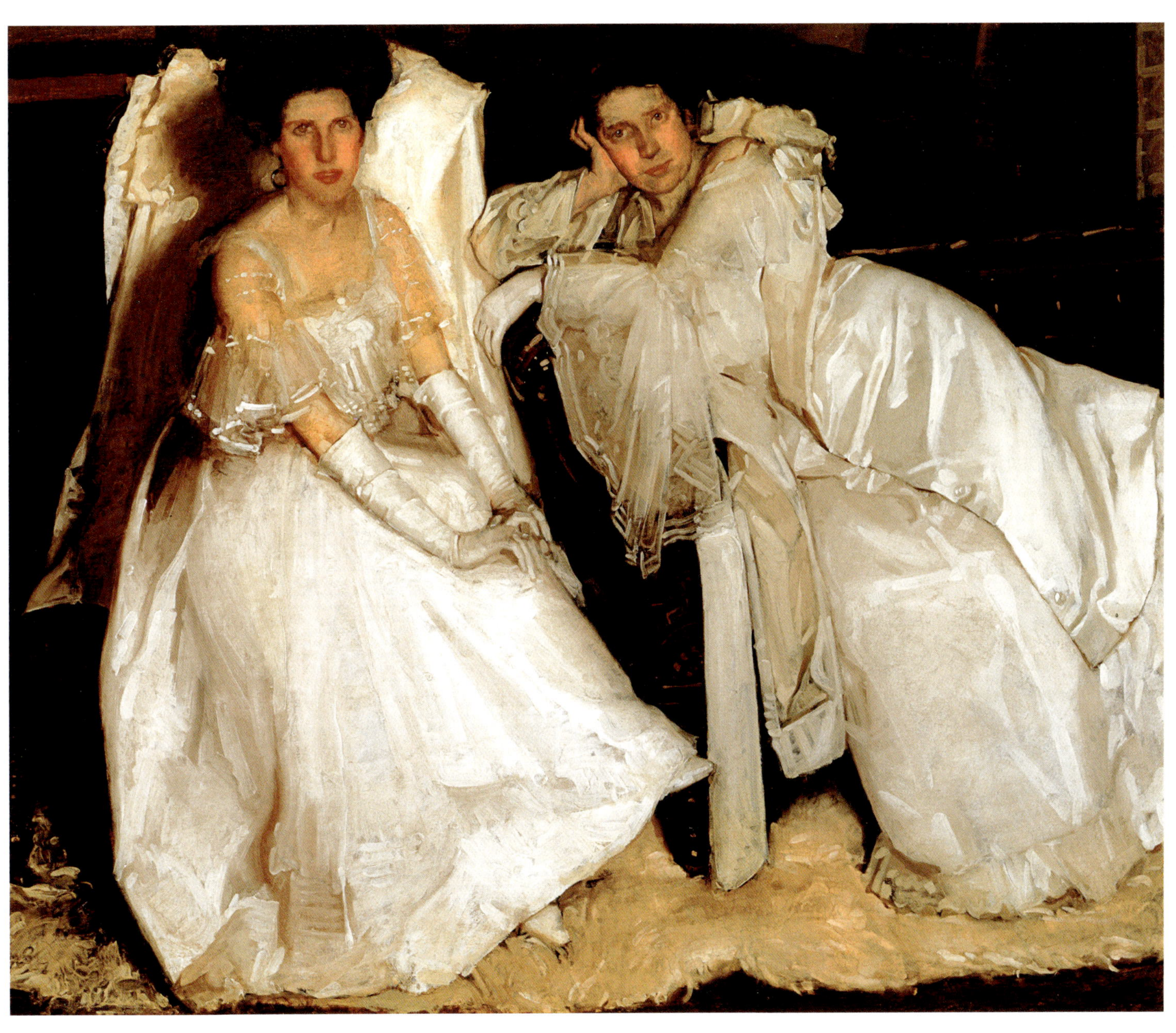

Hugh Ramsay
The Sisters, 1904, mounted oil on canvas, 156 × 176.5 cm (61⅜ × 69½ in)
Art Gallery of New South Wales, Sydney

Peter RINDISBACHER

Emmental, Canton of Berne, 12 Apr 1806 – 13 Aug 1834, St Louis, Missouri
Swiss/Canadian/American, 28 years, 4 months, 2 days

Swiss-born illustrator and watercolourist Rindisbacher received only one year of formal artistic training before he emigrated with his family to the Red River valley in Canada. However, the artist sketched almost continuously from a young age and learned much from his keen observation of nature and people. In 40 watercolour sketches, the 15-year-old Rindisbacher depicted the arduous voyage to Canada during which the ship made its way around glaciers and up rivers, interacting with the local natives.

Upon arrival, the conditions the family faced were harsh and farming was difficult. Rindisbacher supplemented his family's income by working as a clerk and painting watercolours of the settlement and the indigenous people. He also received an important commission from the interim governor of Assiniboia, Andrew H. Bulger, to depict his travels and interactions with the Native American population. Rindisbacher's illustrations attracted much attention in America and abroad for their detailed depiction of the clothing and everyday life of the Cree, Sioux, Chippewa and other Native American tribes. Many copies and prints were made after these works.

The fact that the artist actually lived with the tribes and even used their pigments when his own art supplies were unavailable, has encouraged the view that his scenes are accurate ethnographic, albeit artistic, depictions of native prairie life.[130] *In the Tepee* (c.1825) is a fine example of his watercolours and demonstrates the wider appeal of his art. In 1826, Rindisbacher left Canada for the United States. Living for a time in Wisconsin, he eventually settled in St Louis in 1829 where he established a commercial art studio. The artist added portrait painting to his oeuvre, illustrated magazines, married and had two children, and then died at the age of 28. Rindisbacher may have died of cholera. The fatal epidemic had reached St Louis in 1832 and returned for the subsequent three summers. However, historian Henry Bovay believed he may have had lead poisoning from his compulsive habit of holding his brushes in his mouth.

Rindisbacher's popularity continued as posthumous lithographs after his work were published in notable publications including Thomas McKenney's *History of the Indian Tribes of North America* (1836–44). It is widely thought that had Rindisbacher lived longer he would have become as well known as George Catlin, another painter of 'first contact' Native Americans, who had preceded him. Today, Rindisbacher still fascinates connoisseurs and scholars and is considered an important early painter of Canada and the American West.

Peter Rindisbacher
In the Tepee, c.1825, watercolour and ink on paper, 17 × 21.7 cm (6¾ × 8½ in)
Courtesy of Gilcrease Museum, Tulsa, Gift of the Thomas Gilcrease Foundation, 1955

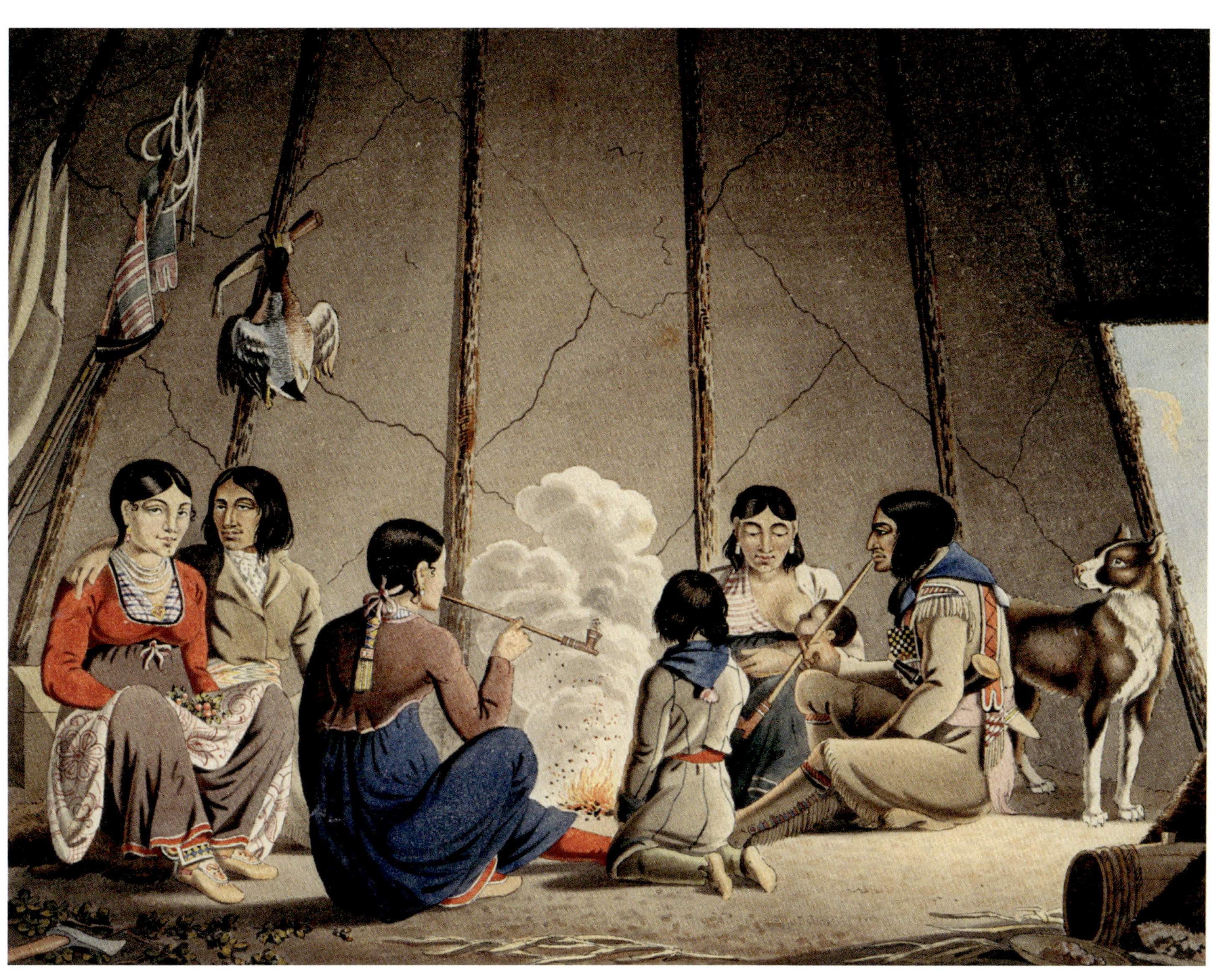

Antonio SANT'ELIA

Como, 30 Apr 1888 – 10 Oct 1916, in Battle of Isonzo near Gorizia
Italian, 28 years, 5 months, 11 days

Sant'Elia was a highly regarded futurist architect and draughtsman whose influence on International Style architecture is considered substantial. Following a degree in construction, Sant'Elia moved to the growing and technologically innovative city of Milan, where he worked as a draughtsman for the Department of Public Works. There, he became aware of the growing needs of a modernising city.

He then studied for a year at the Fine Art Academy in Brera where he became acquainted with future leaders of the Futurist movement. Sant'Elia graduated in architecture from the Accademia di Belle Arti in Bologna in 1912, and the following year established his own office in Milan. Active both artistically and politically, he became a co-founder of the architectural group Nuove Tendenze (New Tendencies) and was elected a city council member for the strident Socialist party.

Ironically, only one building designed by him was ever completed in his lifetime. However, Sant'Elia's fame today derives from the *Manifesto of Futurist Architecture* which he penned in 1914, and architectural drawings that illustrate these futurist ideals.[131] Sant'Elia's greatest achievement is his urban designs for Città Nuova (New City, 1912–14), a machine-age Utopian city of stepped skyscrapers that are interconnected through aerial bridges, skywalks and multi-level transportation routes. His drawing *La Centrale Elettrica* (1914), with its bold design and radiating power lines, displays the energy and excitement for futurist architecture and the achievements of modern technology.

'We must invent and rebuild the Futurist City,' Sant'Elia writes in *Manifesto of Futurist Architecture*.' 'It must be like an immense and tumultuous shipyard, agile, mobile and dynamic in every detail; and the Futurist house must be like a gigantic machine.' Sant'Elia's drawings have been an inspiration to not just later architects but science fiction comic strips such as the *Buck Rogers* and *Flash Gordon* cities of the future (1928 and 1934) and motion pictures, such as Fritz Lang's 1927 film *Metropolis*, and Ridley Scott's 1982 movie *Blade Runner*. In these films, Sant'Elia's architectural concepts are a backdrop for futuristic dystopian societies.

Like many futurists, Sant'Elia welcomed World War I as a means to clear away the old dead order to make room for the future. He enlisted in the Italian army in 1915 and was killed in the eighth Battle of the Isonzo near Monfalcone. His last words are reported to have been: 'Tonight we sleep in Trieste, or in Paradise with the heroes.' Fitting words for a man who is considered a hero in an architectural revolution.

Antonio Sant'Elia
The Power Station (la Centrale Elettrica), 1914, ink, pencil and watercolour paper, 31 × 20.5 cm (12¼ × 8⅛ in)
Private collection

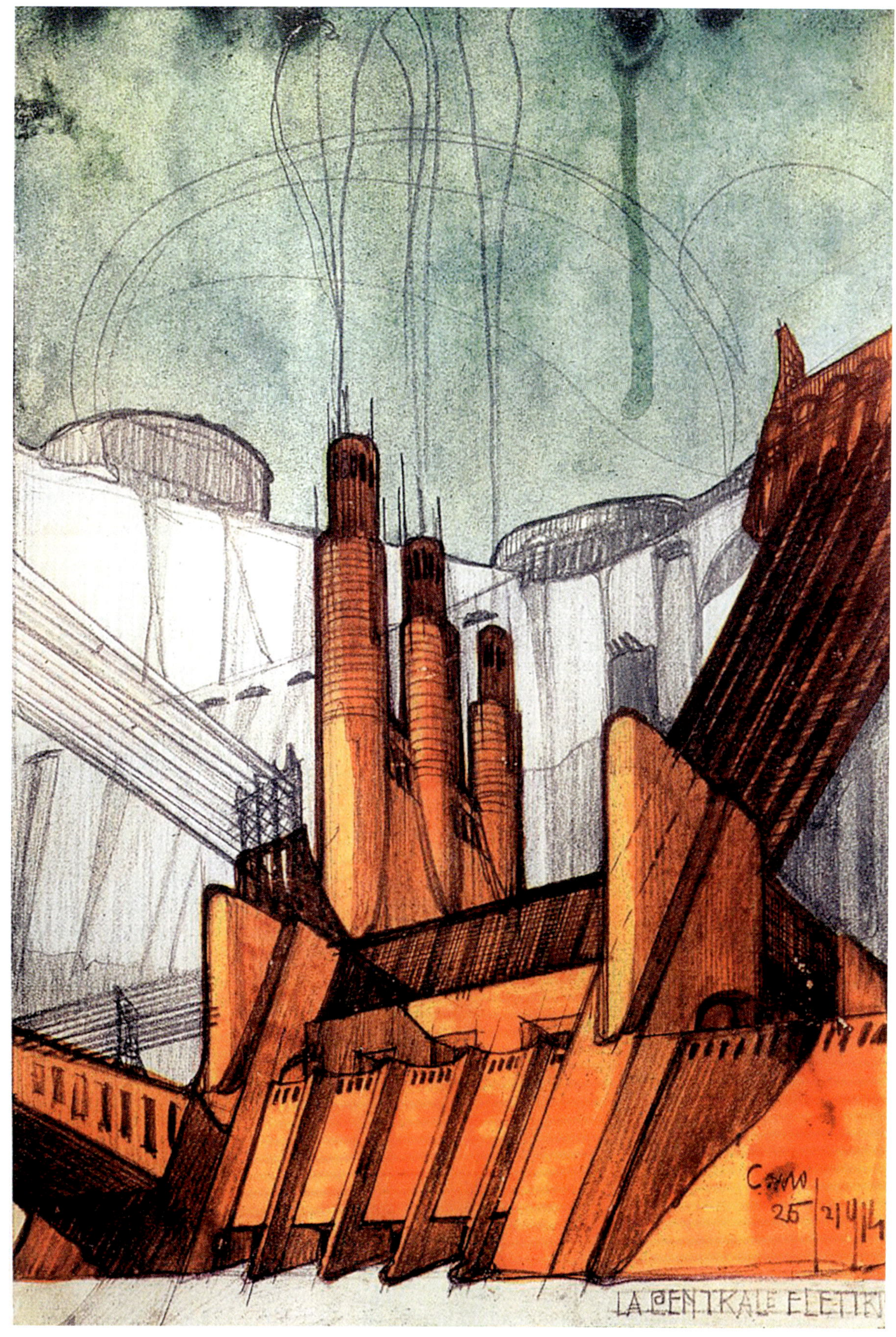

Sant'E
25/2/14
LA CENTRALE ELETTR

Egon SCHIELE

Tulln an der Donau, 12 Jun 1890 – 31 Oct 1918, Vienna
Austrian, 28 years, 4 months, 20 days

A critical player in Austrian expressionism, Egon Schiele studied at the Academy of Fine Arts in Vienna and then began his career as a protégé of Gustav Klimt. Soon, however, Schiele found his own distinctive style. He was very prolific, completing portraits, landscapes, still-lifes and, most controversially, overtly erotic images of contorted, often sexually explicit, nude figures. Schiele's art and lifestyle were frequently at odds with societal norms, beginning with his rumoured teenage incestuous relationship with his younger sister.

Additionally, his studios were often frequented by minors, and even young prostitutes, whom he made the subject of his drawings and paintings. He also lived openly with a young model turned mistress Wally Neuzil. These practices drew criticism and in 1912 he was charged with abducting and seducing an underaged girl. The charges were eventually dropped, but he was sentenced to 24 days in prison for exhibiting erotic art to children – the judge even burning a drawing in court in demonstration. That same year, Schiele painted *Self-Portrait with Chinese Lantern Plant*, presenting himself as self-confident, almost superior, but not immune to the troubles of the outside world. He appears as fragile and delicately balanced as the plant behind him.

In 1915, Schiele decided to make an 'advantageous' marriage with Edith Harms, hoping that his lover Wally would hang around. She did not. Just days after his marriage, he was drafted in World War I. However, he never saw combat and did mostly administrative work, allowing him to continue producing and exhibiting art. In 1917, he returned to Vienna and participated in the 49th Vienna Secession Exhibition in 1918, with great success. However, a short time later Schiele and his pregnant wife contracted the dreaded Spanish flu. Bernard Chambaz writes of their demise:

> On 31 October Edith dies of Spanish flu. She is six months pregnant. Three days later, Egon himself succumbs. He is twenty-eight years old. As for Egon's mother, she has to learn all at once of the death of her son, of her daughter-in-law, whom she didn't like, and of a grandchild whom she did not know existed.[132]

During his short career, Schiele produced around 3,000 drawings, working right up to his death. One of his last drawings is *Edith Schiele on Her Deathbed*, depicting his expiring wife even as he himself is dying. If Schiele had lived longer, would he have continued to push the limits of his taboo subjects to new heights or would his art have become more conservative under the influence of fatherhood and his increased acceptance in the Establishment of the Viennese art world? These are the questions that can never be answered now.

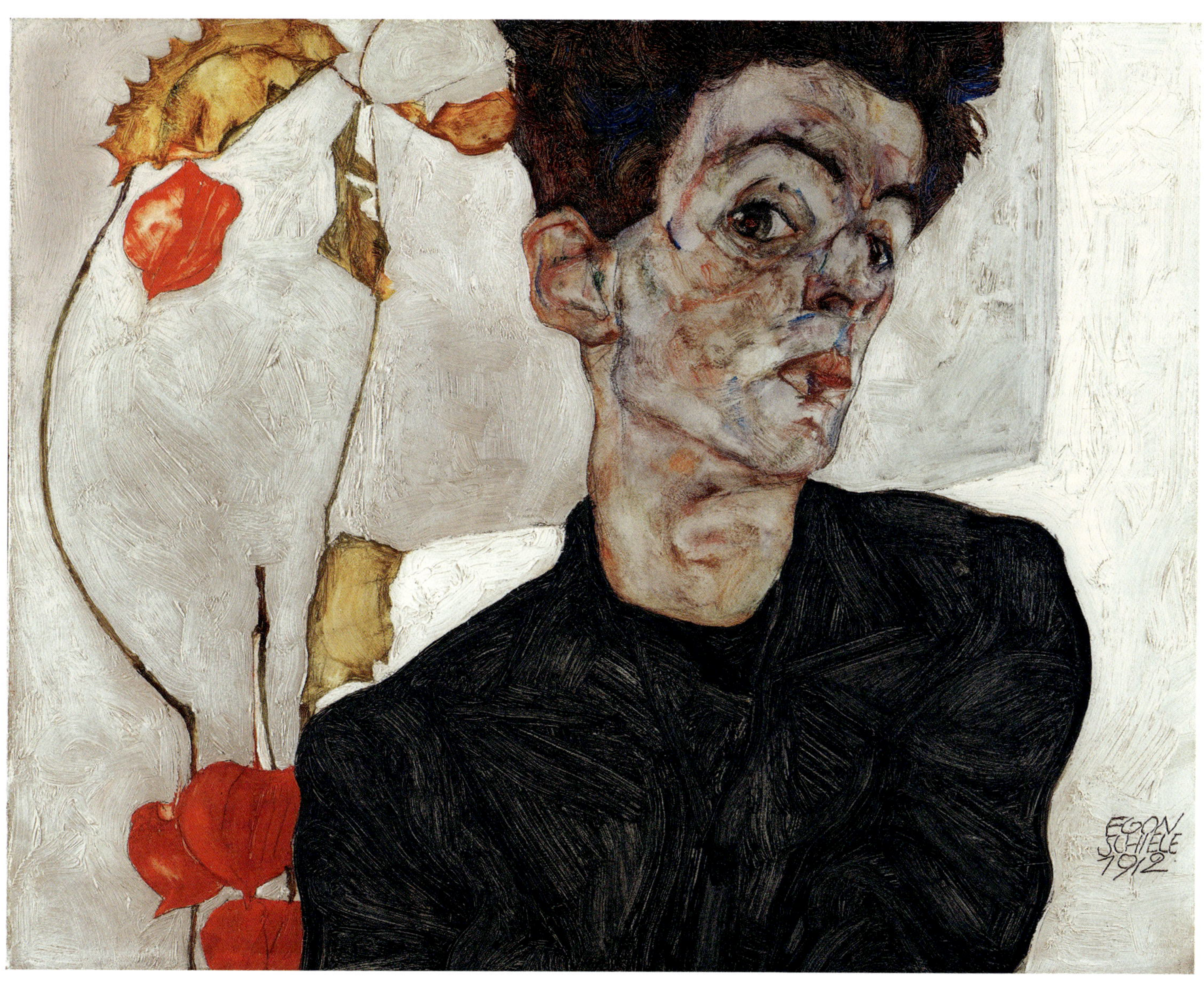

Amrita SHER-GIL

Budapest, 30 Jan 1913 – 5 Dec 1941, Lahore, Pakistan
Indian/Hungarian, 28 years, 10 months, 6 days

Amrita Sher-Gil is widely celebrated as the pioneer of modern art in India. Her distinct bicultural style, convention-flouting life, and mysterious death have made her a modernist icon. In 1976, Sher-Gil was named a National Treasure artist by the Indian government and export of her art became prohibited. Consequently, while her fame in Asia has long been assured, her international recognition has unavoidably suffered. Fortunately, recent scholarship and a 2007 retrospective exhibition of her art at Tate Modern has attempted to correct this oversight, revealing Sher-Gil's original talent and its profound influence. Today her paintings sell for millions; an impressive achievement for an artist who never saw her 29th birthday.

Sher-Gil was born in Budapest to a Hungarian mother and an aristocratic Indian father. Growing up in both Hungary and India, Sher-Gil enjoyed a privileged upbringing. At a young age, she exhibited a precocious talent for art, and in 1929, when Sher-Gil was just 16, her supportive family moved to Paris for her to pursue formal art training. Sher-Gil studied at the prestigious École des Beaux-Arts in Paris. Influenced by Paul Cézanne and Paul Gaugin, she was very productive during her five years in Paris, painting 19 self-portraits alone. For this reason, Sher-Gil is often compared to Frida Kahlo, who was also bicultural and shared her passion for self-portraiture. Christie's notes that Sher-Gil and Kahlo are 'both considered among the greatest avant-garde women artists practicing in the early 20th century.'[133]
In Paris, Sher-Gil lived an unrestrained bohemian lifestyle and pursued numerous love affairs. This led to hardships including abortions, a broken engagement and

venereal disease. However, she also met with acclaim – winning a gold medal in the Salon of 1933 for her canvas *Young Girls* and becoming an Associate of the Grand Salon, a rare distinction for an artist who was just 20 years old.

Nevertheless, by 1934 Sher-Gil longed to return to India. In India she saw the potential to make her mark as an artist, and she was right. She later wrote, 'I can only paint in India. Europe belongs to Picasso, Matisse, Braque … India belongs only to me.' Blending together her European training with inspiration from Indian artistic traditions, her art evolved into a modernist style all her own. Sher-Gil chose as her subjects rural villagers, particularly women, and presented them in a direct, unsentimental manner. Her melancholic canvas *Bride's Toilet* (1937) displays no jubilation for the upcoming arranged nuptials. Instead a sober, almost resigned, mood reigns.

The following year, Sher-Gil married her first cousin Dr Victor Egan, a man who understood her sexually free lifestyle and had procured for her at least two abortions. The pair eventually moved to Lahore. It was there that she became seriously ill and slipped into a coma, dying around midnight on 5 December 1941. The cause of death was unclear. Perhaps it was a result of food poisoning or a botched abortion that led to peritonitis. Sher-Gil's grief-stricken mother blamed Egan for her death. She was cremated just two days later, leaving the circumstances of her death forever a mystery. Despite the brevity of her life, she left a stunning legacy that has inspired Indian artists for generations.

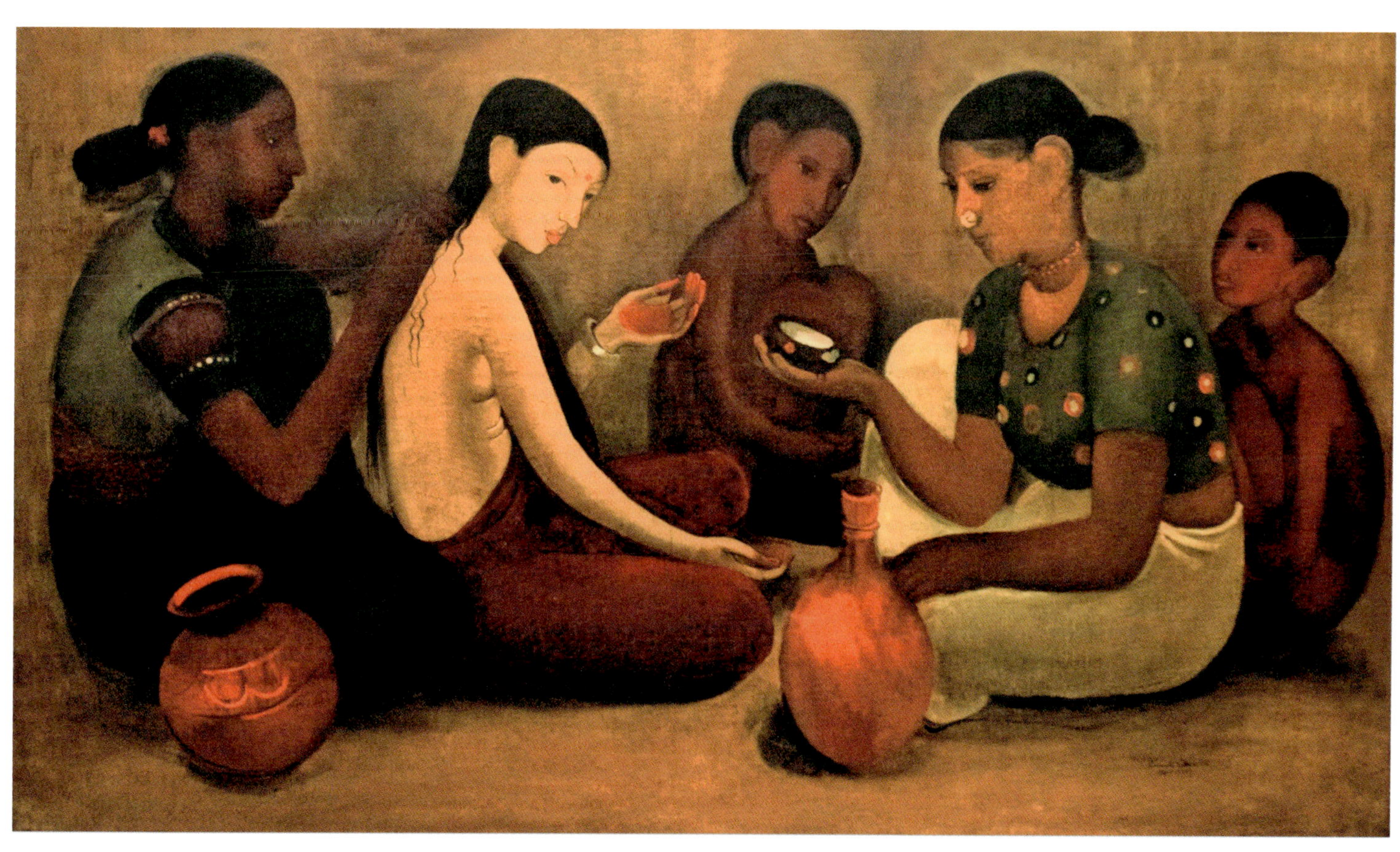

Amrita Sher-Gil
Bride's Toilet, 1937, oil on canvas, 88.5 × 146 cm (34⅞ × 57½ in)
National Gallery of Modern Art, New Delhi

Geertgen tot SINT JANS

Leiden, c.1460/65 – c.1488/93, Haarlem
Dutch, approx. 28 years

This remarkable early Netherlandish oil painter was called 'Geertgen tot Sint Jans' by his chronicler Karel van Mander, meaning 'Little Gerard of St Johns.' We learn from van Mander that Geertgen served as the resident artist for the Knights Hospitallers of St John Monastery in Haarlem. Although not a monk himself, his name 'tot Sint Jans' displays his association with the brotherhood as a lay brother. He painted an altarpiece for them which was partially destroyed following the Spanish Siege of 1573. Its surviving wings, *Lamentation over the Dead Christ* and *Burning the Bones of St John the Baptist* (c. 1484, Kunsthistorisches Gemaldegalerie, Vienna), dazzle with their lustrous enamelled colour, miniature style, and exquisite feeling for detailed flourish and finish.

Geertgen studied with Albert van Ouwater (c.1415–1475) the founder of the Haarlem School of Art. Fortunately, the distinctive quality and warm charm of Geertgen's style has made it possible to attribute around a dozen works to the artist. Works such as *Nativity at Night* with its serene tone or *John the Baptist in the Wilderness* with its contemplative figure in an exquisitely detailed landscape, or *Glorification of the Virgin* with its fanciful concentric rings of angels playing contemporary instruments, make one wish that more works by Geertgen had been produced or at least survived. Unfortunately, the iconoclasms of the Reformation and numerous wars have destroyed some of his small but vital

oeuvre. His paintings are irresistible for their remarkable chiaroscuro, sensitivity to light, natural details, and doll-like figures and animals. It can be argued that Geertgen was one of the most important Netherlandish painters. At least, he has been frequently referred to as the most 'lovable'.[134]

While a range of birth and death dates have been contested, Karel van Mander the only quasi-near-contemporary source, states that the artist died when he was 28 years old and was buried in the monastery graveyard. Was this particularly early death an exaggeration given the quality of his art and apparent length of his career, with some speculating that he flourished between 1480 and 1495? Certainly by 1604, when van Mander's book *Het Schilder-boeck* was published, memories had faded and documents had been destroyed, so his account is necessarily abbreviated and not substantiated. Modern scientific forensics and critical scholarship have been employed to prove his date of birth and the provenance of his oeuvre; however these also have yielded inconclusive results. Therefore, it would be appropriate to accept van Mander's age of 28 years at face value. The cause of Geertgen's early death is unknown.[135] His personal story cannot be told. It does seem incredible that so young an artist could create such mature and influential paintings. Perhaps he was simply a natural born painter, as Albrecht Dürer is claimed to have said, 'Truly he was a painter in his mother's womb.'

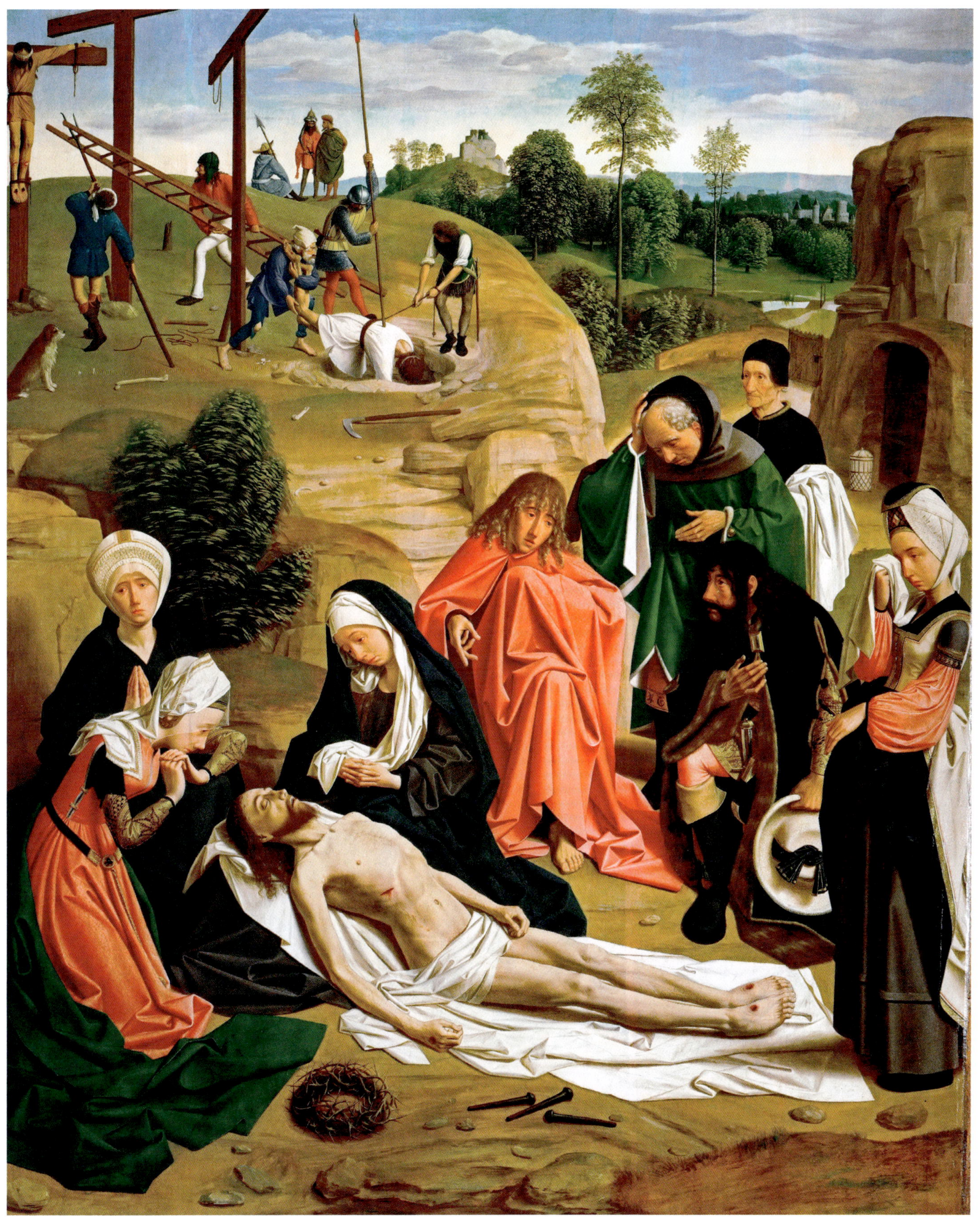

Bob THOMPSON

Louisville, Kentucky, 26 Jun 1937 – 30 May 1966, Rome
American, 28 years, 11 months, 5 days

African-American artist Bob Thompson was a figurative painter influenced by Renaissance, baroque, fauvist, abstract expressionist masters, and jazz music in equal measure. The results of this recipe were paintings of flatly painted, primary coloured, abstracted figures acting out the great narratives of mythology and the Bible on a large scale. *The Deposition* (1961), painted in the year Thompson went to Paris, appropriates compositions from the Old Masters in a new way, based on his personal aesthetic vision.

Even in his short lifetime Thompson's talents were well recognised. He sold his paintings in New York's top galleries; in 1963, the Martha Jackson Gallery held Thompson's first one-man exhibition, and his estate is handled by Michael Rosenfeld Gallery in New York. He had a broad base of friends, including Red Grooms, and participated in many of Grooms's art 'Happenings'. Additionally, Thompson won grants and fellowships that funded extended trips to Europe, where he studied the Old Masters and painted.

Despite these successes, the artist suffered from depression, which cast a constant grey cloud over his young life and career. Following his father's death in a car accident when he was just 13, Thompson went to live with his sister in Boston. He enrolled on a pre-med course at Boston University in 1955 but dropped out after just a year.

His brother-in-law encouraged him to pursue art as a means of dealing with his depression, and Thompson enrolled on the art course at the University of Louisville, where he excelled. Not only did art prove to be Thompson's calling, it was also a kind of therapy for him, which enhanced his ability to communicate with others. In his own words, Thompson explains:

> I paint many paintings that tell me slowly that I have something inside of me that is just bursting, twisting, sticking, spilling over to get out. Out into souls and mouths and eyes that have never seen before. The Monsters are present now on my canvas as in my dreams.

Unfortunately, Thompson also turned to partying, alcohol and drugs as a means of coping with depression. In March 1966, while travelling in Rome with his wife, Thompson underwent emergency gallbladder surgery. Ignoring the doctor's recommendation to recuperate, Thompson resumed his extravagant lifestyle, eventually dying of a heroin overdose later that year. An incessant worker, Thompson completed in his short career an astounding body of work – nearly 1,000 paintings and drawings. Many of these works now hang in the collections of America's pre-eminent museums.

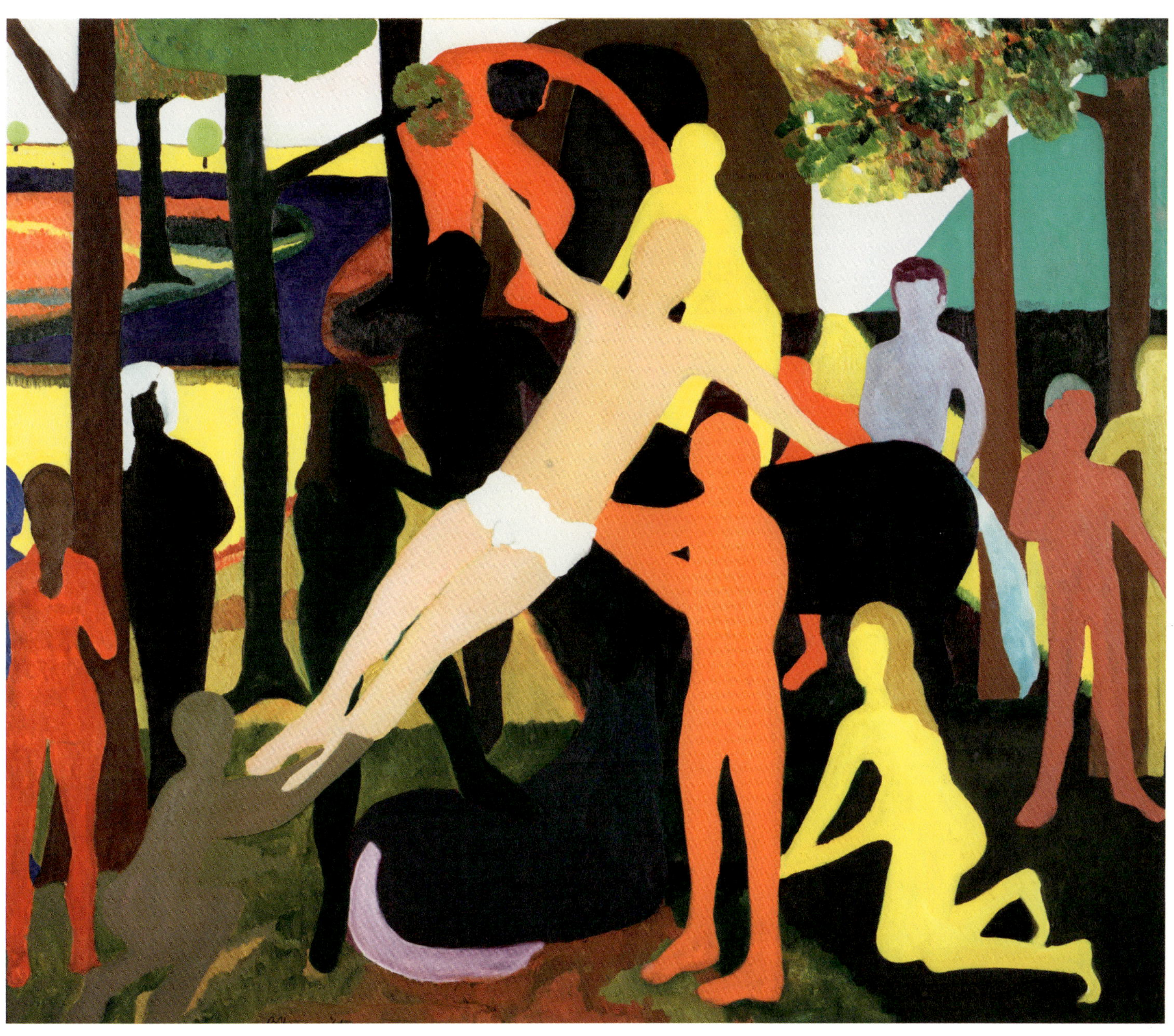

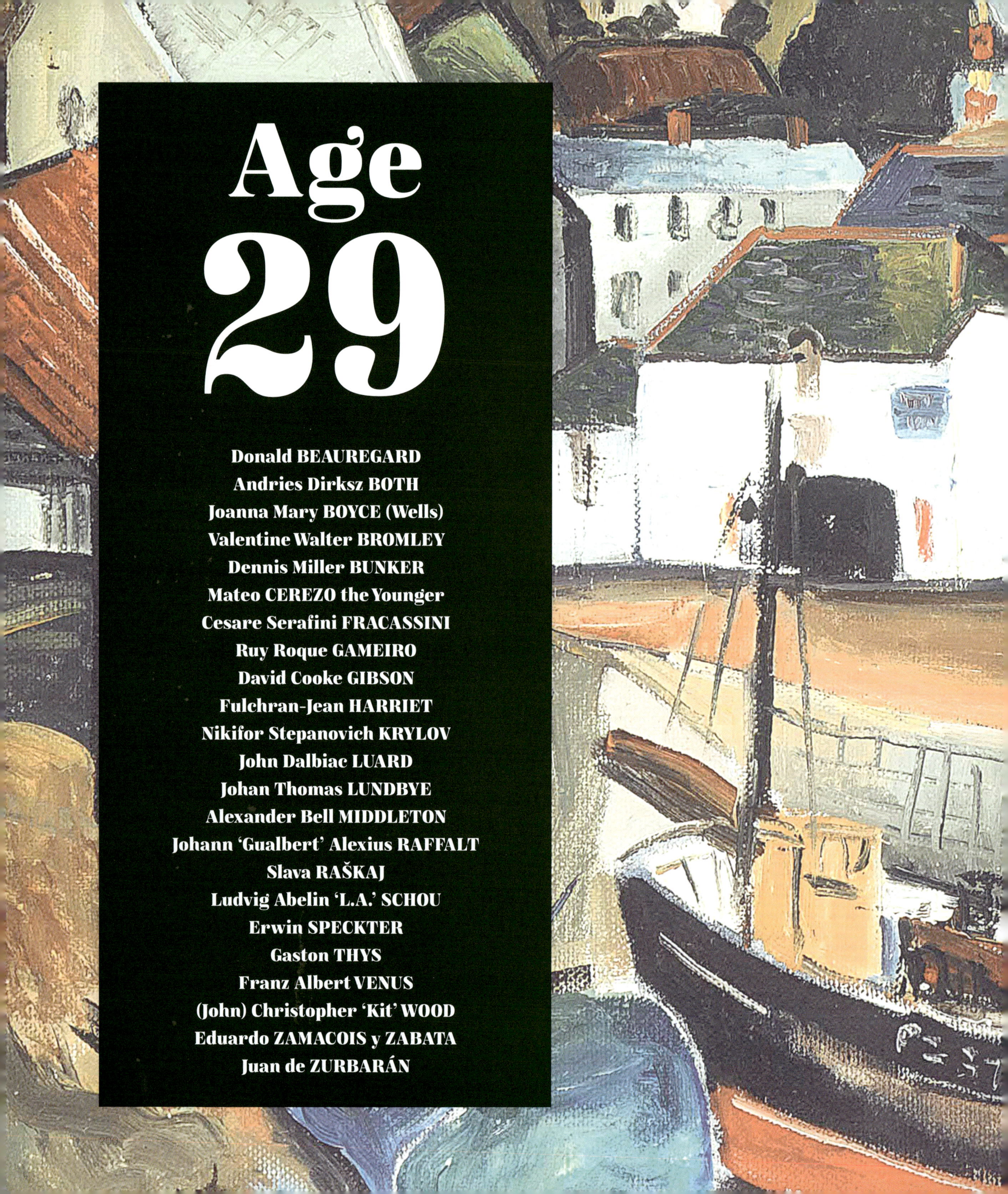

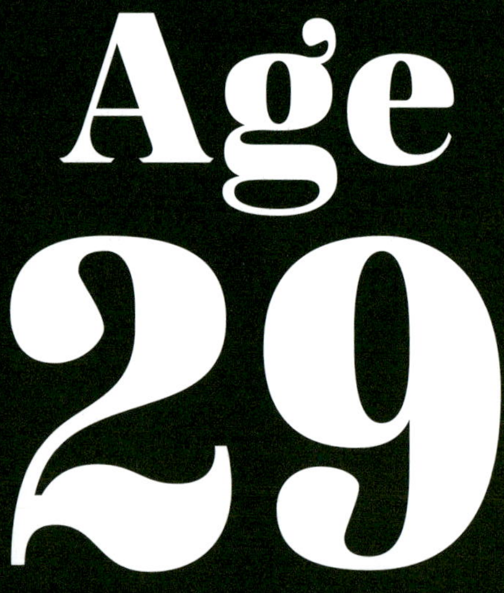

Age 29

Donald BEAUREGARD
Andries Dirksz BOTH
Joanna Mary BOYCE (Wells)
Valentine Walter BROMLEY
Dennis Miller BUNKER
Mateo CEREZO the Younger
Cesare Serafini FRACASSINI
Ruy Roque GAMEIRO
David Cooke GIBSON
Fulchran-Jean HARRIET
Nikifor Stepanovich KRYLOV
John Dalbiac LUARD
Johan Thomas LUNDBYE
Alexander Bell MIDDLETON
Johann 'Gualbert' Alexius RAFFALT
Slava RAŠKAJ
Ludvig Abelin 'L.A.' SCHOU
Erwin SPECKTER
Gaston THYS
Franz Albert VENUS
(John) Christopher 'Kit' WOOD
Eduardo ZAMACOIS y ZABATA
Juan de ZURBARÁN

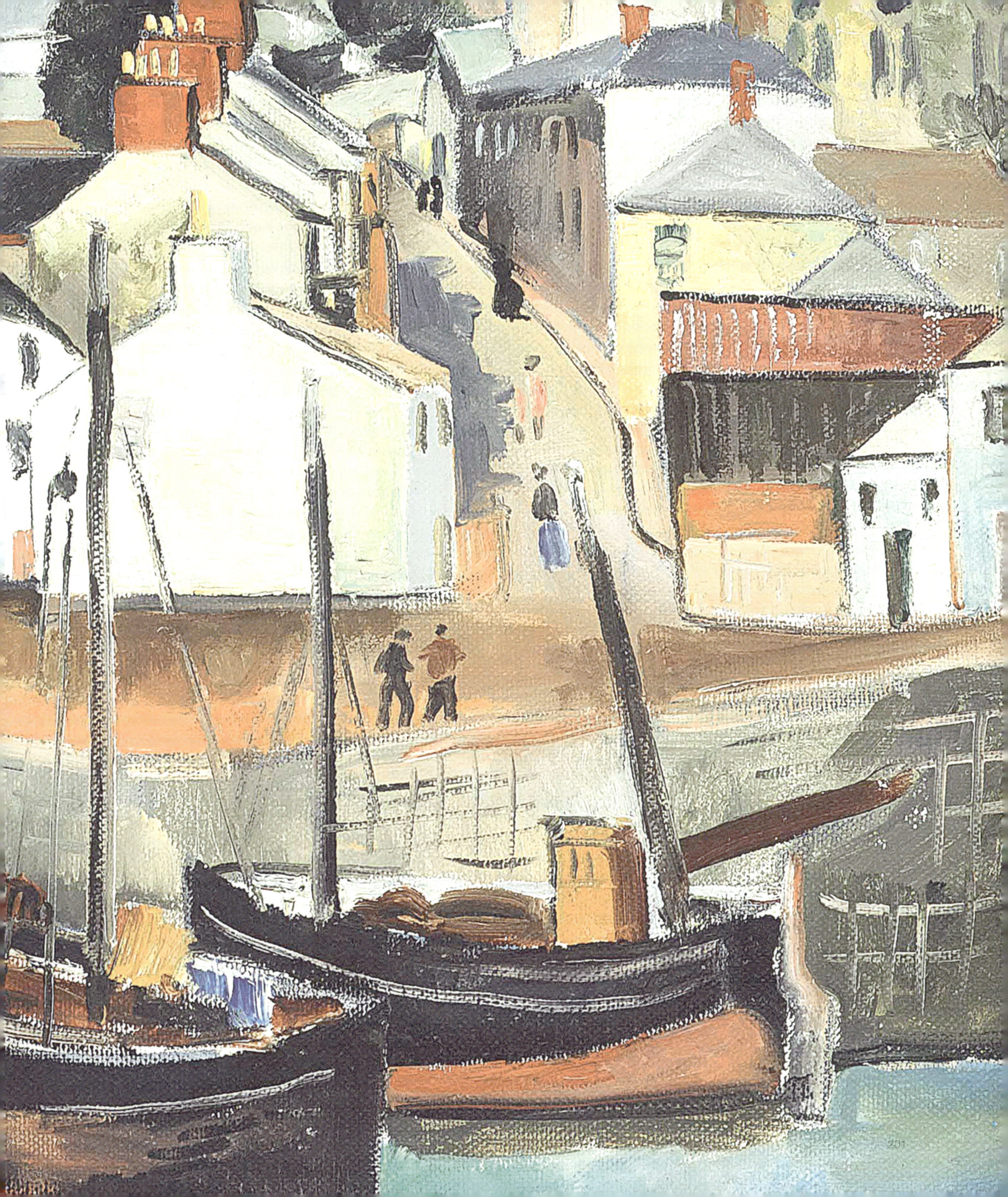

Donald BEAUREGARD

Fillmore, Utah, 17 Aug 1884 – 2 May 1914, Fillmore
American, 29 years, 8 months, 16 days

Beauregard was a figurative painter of cowboy, religious, Native American and landscape subjects. He was born in Fillmore, which had once been Utah's state capital, but by 1884 was a scantily populated wilderness desert and farming community. Somehow, Beauregard had the fortitude to break out and win an art career, if only briefly. He studied at Brigham Young Academy in Provo, then the University of Utah under Edwin Evans, and later at the Académie Julian in Paris (1906–1907) under Jean-Paul Laurens. He then returned to the Western desert, successfully painting in Utah, Arizona and New Mexico. The painterly canvas, *Artist's Father Clearing Sagebrush near Fillmore* (1907) attests to his expressive power of mood and brushwork.

In 1909 and 1910, Beauregard worked with the University of Utah Summer Archaeological Project in New Mexico under Professor Byron Cummings. While on the project he met a gracious benefactor Frank Springer, who appreciated Beauregard's talent and financially assisted him with studying art in Spain, France and Bavaria for two years. In 1912, while in France, Beauregard fell unexpectedly ill. This was the first intimation of the seriousness of an ailment that would cut short his career, just as he was entering his prime.

Beauregard returned to Santa Fe, New Mexico to paint a commissioned work, a mural of the life and influence of St Francis of Assisi for the New Mexico building at the Panama-California Exposition in San Diego. Beauregard worked on the mural from December 1913 until February 1914, but his health forced him to abandon the project after completing just two of the six panels. Alice Klauber writes, 'Mr. Beauregard soon demonstrated that he would win a high place in the world's hall of fame with his work, but the last summons came when he was fairly in the midst of his task.'[136] Consulting a specialist in Denver, Beauregard discovered that he had pancreatic cancer. The weakened artist underwent surgery, but it was too late. Beauregard died at the home of his parents in Fillmore, just eight months after his 29th birthday.[137]

For the local residents, it was a sorrowful scenario to have the most famous native son of Fillmore die just at the moment of his ascendancy. His tombstone touchingly reads: 'What hopes are buried with you my son'. The New Mexico Museum of Art in Santa Fe owns a fine collection of his works, demonstrating that if the artist had lived, he would have been a truly great American Western painter.

Donald Beauregard
Artist's Father Clearing Sagebrush near Fillmore, 1907, oil on canvas, 38.1 × 545.9 cm (15 × 214⅞ in)
Springville Museum of Art

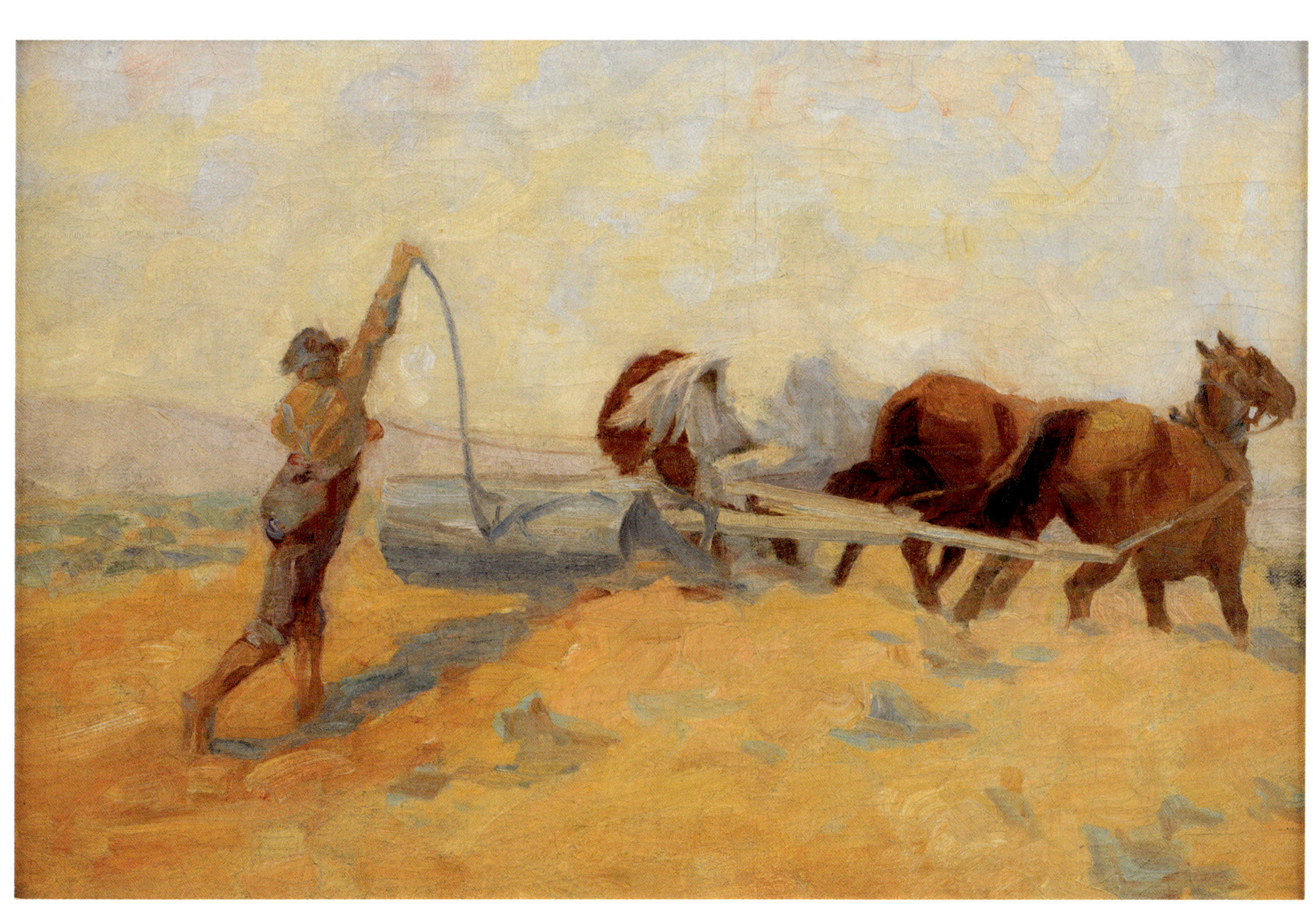

Andries Dirksz BOTH

Utrecht, c.1612/1613 – 23 Mar 1642, Venice
Dutch, approx. 29 years

Andries was the son of Dirck Both, a glass painter, and the brother of the Dutch Italianate artist Jan Both (c.1615–1652). Each of the brothers was exceptionally gifted in their own way, and most probably had their first instruction from their father. Andries subsequently studied with Abraham Bloemaert (c.1564–1651) then travelled through France (especially the Rouen area) before arriving in Rome in 1633. His brother Jan joined him in 1638, and they moved to a studio at the Via Vittoria. The Both brothers joined the highbrow Accademia di San Luca in Rome as well as the less-reputable Bentvueghels (Birds of a Feather), a society of Dutch painters under the influence of Pieter van Laer, which was basically a drinking club.

It was once believed that the two brothers collaborated on Italianate landscape pictures, with Jan painting the landscape and Andries the figures. While this was a common practice at the time, and Jan is known to have collaborated with other artists, the view that the two brothers worked on the same canvas has since fallen out of favour. However, several landscapes bathed in liquid golden light, still bear the attribution to both artists.

Andries is known for his engravings, genre paintings and for being one of the first Bamboccianti ('silly fat babies'). Instead of depicting the great themes of Christendom and antiquity for which Rome was known, the Bamboccianti brought with them the tradition of low-life peasant genre from Netherlandish art and chose to depict the seamier side of Roman life. With their starkly realist and often vulgar pictures, they shocked the more sedate and classical art establishment who preferred a more idealised style of art. However, they found a ready market for their cabinet-sized paintings. These works by Andries, such as *A Concert of Beggars* (c.1634), were humorous and outrageous in their unvarnished reality. Though his life was short, his output was fairly large with 300 works attributed to him.

In 1641, the brothers began their journey home to Utrecht and while en route, they stayed in Venice for a time. Tragically, Andries died in Venice by falling into and drowning in a canal as he was returning from some festivities, probably in a drunken state. Michael Bryan noted: 'his loss is said to have caused his brother great affliction.'[138] Never the same, Jan lived another decade and died in his thirties. With such great studio discipline, Andries would have continued to expand his reputation as a leading painter of the low-life Bambocciati-style genre reminiscent of Adriaen Brouwer.

Andries Dirksz Both
A Concert of Beggars, c.1634, oil on panel, 42 × 53 cm (16½ × 20⅞ in)
Private collection

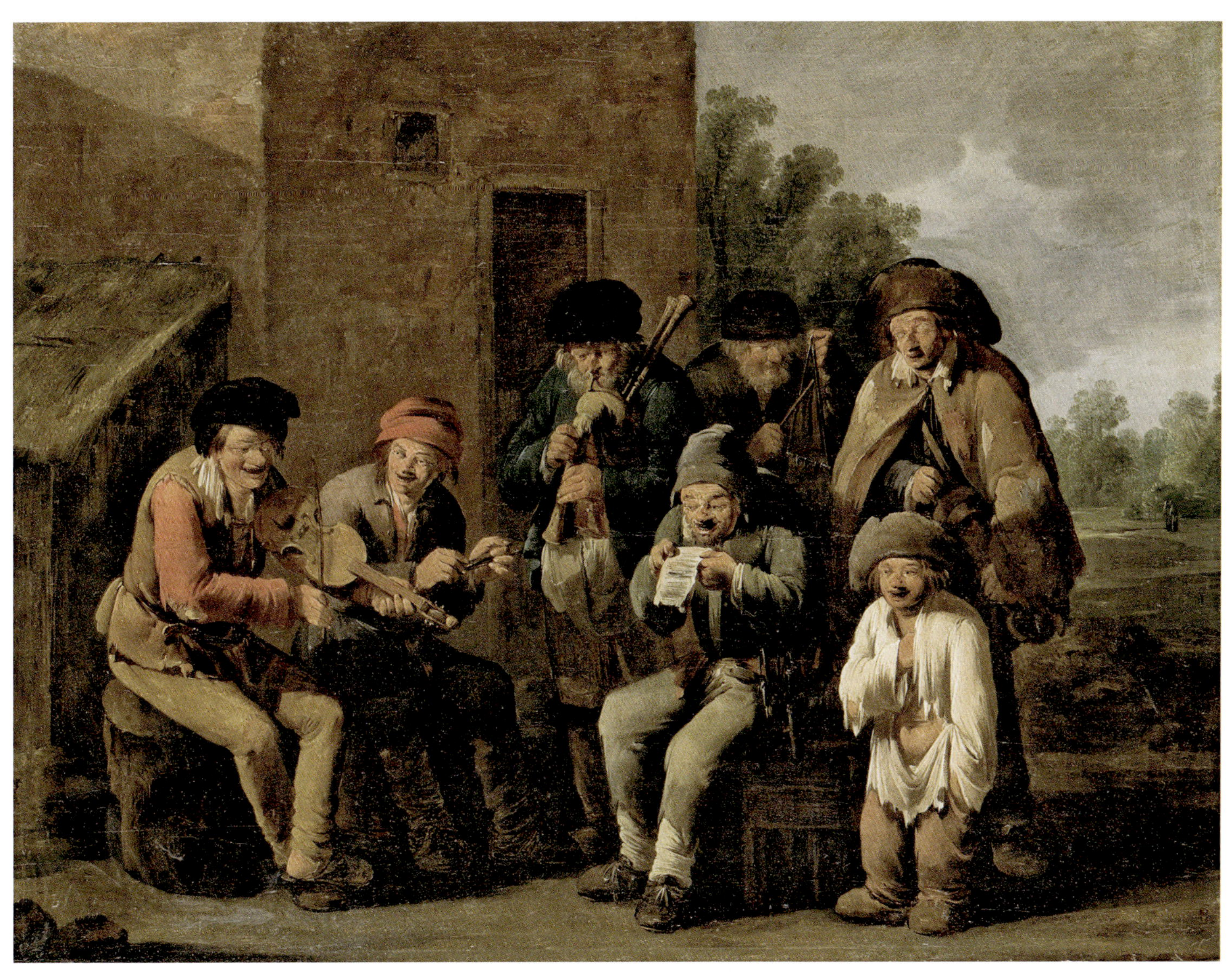

Joanna Mary BOYCE (Wells)

Maida Hill, London, 7 Dec 1831 – 15 Jul 1861, London
British, 29 years, 7 months, 9 days

The portrait, genre and landscape painter Joanna Boyce was the sister of Pre-Raphaelite artist George Price Boyce (1826–1897). From a young age she was artistically gifted but was discouraged by her mother from pursuing art as a vocation. Eventually she began formal training at the Cary Academy, London at the age of 18. Her education was, however, interrupted by family illnesses, during which time she was expected to act as a nurse, and then by the death of her father. In 1853 she finally returned to her studies, this time at the Leigh Academy in London.

In 1855, Boyce attended Thomas Couture's class for female students in Paris, and also exhibited at the Royal Academy, London for the first time. Her submission, a serene head titled *Elgiva*, was widely admired. The famed artist Ford Madox Brown called it, 'the best head in the rooms.' Likewise, John Ruskin wrote of Boyce's potential after viewing *Elgiva*: ' … it seems to me that she might entertain the hope of taking place in the very first rank of painters.'[139]

In 1855 Boyce also received a marriage proposal from the artist Henry Tanworth Wells (1828–1903). Wells fell deeply in love with Boyce, but she initially refused his offer, unwilling to give up her independence for the strictures of Victorian married life. Her art was very important to her, as she wrote in 1857: 'I have talents or a talent and with it the constant impulse to enjoy it, —not for notoriety or fame, but for the love of it and the longing to work.'[140] Wells held out hope, and finally, in December 1857, the two artists married. Thankfully, marriage did not decrease Boyce's output. She exhibited many excellent oils at the Royal Academy, including *The Childs' Crusade: The Departure* (1860), *Homestead on the Surrey Hills*, and *Peep-bo* (1861), amongst others. Her last exhibited work, *Thou Bird of God* (1861), was left complete on her easel at the time of her death and was exhibited at the Royal Academy the following year.

Following the birth of her third child, Boyce died suddenly of puerperal fever, a bacterial infection of the female reproductive tract following childbirth. A *Spectator* obituary reported that 'no English-woman has ever set forth such mastery of style and such subtle qualities of painting as are impressed upon her works.'[141] Years later William Michael Rossetti shared his thoughts on Boyce's passing: 'All the artists whom I best knew and valued, deplored her death as a real loss to art; they had looked upon her as the leading hope for painting in the hands of a woman.'[142] This 'for a woman' attitude would persist for a further 50 years, until women artists would finally be judged squarely against men. When evaluated thus, Boyce is not found wanting. Unfortunately, because of the paucity of her work, she has not been recognised as one of the seven women of Pre-Raphaelitism, but a 2019 National Portrait Gallery exhibition placed her among the 'Pre-Raphaelite Sisters'.

Joanna Mary Boyce (Wells)
Thou Bird of God, 1861, oil on canvas, size unknown
Private collection

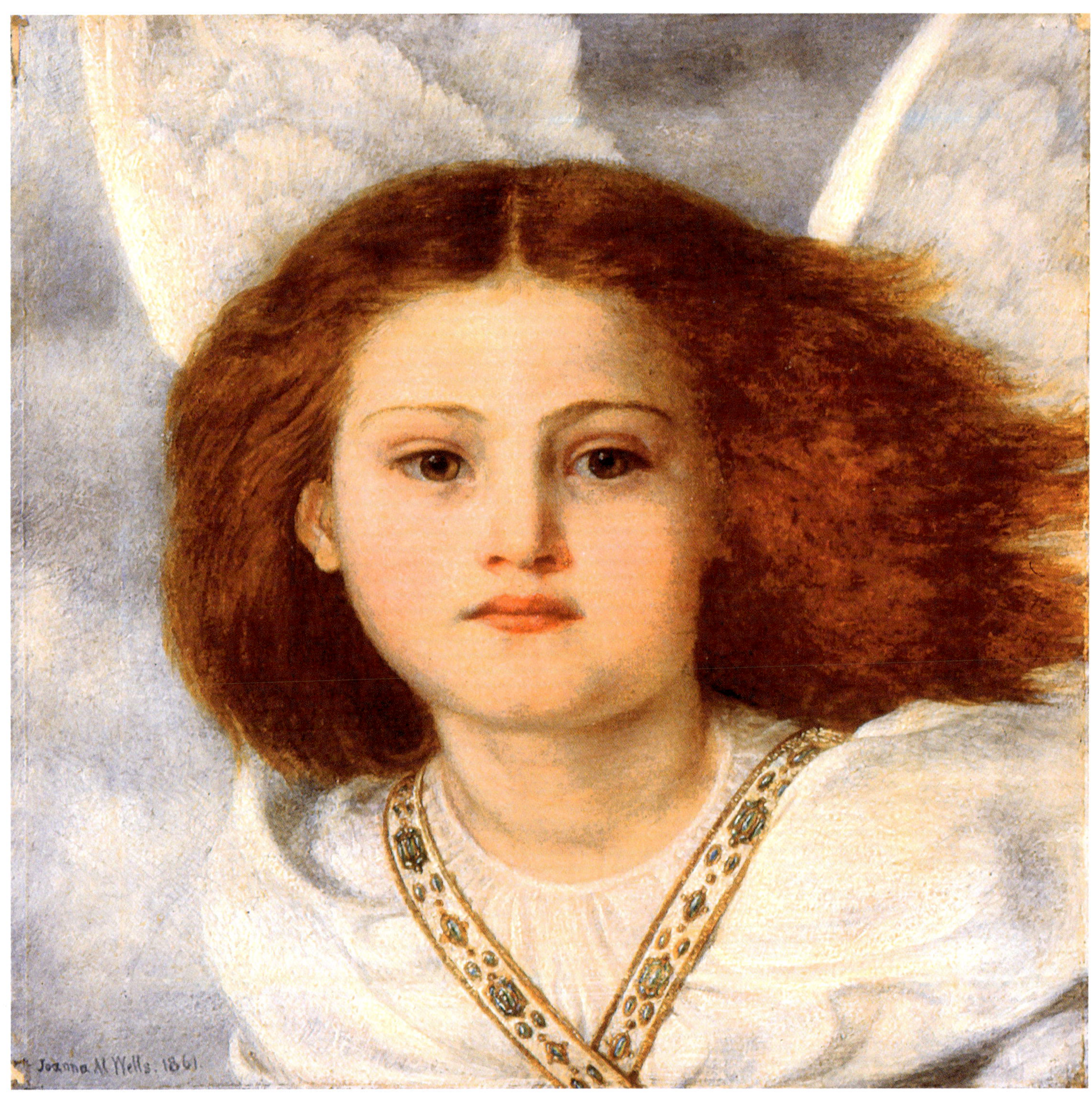

Joanna M Wells. 1861.

Valentine Walter BROMLEY

London, 14 Feb 1848 – 30 Apr 1877, Harpenden
British, 29 years, 2 months, 17 days

Bromley was born into a multi-generational artistic family. His great-grandfather, grandfather and father were all engravers and artists of note. His great-grandfather, William Bromley I, was an associate of the Royal Academy and his father, William Bromley III (active 1838–1888), was well known for his sympathetic portrayals of rustic country life, usually depicting children. Walter Bromley first studied art with his father. Then, by the age of 19 years old, he was so accomplished that he was elected an associate of the Institute of Painters in Water Colours. Later, he exhibited in London at the Society of British Artists, the New Society of Painters in Water Colours and the Royal Academy (1872–1877).

Bromley worked as a staff member and art correspondent for the *Illustrated London News*, for which he produced many fine engravings. The Earl of Dunraven commissioned Bromley to illustrate his book *The Great Divide*. To do so, they travelled to North America in 1874–75 to study Native American tribes, especially the Crow tribe. Bromley's brilliant canvas, *Crow Indian Burial* (1876) is a haunting evocation of the customs among the tribes. His paintings of Native Americans were a significant contribution to the genre even though they were slightly Europeanised. In 1877, the year of his death, he won a gold medal for his oil *Big Chief's Toilet*, at the Crystal Palace Exhibition.

Bromley's broad range was further realised in the large fantasy oil *Flora* (1874) and in such paintings as *The Nearest Way to Church* (watercolour).

After Bromley's return to England, on the eve of working on a series of illustrations of Shakespearean and biblical subjects in his studio at Fallows Green, he became ill with flu-like symptoms. It was soon discovered that he had smallpox, and the attack was swift and fatal.[143] As was typical with smallpox victims, Bromley was buried the same day as his passing, in the parish churchyard 'in the dead of night' – a time when the fewest number of people would have contact with the body.[144] Bromley was a history, literary and genre painter of solid accomplishments for one so young. A notice of his death in the *Art Journal* panegyrises Bromley:

> He was a thorough artist, as full of animation and energy as of talent, and greatly beloved for his affectionate temper and warmth of heart. He had been married only a few months to a lady artist of considerable mark [Ida Forbes-Robertson].[145]

Bromley had a great future, and perhaps would have gained a full RA (Royal Academician) after his name; he simply was that good.

Valentine Walter Bromley
Crow Indian Burial, 1876, oil on canvas, 106.7 × 177.8 cm (42 × 70 in)
Courtesy of American Museum of Western Art – The Anschutz Collection/Photo: William J. O'Connor

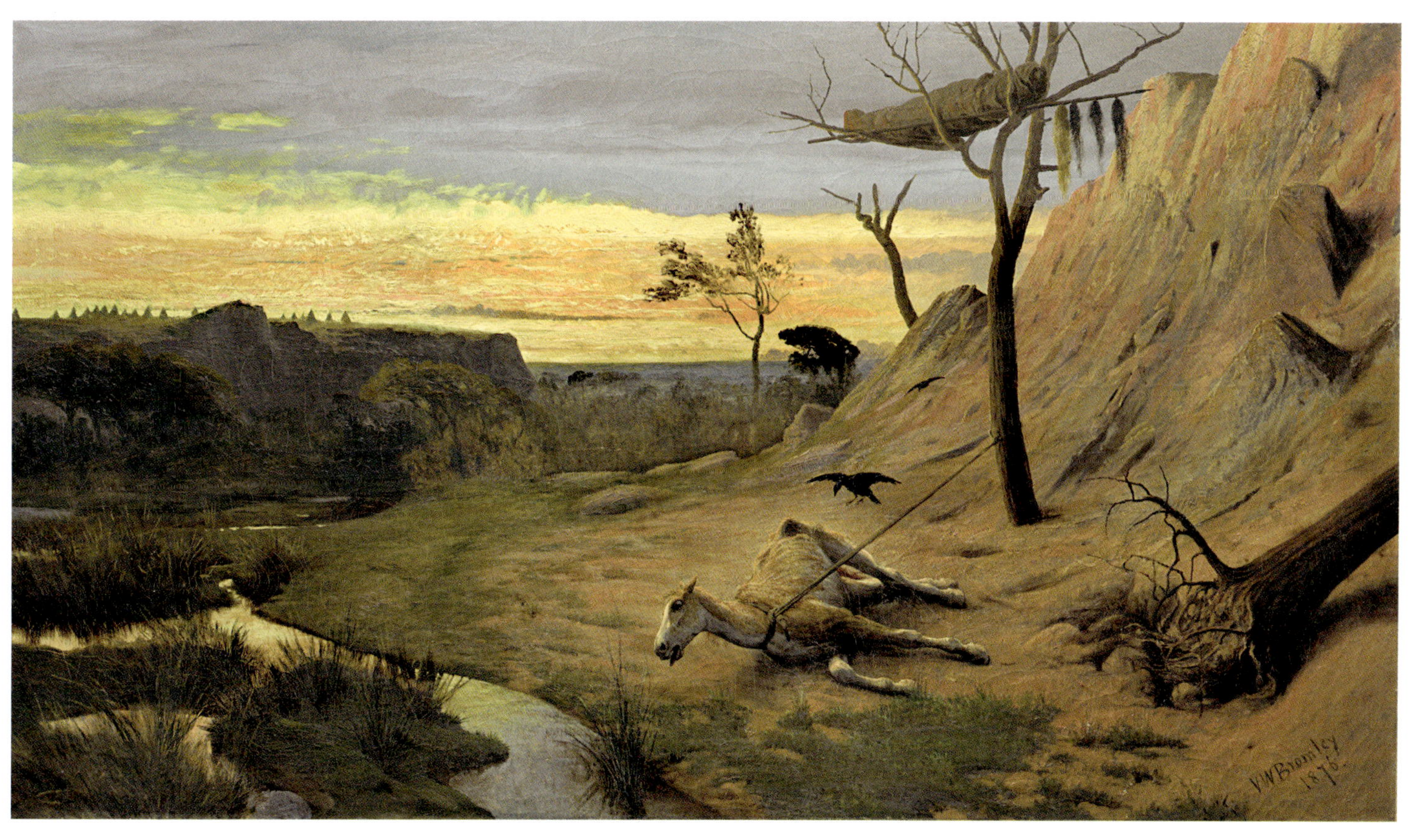

Dennis Miller BUNKER

New York City, 6 Nov 1861 – 28 Dec 1890, Boston, Massachusetts
American, 29 years, 1 month, 23 days

Bunker is widely remembered as one of the first proponents of American impressionism. Studying first at the National Academy of Design and the Art Students League of New York, Bunker concluded his studies at the École des Beaux-Arts in Paris under Jean-Léon Gérôme, where he was trained in consummate academicism. His mature style (1889–90) was informed by his academic training and the new advances of French impressionism. Bunker moved in the circles of New England's most prestigious artists and patrons – accepting commissions from Isabella Stewart Gardner and painting en plein-air with John Singer Sargent at Calcot, to name but a few. He was also an influential art teacher in Boston at the Cowles Art School on Dartmouth Street.

In 1890, the year of his death, Bunker's artistic career and personal life reached an all-time high, and his career was anticipated to climb even further. He began exhibiting his fresh and verdant impressionist landscape paintings, such as *The Pool, Medfield* (1889), and completed several more. New teaching opportunities also presented themselves, with Bunker being offered a position to teach at the Metropolitan Museum of Art and take over William Merritt Chase's class in Brooklyn. Finally, in October 1890, after a lengthy engagement, he married Eleanor Hardy, with whom he was ardently in love. In the early days of their marriage she served as his model for numerous portraits.

Two months later the newlyweds spent Christmas with the Hardy family in Boston. On Christmas Day Bunker complained of feeling chilled. Just three days later he met an unexpected and abrupt end, when he died of heart failure, probably a result of cerebro-spinal meningitis. His death was greatly grieved by his friends and family. The *Boston Post* stating that the 'only possible solace is that he can never grow old.'[146] Augustus Saint-Gaudens and Stanford White designed his tombstone. Friends organised a memorial exhibition of his art in Boston, and raised funds to purchase a portrait of his wife to donate to the Metropolitan Museum of Art.

Unfortunately, like many artists who died before their oeuvre reached critical mass, Bunker and his art became largely forgotten. His wife, Eleanor Hardy Bunker, eventually married artist Charles A. Platt, one of his best friends, and Bunker's reputation dwindled until a student of one of his students, R.H. Ives Gammell, revived his reputation with multiple exhibitions and a 1953 biography. Today, Bunker securely holds a place among the pantheon of forward-thinking impressionists whose influence on later American art is incalculable.

Dennis Miller Bunker
The Pool, Medfield, 1889, oil on canvas, 46.9 × 61.5 cm (18½ × 24¼ in)
Museum of Fine Arts, Boston

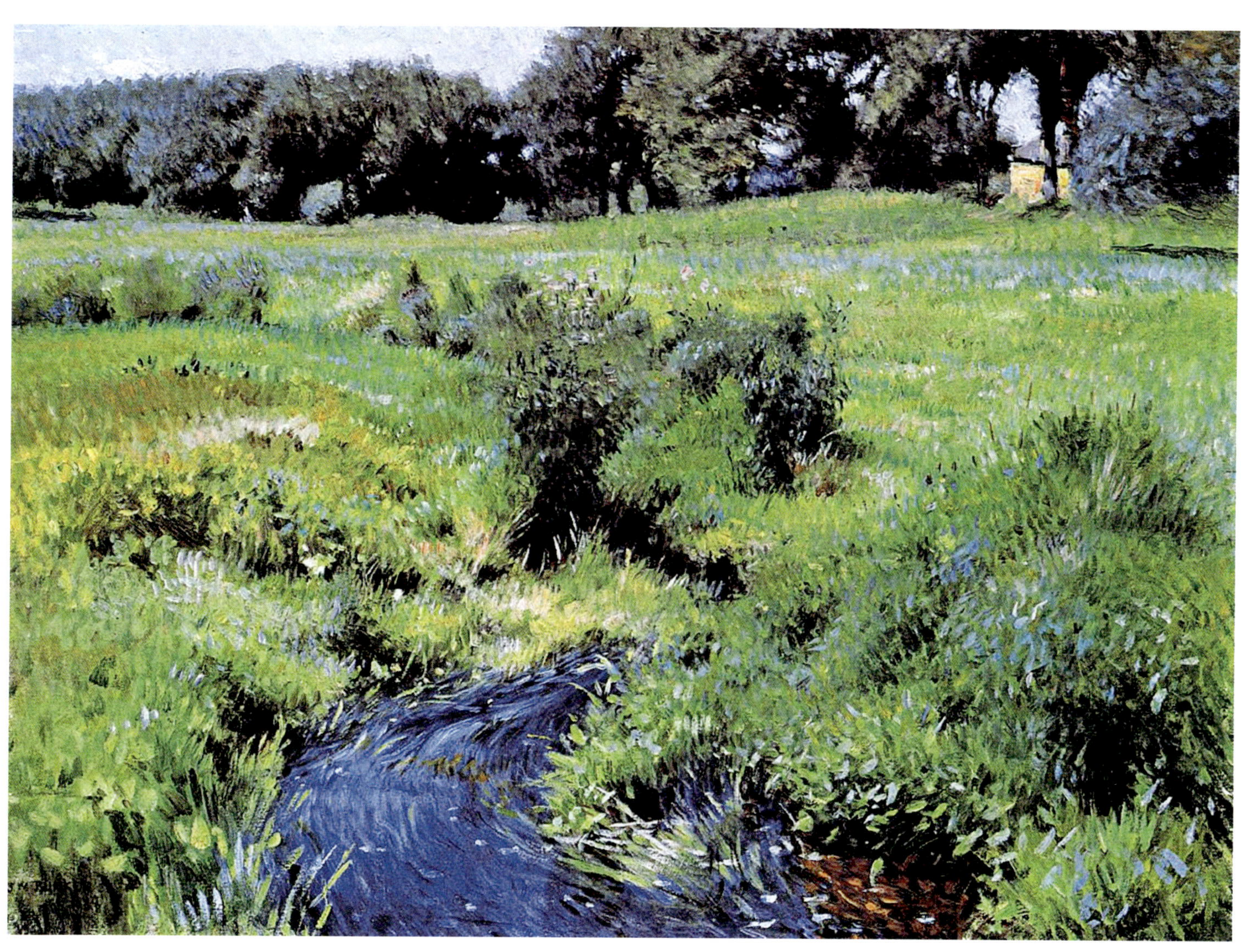

Mateo CEREZO the Younger

Burgos, 19 Apr 1637 – 29 Jun 1666, Madrid
Spanish, 29 years, 2 months, 11 days

It is fortunate that the baroque painter Mateo Cerezo found his vocation so early in life, enabling him to leave a significant body of work before his premature death at the age of 29. Today, his art can be found around the world in the best museums, the Prado in Madrid possessing the largest collection. Most art historians consider him one of the finest Spanish artists of his generation.[147] His father, Mateo Cerezo the Elder, was a devotional painter of modest abilities and was the first to train the young painter.

Then, at the age of 15 he went to Madrid to study in the studio of Juan Carreño de Miranda. After five years with Carreño, he began a successful career painting devotional works and even still-lifes, which 18th-century art scholar Antonio Palomino described as painted 'with such superior excellence that no one could surpass them, or possibly even equal them.'[148] Unfortunately, only two of these still-lifes are known today, but they hint at his abilities.

While Cerezo's earlier art exhibits the stylistic tendencies of Carreño, Titian and Anthony van Dyck, his more mature painting reflects an increasingly personal style. His compositions are elaborately composed, emotional and broadly painted, with dramatic handling of light and atmospheric effects. *Immaculate Conception* (c.1660) in the Prado is a prime example of his technique. In 1664 Cerezo married Maria Fernández Campuzano, a woman who brought no money or property to the marriage, suggesting it was a love match and that Cerezo's career was so successful a large dowry was not essential.

Whatever the case, Cerezo was producing some of his best and most ambitious work during the last two years of his truncated career. According to Palomino his last known painting *Supper at Emmaus* 'exceeds all praise'.[149] His intense work ethic was interrupted by a serious malady, which forced him to give his wife the power of attorney over his estate. Three days later, on 29 June, Cerezo died of an unknown illness, but evidence suggests his death did not come as a total surprise. He was buried at the church of St Martin in Madrid. Biographer Dr Álvaro Piedra Adarves extols, 'His death eclipsed one of the most precocious talents' in Spanish painting.[150]

Mateo Cerezo the Younger
Immaculate Conception, c.1660, oil on canvas, 211.5 × 147.5 cm (83¼ × 58⅛ in)
Museo del Prado, Madrid

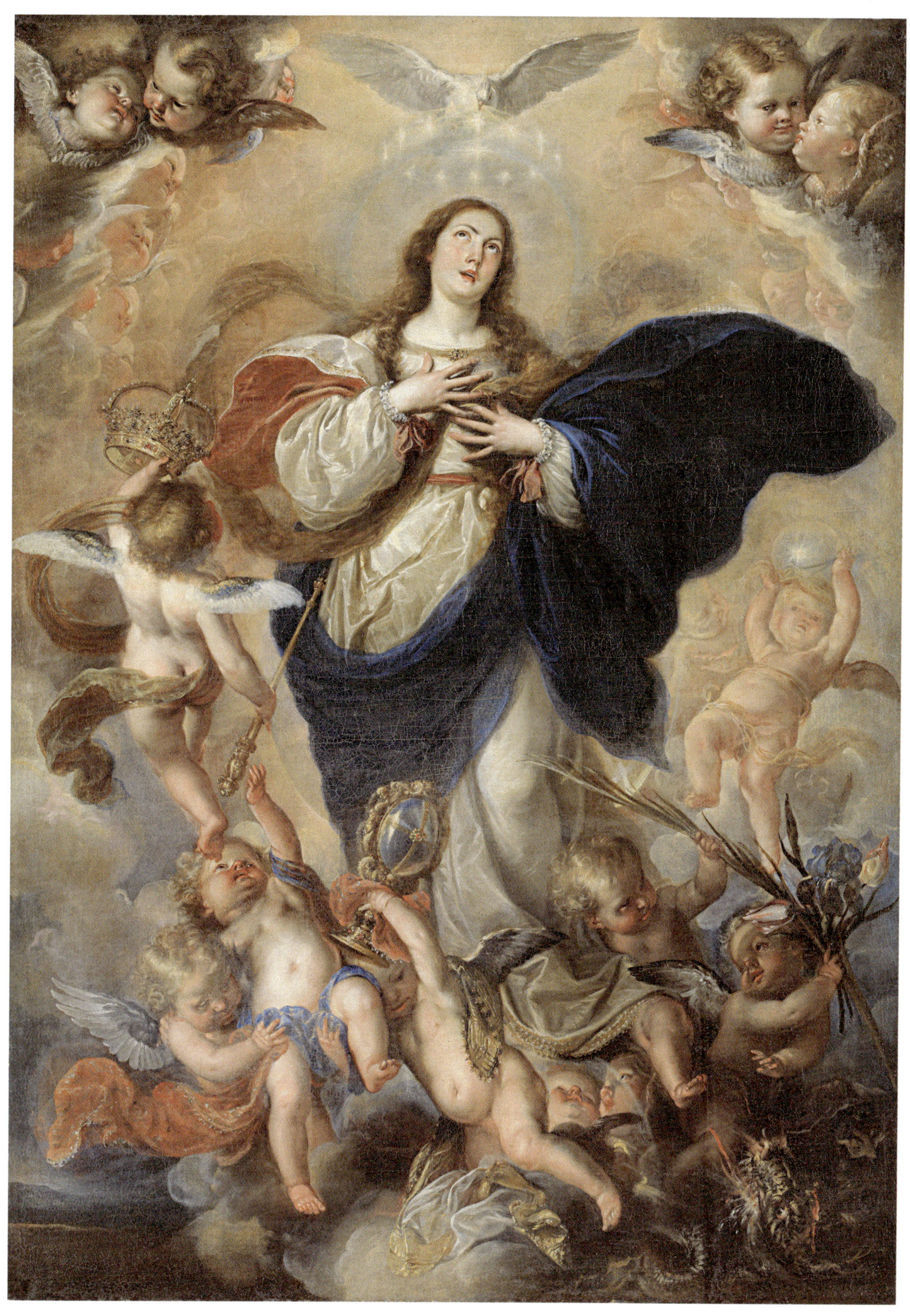

Cesare Serafini FRACASSINI

Orvieto, near Rome, 18 Dec 1838 – 13 Dec 1868, Rome
Italian, 29 years, 11 months, 26 days

Sometimes called 'Fracassi', Fracassini was a painter of large mythological and religious altarpieces, theatre curtains, murals and frescoes, such as *Ordination of San Lorenzo e Stefano*, in the Basilica di San Lorenzo fuori le Mura, Rome. He first studied with Tommaso Minardi in Rome then at the Accademia di San Luca in the same city. In 1857 he was awarded first prize in painting at the Grande Concorso Clementino-Pellegrini competition, which helped propel him in his notable career.

Fracassini was an academic realist, even though he was known for his speed and metre in execution. His most famous painting is the emotionally gripping *The Martyrs of Gorkum* (1867) in the Vatican. The ghastly scene of 19 Catholic monks being hanged by militant Dutch Calvinists during the Eighty Years' War, struck a sympathetic chord with both Catholics and Protestants. Over twenty thousand people flocked to the artist's studio to admire the painting before it was transported to the Vatican. According to the Dizionario Biografico degli Italiani, 'In the eyes of contemporaries, this painting constituted a masterpiece of the artist and of modern Roman painting.'[151]

Fracassini had begun to make a name for himself. The artist married and had two children. He received many commissions in Italy and abroad and was acclaimed by some as 'the new Raphael'.[152] In September 1867, he received the distinct honour of being nominated as a Virtuoso al Pantheon. Then, just as he was becoming successful, Fracassini was struck down with typhoid mere days short of his 30th birthday. Rome's art community mourned greatly at his untimely death. He left unfinished the frescoes for the outside walls of the Basilica di San Lorenzo. These would have to be completed by others.

There was an excellent chance that Fracassini could have been the Roman equivalent of the marvellous Florentine Antonio Ciseri (1821–1891), had he lived. His powerfully expressive religious narrative was forgotten then rejected by a 20th-century art establishment bent on deconstructing the academic milieu, but his famous *The Martyrs of Gorkum* continues to enthrall Vatican visitors to this day.

Cesare Fracassini
The Martyrs of Gorkum, 1867, oil on canvas, approx.300 × 200 cm (118⅛ × 78¾ in)
Sobieski's Room Vatican Museums

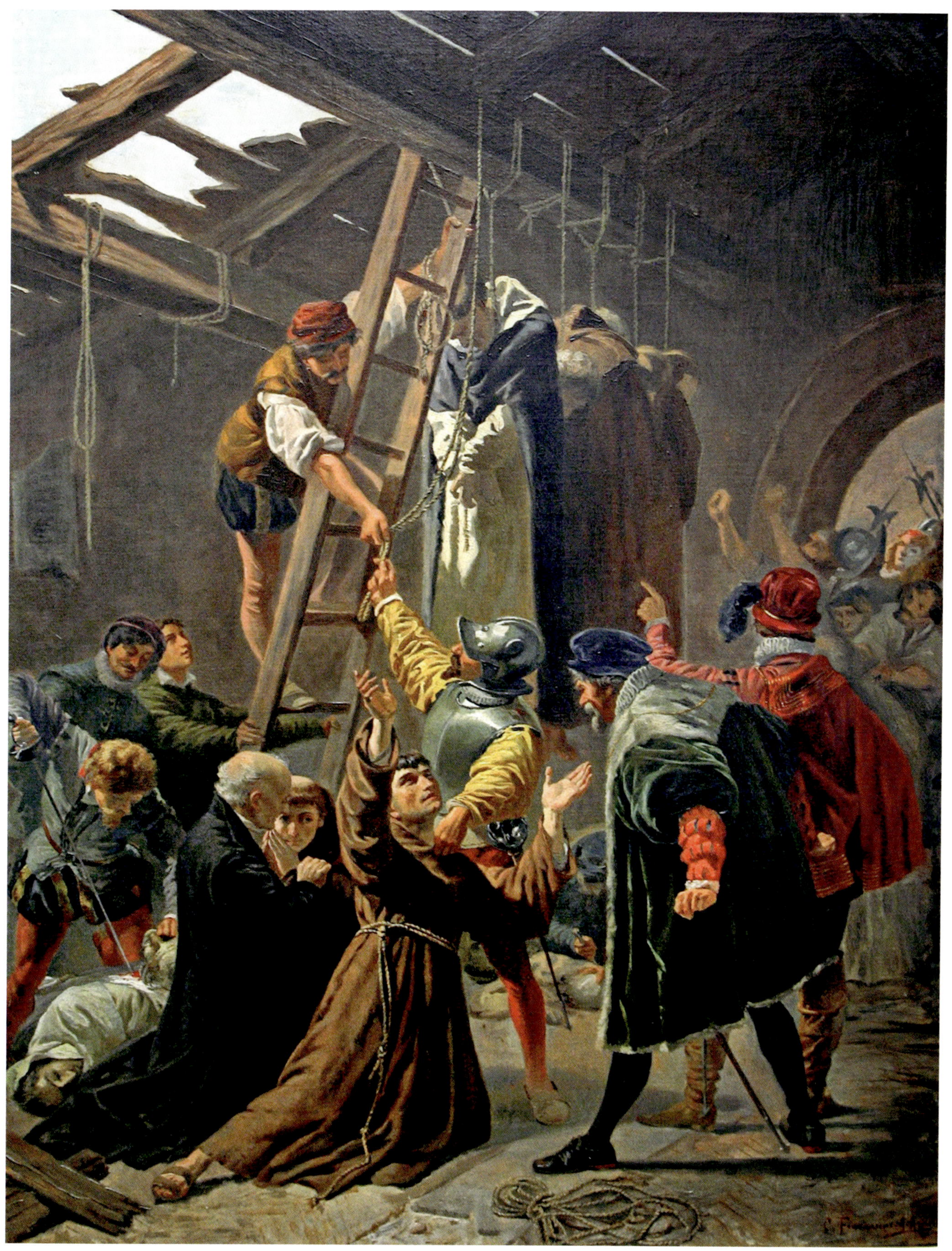

Ruy Roque GAMEIRO

Lisbon, 27 Feb 1906 – 18 Aug 1935, Lisbon
Portuguese, 29 years, 5 months, 23 days

Ruy Gameiro was the youngest of the five children of the revered watercolourist Alfredo Roque Gameiro (1864–1935). All five children became artists, mostly in watercolour, except for Ruy who applied himself in another direction – monumental sculpture. Gameiro was raised in an artistic environment where artists and writers frequented his childhood home. Gifted mechanically, he was initially sent to a trade school to learn auto mechanics. However, by 1921, Ruy recognised art as his calling and enrolled in the Lisbon School of Fine Arts. Nevertheless, he would always maintain an interest in mechanics and motorcycles which would sadly lead to his premature death.

In 1928 Gameiro graduated from the School of Fine Arts with a lauded diploma sculpture titled *Abel and Cain* (1928, marble). The following year, he exhibited for the first time in the Sociedad Nacional de Belas Artes (SNBA), with two sculptures, *Salomé* and a bust of the painter José Tagarro; the latter was soon acquired for the National Museum of Contemporary Art. In 1930 he won the contest for a World War I monument in Abrantes, Portugal. Titled, *Monument to the Dead of the Great War* (1933), it was his first work modelled in concrete.

Gameiro's professional work was executed in a deco-modernist style that displayed power and vitality. In collaboration with the architect Veloso Reis, Gameiro was awarded the first prize for his design of another World War I monument for the city of Maputo in Mozambique. This large memorial was completed in 1934 and delivered to the African island the following year. The sculptor impressively won other commissions for public sculpture, solidifying his reputation as a vital up-and-coming artist. In 1933, Gameiro married and in the same year he modelled statues and bas-reliefs for the design of a monument to Prince Henry the Navigator. These were posthumously displayed at the Paris and New York International Exhibitions in 1938 and 1939.

Tragically, Gameiro and his wife, Maria Helena, were suddenly killed in an accident on Sintra Road, Lisbon. The sculptor and his wife were riding his Ariel 500cc motorcycle and were struck by another vehicle. Gameiro died instantly and Maria followed shortly after. (Curiously, this tragedy occurred just days after the passing of Gameiro's father.) Gameiro's sculptures were well received critically. Even Pablo Picasso praised his work. Gameiro's biographer José Amaro Júnior wrote: 'Rui [sic] Roque Gameiro was a great artist and a great soul. He would have become a great sculptor of Portugal. He was on his way to triumph, that triumph that is great only when one fights hard.'[153] Had he lived, Ruy Gameiro surely would have been Portugal's leading sculptor of his age, making his loss to the world of art particularly heartrending.

Ruy Roque Gameiro
Monument to the Dead of the Great War, 1933, concrete, monumental size
Abrantes, Portugal

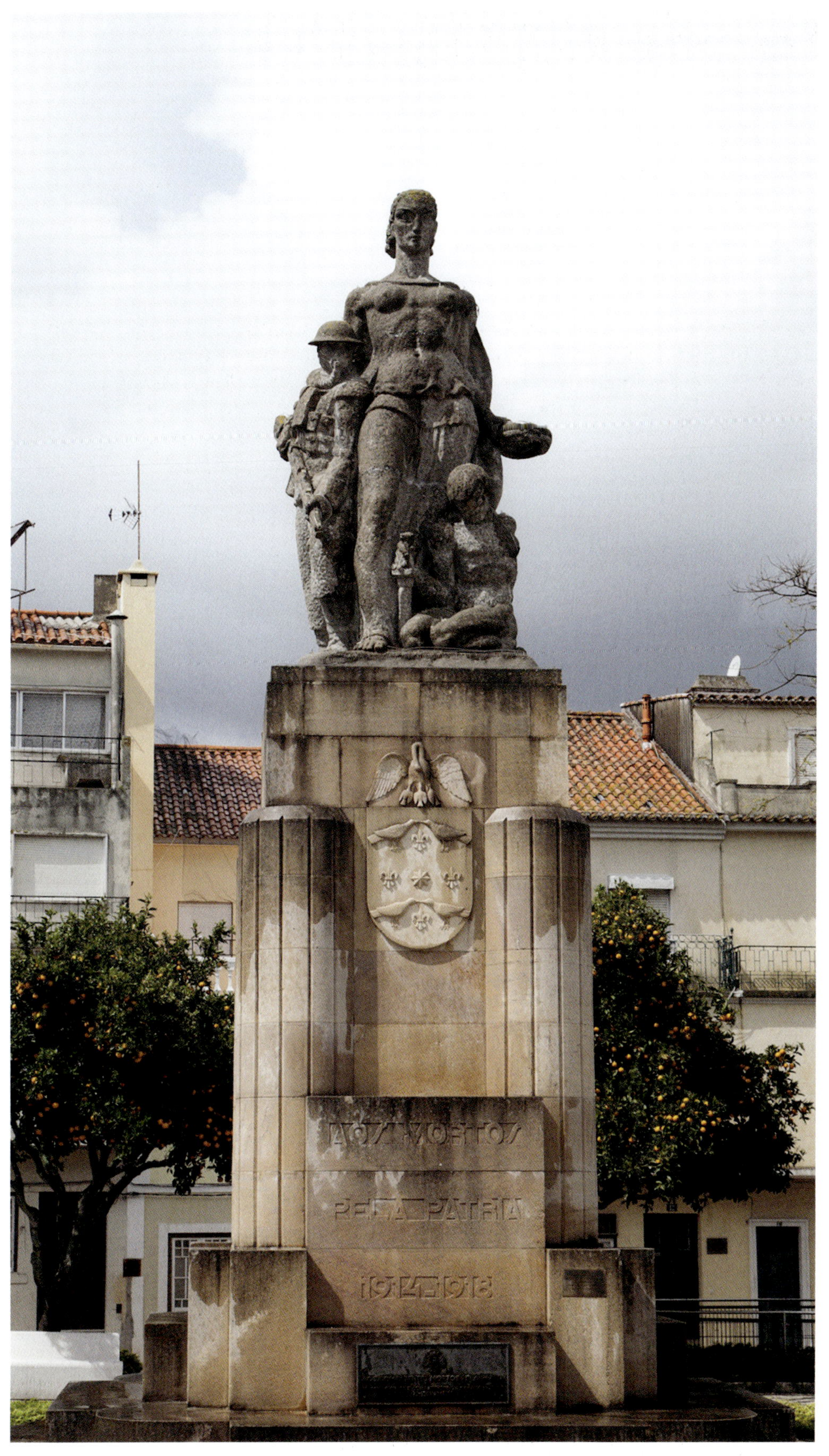

David Cooke GIBSON

Edinburgh, 4 Mar 1827 – 5 Oct 1856, London
Scottish, 29 years, 7 months, 2 days

This artist was the son of a portrait miniaturist and engraver who died early of consumption when the younger Gibson was only 17. The illness affected the entire family; his mother and sister died just a year later of the same disease and David Gibson was, himself, afflicted. He wrote in his journal on 2 December 1845, the day of his mother's death, 'She was the last relation who cared for me.'[154] Now untethered he began his moral decline as he approached adulthood. While he was a social favourite, handsome (though quite short) and liked to dance, he by all accounts approached his art studies with unremitting diligence.

In January of 1846, the 19-year-old Gibson gained three student prizes from the Trustee's Academy of Art in Edinburgh. He earned enough to tour London, Belgium and Paris, assiduously studying in the great galleries and museums. His first major commission was a dual portrait of *Sir Adam and Lady Ferguson* (c.1848, Scottish National Portrait Gallery). This led to a commission from Mr Hope Scott at Abbotsford, the home of Sir Walter Scott. There, he successfully painted two servants' portraits: *John Swanston the Keeper* (1851) and *The Groom Peter Mathieson (1768–1852), with the Pony 'Donald'* (1851).

Gibson moved to London in 1852, where he began to paint high Victorian pictures such as *Unexpected Arrival* (1854). Unfortunately, most of his time in London was either unsuccessful (he was rejected by the British Institution 1853 exhibition) or wasted through debauchery, as biographer, William MacDuff colourfully writes: 'Profligacy, drowned and deadened conscience – that conscience that was once so full of delicate sensitivity … The Bible was scoffed at … night after night in the filth of the purlieus of Drury Lane and the Haymarket, reveling with degraded and degrading minds.'[155]

Recoiling from his lack of success and drunken lifestyle, Gibson retreated to the Highlands of Scotland and to Kirkcaldy on the coast, where his lone art patron (an 'honest, hard-working Christian baker') nurtured his tormented soul back to health. There, in Fife, he found his mother's religion in the autumn of 1854. Sadly, the consumption of his youth had returned, and his doctor advised him to go to Spain for his health. He passed the winter of 1855–56 in Malaga. There his tight academic style opened up in terms of brushwork, light and colour with such pictures as *The Well at Malaga, Spanish Washerwomen*, and *Spanish Gossips at a Well*.

As Gibson's health became manageable, he wrote, 'My illness has been instrumental in leading me to see the necessity and beauty of the religion of Jesus.'[156] The hopeful Gibson returned to England in June of 1856, taking a house in the country, but lingered too long in the damp climate. That October he died of pulmonary tuberculosis (consumption). Had he lived he would certainly have been in the upper echelon of Scottish genre painters.

David Cooke Gibson
The Groom Peter Mathieson (1768–1852), with the Pony 'Donald', 1851, oil on canvas, 59.6 × 46.8 cm (23½ × 18⅜ in)
Courtesy of Abbotsford, The House of Sir Walter Scott

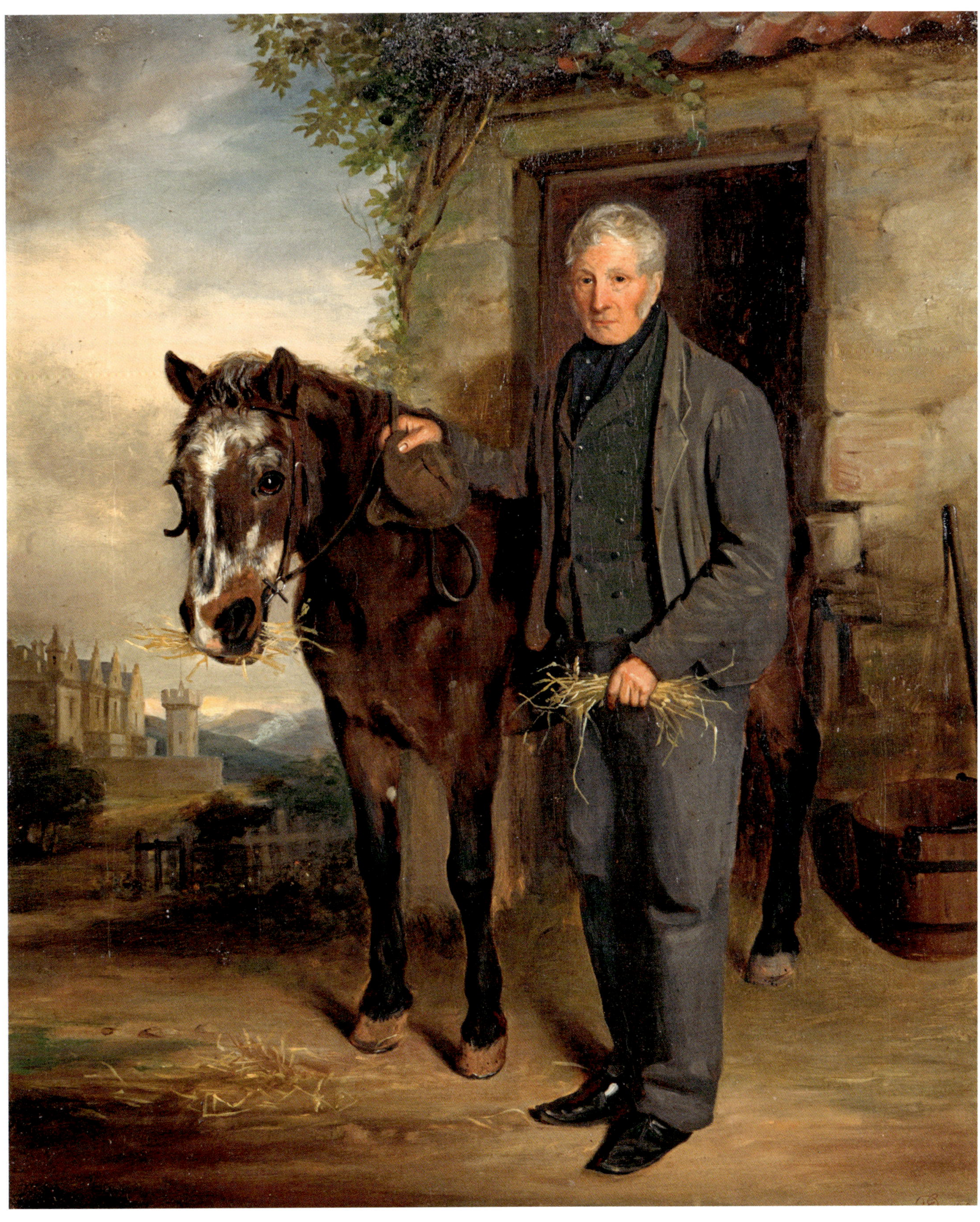

Fulchran-Jean HARRIET

Paris, 1776 – 9 Sep 1805, Rome [157]
French, approx. 29 years

Harriet was a significant hardedge neoclassical painter, designer and student of Jacques-Louis David, the most dominant artistic force of his day. In 1793, Harriet competed for the prestigious Prix de Rome, at the age of only 17, with his much-praised *Brutus Killed in Battle Is Brought Back to Rome*. Narrowly missing the grand prize, the young artist took second place. Because of the political turmoil in France the Prix de Rome was not awarded for three years, then in 1798, Harriet triumphed in winning the grand prize with his diploma oil *Battle of the Horatii and the Curiatii* (1797, ENSBA).

Harriet had to wait for the French Academy in Rome's new location, the Villa Medici, to open before travelling there on scholarship. In the meantime, he exhibited at the Paris Salon from 1796 to 1802. One impressive entry was his *Oedipus at Colonus* (1798), in which Harriet depicts the anguished figure of Oedipus from Sophocles's Greek tragedy. Here, the blind Oedipus rests with his daughter Antigone upon their return to Colonus from exile. Though an ancient tale, the plot had modern relevance in the return of French citizens exiled from their homeland during the French Revolution. The 22-year-old artist's stunning grasp of composition, colour, lighting and human anatomy is particularly evident in this painting.

Finally arriving in Rome around 1802, Harriet would only study there for less than three years before he died. While the exact cause of his passing is unknown, he may have died of malaria, the same illness which is thought to have taken two other Prix de Rome winners, Gaudar de La Verdine and Albert Androt, the year before. Residing in Rome proved to be a top killer for many artists in this book, and France's Villa Medici a prime location. Sadly, Harriet never completed his large oil *Horatius Cocles Defending the Corso Sublicius* (location unknown), although his contemporaries called it a masterpiece.

Following his death, the French Academy in Rome quickly arranged an exhibition of his studio effects, including his major uncompleted canvas. Then, in 1806, a posthumous exhibition of his art was held at the Paris Salon. These exhibitions and the later 1820 statue of him erected in Rome, show the honour his contemporaries had for the young painter. Unfortunately, his excessive neoclassicism without a white-hot passion and limited oeuvre (fewer than 10 surviving known works), would sadly not see him remembered in the pantheon of art.

Fulchran-Jean Harriet
Oedipus at Colonus, 1798, oil on canvas, 157 × 134 cm (61¾ × 52¾ in)
Cleveland Museum of Art, Ohio, Mr and Mrs William H. Marlatt Fund

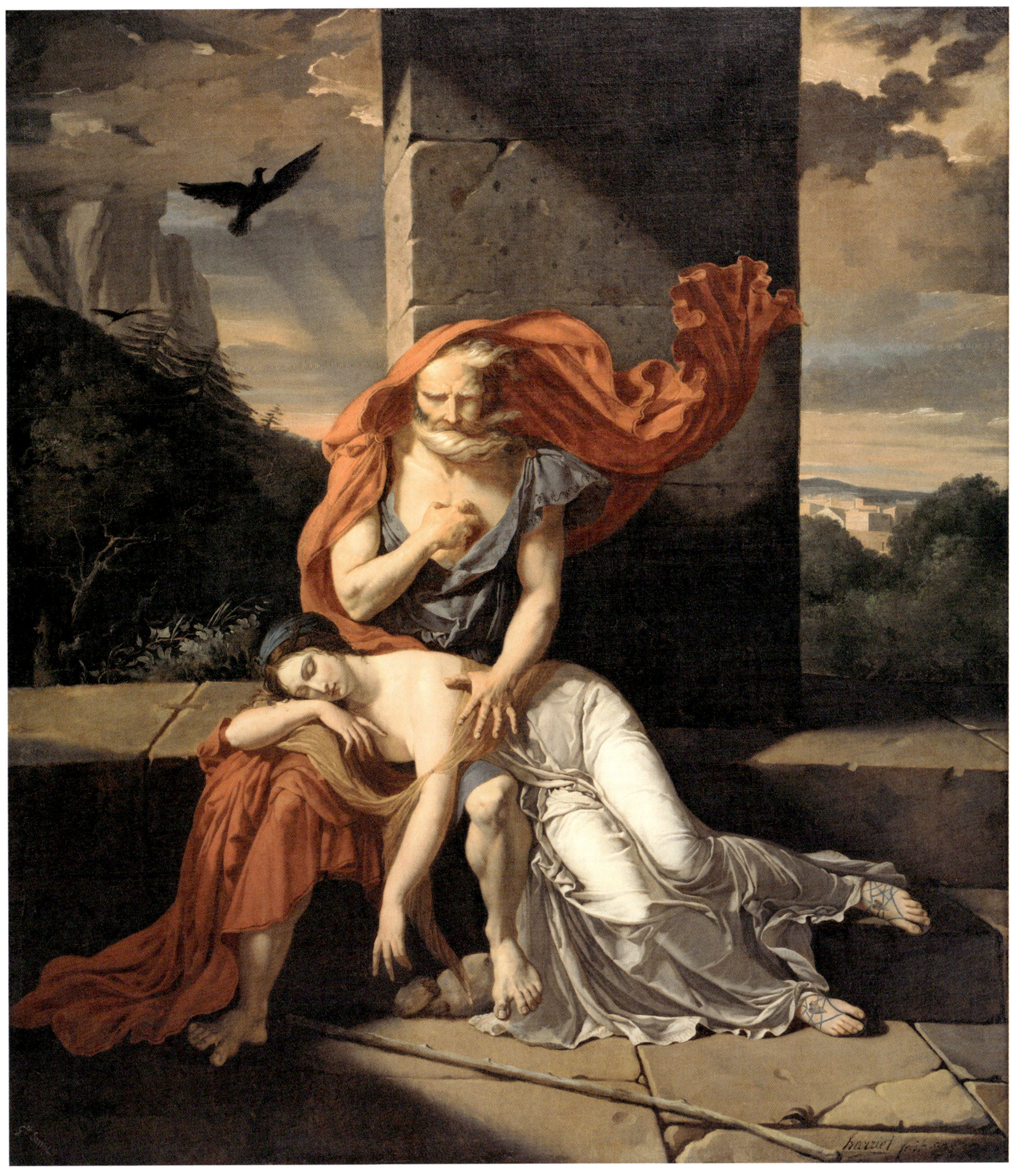

Nikifor Stepanovich KRYLOV

Kalyazin, Tver Oblast, 1802 – 28 Jun 1831, St Petersburg
Russion, approx. 28 or 29 years

Nikifor Krylov began his career as a village painter of icons for churches and the marketplace. Little is known about his early training, but from the early 1820s, Krylov was a part of an Artel (co-operative) of wandering icon painters who worked from village to village. His talent was recognised by the important artist Alexei G. Venetsianov who founded the Safonkovo school of painting and frequently recruited talent from the poorer ranks of society. Beginning in 1823, Venetsianov commenced painting an iconostasis at the Terebensk Monastery in Tver Province. He used Kalyazin icon painters as assistants, and Krylov was the best of them all. From that time forward, Venetsianov became Krylov's mentor and he advised the young icon painter to draw from nature.

Venetsianov invited Krylov to join him in St Petersburg, but Krylov was reluctant, fearing he would be unable to support himself there and would starve to death. Fortunately, with the patronage of the Society for the Encouragement of the Arts, Krylov eventually joined Venetsianov in St Petersburg in 1825. The provincial Krylov was amazed by what he saw at the Hermitage Museum. He simultaneously studied art there while attending drawing classes at the Imperial Academy of Art.

Krylov developed quickly and flourished into a versatile artist. He successfully painted portraiture (see *Portrait of Count Vladimir S. Apraxin*, 1829), genre (see *Russian Woman Feeding Her Baby from a Cow Horn*, 1830), and most notably landscapes. His impressive oil *Russian Winter* (1827) solidified his standing as an artist of repute. Painted beside the banks of the Tosna River, where a wealthy patron provided him with a warm studio to work in for a month, *Russian Winter* is lauded for its authentic presentation of Russian life and sincere realistic approach.

In 1830, Krylov and another Venetsianov student, Zelentsove, became full members of the Academy. In the space of just 10 years, Nikifor Krylov went from being a village icon painter to an academician at St Petersburg's prestigious Academy of Art. His meteoric ascent would probably have continued had a cholera epidemic in St Petersburg not interfered. Krylov was stricken and died at the age of 28 or 29. He is most noted today for his contributions to the concept of nature and truth, holding that whatever was true could not be ugly – 'it is only a question of differing degrees of grace.' Had he lived, Krylov would have become one of the dominant figures of Russian fine art.

Nikifor Stepanovich Krylov
Russian Winter, 1827, oil on canvas, 54 × 64 cm (21¼ × 25¼ in)
State Russian Museum, St Petersburg

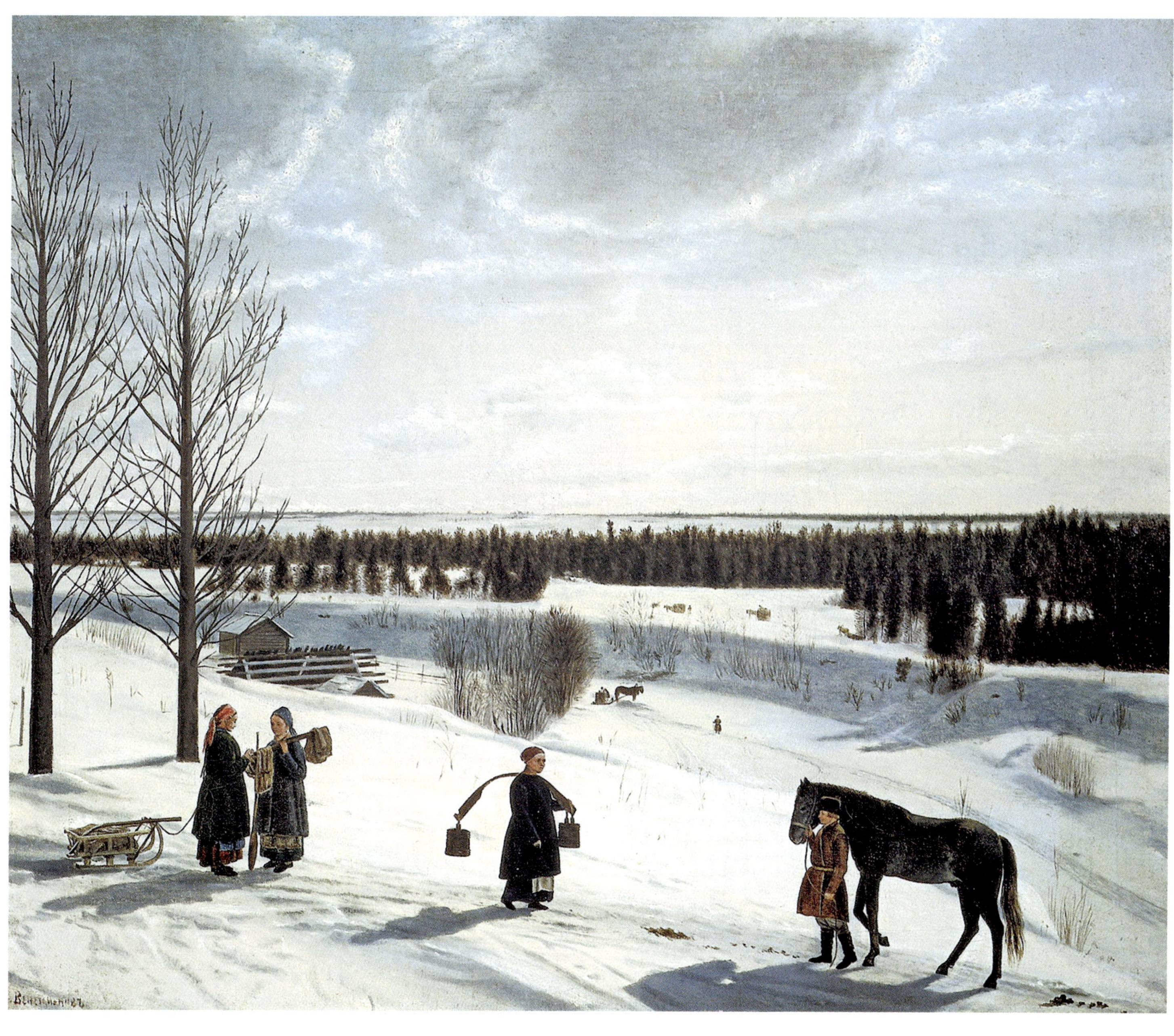

John Dalbiac LUARD

Blyborough, 31 Oct 1830 – 9 Aug 1860, Winterslow near Salisbury
British, 29 years, 9 months, 10 days

The artistic career of John Dalbiac Luard would last but six years, during which time he lived and worked among some of the greatest artistic minds of his generation. Unfortunately, his mental illness and early death would ultimately bar his induction into their immortal ranks. Born into a military, albeit artistic family, Luard began his career by following in their military footsteps. He was educated at the Royal Military Academy at Sandhurst and joined the army in 1848. Luard excelled in military service, although he saw no combat. He was, however, a hero for saving a drowning child who had fallen off a quay at Liverpool. In 1853, Luard became a lieutenant but he could no longer resist his life's calling. In January 1854 he sold his commission to pay for his devotion to art.

Luard first studied under John 'Spanish' Phillip R.A., through whom he met the Pre-Raphaelite painter John Everett Millais. Luard and Millais became good friends and later they shared a studio. Luard quickly found his specialty in military genre subjects. The winter of 1855–56 Luard spent in Crimea with his brother, Captain R.A. Luard, making sketches of the war. By his own admission, Luard was a poor war correspondent and none of his drawings was published. Compounding this disappointment, Luard's 1856 Royal Academy entries were rejected, but he still remained within the lively artistic community that congregated at the Garrick Club. The following year, Luard met with great success at the 1857 Academy exhibition with his Crimean soldier painting *A Welcome Arrival*. He also pursued the theatre, acting beside Charles Dickens in the farce *Uncle John*.

Nearing Home, a painting of an ailing young soldier and his wife returning to England, was exhibited at the RA in 1858, and was widely praised. *The Athenaeum* called it 'The best picture the Indian War has produced.'[158] Sadly, Luard would only paint a few more works, including *The Call to Duty*, a work left unfinished at his death. Correspondence from as early as 1854 hints at Luard's melancholy nature. In September 1859, his father encouraged him to join a voyage to America, hoping it would improve his health and spirits. However, Luard was not a good sailor and returned no better. Soon after he experienced a breakdown.

In July 1860, Luard was admitted to the Fisherton House Asylum, the largest private psychiatric hospital in the UK. There, Luard further weakened, dying the following month. His death certificate states the cause as 'Exhaustion from mania', a terrible end for one of such talents. So little is left of Luard's oeuvre that it is difficult to assess the artist's potential. His biographer Clive Cohen laments that his legacy was 'just seven exhibited paintings, of which four are lost … and much of his other work, including his many Crimean sketches, is also lost.'[159] However, one contemporary obituary claims that Luard would in fact have made a substantial contribution to art. The writer continues: 'As it is, the name of John Luard, claims affectionate remembrance in the pathetic master-roll of Promise whom Fate has snatched away ere full performance could be achieved.'[160] Likewise, the *Art Journal* wrote that he ' … was high on the road to artistic fame, in a path which seemed particularly his own.'[161] If contemporary critics are to be believed, for Luard, greatness was within reach.

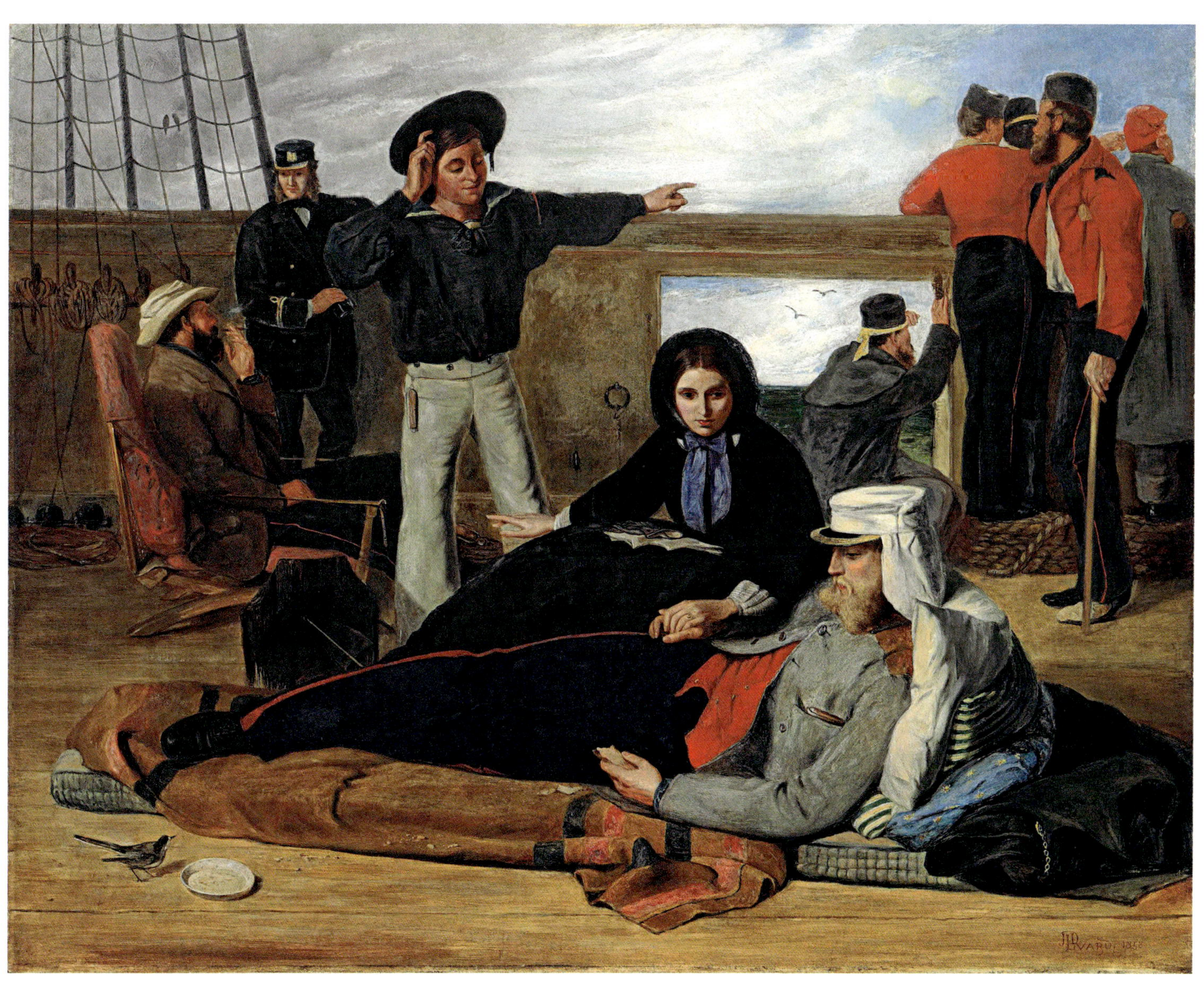

John Dalbiac Luard
Nearing Home, c.1856–58, oil on canvas, 83.8 × 104.8 cm (33 × 41¼ in)
Christie's London

Johan Thomas LUNDBYE

Kalundborg, 1 Sep 1818 – 26 Apr 1848, Bedsted[162]
Danish, 29 years, 7 months, 26 days

Lundbye was an important painter of the Danish Golden Age, a period of artistic flourishing following a series of national tragedies. Influenced by the art critic Niels Laurits Høyen, Lundbye's depictions of Danish landscapes and people can be described as both romantic and nationalistic. The artist was known to have said that his sole wish was to paint 'dear Denmark'.[163] He successfully achieves this in his early oil *Swedish Sledges on Their Way Home after Selling Goods in Copenhagen* (1838). Here, he delightfully captures the moment of departure of Denmark's nearest neighbours, from Skovshoved over the frozen Øresund Strait. The artist takes pains to capture the clear, cold Nordic atmosphere in the frosty icescape which makes this regional mode of transportation possible.

Lundbye was also known for his animal paintings, self-portraits and illustrations of Danish folk-tales. He was highly productive, leaving many oil paintings and nearly 1,500 drawings and watercolours. After studying at the Royal Danish Academy of Art, Lundbye received a travel grant to advance his art in Italy, via Germany and Switzerland. However, his experience abroad was marred by homesickness and he returned to Denmark and settled on a rural farm.

Lundbye suffered from chronic depression, anxiety and disappointment throughout his short life. His journals, which were published over a century after his death, describe his love for a young woman named Louise Marie Neergard. In the five years he knew her, he never had the courage to profess his love. Tragically, the young woman would have reciprocated the artist's feelings but was never given the chance to do so. She died many years later, a spinster.

In 1848, Lundbye enlisted as a soldier in the Three Years' War (Treårskrigen) never anticipating returning home alive. Only eight days later, on 26 April, while stationed in Bedsted, Lundbye took the opportunity to sketch in the fine weather. His subjects were the soldiers' rifles which had been stacked in a pyramidal formation. Unexpectedly, the rifles fell and one fired a bullet which struck Lundbye in the mouth and lodged in his brain. He died immediately, although some suspect he may actually have taken his own life. The young artist never saw the front, but it is believed that the statue of the Danish National Soldier in Fredericia, Denmark by Hermann Wilhelm Bissen depicts the promising artist who died far too young.

Johan Thomas Lundbye
Swedish Sledges on Their Way Home after Selling Goods in Copenhagen, 1838, oil on canvas, 70 × 93 cm (27½ × 36⅝ in)
Øregaard Museum, Hellerup

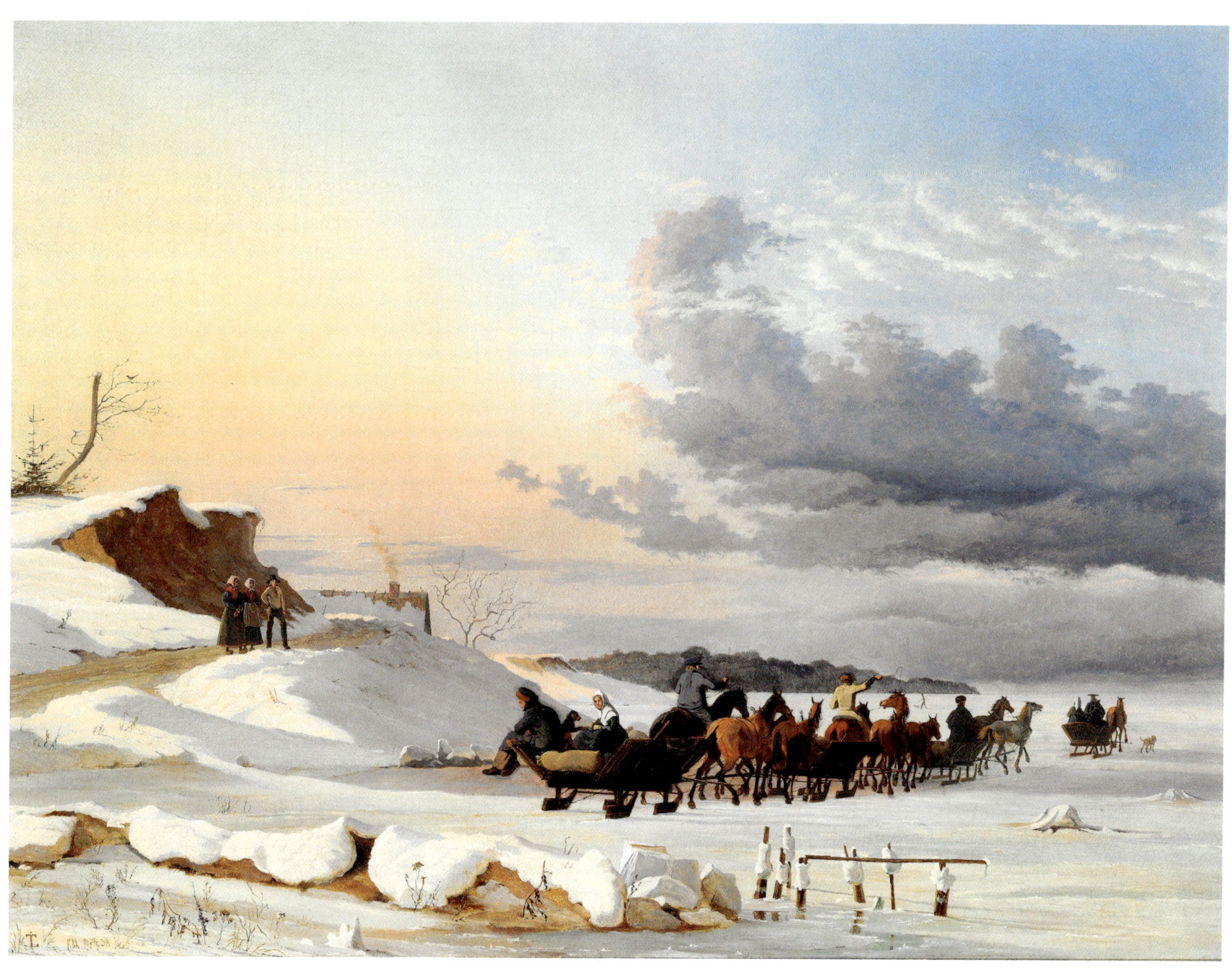

Alexander Bell MIDDLETON

Arbroath, 8 May 1830 – 17 Jan 1860, Arbroath
Scottish, 29 years, 8 months, 10 days

Alexander Middleton had a unique touch as a painter. As he was the only son of a widowed mother and farmer father, he began work at Macdonald & Lowson as a clerk. On Mondays, however, he would go down to Edinburgh to copy paintings at the Royal Society of Arts. We don't know what pretensions he had of becoming an artist but there was in him a true passion for painting. Alexander's obituary says that Patrick Allan-Fraser discovered 'the talents of the quiet clerk.'[164] He may have seen the youthful Middleton's paintings hanging in his clerk's office and recognised his potential.

Patrick Allan-Fraser (1813–1890) and his wealthy wife, the heiress Elizabeth Fraser (he took her name), lived in a castle/mansion at nearby Hospitalfield. They sponsored Middleton to study art at Edinburgh's Trustees Academy (now the Edinburgh College of Art), and he immediately became their favourite artist among the several artists they sponsored.

Middleton sold a number of pictures to Allan-Fraser, which are today in the Hospitalfield House collection. His oil *An Old Woman* (1855), depicting a lady in prayer with her Bible, is unusually good. His most compelling known oil is the charming *The 'Evening-Guide' Sir?* (1858) of a young newspaper-seller offering the evening edition of *The Arbroath Guide*. The work is reminiscent of the American John George Brown's 'Boot Black' paintings. So intent was Middleton in his loyalty to 'nature' that he began to suffer eye problems. In a June of 1852 letter, he complained of weak eyes and was obliged to go to the countryside and swim after drawing sessions.[165] His professors even remarked that he was 'too careful' and urged him to lighten up a bit.

Middleton spent most of his career in Edinburgh's St Cuthbert's where he married and had a child. While there, he remained in almost daily correspondence with Partrick Allan-Fraser mostly discussing art techniques, religious sermons and his health. His letters reveal that he was anxious and highly strung, and suffered from an increasingly painful stomach, much like baroque painter Elisabetta Sirani. His doctor wrote prescriptions to calm this serious disorder, which was perhaps an ulcerous stomach or peritonitis. Middleton writes, '[Dr Simson] advises me to take relaxation and keep my mind easy. This is easier said than done.' His condition worsened over the next few years until he succumbed to its effects. James M. McBain in his book *Eminent Arbroathians* (1897) writes glowingly about the artist:

> The work of Alexander Bell Middleton is not widely known. He was taken away in the early days of his promise; but there is that in his work he has left, which shows that, had length-of-days been granted him, he would have taken high rank in the remarkable groups of artists with which he was associated in Robert Scott Lauder's class in Edinburgh – John Pettie, MacWhirter, Orchardson, Hugh Cameron, George Paul Chalmers, and the rest of them who gave the world the first distinctively Scottish national art of our century.[166]

Alexander Bell Middleton
The 'Evening-Guide' Sir?, c.1858, oil on canvas, 29 × 23 cm (11⅜ × 9 in)
Courtesy of Hospitalfield Arts, Arbroath

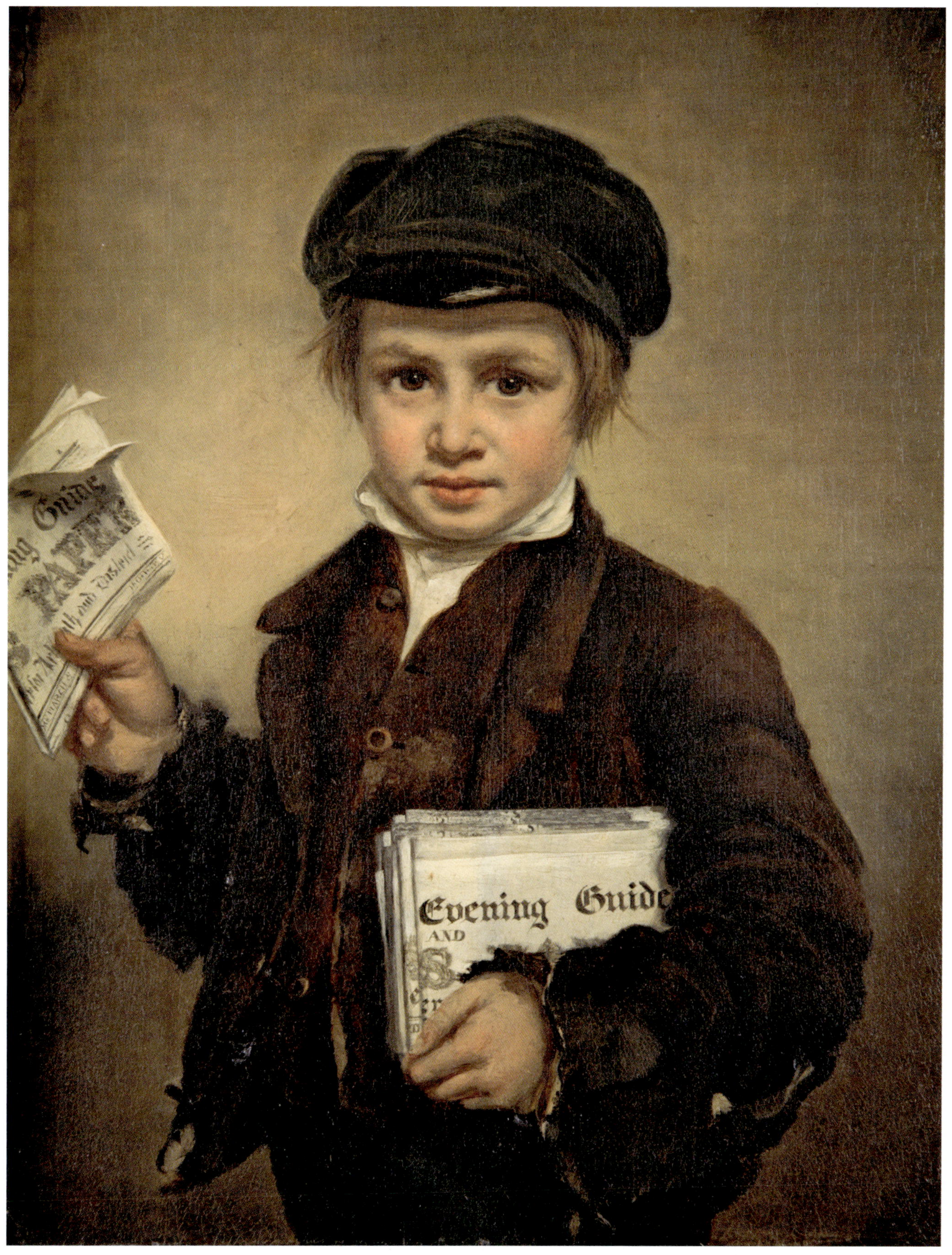
Evening Guide
PAPER
Evening Guide
AND

Johann 'Gualbert' Alexius RAFFALT

Murau, 9 Jul 1836 – 16 Aug 1865, Rome [167]
Austrian, 29 years, 1 months, 8 days

Johann first trained with his father Ignaz Raffalt (1800–1857), a respected artist who painted landscapes and isolated rural genre, often with serene sunsets. Then at the age of 15 he began to study at the Akademie der Bildenden Künste in Vienna (1851–55) under his father's friend August von Pettenkofen (1822–1889). From 1851/52 Ignaz Raffalt and Pettenkofen often travelled south together and painted the plains of Hungary and its nomadic gypsy life. They were joined by Gualbert Raffalt certainly by 1856, if not earlier. The younger Raffalt was inspired by his travels to Dalmatia and then Hungary where he too was drawn to the eastern plains of that country around Szolnok in the Puszta region, and was captivated by its people and culture.

Raffalt's Orientalism, unlike that of most Austrian painters, did not go so far as the Middle East. He prolifically painted the flat landscapes, low horizons, and farm and nomadic life of Hungary. By 1856 Pettenkofen had founded the Szolnok Art Colony of mostly Viennese painters who made a special point to exhibit their 'Hungarian' oils in the Pest Exhibition in Budapest. Szolnok was the final stop on the Monarch's Railways; in the same way that the Newlyn art colony in Cornwall was established near the final southwestern railway stop in England.

Gualbert Raffalt's first major painting from the area was his canvas *Travellers in the Puszta* (1856), and later he painted his most famous work *Market Square in Szolnok.* This painting of a sunbaked dusty frontier town is relieved only by fleecy white clouds and blue sky – a compelling picture. Raffalt painted alongside a number of accomplished Viennese painters and his young talent improved because of it.

In 1861 he travelled to Paris, and in 1863–65 he spent a longer period touring in Dalmatia and Montenegro. Then, in April of 1865, he visited Rome where he died of liver and kidney disease. [168] It is presumed that he may have had cirrhosis caused by alcoholism or viral infections, or that he suffered from chronic dehydration. Whatever the circumstances, it is recorded that he was buried in the former German Cemetery in Rome. The quality and maturity of his work extend beyond his youthful age and his Roman experience certainly would have offered new vistas for his talent, had he lived. His death came just at the point of breaking from the coat-tails of his father and his mentor Pettenkofen. Who knows the road that lay ahead for him?

Johann 'Gualbert' Alexius Raffalt
Market Square in Szolnok, date unknown, oil on canvas, size unknown
Österreichische Galerie Belvedere, Vienna

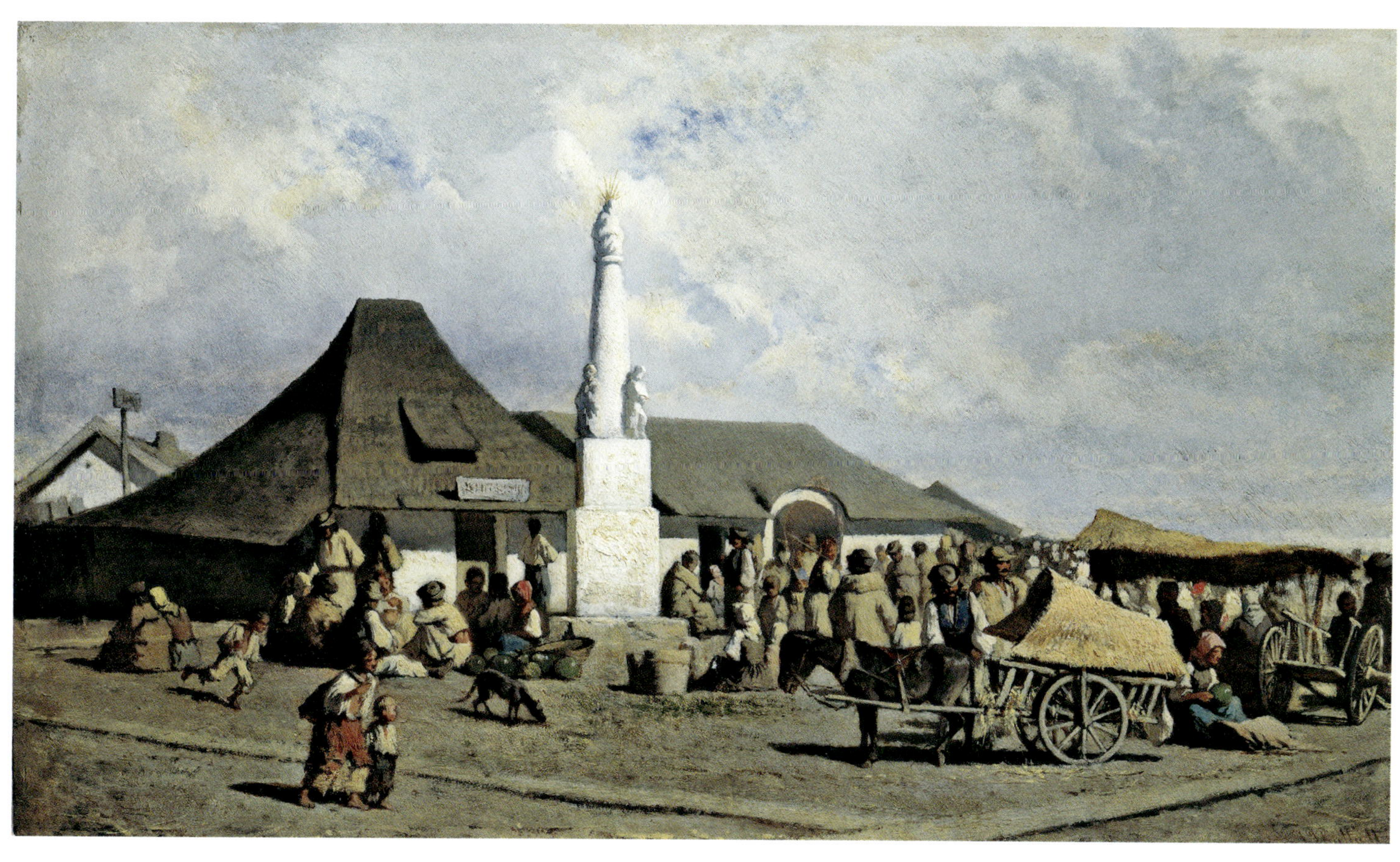

Slava RAŠKAJ

Ozalj, 2 Jan 1877 – 29 Mar 1906, Stenjevec near Zagreb
Croatian, 29 years, 2 months, 28 days

Slava Raškaj's story is a remarkably dramatic one. Deaf and with a speech impairment since birth, she procured a fine education and struck out on what promised to be a modestly successful career. Though the briefness of her career prevented the realisation of her full potential, today Raškaj is a well-known figure in Croatian media and art history for her use of the watercolour medium and her intriguing life. Born into an upper middle class home, Raškaj's mother was herself an amateur artist, and later encouraged her daughter. At the age of eight, Raškaj was sent to a boarding school for the deaf in Vienna, where she received drawing lessons and was tutored in multiple languages. When she returned home to Ozalj, her talent was recognised by a local school master who encouraged her to study art in the capital, Zagreb.

Arriving in Zagreb in 1895, she took up residence at the Zagreb Institute for the Deaf. The supportive director of the institute found her a studio space in a former morgue (an eerie portend for her future), and she commenced her art studies. When the artist Vlaho Bukovac refused her a place in his atelier, Raškaj enrolled in an art course at the Royal Women's Vocational School and studied in the studio of the forceful artist, Bela Čikoš Sesija. While the exact nature of Sesija and Raškaj's relationship has long been debated, Raškaj was trained in drawing and academic oil painting. Although it is thought, by some, that under Sesija's influence her art became rather drab.

Nevertheless, Raškaj soon began to demonstrate her own independent art style, as seen in her penetrating expressionist watercolour *Self-Portrait* of 1898. Her most memorable works are the watercolours she painted en plein-air at Zagreb Botanical Gardens, such as her multiple views of water lilies (1899). Raškaj first exhibited her art in 1898 at the Art Pavilion in Zagreb, followed by exhibitions in St Petersburg, Moscow and the 1900 Paris Exposition Universelle. She also travelled extensively with her mother to Venice, Vienna and Paris. By 1900, Raškaj seemed to possess all the requisite tools to pursue art professionally; but by then she was also showing the initial signs of depression. She continued to work on her art, but her paintings became increasingly dark and confused.

Finally, in 1902 Raškaj was diagnosed with acute depression and aggression. The misguided contemporary view that deaf people usually ended up mentally ill, didn't help her cause either. She was committed to the Psychiatric Hospital at Stenjevec that year, where she lived for more than three years. Although she did have access to her art supplies, she rarely painted. To make matters worse, she had contracted tuberculosis in 1899, and while she had mostly recovered, the awful disease reappeared in 1905. In March of 1906, Raškaj died of the malady. In 2008, the Dvori Gallery in Zagreb held a major retrospective for her, but her art and life remain little known outside Croatia.

Slava Raškaj
Water Lilies II, c.1899, watercolour, 63.1 × 75.4 cm ($24\frac{7}{8}$ × $29\frac{3}{4}$ in)
Moderna Galerija, Zagreb

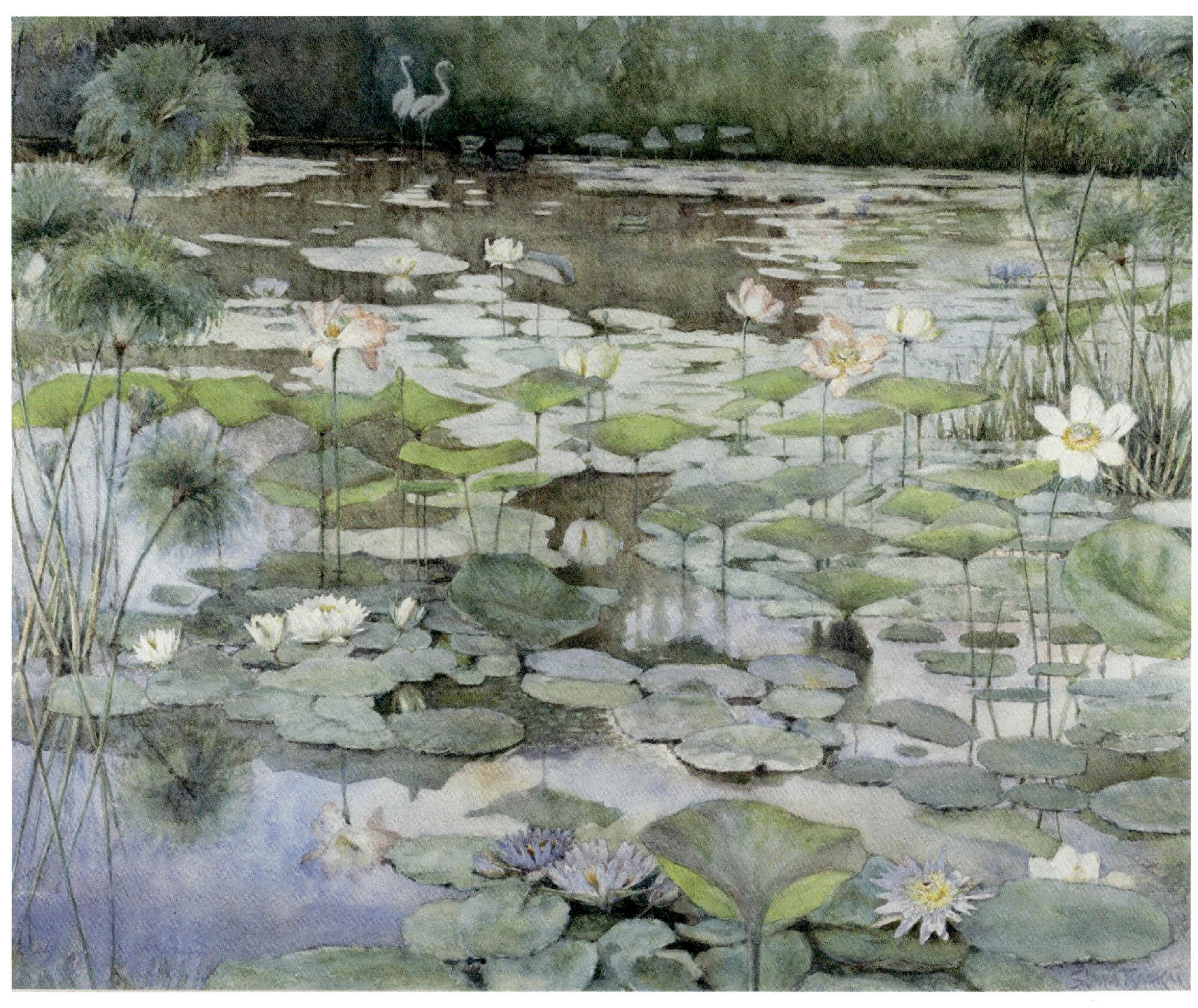

Ludvig Abelin 'L.A.' SCHOU

Slagelse, 11 Jan 1838 – 30 Sep 1867, Florence
Danish, 29 years, 8 months, 20 days

L.A. Schou was a Danish genre and history painter of exceptional talent. Schou's father and grandfather had both studied art before pursuing careers in business, and they shared their passion with the young artist. In 1855, Schou enrolled in the Royal Danish Academy of Arts where he proved to be a gifted student and his art matured greatly. His sensitive oil, *The Good Samaritan* (1863) attests to his skill. However, the artist grew disappointed with his recognition of just silver medals and never gold, and he seriously considered giving up painting completely. Fortunately, a sympathetic uncle revived his ambitions by funding a study trip for Schou to Italy in 1864.

Rome and its environs worked a kind of magic on Schou's art. Although he was chronically ill with liver disease and Rome's climate further compromised his health, Schou produced several remarkable paintings there, including his sensitive social realist portrayal *The Rag Picker (Chiffonier)* (1866) and his rustic genre canvas *Italian Farmers* (c.1865–66). Upon his return to Denmark in the spring of 1866, Schou completed the sensual salon painting *Chione Killed by the Offended Diana* (1866). While these works display the remarkable diversity and quality of his oeuvre, it is said that Schou revealed his 'greatest promise' in a series of drawings depicting the Norse Ragnarok myths.[169]

Restless in Denmark, Schou returned to Rome via Paris in late 1866, where he stayed until the spring. There, he commenced his most ambitious multi-figure painting yet, 'Romans carrying an Imperial statue through the Arch of Titus'. He worked on this painting until just weeks before his death. Unfortunately, that year one of cholera's deadliest pandemics occurred, claiming more than 100,000 lives in Italy alone. The situation in Rome was especially dire, so Schou moved north to Florence in May of 1867. However, Schou was already vulnerable to illness as Charles Been explains: 'With deep contempt for the physical necessities of life, he neglected the needs of his body. He let himself go with lousy, cheap food. He always went inadequately dressed, and he was careless to the extreme. There was then no longer resistance when death suddenly knocked.'[170]

Unfortunately, Schou answered that existential door. Schou lived in Florence with Danish artists Otto Bache and Didrik Frisch (1835–1867). When Frisch became fatally ill with cholera, Schou removed himself to another room in the house, but it was in vain. Schou was already infected with the disease. The next day, Schou died and Didrik followed the next month. As the only cholera victims in Florence, they were hastily and secretly buried in the Protestant cemetery. Thus ended a remarkable artist's career whose paintings were imbued with an 'energy of feeling and greatness of form'. [171] Interestingly, the artist's brother, Peter Alfred Schou (1844–1914), was so stirred by his death, he subsequently took up art himself and became a noted realist-impressionist painter.

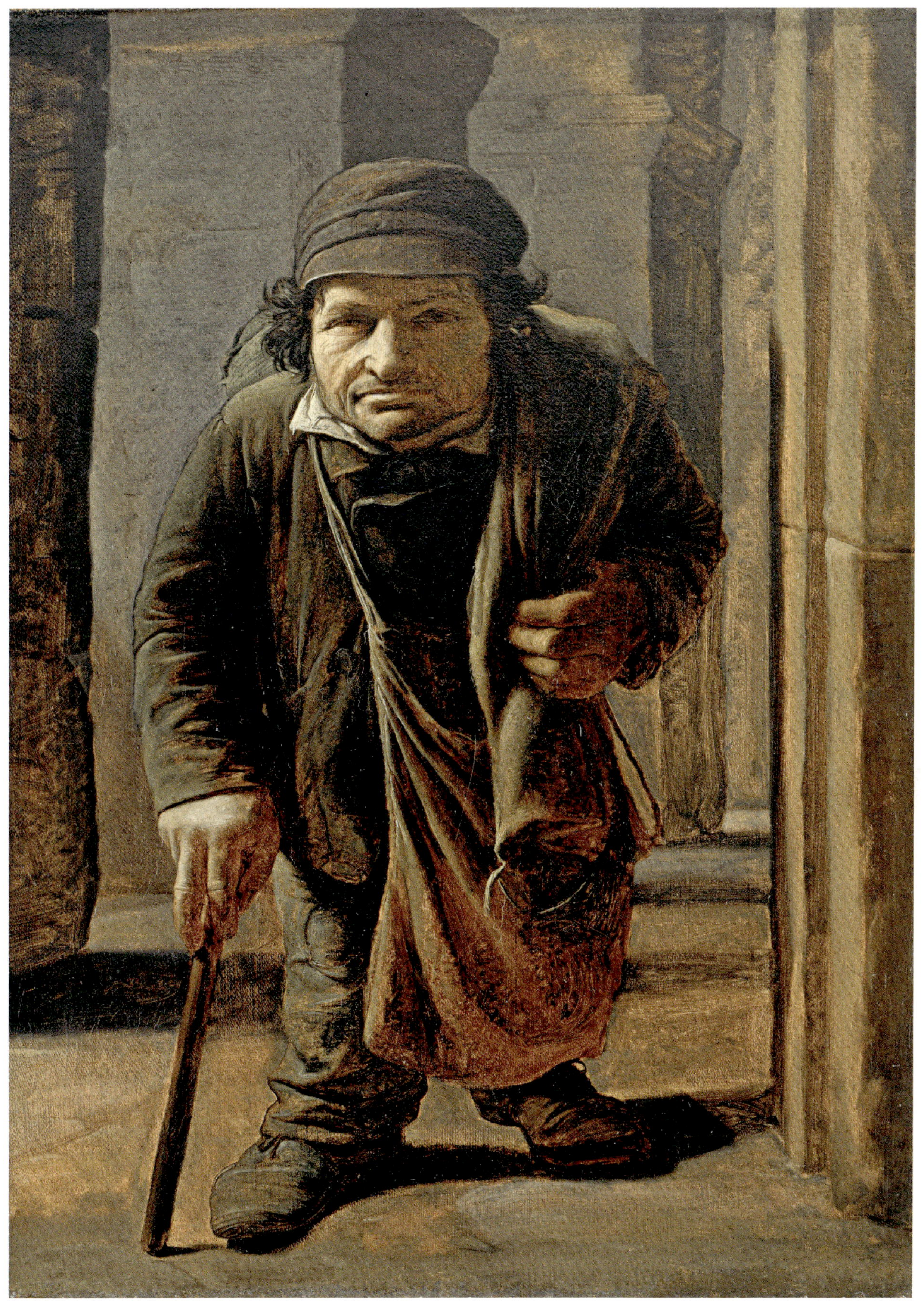

Erwin SPECKTER

Hamburg, 18 Jul 1806 – 23 Nov 1835, Hamburg [172]
German, 29 years, 4 months, 6 days

The painter Erwin Speckter came from a well-known artistic family in Hamburg. His father built a large collection of prints and later founded a lithograph printing business. His home became a meeting place for the city's leading artists, writers, intellectuals and scientists. The seven Speckter children were therefore given early access to the arts, including drawing lessons from the painter Heinrich Joachim Herterich (1772–1852). It is little wonder that Erwin and his brother Otto (1807–1871) pursued art professionally.

Erwin went on to study with several more artists before journeying to Lübeck where he fell under the spell of Germany's modern master, the Nazarene painter Johann Friedrich Overbeck (1789–1869). From 1825 to 1827, Speckter studied at the Academy of Art in Munich with another prominent Nazarene Peter von Cornelius (1784–1867), whom he assisted in painting the loggias at the Pinakothek. Speckter's paintings evolved into a stark Nazarene style, which can be seen in his famous *Jacob Meets Rachel* (1827), while his drawings maintained a delightful naturalism.

From 1830 to 1834 Erwin lived in Italy, where his art greatly matured, and he was filled with enthusiasm and inspiration for future canvases. His letters documenting his impressions were later published as *Letters of a German Artist from Italy* (1846). In 1834 he returned home to Hamburg to paint frescoes in the mayor's home, based upon lofty designs he conceived in Italy, namely 'The Connection of the Gods and Men through the Graces, the Muses and Love'.

However, after completing just one picture of the fresco cycle, Speckter died of an asthma attack – a condition which had plagued him for years, but had grown steadily worse. Fellow artist Louis Asher (1804–1878) painted the young, handsome Speckter on his deathbed wearing a laurel wreath on his head, perhaps in tribute to the victory of his art over his too early death. The beautifully composed inscription on his tombstone states that the ambitious Speckter dedicated the last of his strength to his art, but ultimately followed the 'far-reaching goal of a higher light [Heaven].' It is difficult to know what influence Speckter would have had on German art had he lived. However, the *Deutsche Biographie* laments his death as the passing of 'one of the most promising talents of his generation.' [173]

Erwin Speckter
Jacob Meets Rachel, 1827, oil on canvas, 26.4 × 35.5 cm (10⅜ × 14 in)
Kunsthalle, Hamburg

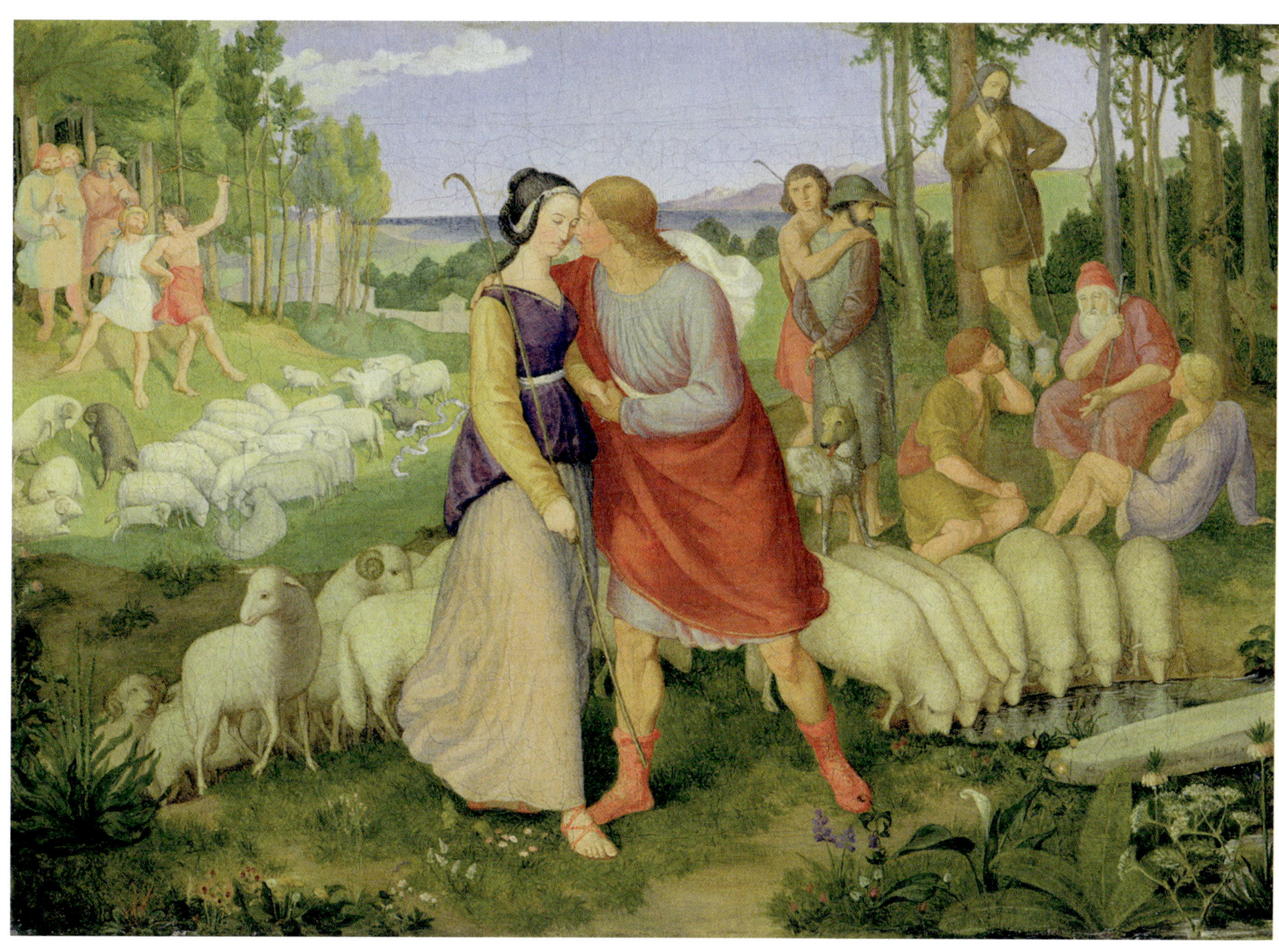

Gaston THYS

Lille, 17 Dec 1863 – 9 Aug 1893, Rome
French, 29 years, 7 months, 24 days

It has been said that Gaston Thys 'naturally possessed the gift of painting.'[174] However, from the fragmentary sources used to reconstruct the story of his life, it would be more accurate to say that his talent came from his dogged determination and hard work. Thys began as a pupil of the painter Alphonse Colas at the Academic Schools of Lille. In 1881, he presented an illustration of the poem *Mazeppa* at the Exposition des Beaux-Arts Lille. Then, in 1883, the artist settled in Paris and joined the School of Fine Arts. There, Thys became the pupil of a stellar array of artists including Léon Bonnat, Ernest Hébert, Luc-Olivier Merson and Gustave Boulanger.

Thys began exhibiting at the Salon de Paris in 1885, mainly with portraits. He also participated in the Prix de Rome competition at the École des Beaux-Arts for six consecutive years, until he finally won in 1889 with an outstanding effort, *Jesus Healing the Paralytic* (oil, ENSBA Paris). The critic of *L'Art Français* was of the opinion that the painting 'has energy and vigor, but the face of his Christ is destitute and his paralytic is quite ill-defined.'[175] In contrast, Eugène Guillaume, Director of the Académie de France in Rome, declared that the painting caused a sensation at the Paris Salon, and that 'everyone appreciated his talent.'[176] Overall, the painting garnered majority support and it became Thys's ticket to Rome.

The following year, Thys joined the French Academy's Villa Medici in Rome, where he was industrious. In 1891, he sent his oil *Les Lavandières* to the Paris Salon, earning himself an honourable mention. In the 1892 Salon, he exhibited *The Bather*, and since Prix de Rome regulations required the artist to produce a painting 'after the masters', Thys painted a copy of Rubens's *Holy Family* at the beginning of 1893.

Unfortunately, Thys's next work, the sweepingly romantic painting *Triumph of Phoebus* was never completed. Only an oil sketch now remains. As Guillaume explains, just 10 days before his funeral 'He had undertaken a large picture full of the most beautiful promises, poetic subject and radiant effect … with an extraordinary enthusiasm.'[177] That night the bleeding began. Thys had long been afflicted with hemoptysis (coughing up of blood), which was a symptom of another undiagnosed illness. But with 'courage' and a 'cheerful humor', he had persevered for years. 'He lived,' Guillaume says, 'only by the love he had for his art.'

In the end, even that love could not delay the inevitable. Thys died and was buried at the Eastern Cemetery in Lille. In July 1894, the Union Art du Nord organised a retrospective of his work, bringing together 146 paintings, drawings and sketches. This was a considerable oeuvre in light of his poor health and young age. While we cannot say he was a brilliant and great talent, through his diligence and industry Thys bequeathed French art a precious endowment. He would undoubtedly have become a consummate fixture in French art.

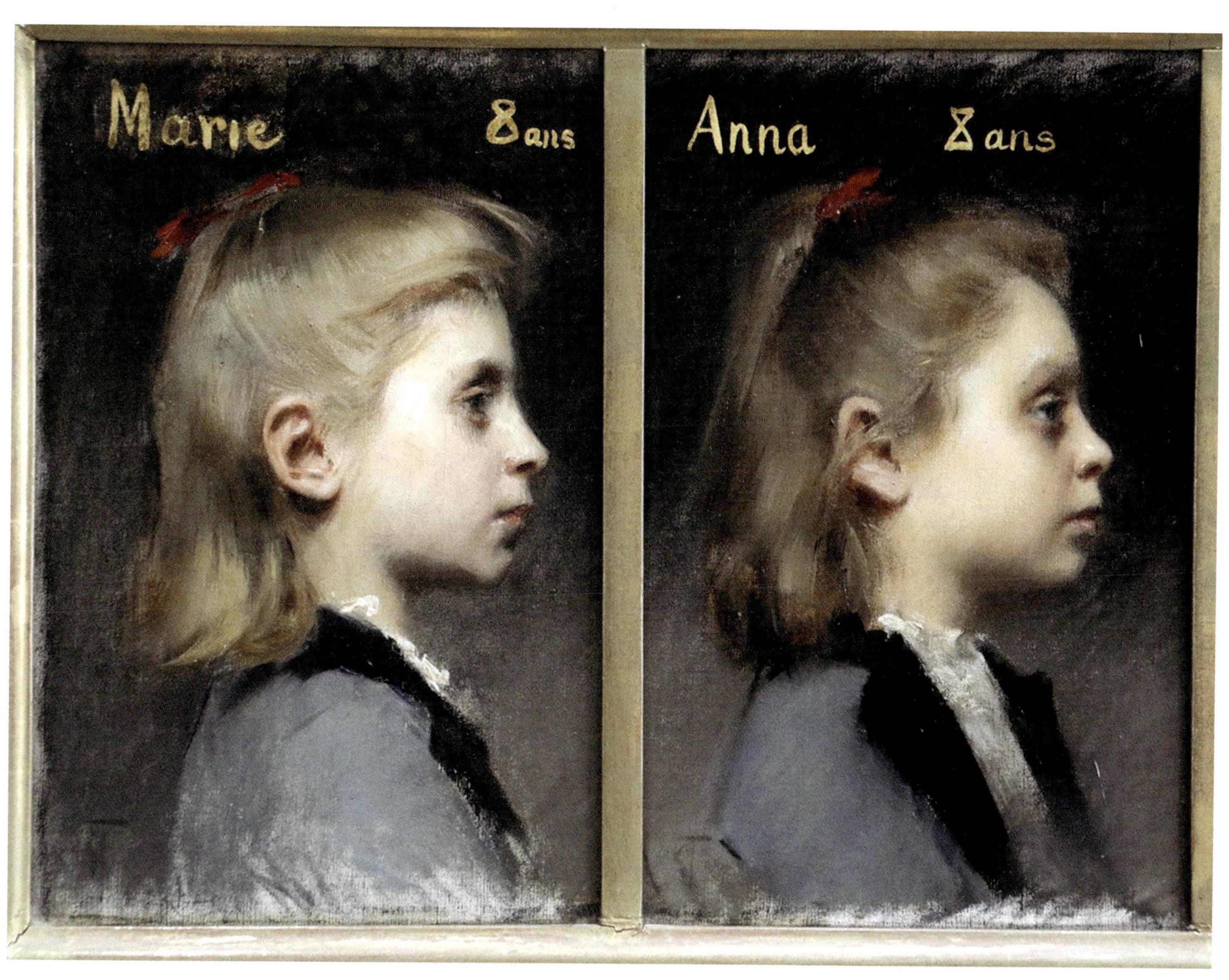

Gaston Thys
The Children, 1885, oil on canvas, 53.4 × 101.6 cm (21 × 40 in)
Leighton Fine Art

Franz Albert VENUS

Dresden, 9 May 1842 – 27 Jun 1871, Dresden
German, 29 years, 1 months, 19 days

Born the son of a footman to Princess Amalia of Saxony, Venus eventually developed into a fine draughtsman, landscape painter and watercolourist. He became an orphan when he was just 10 years old and then went to live at a Catholic orphanage and school. It must have been the art of the Saxon Palace, which housed the orphanage, that spurred his aesthetic interest. At the age of 14, Venus began his studies at the Dresden Royal Academy of Fine Arts.

In 1860 he entered the atelier of the famous painter Ludwig Richter (1803–1884) and developed a close relationship with his mentor. *A Hunting Party* (c.1860–66), which dates approximately to this period, displays Venus's deftness with pencil at this formative stage. Along with fellow students, Venus and Richter went on numerous sketching trips in North Bohemia. Venus's landscapes from this time often reflect his teacher's linear Gothic style.

However, after spending several months studying in Italy in the summer of 1866 – thanks to the patronage of Princess Amalia – Venus's art took on a more personal, atmospheric quality. Upon his return to Dresden, Venus painted his major oil *Thunderstorm in the Roman Campagna* (1868, Crocker Art Museum) based on sketches he made in Italy. *Thunderstorm* won the artist a travel scholarship and he returned to Italy for another year. During this trip Venus produced landscape watercolours, which were beautiful for their subtlety and aerial effects. One such work, *Campagna Landscape on the Via Flaminia* (1869, J. Paul Getty Museum) was painted on the spot with Venus 'applying the medium with wonderful looseness and colouristic clarity.'[178]

In October 1870 Venus married Anna Cäcilie Plaul, and in doing so became the brother-in-law of his important painter friend Carl Wilhelm Müller. However, just eight months later the artist died of pulmonary tuberculosis. Following Venus's death, Ludwig Richter lamented the death of his 'most loved and talented student' and reverently displayed works by the young artist in his studio.[179]

Franz Albert Venus
A Hunting Party, c.1860–66, pen and ink and graphite on paper, 27.5 × 19 cm (10⅞ × 7½ in)
J. Paul Getty Museum, Los Angeles, Digital image courtesy of the Getty's Open Content Program

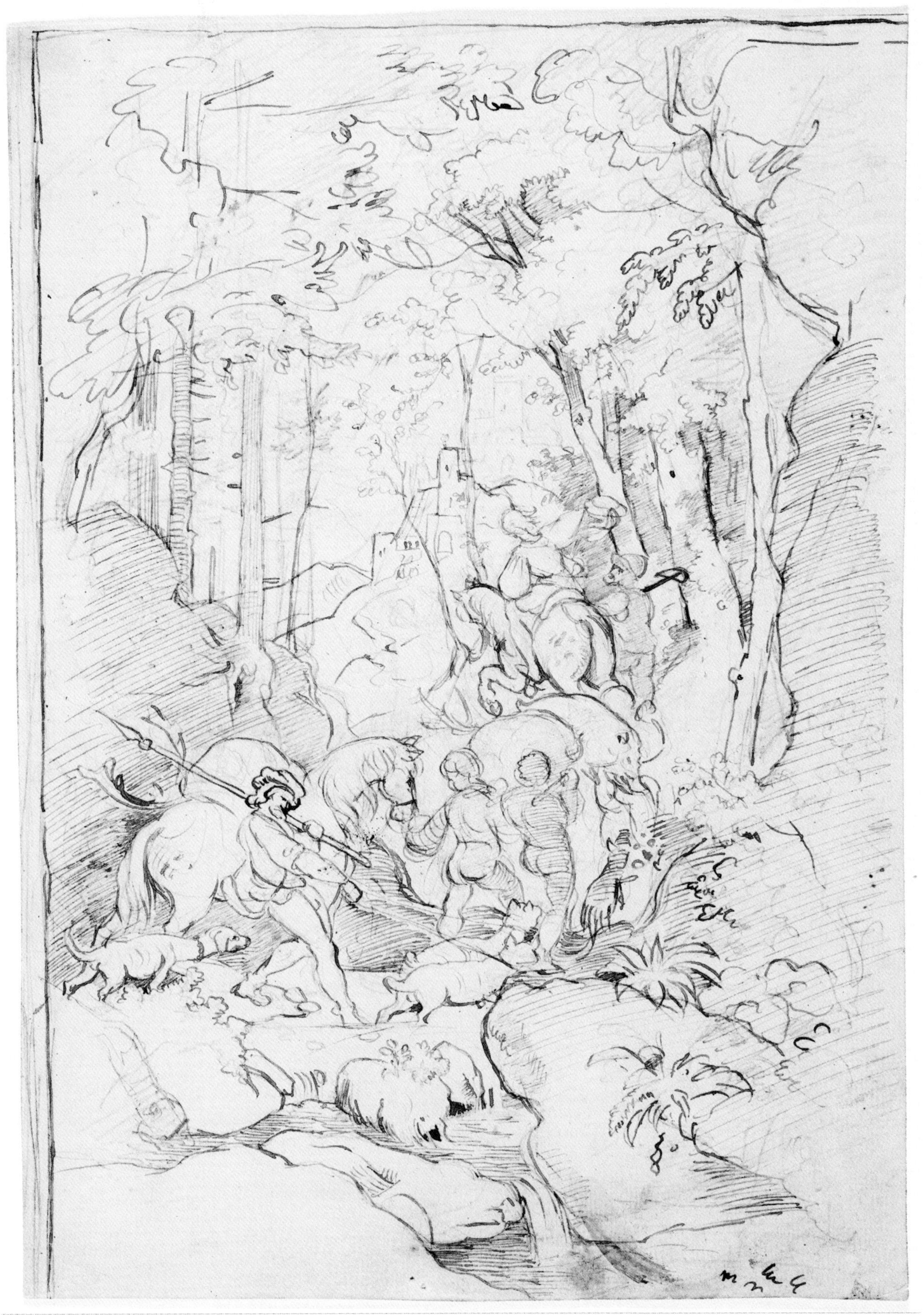

(John) Christopher 'Kit' WOOD

Knowsley, 7 Apr 1901 – 21 Aug 1930, Salisbury
British, 29 years, 4 months, 15 days

Not to be confused with the eminent art historian and dealer Christopher Wood (1941–2009), 'Kit' Wood was an important modern primitivist expressionist. When artists Ben and Winifred Nicholson learned of the death of their dear friend Kit in 1930, they were so shocked they hired a private detective to uncover the true story of his death. However, after the detective's initial report they abandoned the investigation, the evidence of his self-destruction too great to ignore. Although his art appeared to be gaining in strength at the time of his death, his mental health had completely deteriorated, resulting in a dramatic suicide.

Initially, Wood had pursued architectural studies, not art, but on the advice of Augustus John, he made painting his calling. Wood moved to Paris and in 1921 enrolled in the Académie Julian. He unrealistically wrote to his mother: 'I have decided to try and be the greatest painter that has ever lived.' Socially adept, Wood moved freely among Paris's most elite artistic circles as he experimented with various post-impressionist styles, bisexuality and opium. Eventually, Wood became associated with the Seven and Five Society, The London Group and the St Ives School, and was enjoying success,

working both in England and France.

The painting *Fishing Village, Cornwall* (1926) was painted during Wood's first trip to St Ives, Cornwall. The Cornish coast had a deep impact on Wood. Inspired by Cornwall's rocky coastline and simple fishing villages, which contrasted greatly with his bohemian Paris life, Wood finally felt at 'home' in this remote region. Here, he further developed his distinctive naïve style over many subsequent trips.

However, his opium use, financial concerns, and dissolute lifestyle eventually led to serious psychosis. By 1930 he had become paranoid and carried a revolver with him. On 21 August, after lunch with his mother and sister, Wood threw himself on the tracks just as a train was entering Salisbury station, perhaps believing that he was being pursued. The inquest ruled that it was 'suicide while of unsound mind', but was reported as an accident according to his mother's wishes. Despite the brevity of his career, interest in Wood's naïve style has not waned. Wood was an ever-evolving artist. One of his last paintings *Zebra and Parachute* (1930, Tate) hints at the surrealist direction Wood's art may have taken had he lived a little longer.

Christopher 'Kit' Wood
Fishing Village, Cornwall, 1926, oil on canvas, 51 × 61.2 cm (20⅛ × 24⅛ in)
Christie's London

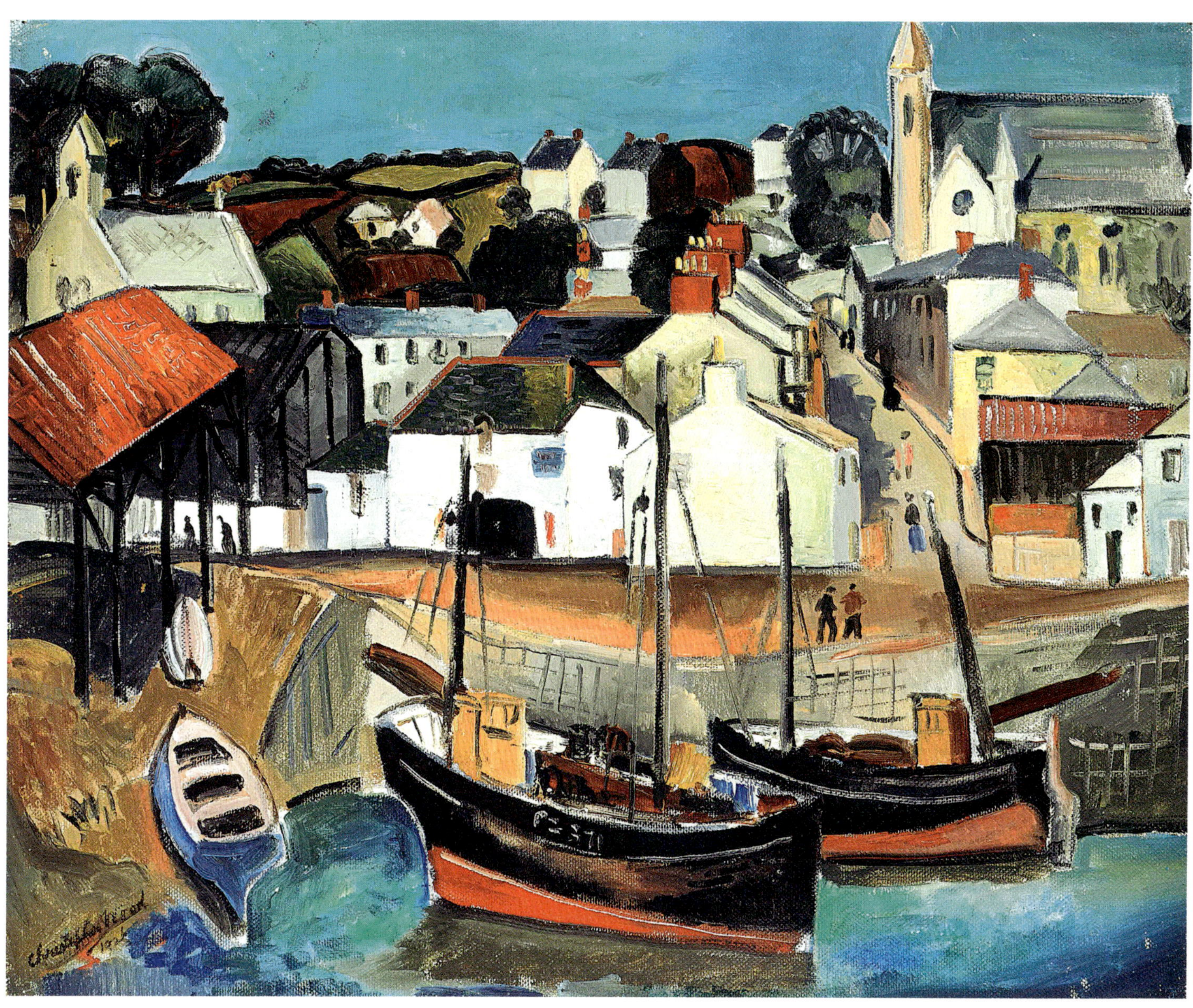

Eduardo ZAMACOIS y ZABATA

Bilbao, 2 Jul 1841 – 12 Jan 1871, Madrid
Spanish, 29 years, 6 months, 11 days

Life began for Eduardo Zamacois in a large and enlightened home. His father was the founder and director of the Santiago de Vizcaya School of Humanities. Both parents were previously widowed, and when the two families were combined and more children added, the grand total came to 23. All highly educated, the Zamacois family made a name for themselves in writing, acting, music and, with Eduardo, visual fine art. Eduardo felt inclined towards painting very early and trained with José Balaca in Bilbao. When the family moved to Madrid in 1856, Eduardo enrolled at the San Fernando School of Fine Arts. He soon became friends with the brilliant Raimundo de Madrazo (1841– 1920), whose father Federico was director of the school.

At Federico's recommendation, Zamacois travelled to Paris in 1861, 'to further his training in contact with the trends and tastes of the modern bourgeois of Paris.'[180] Eventually Zamacois joined the workshop of Ernest Meissonier, where he found his artistic niche, namely small-scale genre paintings called *tableautins*. He painted detailed, humorous paintings of carnival scenes, street musicians, monks and aristocratic pomp in 17th and 18th-century dress.

Art critic Ernest Knauft described the artist thus: 'Zamacois is indeed the prince of the painters … He is moreover prince and jester combined. Being at once a royal colourist and a cultivated wit – a brilliant comic poet.'[181] Paintings such as *The Inopportune Visit* (c.1868), where an artist's nude model shyly hides herself from the unexpected studio visit of a clergyman, delighted collectors.

Zamacois was a regular participant at artistic gatherings, and developed friendships with the foremost painters of the day including Mariano Fortuny, Martín Rico and Jehan Georges Vibert, the latter introducing Zamacois to his future wife. Zamacois often exhibited at the Madrid National Expositions and Paris Salons from 1862 onwards, and in spite of his youth, won awards. In 1868 and 1869, he travelled to Rome where he painted *The Refectory of the Trinitarians*, which was well received at the Paris Salon. His definitive recognition came with a gold medal from the 1870 Paris Salon for *A Prince's Education*, but shortly thereafter the Franco–Prussian War forced Zamacois to leave Paris for Madrid.

He arrived during the cold winter of 1871 in time for King Amadeus's coronation. The artist attended the ceremonies, and the following day became very ill. According to Martín Rico's memoirs, Zamacois contracted 'gangrenous angina' at the coronation ceremonies.[182] This antiquated medical term usually refers to a form of malignant diphtheria, which swept him away in just days, leaving an unusually large-scale history painting incomplete. Sadly, the artist left behind his wife Marie, who was pregnant with a daughter, and a son, Miguel. Miguel Zamacois would follow in his father's cult of genius by becoming a noted writer.

In 1878, the artist's memory was still strong enough for him to be awarded a posthumous diploma by the École des Beaux-Arts and a major retrospective at the Exposition Universelle. Though not a household name, he is remembered as a first-rate artist, and his works hang in public and private collections around the world. In time he might even have competed in fame with the great Fortuny and Jehan Vibert with his cabinet paintings.

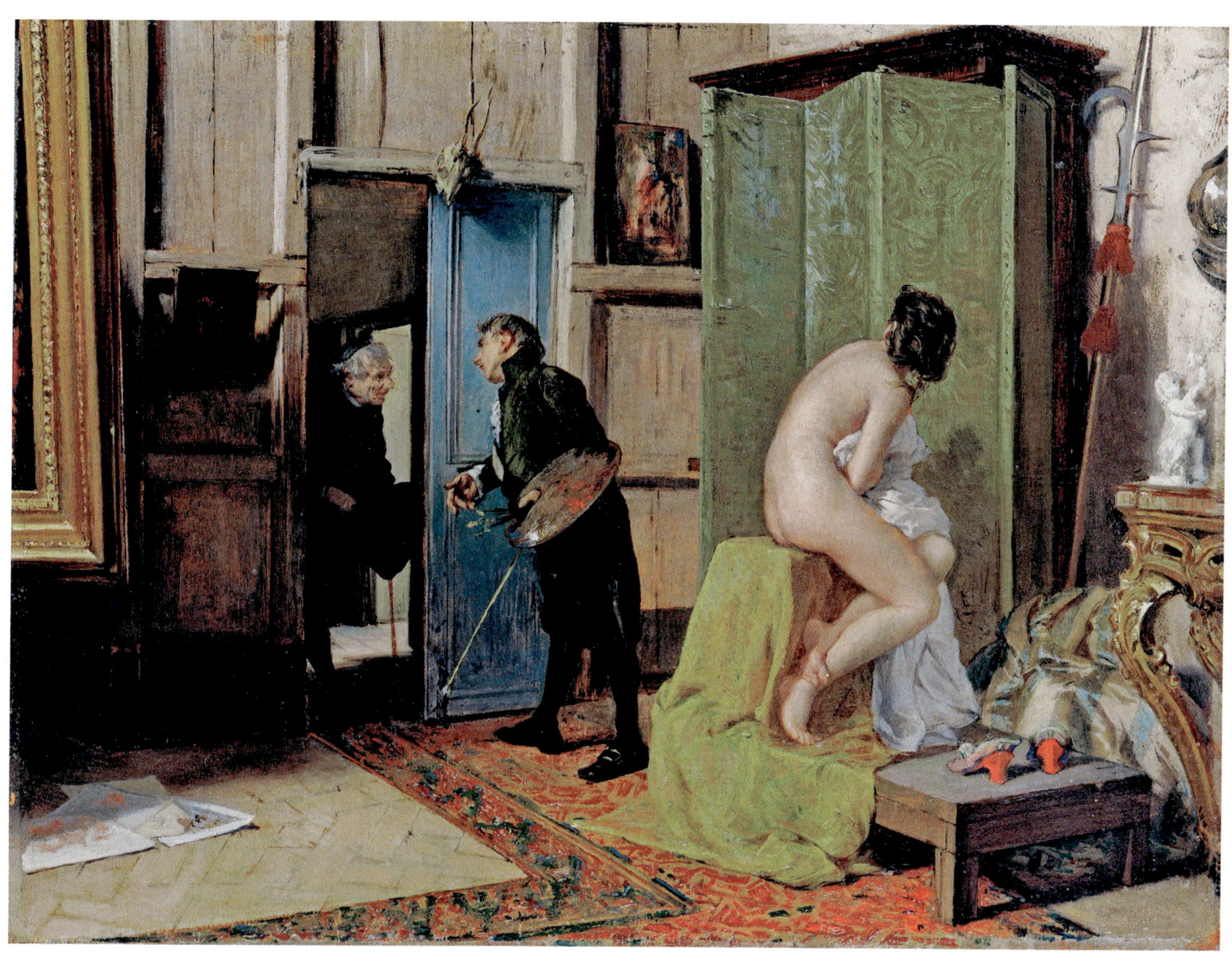

Eduardo Zamacois y Zabata
The Inopportune Visit, c.1868, oil on panel, 23 × 29.5 cm (9 × 11⅝ in)
Bellas Artes de Bilbao

Juan de ZURBARÁN

Llerena, 1620 – 1649, Seville
Spanish, approx. 29 years

This Spanish baroque artist was the son of the renowned religious and still-life artist Francisco de Zurbarán (1598–1664). In 1629, the family moved from Llerena to Seville, where his father came to dominate the artistic scene. Typical in the mediaeval atelier-workshop model, at an early age Juan joined his father's workshop as an apprentice. He was probably no older than 10 to 13 years old at the time, giving him a decided head-start over artists starting out today.

Of course, this meant that Juan would collaborate with his father, whose work was profoundly influential upon him. This tended to make Juan's solo efforts rare and none of his purported religious work has yet to surface. Zurbarán was primarily a table-top still-life artist mostly of fruits. Like much of the tenebrist and Caravaggesque work of the day, his painted backgrounds were invariably dark and the contrast between the shadows and light areas was sharp. The still-life's content, however, was richly painted with close attention to detail.

An example of this can be seen in his canvas, 'Apples in a Wicker Basket with Sliced Pomegranate on Silver Plate and Flowers' (c.1644–49). Beyond his father Francisco, he was also moved by Spanish Netherlandish still-life painter, Juan van der Hamen y León (Madrid, 1596–1632), who died young when Juan was only 12. Dutch, Lombard and Neapolitan still-life painting also had its positive effect on the artist.

The younger Zurbarán was a socially pretentious person, as demonstrated from the signatures on his three known signed paintings, which were presaged with the aristocratic 'don'. He possessed literary talents and wrote sonnets. He studied dance with the most respected dance teacher and became popular for his skills in this artistic medium. In 1641 Juan made a socially brilliant marriage to Mariana de Quadros, the daughter of a procurator in the Real Audiencia of Seville and a rich moneylender. Her dowry was quite substantial, which solidified Juan's social-climbing aspirations. However, she died shortly after the birth of their second child in 1644.

Five years later, Juan contracted Bubonic plague during the epidemic that ravaged Seville and its environs, reaching its height in 1649. Called the Great Plague of Seville (1647-52), the epidemic claimed 150,000 lives – nearly a third of its population. Their deaths were probably avoidable except for the city's lack of precautions to avert the spread of the disease. Because of Juan's early death and working on his father's paintings, his own oeuvre is limited at present to no more than 25 works confidently ascribed to him.[183] Yet, he made important contributions to the bodegón (still-life) tradition in Spain's Golden Age. It is possible to imagine that his fourth decade would have seen him climb to something far more significant than lime-light – he would have been a great artist.

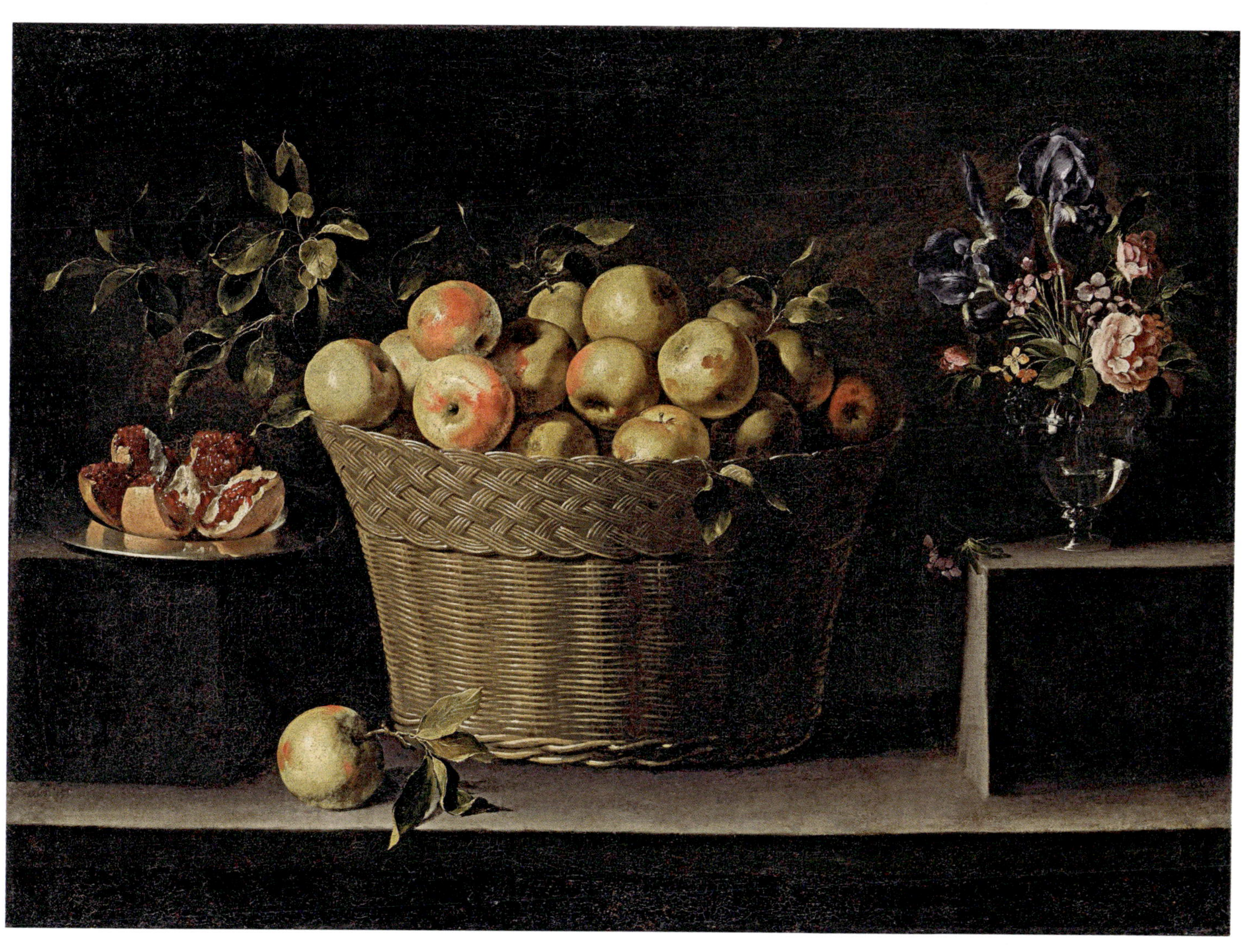

CONCLUSION
Ars Longa, Vita Brevis

This exploration has yielded some surprising results on the early adult mortality of artists. One would think suicide was the leading cause of death, but throughout the course of art history this has not been the case. In fact, of the 109 artists featured in this book, suicide accounts for about 10 deaths, approximately nine percent of these artists. Nearly tied with suicide is violence of another kind – war. However, the greatest killer was tuberculosis, an ailment which thankfully has largely been eradicated by modern medical practice, at least in developed countries. In all instances, these talented individuals were in fact 'gone too soon'. They didn't have time either to wear out, or rust out.

We choke to think of the loss of so many talented souls and their lost contributions to civilisation. As Lord Byron penned, 'Whom the gods love die young' may be good for Heaven but not for this Earth. For the vast majority of artists, death was not a great career move. While some of them are quite famous, other artists, such as Jeanne Hébuterne, Pierino da Vinci, Ernst Klimt and Juan de Zurbarán, are known simply because they were related to famous artists. However, the vast majority of the 'desperately young' were not famous because of the brevity of their careers. A few had said what they had to say with their art and then passed from the scene; but most didn't reach that point. Most still had their strong aesthetic statements or masterpieces still within them. We, the benefactors of their potential, can only mourn their passing and remember these few who could have made a difference.

A number of 'other' artists did not make it into this book because we couldn't uncover enough of their story, or we couldn't find sufficiently high-quality images of their artwork. These include the Spanish painter, Mosen Vicente Bru (1682–1703) who at 21 years was taking commissions to paint cathedrals from older artists – but we couldn't find his artwork. Another was Bonaventura de Bar who was more prolific than talented and just missed the cut. Then there is the story of a Ukrainian artist named Max Rausher (c.1920–1941) who may be credited for the authors' desire to write this book.

Leonid Steele remembers his fellow-student at Kharkov Art Academy as a blinding painter and spectacular talent. Rausher was all the rage amongst the students and faculty. Sadly, none of his works are known to exist today. He was of German descent and when the war came German nationals were forbidden to enter the army. He convinced the recruiting station he was Jewish and not German, and so he was inducted into the army. He was killed in his first action during the Great Patriotic War (WWII). In pain of this, Leonid's son Alexey Steele recounts:

> Ever since, my dad couldn't talk about him in a straight voice. The artists all had dreams. They all loved Velázquez and Rembrandt, Repin and Serov. They all wanted to give everything to Art and hoped their names wouldn't be forgotten. They just never had a chance.

OTHER ARTISTS
Gone too Soon

Phineas Howe YOUNG
(31 Dec 1847–13 Mar 1868) American, 20 years
Mosen Vicente BRU
(1682–1703) Spanish, approx. 21 years
Max RAUSHER
(c.1920–1941) Ukrainian, approx. 21 years
Jan Vuuring van DRIELST
(11 Oct 1789–8 Mar 1813) Dutch, 23 years
Karl Heinrich Hermann STAHL
(13 May 1824–13 Nov 1848) German, 24 years
Vasili Nikolaevich CHEKRYGIN
(19 Jan 1897–3 Jun 1922) Russian, 25 years
Jean HILLEMACHER
(15 Jun 1889–6 Sep 1914) French, 25 years
Jens Adolf Emil JERICHAU
(11 Dec 1890–16 Aug 1916) Danish, 25 years
Alfredo RICCI
(24 Jan 1864–9 Sep 1889) Italian, 25 years
Josef BAYER
(1805–17 Nov 1831) Austrian, approx. 26 years
Il'ya Grigorevich CHASHNIK
(26 Jun 1902–4 Mar 1929) Latvian, 26 years
Adolphe LULLIN
(1 Feb 1780–28 Feb 1806) Swiss, 26 years
Jacobus de BAEN
(1673–1700) Dutch, approx. 27 years
Charles Octave BLANCHARD
(12 Aug 1814–12 Jul 1842) French, 27 years
Francesco 'Franceschino' CARRACCI
(1595–3 Jun 1622) Italian, approx. 27 years
Giovanni Paolo CERVETTO
(c.1630–1657) Italian, approx. 27 years
Robert HOWLETT
(3 Jul 1831–2 Dec 1858) British, 27 years
Miroslav KRAJEVIĆ
(14 Dec 1885–16 Apr 1913) Croatian, 27 years
Matthew James LAWLESS
(1837–6 Aug 1864) Irish, approx. 27 years
Jean-Louis SAUCE
(1760–9 Jan 1788) French, approx. 27 years
Raffaello SERNESI
(25 Dec 1838–9 Aug 1866) Italian, 27 years
Dash SNOW
(27 Jul 1981–13 Jul 2009) American, 27 years

François Van Der VERDONK
(1848–1875) Belgian, approx. 27 years
Ulrika Sofia Sparre af Sundby ADLERFELT
(21 Jul 1736–23 May 1765) Swedish, 28 years
Ferdinand Henricus De BRAEKELEER II
(29 Aug 1828–11 Feb 1857) Belgian, 28 years
Charles DARCHE
(3 Jan 1810–22 Mar 1838) French, 28 years
(Johann) Adam EBERLE
(27 Mar 1804–15 Apr 1832) German, 28 years
Adriaen Van GAESBEECK
(baptised 22 Aug 1621–buried 11 Feb 1650) Dutch,
28 years
George HEPPER
(baptised 26 May 1839– Jan 1868) British, approx.
28 years
Urban JANKE
(12 Feb 1887–1915) Austrian, approx. 28 years
Maningning MICLAT
(1972–2000) Filipino, 28 years
Sigismondo NAPPI
(1804–5 Sep 1832) Italian, approx. 28 years
Amable-Louis-Claude PAGNEST
(9 Jun 1790–25 May 1819) French, 28 years
Thomas PEMBROKE
(c.1658–c.1686) British, approx. 28 years
Wladyslaw PODKOWINSKI
(4 Feb 1866–5 Jan 1895) Polish, 28 years
Maurice VEZOUX
(1872–Jun 1900) French, approx. 28 years
Bonaventure de BAR
(1700–1 Sept 1729) French, approx. 29 years
Claude Michel 'Amon' HAMON-DUPLESSIS
(1770/71–1799) French, approx. 29 years
Moriz JUNG
(22 Oct 1885–11 Mar 1915) Czech, 29 years
John MIDDLETON
(9 Jan 1827–11 Nov 1856) British, 29 years
Marie H. Guise NEWCOMB
(1865–23 Jun 1894) American, approx. 29 years
Ludwig Hermann Alfred von SCHÜSSLER
(7 Apr 1820–22 Nov 1849) German, 29 years
Henry 'Harry' WARD
(1844–1873) British, approx. 29 years

ENDNOTES

1. Sandy Askey-Adams, 'Past Great Artists Who Died Young' Happily an Artist, posted 2012, sandyaskeyadams.com/blog.

2. Both's dates vary and are listed as between 1611 and 1642.

3. B.H. Roberts, 'Funeral Oration for John Hafen' (Springville, Utah on 10 July 1910).

4. Constance Moes and Nine Wevers, *De Familie Koekkoek: Vier Generaties Schildertalent* (Ede, Netherlands: Simonis & Buunk Kunsthandel, 2003), 17.

5. Jan Patience, 'Paisley High Street Museum', *The Herald*, 22 Jun 2019.

6. All Ruess quotes found in David Roberts, *Finding Everett Ruess* (New York: Broadway Book, 2011), xii, 72, 101, 189.

7. 'Everett Ruess', Utah Division of Arts and Museums, accessed 22 Jan 2020, https://artsandmuseums.utah.gov/block-prints-by-everett-ruess/.

8. '5 minutes with… Autoportrait (Self-Portrait) by Jeanne Hébuterne' Christie's, posted 2 October 2018, https://www.christies.com/features/5-minutes-with-Autoportrait-by-Jeanne-Hebuterne-9415–1.aspx.

9. While some sites, including London Art Council, list his death as 1874, the 'Archive Baker Family of Birmingham and Stratford-upon-Avon' and 'Christopher Wood', *Dictionary of Victorian Art* (1995), 4:33 say his death was in 1872.

10. 'The Birmingham Autumn Exhibition', *Art Journal* 34 (1 Sep 1872): 264.

11. *Birmingham Museum of Art, Illustrated Catalogue with Descriptive Notes* (Birmingham: Guild Press, 1899), 6.

12. Phillip Dieffenbach, *Das Leben des Malers Karl Fohr: Zunächst für dessen Freunde und Bekannte Geschrieben* (Darmstadt: Verlag von Joh Wilm Heuer, 1823), VI.

13. Dieffenbach, *Das Leben*, XIV.

14. Paul G. Stein, 'The Prodigy', last update 27 May 2014, Artfixdaily.com.

15. Stein, 'The Prodigy'.

16. *The Sixth Annual Report of the Artists' Fund Society 1865-66* (New York, 1866), 10–11.

17. Harry Willard French, *Art and Artists of Connecticut* (New York: Lee and Shepherd, 1878), 153.

18. 'Kaita Murayama, the Enigmatic Artist Who Died 100 Years Ago at 22', Spoon & Tamago, accessed 24 May 2019, http://www.spoontamago.com/2019/05/24/kaita-murayama-artist/.

19. William Jefferson Tyler, *Modanizumu: Modernist Fiction from Japan, 1913–1938* (Honolulu: University of Hawaii Press, 2008), 66.

20. Tyler, *Modanizumu*, 66.

21. 'Deaths', *The Cork Constitution*, 2 August 1828, as quoted on 'Samuel Forde "An Ornament of His Native City"'. The Samuel Forde Project, last updated 29 July 2014, samuelforde.wordpress.com.

22. 'Samuel Forde', *The Freeholder*, 31 July 1828 as quoted on 'Samuel Forde "An Ornament of His Native City"'. The Samuel Forde Project, last updated 29 July 2014, samuelforde.wordpress.com.

23. Waldron, Michael and Shane Lordan. 'A Vision of Tragedy', *Irish Arts Review* vol. 30, no. 4 (2013): 125. JSTOR, www.jstor.org/stable/23611561.

24. Encyclopædia Britannica, 'Henri Gaudier-Brzeska', last updated 30 Sept 2019, https://www.britannica.com/biography/Henri-Gaudier-Brzeska.

25. Ezra Pound, *Gaudier-Brzeska: A Memoir* (London: John Lane, 1916), 3.

26. 'F. Trevelyan Goodall 1848–1871', The Goodall Family of Artists, accessed 7 January 2020, www.goodallartists.ca.

27. 'Frederick Trevelyan Goodall', *The Art Journal* 33 (1871): 166.

28. 'Exhibition of the Royal Academy', *The Art Journal* 35 (1873): 198.

29. 'H. Goodall', *The Art Journal* 36 (1874): 60.

30. Yemima Hovav, 'The Many Faces of Maurycy Gottlieb', *Segula: The Jewish History Magazine*, accessed 21 January 2020, https://segulamag.com/en/.

31. Quoted on 'Hermann Stenner', Hermann Stenner Freundeskreis e.V., accessed on 17 May 2019, www.hermann-stenner.de.

32. Dr W. Sch., *Düsseldorfer Generalanzeiger* 13 Nov 1917, quoted on 'Hermann Stenner', Hermann Stenner Freundeskreis e.V., accessed on 17 May 2019, www.hermann-stenner.de.

33. The above are Vasilyev's New Style (N.S.) dates. The artist's Old Style (O.S.) dates are 10 Feb 1850–24 Sep 1873.

34. Giorgio Vasari, 'Life of Pierino (Piero) Da Vinci Sculptor', in *The Lives of the Most Excellent Painters, Sculptors, and Architects*, 1568.

35. Vasari, 'Life', 1568.

36. 'Harry Leslie Baldry', Suffolk Artists, accessed 20 January 2020.

37. 'The Week', *The Speaker* 2 (6 September 1890): 270.

38. C. Marchille, 'Notice sure Mathieu Cochereau Peintre Beauceron', in *Mémoires de la Société archéologique d'Eure-et-Loir* (Chartres: Société Archéologique d'Eure-et-Loir, 1876), 50.

39. M. Therese Southgate, 'The Interior of David's Studio at the Collège des Quatre Nations, Paris 1814', *JAMA: The Journal of the American Medical Association* 284, no. 9 (6 September 2000): 1065.

40. C. Marchille, 'Notice', 53.

41. While death dates of 15 Feb 1788 and 15 Jul 1788 have been proposed, 13 Feb 1788 is the most widely accepted.

42. John D. Bandiera, 'The Shepherd Paris of Jean-Germain Drouais', *Annual Bulletin* 7 (1983–84).

43. Balthasar Hunold, *Jakob Fink, der Maler aus dem Bregenzerwalde. Ein Künstler-Lebensbild* (Veröffentlichungen des Tiroler Landesmuseums Ferdinandeum, 1880), p. 7.

44. Hunold, *Jakob Fink*, p. 4.

45. C. Debray and A. Gilet, *Gaudar de Laverdine: 1780–1804: une oeuvre inachevée* (Châteauroux: Ville de Châteauroux, 1999), pp. 7, 12, 23.

46. Ford, Brinsley and R.B.F. 'The letters of Jonathan Skelton written from Rome and Tivoli in 1758', *The Volume of the Walpole Society*, vol. 36 (1956): 23.

47. 'View of Ariccia, Italy', The Metropolitan Museum of Art, accessed 3 May 2019, www.metmuseum.org/art/collection/search/359574.

48. While she was born in 1858, her mother falsely claimed it as 1860 to make her appear more precocious.

49. G.H. Perris, 'Introduction', in *The Last Confessions of Marie Bashkirtseff and Her Correspondence with Guy de Maupassant* (New York: Frederick A. Stokes, 1901), 16.

50. S. Wilson and L. Barton, 'Beardsley, Aubrey', Grove Art Online, retrieved 20 Jan 2020, www.oxfordartonline.

51. Ibid.

52. Miguel Cullen, 'The convert ashamed of his "obscene" drawings', *Catholic Herald*, 14 Jan 2016.

53. Matthew Sturgis, 'The death of Aubrey Beardsley', *The Princeton University Library Chronicle*, vol. 60, no. 1 (Autumn 1998): 82.

54. 'Richard Parkes Bonington' The National Gallery, accessed 10 September 2019, http://www.nationalgallery.org.uk.

55. 'Richard Parkes Bonington', Encyclopaedia Britannica, published 21 Oct 2019, www.britannica.com/biography/Richard-Parkes-Bonington.

56. Patrick Noon, 'Bonington, Richard Parkes (1802–1828), Landscape Painter', Oxford Dictionary of National Biography, retrieved 31 Oct. 2019, www.oxforddnb.com/view/10.1093/ref:odnb/9780198614128.001.0001/odnb-9780198614128-e-2845.

57. Most auction sources say that he died on 8 March. However, Grove and many other sources agree on 8 July instead.

58. Willoch, Sigurd, 'August Cappelen', Norsk Kunstner Leksikon, accessed 14 Nov 2019, https://nkl.snl.no/August_Cappelen.

59. Arnold Houbraken, *Degroote Schouburgh der Nederlantsche Konstschilders en Schilderessen* (1718).

60. Dr Jonathan Bikker, *Willem Drost: A Rembrandt Pupil in Amsterdam and Venice* (New Haven: Yale University Press, 2005), 40.

61. Otto Breicha, 'Richard Gerstl', Grove Art Online, 2003, accessed 10 March 2019, http://www.oxfordartonline,

62. According to some sources he disembowelled himself; another says he stabbed himself in the chest.

63. Karolina Dzimira-Zarzycha, 'Ghost, City and Night "Paris at Night"'. Herbst Palace Museum, Lodz (2018) exhibition catalogue.

64. Dzimira-Zarzycha, 'Ghost'.

65. 'Achille-Etna Michallon', The National Gallery Website, accessed 27 Oct 2019, *www.nationalgallery.org.uk/artists/achille-etna-michallon.*

66. Eugène Guillaume, *Allocutions et Discours* (Paris: Société Française d'éditions d'art, 1899), 271–73.

67. Harriet Grote, *Memoir of the Life of Ary Scheffer* (London: John Murray, 1860), 39.

68. Anastasia Easterday, 'Labeur, Honneur, Douleur: Sculptors Julie Charpentier, Félicie De Fauveau, and Marie D'Orléans'. *Woman's Art Journal* 18, no. 2 (1997): 15.

69. Grote, *Memoir of the Life*, 38.

70. 'Henrique Pousão', Wikipedia, accessed 5 September 2019, https://pt.wikipedia.org/wiki/Henrique_Pous%C3%A3o.

71. Sabido, Maria do Carmo. 'Pousão, Henrique', Grove Art Online, 2003, accessed 5 September 2019, www.oxfordartonline.

72. Alfred Trumble, *Representative Works of Contemporary American Artists* (New York: Garland Publishing Co., 1887, reprint 1978), Introduction.

73. While some sources claim he died of a cold following the ice-skating accident, the contemporary *Menands, New York, Albany Rural Cemetery Burial Cards* list his death as 'Dis. of Spine'. www.ancestry.com.

74. 'William Bliss Baker', *Harper's Weekly* 30 (4 Dec 1886): 785.

75. William Michael Rossetti, 'Mr. W. H. Deverell', *Spectator* (11 Feb 1854): 159.

76. 'Artists Resting in the Mountains' Google Arts & Culture, accessed 14 Jan 2020, https://artsandculture.google.com.

77. Aloys Apell, *Das Werk von Johann Christoph Erhard, Maler und Radirer* (Dresden: Verlag Aloys Apell, 1866), 25.

78. 'Johan Christoph Erhard', *Allgemeines Künstlerlexikon* (KG Saur, 2002), 34: 323–25.

79. Bruce Coe, 'Masaccio' Encyclopædia Britannica, accessed 3 Nov 2019, https://www.britannica.com/biography/Masaccio.

80. Cath Pound, 'Tragedy and the Will to Live: The Obsessive Art of Charlotte Salomon', *The New York Times*, 23 Oct 2017.

81. 'Charlotte Salomon's 'Life? Or Theatre?' Film created for the exhibition at the Jewish Historical Museum, Amsterdam, posted October 2017, https://www.youtube.com/watch?v=F9wRMQ81Y_g.

82. Ernst Forster, *Denkmale deutscher Baukunst, Bildnerei und Malerei von Einfu hrung des Christenthums bis auf die neueste Zeit* (Leipzig: T.O. Weige, 1861), 3: 19.

83. 'Jean-Michel Basquiat', Sotheby's, accessed 16 May 2019, https://www.sothebys.com/en/artists/jean-michel-basquiat.

84. Francis E. Hyslop, *Henri Evenepoel Belgian Painter in Paris 1892–1899* (University Park: The Pennsylvania State University Press, 1975), 24–25.

85. Ewa Micke-Broniarek, 'Maksymilan Gierymski', Culture.PL, posted December 2004, www.culture.pl/en/.

86. Gary Longbottom, 'Mr. Turner and Mr. Girtin: The Young Masters', *The Yorkshire Post*, Sunday 10 May 2015, https://www.yorkshirepost.co.uk/what-s-on/entertainment/mr-turner-and-mr-girtin-the-young-masters-1-7244688.

87. Michael Bryan, *Biographical and Critical Dictionary of Painters and Engravers* (London: H.G. Bohn, 1853), 374.

88. Mieczysiaw Wallis, *Polish Art of the Interwar Period*, (Warsaw 1959), 79.

89. 'El pintor Francisco de Palaciosalgunas noticias sobre su vida y su obra', *Boletín del Seminario de Estudios de Arte y Arqueología* (1987), 425–35.

90. A. Antonio Palomino de Castro y Velasco, '150. Francisco de Palacios', in *An Account of the Lives and Works of the most Eminent Spanish Painters, Sculptors and Architects* (London: Sam Harding, 1739), 93.

91. Lucy H. Hooper, 'Henri Regnault', *The Art Journal* 37 (1875): 378.

92. Hooper, 'Henri Regnault', 378.

93. Lucy Paquette, 'The Future of French Art: Henri Regnault (1843–1871)', The Hammock, accessed 20 Mar 2020, https://thehammocknovel.wordpress.com/2013/03/25/the-future-of-french-art-henri-regnault–1843–1871/.

94. Sirani's death date is sometimes listed as 25 August 1665. Laura Ragg records her funeral on 14 November.

95. Laura Ragg, *The Women Artists of Bologna* (London: Methuen & Co., 1907), 242.

96. Carlo Cesare Malvasia, *Fesina pittrice: vite de'pittori bolognesi (Lives of the Bolognese Painters)*, 1678.

97. 'Elisabetta Sirani: The Mysterious Death of a Young Art Teacher', Art History Project, accessed 10 September 2019, www.thearthistoryproject.com.

98. The RKD (Netherlands Institute for Art History) firmly says she died in 1565. Her birth date is harder to pin down. The *Union List of Artists Names* (Getty Research Institute) says that her birth occurred between 1536 and 1538. The researchers of *Female Artists in History* say that c.1537 is the closest approximation for her birth date. Most references say she was born c.1536–40 and died 1565–68.

99. Delia Gaze, *Dictionary of Women Artists: Artists, J-Z* (Chicago: Fitzroy Dearborn, 1998), 2: 190.

100. 'Lot 358 Lucia Anguissola, Old Masters 27 January 2005 Sale', Sotheby's, accessed 9 Oct 2019, http://www.sothebys.com/en/auctions/ecatalogue/2005/old-master-paintings-n08061/lot.358.html?locale=en.

101. Peter Schjeldahl, 'Frédéric Bazille's Short Career, Reconsidered', *The New Yorker*, posted 10 April 2017, https://www.newyorker.com/magazine/2017/04/17/frederic-bazilles-short-career-reconsidered.

102. Jean Renoir, *Renoir: My Father* (New York: New York Review Books, 2001), 129.

103. Andreas Røder, *Maleren W. Bendz* (København: Kommission Hos Karl Køster, 1905), 53.

104. While Wikipedia states he died of a lung infection, the description of his last hours of feverish delirium reported in 'Breve Fra Danske Kunstnere', *Kunstbladet* (1898): 21–22, is conclusive that he died of typhoid fever.

105. Getty and Wikipedia state date of birth as 1632. RKD also states 1629, although it acknowledges that Gavazza / Rotondi Terminiello 1992, p. 98 lists it as 1632.

106. F. Lamera, 'Biscaino, Bartolomeo', Grove Art Online, 2003, accessed 17 Dec. 2019, www.oxfordartonline.com.

107. Rob Baker, *Beautiful Idiots and Brilliant Lunatics: A Sideways Look at Twentieth-Century London* (Stroud: Amberley Publishing Limited, 2015), 38.

108. M.S. Taylor, 'Herman Corrodi', *The Magazine of Art* 12 (London, 1889): 220.

109. 'Ilse D'Hollander', ArtNet Biographies, accessed 10 October 2019, http://www.artnet.com/artists/ilse-dhollander/.

110. Laura Cumming, 'Ilse D'Hollander; Fiona Tan: Elsewhere – Review', *The Observer* 18 Nov 2018.

111. Mary Olive Hussey, 'Thomas Foster', *A Century of Dublin Portrait Painters, 1750–1850*, Dublin Historical Record, vol. 18, no. 4 (Sep 1963): 109–110.

112. Walter G. Strickland, 'Thomas Foster, A.R.H.A', in *A Dictionary of Irish Artists* (Dublin: Maunsel & Co., 1913), 1: 379.

113. Sarah MacDougall, 'The Lives of Others: Eva Frankfurther (1930–1959)', Ben Uri Gallery, accessed 2 Nov 2019, https://evafrankfurther.benuricollection.org.uk/biography.php.

114. 'Eva Frankfurther (1930–1959)', Ben Uri Gallery, accessed 6 Nov 2019, https://evafrankfurther.benuricollection.org.uk/.

115. 'Brian Hatton', Brian Hatton: The Life and Death of a Young Artist, accessed 8 June 2019, *https://brianhatton.herefordshire.gov.uk/biography/biographical-note/*.

116. Walter Shaw Sparrow, 'Brian Hatton: young painter of genius killed in the war', *Walker's Quarterly* issue 17 (London: Walker's Galleries, 1926). Quoted on 'The Outcast by Brian Hatton', My Daily Art Display, accessed 13 Jan 2020, https://mydailyartdisplay.wordpress.com/2012/10/28/the-outcast-by-brian-hatton/.

117. Sabine Rewald, 'August Heinrich: Poet of Loschwitz Cemetery', *Master Drawing* 39, no. 2 (Summer, 2001): 148.

118. Casper David Friedrich called him an artist of 'future promise' when he viewed his 1820 oil painting *Rock Canyon in Utterwalder Valley*, as quoted by Rewald, p. 148.

119. Em, N., 'Jacquot-Defrance', *La Lorraine* no. 15 (1 August 1902): 228.

120. Em, N., 'Jacquot-Defrance', 232.

121. Em, N., 'Jacquot-Defrance', 230.

122. Lynne Millman-Weidenger, 'Dean Allen Millman (1948–1977) – Biography', Millmann Studios, accessed 7 January 2020, http://www.millmanstudios.com/dean/.

123. Weidenger, 'Dean Allan Millman'.

124. Alexey Petrovich Novitsky, 'Petrovsky, Petr Stephanovich', in A.A. Polovtsov, *Russian Biographical Dictionary* (St Petersburg: Imperial Russian Historical Society, 1901), 13: 648.

125. 'Paulus Potter', J. Paul Getty Museum, accessed 9 Nov 2019, www.getty.edu/art/collection/artists/259/paulus-potter-dutch–1625–1654/.

126. Timothy Cole, 'Old Dutch Masters – Paulus Potter', *Century Magazine* 48, no. 6 (Oct 1894): 840.

127. A. Wheelock Jr, 'Paulus Potter', National Gallery of Art, posted Apr 2014, https://www.nga.gov/collection/artist-info.1797.html.

128. P. Fullerton, 'Hugh Ramsay', accessed 8 Jan 2020, www.hughramsaypainter.com.au.

129. Fullerton, 'Hugh Ramsay'.

130. 'Rindisbacher, Peter', *Benezit Dictionary of Artists*, 31 Oct 2011, accessed 11 Nov 2020, https://www.oxfordartonline.com/.

131. There is debate over whether Sant'Elia wrote the *Manifesto of Futurist Architecture* alone or if other Futurist colleagues contributed.

132. Bernard Chambaz, *The Last Painting* (Woodbridge: ACC Art Books, 2018), 150–51.

133. 'Amrita Sher Gil: Revolution Personified', Christie's, posted 26 May 2015, www.christies.com/features/Amrita-Sher-Gil-6132–1.aspx.

134. James Snyder, 'Geertgen tot Sint Jans', Grove Art Online, 2003, accessed 18 April 2019, www.oxfordartonline.com.

135. The population of Haarlem was 11,367 in 1477, then in 1493–94 the population of the city suddenly drops by a quarter of a percent to 10,917 (about 400 people). Could there have been a moderate flu epidemic that caused a larger than average drop and took Geertgen's life?

136. Alice Klauber, 'The Painting of Donald Beauregard', *Art & Archaeology: The Arts throughout the Ages* 7 (Jan–Feb 1918): 82.

137. During the early 1990s, Dr Vern G. Swanson, author of the book *Utah Painting and Sculpture*, conducted interviews with family members in Fillmore. The elderly surviving sister recounted the family legend that the cause of his death was that Beauregard had another person growing inside his body. That, as he aged, this other body in parasitic fashion robbed him of his strength, leading to his death. This might have been a garbled way of describing the cancer that slowly overtook him.

138. Michael Bryan, *Dictionary of Painters and Engravers: Biographical and Critical* (London: George Bell & Sons, 1886), 1: 163.

139. John Ruskin, 'Academy Notes 1855', in E.T. Cook and Alexander Wedderburn, eds, *The Complete Works of John Ruskin* (London: George Allan, 1904), 31.

140. Sue Bradbury, ed., *The Boyce Papers: The Letters and Diaries of Joanna Boyce, Henry Wells and George Price Boyce* (Woodbridge: The Boydell Press, 2019), 1: 529.

141. 'The Life of Mrs. H.T. Wells', *Spectator*, 20 July 1861, 19.

142. William Michael Rossetti, *Some Reminiscences of William Michael Rossetti* (New York: Charles Schribner & Sons, 1906), 1:154.

143. *Richard Garnett,* 'Valentine Walter Bromley', *Dictionary of National Biography, 1885–1900* (New York: Macmillan & Co.,1886) 6:403. Errata appended in 1904 to read 'smallpox'. William Michael Rossetti in his letters of 2 May 1877, sorrowfully writes of Bromley's death by smallpox. Roger W. Peattie, ed., *Selected Letters of William Michael Rossetti* (University Park: Pennsylvania State University Press, 1986), 358.

144. Edwin Grey, *Cottage Life in a Hertfordshire Village: How the Agricultural Labourer Lived and Fared in the Late '60's and the '70's* (St Albans: Fisher, Knight & Co., 1935), p. 172.

145. 'Valentine Walter Bromley', *Art Journal* 39 (5 May 1877): 205.

146. As quoted in Erica E. Hirshler, *Dennis Miller Bunker: American Impressionist* (Boston: Museum of Fine Arts, 1994) 81.

147. Jesús Ángel Sánchez Rivera, 'Mateo Cerezo 'el Joven' y su padre en el convento santiaguista de Madrid: nuevas pinturas e hipótesis de su presencia', in La Clausura Femenina en el Mundo Hispánico: Una Fidelidad Secular. Simposium (San Lorenzo del Escorial: Instituto Escurialense de Investigaciones Históricas y Artísticas, 2011), 1028.

148. A. Antonio Palomino de Castro y Velasco, '145. Matheo Cerezo, Painter', in An Account of the Lives and Works of the Most Eminent Spanish Painters, Sculptors and Architects (London: Sam Harding, 1739), 90.

149. A. A. Palomino, '145. Matheo Cerezo', 90.

150. Álvaro Piedra Adarves, 'Mateo Cerezo Delgado', Diccionario Biográfico Español, Real Academia de la Historia, accessed 21 Jan 2020, http://dbe.rah.es/biografias/16368/mateo-cerezo-delgado.

151. Alessandra Imbellone, 'Serafini Fracassini, Cesare Salvatore', *Dizionario Biografico degli Italiani* 92 (2018), http://www.treccani.it/enciclopedia/serafini-fracassini-cesare-salvatore_(Dizionario-Biografico)/Imbellone, 'Serafini Fracassini'.

152. Imbellone, 'Serafini Fracassini'.

153. Fernando de Pamplona, 'Gameiro (Rui)', in *Divionário de Pintores e Escultores Portugueses ou que trabalharam em Portugal*, 2nd Edition (Porto: Livraria Civilização Editora, 1988), 3:18. For more information on the Gameiro family, consult the excellent Roque Gameiro website http://www.roquegameiro.org/.

154. Cecilia Lucy Brightwell, 'David Gibson', in *Men of Mark: A Book of Short Biographies* (London: Book Society, 1872), 245.

155. William MacDuff, *The Struggles of a Young Artist: Being a Memoir of David C. Gibson by a Brother Artist* (London: James Nisbit, 1858), 4, 18, 48–49, as quoted in Joe Law and Linda K. Hughes, eds, *Biographical Passages: Essays in Victorian and Modernist Biography* (Colombia and London: University of Missouri Press, 2000), 71.

156. Law and Hughes, *Biographical*, 71.

157. Multitudinous sources give us two dates – 1776 and 1778 – for Harriet's birthdate. However, 1776 is more dominant. We have sided with the majority of credible sources.

158. Cohen, Clive, 'The Life and Works of John Dalbiac Luard (1830–1860). Soldier and Artist: Part 1 – Life', *Journal of the Society for Army Historical Research* 93, no. 375 (2015): 193–209. Accessed 13 January, 2020, www.jstor.org/stable/44233187.

159. Cohen, Clive, 'The Life and Works of John Dalbiac Luard (1830–1860) Soldier and Artist Part 2 – Works', *Journal of the Society for Army Historical Research* 93, no. 376 (2015): 285–306. www.jstor.org/stable/44233205.

160. *The Critic*, 1861, p. 318.

161. 'Mr. John Dalbiac Luard', *The Art Journal* 23 (1861): 119.

162. There is some confusion over whether he died on 25 or 26 April. However, his gravestone lists 26 April.

163. Jens Peter Munk, 'Lundbye, Johan Thomas', Grove Art Online, 2003, accessed 10 Jan 2020, www.oxfordartonline.com.

164. T. Bunelt, 'Obituary of Alexander Bell Middleton', *The Arbroath Guide*, 19 Jan 1860.

165. Letter dated 7 Jan 1851, *Letters to Patrick Allan Fraser from Alexander Bell Middleton*, Hospitalfields Library Archives.

166. James M. McBain, *Eminent Arbroathians: Being Sketches, Historical, Genealogical and Biographical* (Arbroath: Brodie & Salmond, 1897), 28.

167. The death date of 9 August 1865 is put forward in Constantin von Wurzbach, *Biographisches Lexikon des Kaiserthums Oesterreich* (Wien: Kaiserlich-königlichen Hof-und Staatsdruckerei, 1872) 24: 220, but this is the minority view.

168. 'Johann Gaulbert Raffalt', Vladimir Aichelburg: 150 Years of Vienna Painters (1861–2011), accessed 16 Jan 2020, http://www.wladimir-aichelburg.at/kuenstlerhaus/mitglieder/verzeichnisse/mitglieder-gesamtverzeichnis/#r.

169. Charles Arnold Been and Emile Hannover, *Danmark's Malerkunst* (København: Det Nordiske Forlag,1902), 218.

170. Been and Hannover, *Danmark's*, 219.

171. Carl Frederik Bricka, *Dansk Biografisk Lexikon* (Kjøbenhavn: Gyldendalske Boghandels Forlag (F. Hegel & Søn), Græbes Bogtrykkeri, 1901), 15: 263.

172. Many sources list his death date as 23 December 1835, however his tombstone indicates he died on 23 November 1835.

173. Börsch-Supan, Helmut, 'Speckter, Erwin', in *Neue Deutsche Biographie* 24 (2010), 640. Online version, accessed 21 Mar 2019, URL: https://www.deutsche-biographie.de/pnd117482358.html#ndbcontent.

174. Eugène Guillaume, *Allocutions et Discours* (Paris: Société Française d Éditions D'Art, 1899), 264.

175. Firmin Javel, 'Les Prix de Rome: Peinture', *L'Art Francais Revue Artistique*, no. 119 (2 August 1889): unpaginated.

176. Guillaume, *Allocutions*, 264.

177. Guillaume, *Allocutions*, 265.

178. '*Campagna Landscape on the Via Flaminia*', The J. Paul Getty Museum, accessed 14 Jan 2020, www.getty.edu/art/collection/objects/248174/franz-albert-venus-campagna-landscape-on-the-via-flaminia-german–1869/.

179. Quote by Richter 'liebsten u. talent-vollsten Schüler' from Ulrich Thieme and Felix Becker, *Allgemeines Lexikon der bildenden Künstler: von der Antike bis zur Gegenwart* (Leipzig: Seemann, 1926), 34: 219.

180. Miguel Zugaza, 'Eduardo Zamacois y Zabla', Museo Carmen Thyssen, Màlaga, accessed 9 Jan 2020, https://www.carmenthyssenmalaga.org/en/artista/eduardo-zamacois-y-zabala.

181. Ernest Knauft, 'Art Talk' *The Theatre* 2, no. 26 (14 March 1887): 440.

182. Miguel Zugaza, 'Eduardo Zamacois y Zabla.'

183. 'Juan de Zurbarán', National Gallery, London, accessed 10 Jan 2020, https://www.nationalgallery.org.uk/artists/juan-de-zurbaran.

ABOUT THE AUTHORS

Angela Swanson Jones, daughter of Vern Swanson, was practically raised in an art museum and followed her father around the world, visiting libraries, galleries and auction houses. She is a graduate of Brigham Young University and holds an M.A. from the Courtauld Institute of Art, University of London. During her training she gained work experience at both Sotheby's in New York and Christie's in London, and is now Director of Swanson-Jones Fine Art Consulting. An avid collector and writer in her own right, her topics of research include Newlyn School painting and 19th and 20th-century religious art. She is currently writing a biography and catalogue raisonné on the German painter, Heinrich Hofmann (1824–1911). She has published essays and articles with *Fine Art Connoisseur*, among others. After living for 10 years in Europe, Angela currently resides in Dallas, Texas.

Dr Vern Grosvenor Swanson, native of Central Point, Oregon, studied at Brigham Young University and the University of Utah. He received his doctorate at the Courtuald Institute of Art, University of London. Swanson has worked at the National Gallery, Washington, D.C. and is a former associate Professor of art history at Auburn University, Alabama. Since 1973 he has been researching, authenticating and cataloguing British and Continental, classical and academic paintings. He was Museum Director of Springville Museum of Art, Utah for 32 years until his retirement in 2012. His authored publications include *J.W. Godward: The Eclipse of Classicism*, as well as two major books on Sir Lawrence Alma-Tadema, six books on Russian and Soviet art, and five books on Utah painting and sculpture.

The authors care to hear of other worthy artists who died before their time, and details of how they died. They also welcome correction or additional information to those artists included in this book. Information may be sent to: angsjonesjones@gmail.com and verngswanson@gmail.com.